The Fourteen Qurʾānic Readings

Impact on Theology and Law

أثر إختلاف القراءات الأربعة عشر في مباحث العقيدة والفقه

The Fourteen Qurʾānic Readings

Impact on Theology and Law

Dr. Waleed Edrees Al-Meneese

Translation and critical annotation

Dr. Abu Zayd

Quran Literacy
PRESS

(ICNA—Islamic Circle of North America)
1320 Hamilton St
Somerset, NJ 08873
Quranliteracy.org
quranliteracypress@gmail.org

ISBN 978-1-7338374-2-2

الناشر

دار الجامعة الإسلامية بولاية مينيسوتا للنشر والتوزيع

الطبعة الأولى 1442 هـ - 2021 م

Co-published by:

Islamic University of Minnesota, 1442/2021.
8201 Park Ave South
Bloomington, MN 55420
iuminnesota@gmail.com

DEDICATION

To my teacher, my inspiration, my beloved

Shaykh Waleed Edrees

حفظه الله من كل سوء

‘The Qur’ānic readings are like a precious treasure-chest filled with concealed pearls which require extraction by qualified individuals.’

— Shaykh Waleed Edrees

Contents

Translator's Foreword i

Author's Introduction 1

Chapter 1: Introduction to the Qur'ānic Readings................. 6

- Towards Defining the Qur'ānic Readings.................................... 7
- Qur'ān Readers: Some Related Terms....................................... 11
- Significance and Rationale of the Multiple Readings 13
- The Seven Modes of Revelation 15
- History of the Qur'ānic Readings 27
- Pillars of an Authentic Reading.. 33
- Shādh Readings... 39
- Differences Complementary not Contradictory 41

Chapter 2: History and Chains of the Qur'ānic Readings...... 44

- Importance and Value of Isnād.. 45
- Highest Qur'ānic Isnāds 46
- The Great Practice of Memorizing the Qur'ān............................ 47
- Qur'ān Memorizers Among the Companions 53
  - The First Tier: Those Who Learned from the Prophet............. 59
  - The Second Tier: Those Who Learned from Companions 64
- Qur'ānic Teaching Circles of Companions.................................. 68
- Specific Readings Attributed to the Prophet 73
- Attribution of a Reading to an Individual.................................... 74
- The Fourteen Imāms and their Isnāds 75

1. Imām Nāfiʿ of Madīnah (d. 169/785) 75
2. Imām Ibn Kathīr of Makkah (d. 120/737) 77
3. Imām Abū ʿAmr of Baṣrah (d. 154/770) 78
4. Imām Ibn ʿĀmir of Damascus (d. 118/736) 79
5. Imām ʿĀṣim of Kūfah (d. 127/745) 80
6. Imām Ḥamzah of Kūfah (d. 156/773) 82
7. Imām Kisāʾī of Kūfah (d. 189/804) 84
8. Imām Abū Jaʿfar of Madīnah (d. 130/738) 86
9. Imām Yaʿqūb of Baṣrah (d. 205/821) 86
10. Imām Khalaf of Baghdad (d. 229/844) 87
11. Imām Ibn Muḥayṣin of Makkah (d. 123/740) 89
12. Imām Yazīdī of Baṣrah (d. 202/817) 89
13. Ḥasan al-Baṣrī (d. 110/728) 90
14. Aʿmash (d. 147/764) 91
Examples of Contemporary Isnāds 92
Isnād of Ḥafṣ from ʿĀṣim 92
My Isnād of the Ten Readings 93
My Isnād of the Four Shādh Readings 94
Historical Survey of the Qurʾānic Readings 95
Worldwide Readings in the Time of Ibn Mujāhid 95
Shuʿbah dominated Ḥafṣ, and Ḥamzah over ʿĀṣim, in Kūfah ... 95
Post-Ibn Mujāhid Yaʿqūb Predominance in Baṣrah 96
Syrian Reading of Ibn ʿĀmir Replaced by Abū ʿAmr 96
Warsh and Qālūn Dominate North Africa 96
Rise of Abū ʿAmr in the Heartland 97
Ḥafṣ Rises in the East to Eclipse All Others 98

Chapter 3: The ʿUthmānic Codex and the Qur'ānic Readings100
Writing the Qur'ān in the Prophetic Era 101
The First Compilation of the Qur'ān 102
The ʿUthmānic Codex Project.. 105
The Number of ʿUthmānic Copies.. 109
Abrogation in the Qur'ān 112
Skeletal Script of the ʿUthmānic Codices 117
Conformity of the ʿUthmānic Orthography with the Readings.. 120
Necessity of Following ʿUthmānic Orthography 122
Chapter 4: The Influence of Variant Readings on Theology126
ʿAqīdah and the Qur'ānic Readings.. 127
Part 1: The Fourteen Readings and Belief in God 129
Establishing Allah's Beautiful Names and Their Variants....... 129
Establishing Additional Names of Allah 132
Establishing Allah's Attributes of Action 141
Understanding Tawḥīd through Variant Readings................. 171
Part 2: The Readings and Belief in Angels and Scripture 186
Part 3: The Readings and Belief in Prophethood 190
The Names of Prophets.. 193
The Selection of the Prophet 195
The Infallibility of Prophets... 195
The Finality of Prophethood 200
The Father of Ibrāhīm 203
The Unity of the Prophetic Messages 204
Part 4: The Readings and Belief in the Last Day......................... 206
Descent of ʿĪsā 206

Emergence of the Beast 207
Blowing of the Trumpet..209
Part 5: The Readings and Belief in Predestination 212
Creation Perform Their Actions in Reality 212
Allah is the Creator of the Actions of Creation.......................215
Part 6: The Readings and Other Beliefs......................................217
Faith Being Statement and Action..217
Obligation of Accepting All of the Sharīʿah.............................218
Prior Good Deeds of Disbelievers...220
How a Disbeliever is Deemed Muslim 222
The Faith of Minors 225
Magic 228
Taqiyyah...229
Companions..231
Chapter 5: Influence of Variant Readings on Jurisprudence..........234
The Meaning of Fiqh 235
The Readings and the Rulings of Fiqh..236
Relying on Shādh Readings..238
Part 1: Issues of Purification 240
Sexual Relations and the Cessation of Menses 240
Washing the Two Feet in Ablution 242
Does Touching a Female Nullify Ablution?.............................245
Part 2: Matters Related to Prayer 249
The Obligation of Istiʿādhah in Ṣalāh......................................249
The Wording of Istiʿādhah 251
Verbalizing Istiʿādhah Aloud 253

Istiʿādhah for Each Rakʿah 253
The Place of Istiʿādhah 254
Qurʾānity of Basmalah 255
Reciting Basmalah in the Beginning of Each Sūrah 256
Reciting Basmalah Between Two Sūrahs 256
Reciting from within a Sūrah 257
Basmalah with Sūrah al-Tawbah 257
Audible Basmalah in Prayer 258
Takbīr in the Final Sūrahs 262
Reciting Certain Readings in Prayer 264
Reciting Anomalous Readings in Prayer 268
Combining Multiple Readings in Recitation 271
Reading Mistakes 273
Pagans Maintaining the Mosques 276
Part 3: Issues Related to Fasting 279
The Obligation of Fasting 279
Iʿtikāf in other than the Three Mosques 279
Part 4: Matters Pertaining to Ḥajj 283
Argument during Ḥajj 283
Two Rakʿahs after Ṭawāf 285
The ʿUmrah 286
Part 5: Matters Pertaining to Sales 288
The Scribe and Witness to the Debt Contract 288
Part 6: A Case of Inheritance Law 289
Part 5: Matters Pertaining to Marriage and Divorce 291
Consent in the Marriage Contract 291

The Need for a Judge in Khulʿ Divorce 292
Part 6: Matters Pertaining to Vows 295
Oaths Requiring Expiation 295
Agreements of Disbelievers 296
Conclusions 301
Broad Conclusions 301
Conclusions in Theology 302
Conclusions in Jurisprudence 302
Proposals for Research 302
Index 305
Bibliography 309

Translator's Foreword

The readings of the Qur'ān are a matter that either draws you in completely or repels you away indefinitely. There is no middle ground. Students of Islamic sciences find themselves so fascinated and enthralled that it winds up consuming their entire life efforts, or so intimidated and confused that they avoid the topic entirely. There is a third group: those who are wholly unaware, perhaps even blissfully so, of such a thing as multiple ways of reciting the Qur'ān.

I strongly believe that our beloved teacher and guide Shaykh Dr. Waleed Edrees Al-Meneese is one of the foremost people of the first group: a pioneer in this complex field who paved the road decades before the current renewed interest in the Qur'ānic readings. For that, he played no small part in this global revival. As a child, I do fondly recall his leading us in prayer in our mosque through his crisp and clear recitation with articulations that were sometimes unfamiliar to us. My late grandfather Dīn Muḥammad, a man of great piety and commitment, used to visit us from his native Pakistan and pray behind him, never missing a prayer while he was here. He once remarked to me on a drive back from Al-Tawheed Islamic Center that this imām was a rare expert in what he called the *'riwāyāt'* (narrations) of the Qur'ān. Of course, I had no idea what my grandfather was referring to at the time, but my interest was sparked nonetheless.

Once I came to know of the readings, I was among those drawn in entirely. I had spent my youth captivated for hours on end in my dusty basement playing cassettes of legends like Shaykh ʿAbd al-Basit ʿAbd al-Ṣamad and Muḥammad Ṣiddīq Minshāwī until those tapes would get caught in the old players and require unrolling with delicate pencil extraction procedures, often unsuccessfully. Discovering the qirāʾāt added another entirely new dimension to that passion that I never knew existed.

As I got started on my journey learning the readings, I found myself searching for direction. Shaykh Waleed happened to be visiting for a major conference (by that time he had long since left our community). The conference was only in Arabic, and when the time for written questions came, I mustered up the little Arabic I knew to compose a question about those who disparaged the study of Qur'ānic readings as representing *shahwat al-ʿilm* (vain or fruitless knowledge). I cannot recall now where I had heard that accusation and I don't even remember the full answer. I do recall, though, the very moment when he read out my question, alongside Shaykh Dr. Hatem Al-Haj, who was serving as his translator and co-presenter. Both of them smiled to one another and made a comment about my broken Arabic, along the lines of—as I imagined, at least: 'This person must be learning Arabic!' Of course, they must have said it with love, but I was mortified, nonetheless. To this day, I haven't mentioned this to either of them. I interpreted his answer, though I don't recall its details, to validate my interest.

FOREWORD

A defining moment in my journey occurred when I found an opportunity to study the Qur'ān one-on-one with a student and colleague of Shaykh Waleed and great scholar in his own right: Shaykh Saad Hassanin. I do remember frequently seeing Shaykh Saad with Shaykh Waleed, the two of them sitting alone in the mosque, reciting Qur'ān and discussing matters. Over a period of a few years, Shaykh Saad gave my wife and I exclusive time (by this time I had gotten married) and trained us in his characteristic tajwīd precision. Over hundreds of hours, alongside learning tajwīd and other matters relating to the science, both of us had recited every single word of the Qur'ān until the Shaykh was fully satisfied. In addition, I had managed by this time to translate the popular tajwīd poem *Tuḥfat al-Aṭfāl* and compose a textbook entitled *Childrens Bequest: the Art of Tajwīd.* Shaykh Sa'd meticulously read every single line and gave me valuable corrections which I incorporated before publishing the final product. By the end, my wife and I received our first ijāzah in the Qur'ān in the transmission of Ḥafṣ from ʿĀṣim through the path of Fīl.

After this milestone I found myself once again looking for direction. Exhausting the Qur'ān through one single reading is daunting enough, but this really represents only one of two transmissions from one of ten Imāms. How does one proceed through the remaining nineteen transmissions, all which have simultaneous two-pronged approaches: a summarized path (known as *al-ʿashr al-ṣughrā*) and a comprehensive one (*al-ʿashr al-kubrā*)? A search for answers led me to an invaluable article written by one Abū Khālid al-Sulamī, which I took to heart and utilized to advance my journey. When I subsequently learned that Abū Khālid was none other than our own Shaykh Waleed, well, you can imagine my feelings.

My journey led me to a number of other teachers, including my beloved Shaykh Usāma ʿAbd al-ʿAzīz Ḥasan, with whom I spent nearly a decade reciting each of the twenty transmissions separately. I marveled at his incredible patience with me over long hours that quickly melted into years.

I met many other teachers over time, but I can say with a fair amount of confidence that my entire Islamic career—as meager as it is—and that of countless others has been under the nurturing shadow of Shaykh Waleed's legacy. I would like to reproduce here a remark I made when introducing another teacher of mine, the esteemed Dr. Muḥammad Akram Nadwī, before an audience at Shaykh Waleed's Islamic University of Minnesota. I related that the grammarian Yūnus b. Ḥabīb once said about his teacher Abū ʿAmr of Baṣrah, one the ten Imāms of the Qur'ānic readings: 'If there were any one from whom every single matter is accepted, it would be him.' I admitted that I had frequently said these very words about my own teacher and mentor Shaykh Waleed.

This Book

This work in your hands is essentially a translation of Dr. Waleed's masters dissertation which earned him an honors distinction and was transformed into a book published by Maktabah Dār al-Ḥijāz of Cairo in 1436/2014 entitled *Athr ikhtilāf al-qirā'āt al-arba'ata 'ashar fī mabāḥith al-'aqīdah wa al-fiqh (The impact of the differences of the fourteen readings on theological and legal studies).* The work is meant to explore how the variant readings impact and enhance our understandings on various issues, which Dr. Waleed broadly divided under the categories of 'aqīdah (creed) and fiqh (jurisprudence). In that, it fills a major void in the Islamic library. There have always existed multiple works based upon the Qur'ān that range from tafsīr and translations to jurisprudential and theological works. Few of them, however, venture beyond a single reading of the Qur'ān, leaving gaps in understanding. Admittedly, there is a genre of works known as *tawjīh al-qirā'āt* ('guidance from the readings'), but it is comparatively limited in scope and depth when you place that against the ample works of theology or jurisprudence, for example. Dr. Waleed's work is thus a valuable addition to the field.

What I found particularly invaluable was his summary of the complex matter of the Qur'ānic readings, which has enjoyed much recent interest along with no small measure of controversy. I sensed a benefit in highlighting and expanding this introductory section in some way. *Athr ikhtilāf al-qirā'āt* was intended to explore the ramifications of the readings on theology and law, and hence was written with a different focus. Exploring the impact of the readings on secondary issues is less meaningful when there is massive confusion as to what the readings are in the first place. To make my vision work within the canopy of Dr. Waleed's own work, I had to turn to some of his other books.

With approval from Shaykh Waleed, I supplemented this translation with relevant portions from three of his related works. The first is *al-Qamar al-munīr fī sharḥ al-zamzamīyah wa mutammimatuhā fī uṣūl al-tafsīr,* published by the Islamic University of Minnesota in 2020, representing an exhaustive commentary on a 158-line poem listing all the branches that comprise the study of the Qur'ān by 'Abd al-'Azīz al-Zamzamī of Makkah (d. 976 AH). Zamzamī versified the branches of 'ulūm al-Qur'ān that were listed by Imām al-Suyūṭī in his brief work entitled *al-Nuqāyah* (also pronounced *al-Naqāwah* and *al-Nuqāwah*).

This was Suyūṭī's first work on the topic (listing 55 Qur'ānic subdisciplines), which he later expanded on in *al-Taḥbīr fī 'ulūm al-Qur'ān* (listing 102 subdisciplines), and even later in *al-Itqān fī 'ulūm al-Qur'ān* (his final and most comprehensive work, listing a total of 300 subdisciplines organized under eighty broader categories). Since the *Itqān* contained much material not mentioned in the *Nuqāyah,* Shaykh Waleed included all of this additional content at the end of his commentary, versifying and organizing it in the style of Zamzamī.

The second work is a valuable research paper entitled *al-Iqrā' 'inda al-ṣaḥābah*, prepared by Shaykh Waleed on 30 Rabi al-Awaal 1438/Dec 30, 2016 for the 3rd annual conference on the Qur'ānic Readings organized in Morocco by Markaz Imām Abū 'Amr al-Dānī. In this paper, the author discussed the involvement of the Companions, as a uniform generation, in learning and teaching the Qur'ān to subsequent generations. He organized the most important Companions in Qur'ānic teaching into two major tiers, highlighted the prominent Qur'ānic isnāds that persist to this day, and attempted to develop a coherent understanding of what their Qur'ānic teaching circles looked like.

The third is *al-Khayr al-kathīr sharḥ al-naẓm al-ḥabīr fī 'ulūm al-Qur'ān wa uṣūl al-tafsīr,* published by the Islamic University of Minnesota in 1438/2016. This represents a commentary on a small but comprehensive poem on Qur'ānic sciences by the Imām of Masjid al-Ḥarām in Makkah Dr. Sa'ūd al-Shuraym.

Beyond these four works, where I felt there was a need for additional discussion or clarification, I reached out to Shaykh Waleed who quite graciously and promptly provided responses and modifications which I did not hesitate to include.

Distinctions of Shaykh Waleed's Work

In the end, this current book really represents a translation of these four books of Dr. Waleed along with additional material received from him, reorganized into a coherent narrative on the Qur'ānic readings. At its heart, *this is a critical and honest traditional account of the readings* by an individual who has been immersed in them for most of his life.

In my opinion, Shaykh Waleed's perspective on this matter is invaluable for a number of important reasons. First, there is his expertise in the Arabic language which serves to sharpen insight into the readings which are at their heart a linguistic phenomenon. Dr. Waleed's qualifications in this regard include a Bachelor's degree in Arabic language from the College of Literature, Alexandria University in Egypt, along with extensive traditional immersion in poetry, literature and Arabic language-disciplines. Students will testify how they have been enlightened by his frequent quotations of Arabic verses, his drawing on the deeper meanings of Arabic terms, his pointing out the inter-connection of remotely related words (ishtiqāq kabīr), and more. His publication of poems in various Islamic fields along the patterns of the great classics bears testimony to his linguistic mastery.

Second, he has been practically immersed in the Qur'ānic readings on the ground through learning from some of the great authorities of transmission from past generations. Discussing this topic is no theoretical or academic matter for him, but one for which he has intimate familiarity in traditional terms, having taken each Qur'ānic variant from mouth-to-mouth with connected chains that are some of the highest in the world. For this, Shaykh Waleed is one of the most sought-after individuals in the world for purposes of recitation and consultation regarding the Qur'ān, as demonstrated by his constant attendance in numerous conferences and Qur'ān competitions around the world.

Third, Shaykh Waleed is a prolific traditional scholar par excellence. Having memorized the Qur'ān at the ripe age of fourteen, he then absorbed the knowledge—through study of classical texts—of his native Alexandria from individuals such as the late Muḥammad Najīb al-Muṭīʿī, the late Shaykh ʿAbd al-ʿAzīz Burmāwī and Sayyid Saʿd al-Dīn al-Ghubāshī. He then began his travels around the world which started with a decade spent in Saudi Arabia where he studied with some of the renowned scholars of the region, including the late Grand Muftī Shaykh ʿAbd al-ʿAzīz b. Bāz, the late Shaykh ʿAbd al-Razzāq ʿAfīfī (with whom he spent a total of five years), Muḥammad b. Ṣāliḥ al-ʿUthaymīn, Ṣāliḥ Āl al-Shaykh, Ismāʿīl al-Anṣārī, Ṣāliḥ b. Fawzān, the late ʿAbdullah b. Jibrīn, ʿAbdullah b. Quʿūd, the late ʿAbdullah b. Ghudayān and many others.

Shaykh Waleed has received Ijāzah from over a hundred scholars worldwide, which he has published in a work entitled *Inʿām al-Mālik al-Quddūs bi Asānīd Walīd b. Idrīs*. He has some of the highest chains in Qur'ān and ḥadīth attainable today. Some of the foremost senior scholars who have granted him Ijāzah include the late Shaykh Ismāʿīl al-Anṣārī, ʿAbd al-Qādir Karāmatullāh, ʿAbd al-Raḥmān al-Mullā al-Aḥsā'ī, ʿAbd al-Qayyūm al-Raḥmānī, Ẓahīr al-Dīn Mubarakpūrī, Ṣafiyy al-Raḥmān Mubarakpūrī, Muḥammad Isrā'īl Nadwī, ʿAbd al-Raḥmān b. ʿAbd al-Ḥayy al-Kittānī, and many others.

Fourth, apart from his traditional background, he has also attained a high level of modern academic training which allows him to research and critically analyze. His formal degrees include a Bachelor's in Arabic language from Alexandria University; a Master's degree in Islamic jurisprudence from the American Open University with the highest honors (summa cum laude), and a PhD in Islamic jurisprudence from the Graduate Theological Foundation. His master's dissertation, as previously mentioned, is the basis for this book. His PhD was a study of the jurisprudential rules pertaining to the means of communication. Though predominantly traditional in his manner and style, Shaykh Waleed has the analytic ability to be critical when needed and to help chart new directions. He has researched numerous contemporary and past issues for the American Muslim Jurists Association (AMJA) and other bodies.

These factors among others makes for an extremely valuable contribution on the Qur'ānic readings. His starting chapter on definitions, for instance, starts by drawing on his linguistic ability to build an understanding of terms, before discussing and critiquing prevailing definitions and coming up with his own solid definition of the Qur'ānic readings which is worthy of note:

> The broad discipline that studies the exact manner of articulating and writing the words of the Qur'ān, the identification of points of agreement and variation among the transmitters of the Qur'ān, the referencing of each variant to its particular transmitter, and the examination all that is transmitted as Qur'ān in order to distinguish what is soundly transmitted—either through solitary or mass-transmission—from what is not.

His explanation of the reason for the multiplicity of readings by pointing to the notion of personal selections and then comparing them to combinations and permutations in mathematics is brilliant. His discussions on isnād reveal his practical training and his survey of the historical landscape of the Qur'ānic readings across the Muslim world is also extremely insightful. His chapter on the Qur'ānic codices, an extremely complex and technical topic, is remarkable in managing to convey a narrative that is organic, highly coherent and full of insight without compromising essential and technical details.

He is also honest and critical where needed while maintaining deference to the Islamic scholarly tradition. He does not deny inadequacies of some aspects of traditional accounts such as the tawātur of the readings (they are not exactly), the 'Final Rehearsal' of the Prophet (there is no strong evidence that any Companion was physically present), the notion of mixing multiple readings (not exactly forbidden), and more.

At the heart of Shaykh Waleed's manner and style is his conciliary spirit: he will always endeavor to reconcile available evidence and explore the motives behind various positions and competing definitions in order to understand them better and minimize clash and conflict. This is readily illustrated throughout the book, including how he masterfully explained, for instance, the reported differences on the number of 'Uthmānic codices and the contradictory reports about the number of Companions who memorized the Qur'ān.

Admitting that the seven and ten readings do not exactly conform to the technical, uṣūlī definition of tawātur (concurrent, mass-transmission) and are rather transmitted through āḥād (solitary) channels of transmission, he then justifies the use of the term tawātur for the readings through coopting a different usage:

> It must also be pointed out that the usage of tawātur does not necessitate that it refer to technical tawātur of a massive group at each level of the isnād until the end. It has become convention in latter times to refer to the ten readings as mutawātir readings, in light of the fact that the readings contain elements that are mutawātir and elements that are less than that but still widespread. The elements of tawātur within the readings allow the ten readings as a whole to be referred to as mutawātir.

Finally, his drawing on the fourteen readings throughout the work, whereas most scholars would restrict themselves to seven or ten readings, reflects his strong understanding on the issue and his awareness that these four additional readings known as anomalous (shādh) ones are also soundly transmitted and part of the Islamic tradition, albeit with their own caveats.

My Work in the Book

I have taken the liberty of reorganizing Dr. Waleed's research into chapters that are more coherent for an English language work. The result is a book containing five basic chapters of vastly different lengths. I have sacrificed uniformity for the sake of stronger thematic arrangement. Chapter 1 captures all introductory material related to the Qur'ānic readings. This includes basic definitions, the rationale and wisdom behind this Qur'ānic multiplicity, the matter of the aḥruf, the qirā'āt, their relationship, and much more. I have dedicated chapter 2 to the history of the readings and included all isnād-related topics. Chapter 3 is exclusively about the 'Uthmānic codices. Though the shortest of the chapters, I still found it beneficial to separate the discussion on the codices rather than leaving it scattered throughout other sections. Chapter 4 and 5 are the bread and butter of Dr. Waleed's research, though I found the other chapters equally invaluable, if not more so.

Some methodological points are in order. I have eliminated many Arabic expressions for smoother English: 'Qur'ān' for all descriptions of Allah's Book, Noble Qur'ān, etc.; 'the Prophet' for Allah's messenger, Prophet of Allah, etc.; and their likes. A number of terms specific to this discipline have been generally translated as follows—with occasional modifications made based upon the context: 'mode' for *ḥarf*, 'readings' for *qirā'āt*, 'Qur'ānic expert' for *imām*, 'transmission' for *riwāyah*, 'path' for *ṭarīq*, 'option' for *wajh*, and 'mass transmission' for *tawātur*.

I have also consulted additional invaluable works from other authors which guided me in this entire process. These are listed in the bibliography, which contains not only Shaykh Waleed's sources but also some of my own as well. This supplementary material that is not from Dr. Waleed has been introduced entirely in the footnotes and is not part of the text of this book in any way. Generally, the material in the footnotes is my own, apart from the references from Dr. Waleed and some of the biographical information.

I must point out my indebtedness to a great Qur'ān translation project that more people need to be aware of: the UK-based Bridges Foundation translation of the ten qirā'āt supervised by Imām Fadel Soliman. Available in print form as well as app, this is the first major translation in English that incorporates the variant readings within the translation. I am grateful to Fadel Soliman for replying to some of my queries.

Finally, I must confess a great uncertainty I have always felt in translating works from great authors. To what extent does the translation represent the work of the original author and how much of the ideas are those of the translator? The original author has written in an entirely different language with its own set of idioms and using words with their own particular meanings and implications. How do you convey not only the literal words but also these implications and subtleties into a new language? Admittedly, translation is very much an act of reading and interpretation as Dr. Ebrahim Moosa aptly observes: 'Translation is nothing but an intense or more demanding form of what we do whenever we are engaged in reading.' For that, it is as critical for the reader/translator/commentator to understand what lies behind the author's words as the meanings of the words themselves. Out of his humility, Shaykh Waleed even suggested that I place my name as a coauthor. Of course, I declined, for surely this was not my work. The content is entirely his, though some of its arrangement and choice of words may be mine. I found some ease to my dilemma from a recent work of Dr. Muḥammad Akram Nadwi, *Foundation to Ḥadīth Science,* where he states in the chapter "Transmission of Books from their Authors":

> Many works represent the transmission in book form of ideas and teachings from certain individuals, who are the proponents of those teachings but not the authors of those books. . . Examples included Abū Ḥanīfah's Kitāb al-Āthār and the Musnad works of Abū Ḥanīfah and Shāfiʿī.

In the end, I have tried my best to faithfully transmit Dr. Waleed's ideas. I am fairly certain that despite my best efforts, many a mistake must have inevitably found its way into this book. My greatest fear is that Dr. Waleed be tainted by these in any way. Therefore, all potential mistakes and issues should be assumed to be from my own mistranslation or misunderstanding. For that I seek Allah's forgiveness and I have already apologized to Dr. Waleed. For me, any association with the likes of him is well worth it, despite these challenges. It is as the great Imām Shāfiʿī put it:

أُحِبُّ الصَّالِحِينَ وَلَسْتُ مِنهُم   لَعَلِّي أَن أَنالَ بِهِم شَفَاعَه
وَأَكرَهُ مَن تِجَارَتُــهُ المَعَاصِي   وَلَو كُنَّا سَوَاءً فِي البِضَاعَه

I love the pious ones in full
Though in their ranks I'll never be

I'm hoping they would plead for me
Though worthy I will never be

I hate so much who trades in sin
Though I own the same commodity.

Dr. Abu Zayd
Obaidullah Choudry
New Jersey, USA
Dec 1, 2020 / 15 Rabīʿ al-Ākhar 1442

FOREWORD

Author's Introduction

إن الحمد لله نحمده ونستعينه ونستغفره، ونعوذ بالله من شرور أنفسنا ومن سيئات أعمالنا، من يهده الله فلا مضل له، ومن يضلل فلا هادي له، وأشهد ألا إله إلا الله وحده لا شريك له، وأشهد أن محمدًا عبده ورسوله

All praise is for Allah, Who we praise and Whose assistance and forgiveness we seek. We seek refuge in Him from the evil within ourselves and the evil of our actions. Whomever Allah guides, there is none to misguide them. Whomever Allah allows to be misguided, there is none to guide them. I testify that there is no one worthy of worship but Allah alone, without any partners. And I testify that Muḥammad ﷺ is His servant and messenger.

Surely the Qur'ān is the firm rope of God which saves those who grasp it and destroys those who turn away from it. It is clear light and healing for the hearts. He who revealed it says: ﴿*People of the Book! Our Messenger has come to you: he makes clear to you many things of the Book which you were wont to conceal, and also passes over many things. There has now come to you a light from Allah, and a clear Book through which Allah shows to all who seek to please Him the paths leading to safety. He brings them out, by His leave, from darkness to light and directs them on to the straight way.*﴾ (5:15-6)

For this reason, Muslims have devoted great attention and care to the Book of their Lord while scholars expended their life-efforts in service to this Mighty Book, preserving its words as well as its meanings.

Allah revealed His Book in seven modes (aḥruf), each of them sufficient and complete. In that, there exists an ideal distinctiveness and amazing brevity, as a single word through its variant readings encompasses a multiplicity of meanings each of which explains and complements the others. The multiplicity of readings also had a great effect on making the process of memorizing, preserving and transmitting the Qur'ān easier, because memorizing one word that has multiple ways of reading is far easier than memorizing many words or sentences that would encompass those same meanings.

Thus, the multiplicity of readings is one of the greatest miracles of the Qur'ān, and the Islamic library is in great need for further studies that elucidate this. It is for this very reason that I authored this book— *Athr ikhtilāf al-qirā'āt al-arba'ata 'ashar fī mabāḥith al-'aqīdah wa al-fiqh (The impact of the differences of the fourteen readings on theological and legal studies)*—so that it may be one additional brick in the building blocks of Qur'ānic studies and participate in the raising of this structure. This book is based upon research that served as my master's dissertation and earned an honors distinction.

The subject of this research was to explore the effects of the variant Qur'ānic readings upon theological and jurisprudential issues. In the realm of theology, it involved uncovering additional evidence for the validation of the approach of the pious predecessors in various issues of creed and for the refutation of some of the doubts of those who diverged from this approach. In jurisprudential matters, it involved examining how those differences could provide evidence for specific juristic rulings or serve as the basis for preferring some of these over others in matters of dispute.

The fourteen Qur'ānic readings are the ten mass-transmitted readings along with the readings of Ibn Muḥayṣin, Yaḥyā al-Yazīdī, Ḥasan al-Baṣrī, and Aʿmash. These latter four readings continue to be transmitted with authentic and continuous chains despite them not reaching the level of mass-transmission. Because of that, I decided to include them in my study along with those of the ten mass-transmitted readings. For this study, I was motivated by the following:

1. The great importance of this issue due to its connection with some of the greatest Islamic disciplines: Qur'ānic readings, theology, and Islamic jurisprudence
2. The desire to serve Allah's Book, ponder over its verses and live under its shade
3. The need to gather the scattered studies that existed on this topic into a single one for greater accessibility and benefit
4. Demonstrating that Islamic sciences are not separate and independent but firmly interconnected and emanating from one common source
5. Revealing more aspects of the wisdom and benefit that stem from the multiplicity of Qur'ānic readings
6. Since Allah graced me with memorizing His Book and reciting it through all fourteen readings to a number of leading scholars worldwide who granted me license (ijāzah) through their connected chains to Allah's Messenger ﷺ and then to the Lord Himself, I wanted to participate in that noble process through this research connected to serving Allah's Book and its variant readings
7. The paucity of what has been written on this subject—despite its importance—and the lack of comprehensive inclusion in any single work of all these issues. This topic is scattered across early books of tafsīr (Qur'ānic commentary) and variant readings. Furthermore, the books on the

Qur'ānic readings predominantly deal with their linguistic and grammatical aspects, whereas their theological and juristic aspects are dealt with only through fleeting references. As for contemporary writings on the issue, I have come across only two, each of which is not fully comprehensive, on the influence of the fourteen readings upon matters of theology and law. These two books are:

a. *The Qur'ān Readings and their Effects on Tafsīr and Rulings* by Dr. Muḥammad 'Umar Bāzmūl,[1] which is the more comprehensive of the two and deeper in scholarship and research. I have benefited from this book greatly and desire that my work serve as a completion to his, serving to cover what is missing from it.
b. *The Effect of the Qur'ānic Readings on Islamic Fiqh* by Dr. Ṣabrī 'Abd al-Ra'ūf.[2]

I have divided my research into five chapters. In the first, I have dealt with defining the Qur'ānic readings and discussing their importance, divisions, and rationale. I have also discussed the seven modes of revelation and their relation to the readings, the pillars of an authentic reading, and the fact that the differences of the variant readings are complementary and not contradictory.

In the second chapter, after highlighting the value and importance of the isnād, I have discussed the chains of the Qur'ānic readings and the fact that they are evaluated through their transmitters as in the case of ḥadīth chains. I have also introduced the fourteen Qur'ānic scholars that are the sources for these chains and clarified that these isnāds continue to be transmitted in an authentic and connected manner until our times.

In the third, I have clarified the relationship of the 'Uthmānic Qur'ānic codex (muṣḥaf) with the Qur'ānic readings. I have gone through the stages of writing and compiling the Qur'ān, the methodology of the Companions in producing this codex in the era of 'Uthmān, and the number of copies produced. I have clarified that the 'Uthmānic manuscripts were compiled in concordance with the Qur'ānic readings, not that the readings emanate from the differences in these manuscripts as many Orientalists presume. I have also listed some key features of the 'Uthmānic orthography and the fact that it is divinely determined (tawqīfī) and hence, fully binding.

The fourth chapter discusses the influence of the variant readings on theological studies. I have discussed a number of such issues that could be affected by the

---

[1] Bāzmūl, Muḥammad b. 'Umar. *Al-qirā'āt wa athruhā fī al-tafsīr wa al-aḥkām*. PhD dissertation. Makkah: Umm al-Qurā University. 1413/1993.

[2] 'Abd al-Ra'ūf, Ṣabrī. *Athr al-qirā'āt fī al-fiqh al-islāmī.* Riyad: Aḍwā' al-Salaf. 1997.

variant readings in terms of providing evidence for mainstream Sunni positions or removing some ambiguity or doubt from them.

The final chapter concerns the influence of the fourteen readings on matters of jurisprudence. I have mentioned a number of juristic issues that are impacted, or potentially impacted, by the readings. I have paid particular attention to referencing the Qur'ānic verses to their relevant chapters, tracing the noble Prophetic ḥadīth to their primary sources, and verifying the attribution of juristic views to their sources. In light of the numerous personalities mentioned in this work, I have provided brief biographies for most of them but left out those of the well-known Companions and other that were beyond the need for such.

I end the work by summarizing the main conclusions of the work, while asking Allah for success, help and pardon from errors, and relying on His grace and generosity, for He is Ever-Generous and Ever-Noble. I ask Him to accept this work, keep its motives sincere, and make it beneficial for Muslims.

In the end, all praise belongs to Allah, Lord of the worlds, and peace and blessings be upon the seal of the prophets ﷺ and upon his family and companions.

Chapter 1: Introduction to the Qur'ānic Readings

القراءات

Towards Defining the Qur'ānic Readings

Linguistically,[1] *reading* (singular *qirā'ah*, plural *qirā'āt*) is the verbal noun of the root verb to *read* (*qara'a*), or, according to many, the root word *qariya* (q-r-y), which means to *gather*.[2] For that reason, a village is called *qaryah*, because it gathers people in it. To say that I have read (*qara'tu*) something is to say I have gathered it and joined one part of it to another.

In a ḥadīth report that relates the story of the conversion of Abū Dharr al-Ghifārī, a poet named Unays responded to accusations that the Prophet was a poet, soothsayer and magician by saying the following: 'I have heard the words of soothsayers but his words in no way resemble them. I have also compared his words to the various modes (*aqrā'*) of poetry but such words cannot be uttered by any poet. By Allah, he is truthful, and they are liars.'[3] Here the word *aqrā'*, singular *qarī*, refers to the range of meters and modes that encompass all types of poetry.

Ibn al-Athīr (d. 606/1210)[4] states: 'Everything that you gather is that which you have read. The Qur'ān is named such because it has gathered stories, directives, prohibitions, warnings, exhortations, verses, and chapters, all of which are connected to one another.'[5] Zayn al-Dīn al-Rāzī (d. 666/1261)[6] says: 'The term *Qur'ān* can refer to reading a book and also to gathering or joining something. Allah's words: ﴿*Behold, it is for Us to gather it and to cause it to be read*﴾,[7] refers to this usage of reading. The word is also used for a person conveying his greetings to another (*qara'a 'alayka al-salām/aqra'a 'alayka al-salām*).'[8]

The term *Qur'ān* is a noun on the pattern of *fa'lān* derived from the same root and is used because the Qur'ān contains content (verses and chapters) that is gathered together, or parts (chapters) that are connected, one to another. The

---

[1] This section is supplemented with content translated from Shaykh Waleed's *al-Iqrā' 'inda al-ṣaḥābah.*

[2] A chronological review of Shaykh Waleed's works indicates that he considers the real root to be *qariyah.* In *Athr ikhtilāf al-qirā'āt al-arba'at 'ashr,* the basis for this current translation and the first of his works (serving as his masters decades ago until finally being published in 2014), he lists the root as *qara'a.* In his early 2016 work *al-Khayr al-Kathīr,* it is listed as both, and in his late 2016 *al-Iqrā' al-ṣaḥābah* it is listed as *qariya.*

[3] Ṣaḥīḥ Muslim: Kitāb faḍā'il al-ṣaḥābah—Bāb min faḍā'il Abī Dharr

[4] Majd al-Dīn Abū al-Sa'ādāt al-Mubārak b. Muḥammad b. Muḥammad b. 'Abd al-Karīm al-Shaybānī al-Jazarī, better known as Ibn al-Athīr, was a great scholar and historian from Mosul, Iraq, who authored *Jāmi' al-Uṣūl, al-Nihāyah,* among other works. He was the eldest of three brothers, all of them authors known as Ibn al-Athīr. The most famous of the brothers was the historian 'Alī b. al-Athīr (d. 630/1233), author of *al-Kāmil fī al-tārīkh.*

[5] Ibn al-Athīr, *Al-nihāyah fī gharīb al-ḥadīth wa al-athar,* vol 4, p 30.

[6] Zayn al-Dīn Abū 'Abdullah Muḥammad b. Abī Bakr b. 'Abd al-Qādir al-Rāzī was a Ḥanafī scholar and linguist from Rayy whose most famous work was on Arabic linguistics entitled *Mukhtār al-ṣiḥāḥ,* essentially a summary and refinement of Jawharī's *Kitāb al-Ṣiḥāḥ.*

[7] Qur'ān 75:17.

[8] Al-Rāzī, *Mukhtār al-ṣiḥāḥ,* vol 1, pg 249.

technical definition of the Qur'ān is: *the speech of Allah revealed upon his Prophet Muḥammad ﷺ whose recitation is used in worship*.[9]

Thus, the essence of the term *qirā'ah* has to do with joining or gathering. Linguistically, it refers to the act of reading or reciting. As for the technical term *qirā'āt,* used for the Qur'ānic readings, it has been formally defined in various ways by a large number of scholars, and the best of these definitions are as follows:

1. Abū Ḥayyān of Andalus (d. 745/1344):[10] The science that studies how to articulate the words of the Qur'ān.[11]
2. Badr al-Dīn Zarkashī (d. 794/1392):[12] the Qur'ān is the revelation sent down to Muḥammad for expressing meanings and demonstrating a miracle, while the readings are the variation of the words of revelation in the writing of their letters or in their articulation, such as heaviness and lightness.[13]
3. Ibn al-Jazarī (d. 833/1429):[14] The science concerning the exact articulation of the words of the Qur'ān along with their variations, with referencing of each to its transmitters.[15]
4. 'Abd al-Fattāḥ al-Qāḍī (d. 1403/1983):[16] The science which reveals the manner of articulating the Qur'ānic words and the manner of pronouncing them proficiently along with their variations, while referencing each difference to its transmitter.[17]

---

[9] *Al-Khayr al-kathīr,* pg 16.

[10] Abū Ḥayyān Muḥammad b. Yūsuf Athīr al-Dīn of Granada, Andalus was a great scholar of Qur'ān and Arabic who migrated from Andalus to Egypt, where he settled until his death. His magnum opus was *Tafsīr al-baḥr al-muḥīṭ.*

[11] Abū Ḥayyān al-Andalusī, *Tafsīr al-baḥr al-muḥīṭ*, vol 1, pg 10.

[12] Abū 'Abdullah Badr al-Dīn Muḥammad b. Bahādur b. 'Abdullah al-Zarkashī was a noted Shāfi'ī jurist and author of the famed book on Qur'ānic sciences *Al-burhān fī 'ulūm al-Qur'ān* who lived in Mamluk-era Egypt.

[13] Al-Zarkashī, *Al-burhān fī 'ulūm al-Qur'ān*, vol 1, pg 318.

[14] Abū al-Khayr Shams al-Dīn Muḥammad b. Muḥammad b. Muḥammad b. al-Jazarī was one of the most—if not the single-most—prominent scholar of the Qur'ānic readings who is considered a reference and authority in the field. The appellation al-Jazarī refers to Jazīrah Ibn 'Umar, Romanized as Cizre, a city in southeastern Anatolia located on the Tigris River on the border of Syria-Turkey-Iraq.

[15] Ibn al-Jazarī, *Al-munjid al-muqri'īn wa murshid al-ṭālibīn*, pg 9.

[16] 'Abd al-Fattāḥ b. 'Abd al-Ghanī al-Qāḍī was an Egyptian Azharī (alumni of Azhar University) scholar of the Qur'ānic readings and author of one of the most significant commentaries on the Shāṭibīyyah poem entitled *Al-budūr al-zāhirah fī al-qirā'āt al-'ashr al-mutawātirah min ṭarīqay al-shāṭibīyyah wa al-durrah.*

[17] al-Qāḍī, *Al-budūr al-zāhirah fī al-qirā'āt al-'ashr al-mutawātirah min ṭarīqay al-shāṭibīyyah wa al-durrah,* pg 5.

The summary of these definitions is that the science of the Qur'ānic readings is a discipline that includes the following:

1. The exact manner of articulating the words of the Qur'ān
2. The exact manner of writing the words of the Qur'ān
3. Identifying the places of agreement and difference among the Qur'ānic transmitters
4. Referencing each difference of articulation to its transmitters
5. Distinguishing what is sound—either through mass transmission[18] or otherwise—from the material transmitted as the Qur'ān.

Several matters must be noted here. Some of these individuals have defined the readings with the same definition that applies to the sciences of tajwīd (articulation) and Qur'ānic orthography, whereas the truth is that the discipline of the readings is actually much broader than these while encompassing most of their topics.

Furthermore, the conflation of the Qur'ān expressed through its variant readings with the readings in whole as a single discipline has led certain scholars like Zarkashī to restrict their definition to the differences of articulation. The other definitions, on the other hand, are inclusive of both differences as well as points of concordance. This is perhaps more correct since what is meant, for example, by the reading of Nāfi' or that of 'Āṣim is their reading of the entirety of the Qur'ān, which included all that they agree upon and differ over.

Also, these traditional definitions do not adequately highlight the conventional technical classifications of Qur'ānic transmitters, as their transmissions are at times referred to as a *reading* (*qirā'ah*), or a *transmission* (*riwāyah*), *path* (*ṭarīq*), or *option* (*wajh*).

Dr. Muḥammad 'Umar Bāzmūl[19], after relating a number of traditional definitions, points out the same shortcomings and endeavors to provide his own definition free of these issues:

> The definition of the Qur'ānic readings as a codified science is the following: all issues relating to the variations among transmitters of Allah's Book, in terms of omission or affirmation of specific elements, the existence or absence of vowels on letters, the separating or joining of words and verses, and all other matters pertaining to the exact manner of articulation and varying sounds.

---

[18] The term *tawātur* (adjective, *mutawātir*) is a ḥadīth-specific terminology that arose in latter times to describe a report that is transmitted en masse from generation to generation, such that its veracity becomes certain. Its place in the Qur'ānic sciences, and ḥadīth, has been heavily contested. The term will be discussed later in the conditions for a sound reading.

[19] He is a contemporary Saudi scholar and prolific author whose PhD dissertation at Umm al-Qurā University of Makkah served as the stimulus and starting point for this current work.

> It could also be defined as all issues relating to variations among transmitters of the Qur'ān from the perspective of language and grammar, omission and affirmation, or separating and joining, as it pertains to transmission.
>
> It could also be defined as all issues relating to the articulation of Qur'ānic words and the exact manner of this articulation with all variants attributed to their transmitters.[20]

It should be noted that the first two definitions of Dr. Bāzmūl are also restricted to the differences among readings. In addition, the first one is quite verbose, as he lists a number of specific differences for no clear reason while alluding to the rest with: 'and all other matters.' The second definition has confined the variations to several specific matters, which, in my view, is not all-encompassing and misses out on other types of differences such as the madd vowel. It may be argued, of course, that these missing elements could be considered inclusive under the listed category of 'language and grammar,' but that could also apply to the other mentioned differences. As for his third definition, it does not adequately exclude the disciplines of Arabic language, such as grammar and morphology, from being part of it.

In my opinion, defining the science of Qur'ānic readings in a manner entirely free of criticism is quite difficult, for the discipline by its nature is inclusive of a variety of additional sciences in their entirety, like tajwīd, as well as portions of others, such as the Arabic language. All of that notwithstanding, my preferred definition of the Qur'ānic readings is the following:

> The broad discipline that studies the exact manner of articulating and writing the words of the Qur'ān, the identification of points of agreement and variation among the transmitters of the Qur'ān, the referencing of each variant to its particular transmitter, and the examination all that is transmitted as Qur'ān in order to distinguish what is soundly transmitted—either through solitary or mass-transmission—from what is not.

---

[20] Bāzmūl, *Al-qirā'āt wa athruhā fī al-tafsīr wa al-aḥkām,* vol 1, pg 112.

Qur'ān Readers: Some Related Terms

The term *qāri'* is the active participle of the trilateral verb *qara'ah* ('to read') and refers to the one who has memorized the Qur'ān. See chapter 2 for an expanded discussion.

In the discipline of Qur'ānic sciences, the term *qāri'* has been further qualified to become part of a two-tier way of looking at Qur'ān memorizers. The beginner is one who has learned one to three readings, while the expert is the one who has mastered most or all of them. The term *muqri'* is the active participle of the quadrilateral root *aqra'ah* and is used for the scholar of all the readings who narrates them orally. The latter term is more specific [and a higher level], for every *muqri'* is a *qāri'* but not vice versa. Ibn al-Jazarī says the following:

> The discipline of the qirā'āt is the exact manner of articulating the words of the Qur'ān and preserving their differences by referencing each variant to its transmitter. It excludes grammar, language, tafsīr and similar topics.
>
> The *muqri'* is the scholar of the readings who relates them orally. If one memorizes the book *al-Taysīr,* for instance, he cannot start teaching it unless he learned it direct from his teachers from their teachers in a continuous way, because the readings are not mastered except through hearing and direct oral transmission.
>
> The *qāri'* who is a beginner is one who has started his studies until he has learned three readings, while the advanced *qāri'* is one who relates most of them, or, at least, the most popular ones.
>
> It is important that the *muqri',* before he devotes himself to teaching the readings, learns the Islamic sciences, especially an understanding of fiqh that is sufficient to rectify their own religious practice, and some more in order to guide others. He also must know enough foundational principles to ward off doubts concerning the readings. He must also know enough grammar to distinguish the reasons for reading variants. These are important, for without them many mistakes are bound to occur in matters such as rules of stopping, ḥamzah, and imālah.[21] He must also know a bit of language and tafsīr, but the knowledge of verse abrogation is not essential as stipulated by Imām Ja'barī. He must have memorized the Qur'ān in a way inclusive of the details of the readings, or else many mistakes are bound to happen.[22]

---

[21] See footnote 27 on page 14.

[22] Ibn al-Jazarī, *Munjid al-muqri'īn wa murshid al-ṭālibīn*, pg 9.

There are a number of related terms concerning the basic process of learning the Qur'ān.[23] The term *iqrā'* refers to the practice of Qur'ānic teachers listening to the recitation of students in order to correct their errors and then grant them permission (ijāzah) to teach others in the same manner so long as they were worthy of that, and permission to narrate the Qur'ān from them with their isnād back to the Prophet ﷺ. The term *iqrā'* (literally, 'having someone recite') is used for this practice from the angle of the teacher, while the term *qirā'ah* ('recitation') is used to describe the student who is reciting Qur'ān to his teacher.

It should be noted that the process of learning the Qur'ān traditionally has always involved students reciting the Qur'ān to teachers who would correct them. Unlike the field of ḥadīth, it was not enough for a student to hear the Qur'ān from a teacher. Listening to the entire Qur'ān from a master like Ḥuṣarī, for instance, does not ensure that a person would be able to recite with Ḥuṣarī's proficiency and mastery. Rather, the student must go through the process of actively reciting the Qur'ān to a teacher.

However, for the first generation only, it was acceptable for the Companions to hear the Qur'ān from the Prophet ﷺ and then transmit it like they had heard it due to their mastery and proficiency over pure Arabic. This did not apply to any subsequent generation, who were bound to recite the Qur'ān to their teachers.

---

[23] This entire section is not found in any of Shaykh Waleed's works but was taken by the translator from him directly on 11/1/2020.

Significance and Rationale of the Multiple Readings

The multiple readings were considered to be of great significance in the past and included important benefits. Qasṭallānī (d. 923/1517)[24] states: 'Scholars have not ceased to extract from every variation of a transmitter some meanings not found in other readings, and the Qur'ānic readings are surely evidence for jurists in extracting rulings and their recourse in finding the right path.'[25] The best and most comprehensive discussion of the wisdom of these variant readings is from Ibn al-Jazarī, who summarized as follows:

1. *Providing ease and facilitation for the ummah*: Since every people have their own individual dialects which are easier for them while being difficult for others, the variant readings encompassed multiple dialectical ranges so that a Muslim could choose whatever is easier to recite for them.
2. *Demonstrating maximal eloquence and uniqueness while maintaining perfect brevity*: Multiple word variations exist for many expressions rather than having multiple verse variations, which would have made the Qur'ān far lengthier to achieve the same result.[26]
3. *Maintaining perfect uniformity across its multiplicity*: The variant readings through their multiplicity still manage to affirm and support one another, demonstrating that all of them represent one essential form in their meaning and eloquence. This is a decisive evidence of the Qur'ān being from God as no human being can achieve anything similar to this.
4. *Allowing ease of memorization and transmission*: Memorizing and preserving a single word with some variations is far easier than retaining multiple sentences that convey the same meanings as those readings.
5. *Magnifying the rewards of this ummah*: Muslims have expended their utmost efforts in extracting wisdom and rulings from the implications of every word, thereby uncovering its hidden secrets and allusions. Allah says: ﴿*Their Lord answered the Prayer thus: 'I will*

[24] Aḥmad b. Muḥammad b. Abī Bakr b. ʿAbd al-Malik al-Qasṭallānī was a great Shāfiʿī scholar of Qur'ān and ḥadīth, contemporary of Suyūṭī, and author of a commentary on Ṣaḥīḥ Bukhārī entitled *Irshād al-Sārī*. He was born in 851 AH and died in Cairo in 923/1517.

[25] Qasṭallānī, *Laṭā'if al-ishārāt li funūn al-qirā'āt,* vol 1, pg 171.

[26] What this means is that the Qur'ān through this structure of a single text encompassing variant readings achieved a type of brevity (*iqtiṣār*) while encompassing a broad range of eloquent meanings (*balāghah*) in a way that is unparalleled and unmatched (*iʿjāz*).

not let the work of any of you, male or female, to go to waste; each of you is from the other.﴿' (3:195).

6. *Highlighting a unique distinction for this nation*: Since it received its scripture in this manner, this ummah has not failed to preserve a single vowel or lack thereof (sukūn), or a single case of a letter pronounced in heavy or light manner, even to the extent of preserving the exact lengths of certain vowels and their precise form of vowelization such as imālah.[27] No other nation has done this with their religious Book.
7. *Preserving the Qur'ān itself*: The multiplicity of readings was a stimulus for the preservation of the chains of these readings due to the obvious need for the ummah to authenticate these readings by rigorously referencing them to these scholars. That led to the preservation of the chains of transmission for the Qur'ān itself, which is another distinction of this nation.

---

[27] Imālah is the articulation of the alif sound closer to the yā. Examples of the normal alif sound would the middle vowels of the words *rot* and *drop*, while the imālah of those sounds would be like the words *rate* and *drape*.

The Seven Modes of Revelation

Qur'ān Revealed in Seven Modes

Allah revealed His Noble Book in seven modes (*aḥruf*),[28] as indicated by a mass-transmitted ḥadīth from Allah's Messenger ﷺ narrated through a large group of Companions including ʿUmar, Ubayy b. Kaʿb, Ibn Masʿūd, Ibn ʿAbbās, Ḥudhayfah, Abū Bakrah, and ʿUbādah b. al-Ṣāmiṭ. Many of these reports appear in the Ṣaḥīḥayn (Bukhārī and Muslim).

Here I will relate three sound transmissions of this ḥadīth which adequately serve to reveal what these modes mean and the wisdom behind their number. They also demonstrate that the term seven is a literal number and not representative of general multiplicity, and that these revealed modes were a phenomenon of Madīnah.

The first report is that of Ubayy b. Kaʿb:

Ubayy b. Kaʿb reported that the Messenger of Allah ﷺ was near the pond of the Ghifār clan when Jibrīl came to him and said: 'Allah has ordered for you that your people recite the Qur'ān in one mode (ḥarf).' Upon this, the Prophet ﷺ replied: 'I ask Allah's pardon and forgiveness! My people are not capable of doing that.' Jibrīl then came for the second time and said: 'Allah has ordered for you that your people recite the Qur'ān in two modes.' Upon this, the Prophet ﷺ again said: 'I seek pardon and forgiveness from Allah, for my people would not be able to do so.' Jibrīl came for the third time and said: 'Allah has ordered for you that your people recite the Qur'ān in three modes.' Upon this he again said: 'I ask pardon and forgiveness from Allah! My people would not be able to do it.' He then came to him for the fourth time and said: 'Allah has commanded for you that your people recite the Qur'ān in seven modes, and in whichever mode they recite, they would be correct.'[29]

عَن أُبَيِّ بنِ كَعبٍ، أَنَّ النَّبِيَّ صلى الله عليه وسلم كَانَ عِندَ أَضَاةِ بَنِي غِفَارٍ قَالَ فَأَتَاهُ جِبرِيلُ عَلَيهِ السَّلاَمُ فَقَالَ إِنَّ اللَّهَ يَأمُرُكَ أَن تَقرَأَ أُمَّتُكَ القُرآنَ عَلَى حَرفٍ. فَقَالَ أَسأَلُ اللَّهَ مُعَافَاتَهُ وَمَغفِرَتَهُ وَإِنَّ أُمَّتِي لاَ تُطِيقُ ذَلِكَ. ثُمَّ أَتَاهُ الثَّانِيَةَ فَقَالَ إِنَّ اللَّهَ يَأمُرُكَ أَن تَقرَأَ أُمَّتُكَ القُرآنَ عَلَى حَرفَينِ فَقَالَ أَسأَلُ اللَّهَ مُعَافَاتَهُ وَمَغفِرَتَهُ وَإِنَّ أُمَّتِي لاَ تُطِيقُ ذَلِكَ. ثُمَّ جَاءَهُ الثَّالِثَةَ فَقَالَ إِنَّ اللَّهَ يَأمُرُكَ أَن تَقرَأَ أُمَّتُكَ القُرآنَ عَلَى ثَلاَثَةِ أَحرُفٍ. فَقَالَ أَسأَلُ اللَّهَ مُعَافَاتَهُ وَمَغفِرَتَهُ وَإِنَّ أُمَّتِي لاَ تُطِيقُ ذَلِكَ. ثُمَّ جَاءَهُ الرَّابِعَةَ فَقَالَ إِنَّ اللَّهَ يَأمُرُكَ أَن تَقرَأَ أُمَّتُكَ القُرآنَ عَلَى سَبعَةِ أَحرُفٍ فَأَيُّمَا حَرفٍ قَرَءُوا عَلَيهِ فَقَد أَصَابُوا.

[28] For another excellent discussion on the seven modes, see Yasin Dutton. ORALITY, LITERACY AND THE 'SEVEN AḤRUF' ḤADĪTH. Journal of Islamic Studies 23:1 (2012).

[29] Ṣaḥīḥ Muslim: Kitāb ṣalāt al-musāfirīn wa qaṣrihā—Bāb bayan anna al-Qur'āna ʿalā sabʿat aḥruf wa bayan maʿnāhā; Also related by Abū Dāwūd, Tirmidhī, and Nasā'ī.

The second report comes from Ubayy b. Ka'b, Abū Bakrah, and 'Ubādah b. al-Ṣāmiṭ:

The Prophet ﷺ said: Jibrīl and Mikā'īl, peace be upon them, came to me, and Jibrīl sat on my right while Mikā'īl on my left. Jibrīl said: 'Recite the Qur'ān with one mode of recitation.' Mikā'īl kept saying: 'Teach him more, teach him more,' until there were seven modes of recitation, each of which is whole and sufficient.[30] [31]

قَالَ النَّبِيُّ صَلَّى اللهُ عَلَيهِ وَسَلَّمَ إِنَّ جِبرِيلَ وَمِيكَائِيلَ عَلَيهِمَا السَّلَامُ أَتَيَانِي، فَقَعَدَ جِبرِيلُ عَن يَمِينِي، وَمِيكَائِيلُ عَن يَسَارِي، فَقَالَ جِبرِيلُ عَلَيهِ السَّلَامُ: اقرَأِ القُرآنَ عَلَى حَرفٍ، قَالَ مِيكَائِيلُ: استَزِدهُ استَزِدهُ، حَتَّى بَلَغَ سَبعَةَ أَحرُفٍ، فَكُلُّ حَرفٍ شَافٍ كَافٍ.

The third report comes from 'Umar b. al-Khaṭṭāb:

Narrated 'Umar b. al-Khaṭṭāb: I heard Hishām b. Ḥākim b. Ḥizām reciting Sūrah al-Furqān during the lifetime of Allah's Messenger ﷺ and I noticed that that he recited in several different ways (aḥruf) which Allah's Messenger had not taught me. I was about to jump over him during the prayer, but I waited until he finished. I put his upper garment around his neck, seized him by it and asked, 'Who taught you this sūrah which I heard you reciting?' He replied, 'Allah's Messenger ﷺ taught it to me.' I replied, 'You have told a lie, for by Allah, Allah's Messenger has taught it to me in a way different from yours.'

So I dragged him to Allah's Messenger ﷺ while holding him and said to the Prophet, 'I heard this person reciting sūrah al-Furqān in a way

عَن عُمَرَ بنَ الخَطَّابِ يَقُولُ: سَمِعتُ هِشَامَ بنَ حَكِيمٍ يَقرَأُ سُورَةَ الفُرقَانِ فِي حَيَاةِ رَسُولِ اللهِ صَلَّى اللهُ عَلَيهِ وَسَلَّمَ، فَاستَمَعتُ لِقِرَاءَتِهِ، فَإِذَا هُوَ يَقرَأُ عَلَى حُرُوفٍ كَثِيرَةٍ لَم يُقرِئنِيهَا رَسُولُ اللهِ صَلَّى اللهُ عَلَيهِ وَسَلَّمَ، فَكِدتُ أُسَاوِرُهُ فِي الصَّلَاةِ، فَتَصَبَّرتُ حَتَّى سَلَّمَ، فَلَبَّبتُهُ بِرِدَائِهِ فَقُلتُ: مَن أَقرَأَكَ هَذِهِ السُّورَةَ الَّتِي سَمِعتُكَ تَقرَأُ؟ قَالَ: أَقرَأَنِيهَا رَسُولُ اللهِ صَلَّى اللهُ عَلَيهِ وَسَلَّمَ، فَقُلتُ: كَذَبتَ، أَقرَأَنِيهَا عَلَى غَيرِ مَا قَرَأتَ ، فَانطَلَقتُ بِهِ أَقُودُهُ إِلَى رَسُولِ اللهِ صَلَّى اللهُ عَلَيهِ وَسَلَّمَ ، فَقُلتُ: إِنِّي سَمِعتُ هَذَا يَقرَأُ سُورَةَ الفُرقَانِ عَلَى حُرُوفٍ لَم تُقرِئنِيهَا، فَقَالَ: أَرسِلهُ، اقرَأ يَا هِشَامُ فَقَرَأَ القِرَاءَةَ الَّتِي سَمِعتُهُ، فَقَالَ رَسُولُ اللهِ صَلَّى

---

[30] Sunan al-Nasā'ī: Kitāb al-Iftitāḥ—Bāb Jāmi' mā jā'ā fī al-Qur'ān. Also related in Musnad Aḥmad. It was authenticated by Albānī in *al-Silsilah al-ṣaḥīḥah* (843) and *Ṣaḥīḥ al-jāmi'* (78).

[31] The seven aḥruf have been described in this report by two adjectives *kāf* (literally, 'sufficient') and *shāf* (literally, 'healing') which have been subject to some scholarly discussion. For some scholars kāf means enough to establish the Qur'ān's inimitable eloquence, or proof for the truthfulness of the Prophet, while shāf means that it is a healing for the hearts or erasing of sins. It should be noted that compound expressions in Arabic create new meanings independent of each individual term. In this sense, Mullā 'Alī Qārī has described—and 'Ubaydullah Mubārakpūrī agreed—that kāf means sufficient for establishing proof and judgement against disbelievers while shāf means sufficient in achieving the believer's goals in reciting it, i.e. rectifying the hearts. The combined sense is that each mode is complete and whole for the Qur'ān's purposes.

different from the way you taught me.' The Prophet ordered me to release him and asked Hishām to recite it. When he recited it, Allah's Messenger said, 'It was revealed in this way.' He then asked me to recite it, and when I did, he said, 'It was revealed in this way. Indeed, the Qur'ān has been revealed in seven different modes, so recite it in the way that is easier for you.'[32]

اللهُ عَلَيْهِ وَسَلَّمَ: كَذَلِكَ أُنْزِلَتْ ثُمَّ قَالَ رَسُولُ اللهِ صَلَّى اللهُ عَلَيْهِ وَسَلَّمَ: اقرأ يَا عُمَرُ فَقَرَأْتُ الَّتِي أَقْرَأَنِي ، فَقَالَ: كَذَلِكَ أُنْزِلَتْ، إِنَّ هَذَا القُرْآنَ أُنْزِلَ عَلَى سَبْعَةِ أَحْرُفٍ، فَاقْرَءُوا مَا تَيَسَّرَ مِنْهُ.

There are also many other similar reports, including one in which a difference between Ubayy b, Ka'b and Ibn Mas'ūd was brought to the Prophet's attention, and he uttered similar words. What these reports teach us is that Allah revealed the Qur'ān in seven modes, all of which the Prophet ﷺ recited himself and taught to his Companions. The Qur'ān was revealed in seven variations, or types of differences, or languages. From the range of these multiple modes of revelation, the Prophet taught each Companion one particular mode.

In addition, what is certain is that the seven popular readings are different from these seven modes. The Qur'ān was revealed according to these modes which the Prophet recited and taught. This was long before the birth of the seven Imāms who chose specific selections from these modes for their own recitation (thus popularizing the specific readings that bear their names).[33]

Abū Shāmah (d. 665/1268)[34] stated: Some people supposed that the seven readings currently widespread are intended by this ḥadīth, but this contradicts the consensus of scholars and is the view of only the ignorant ones.[35]

What Are the Seven Aḥruf?

As for the seven modes alluded to it in these ḥadīth reports, scholars differed over them extensively to the point of producing as many as forty views. However, many of these opinions overlap, and the proponents for some of them are not known for sure. For this reason, I will confine myself to two of the most popular views on this matter:

---

[32] Ṣaḥīḥ Bukhārī: Kitāb al-ashkhāṣ wa al-khuṣūmāt—Bāb kalām al-khuṣūm ba'ḍuhum fī ba'ḍ; Kitāb faḍā'il al-Qur'ān—Bāb unzila al-Qur'ān 'alā sab'at aḥruf and Bāb man lam yara ba'san an yaqūl sūrat al-baqarah wa sūrat kadha wa kadha; Kitāb al-tawḥīd—Bāb qawl Allah faqra'ū mā tayassara min al-Qur'ān; Ṣaḥīḥ Muslim: Kitāb ṣalāt al-musāfirīn wa qaṣrihā—Bāb bayan anna al-Qur'āna 'alā sab'at aḥruf wa bayan ma'nāhā

[33] More on this in chapter 2.

[34] Abū al-Qāsim Shihāb al-Dīn 'Abd al-Raḥmān b. Ismā'īl b. Ibrāhīm, native of Palestine, resident of Damascus, was a noted Qur'ān scholar and historian with five surviving works.

[35] Abū Shāmah, *al-Murshid al-wajīz*, pg 146.

The first view is that these modes refer to seven languages or dialects of early Arabs. This was the opinion of Sufyān b. ʿUyaynah (d. 198/814),[36] ʿAbdullah b. Wahb (d. 197/813),[37] Ibn Jarīr al-Ṭabarī (d. 310/923),[38] Abū Jaʿfar al-Ṭaḥāwī (d. 321/933)[39] and others. The details of these dialects, however, were not agreed upon. Abū ʿUbayd al-Qāsim b. al-Sallām (d. 224/838),[40] for one, stated that they are specific dialects of the clans of Quraysh, Hudhayl, Hawāzin, Tamīm, Kinānah, Thaqīf, and al-Yaman. Abū Ḥātim of Sijistān (d. 255/869)[41] believed that they represented the dialects of Azd, Rabīʿah, Saʿd b. Bakr, Quraysh, Hudhayl, Hawāzin and Tamīm.[42] There was also other variations of this view.

The second view is that these modes refer to seven types of variations, and this was the opinion of Ibn Qutaybah (d. 276/889)[43] and Ibn al-Jazarī. The word *ḥarf* in Arabic is often used for type or variety. It is used in this sense in: ﴾*And there is, too, among men many a one who worships God on the border-line of faith (ḥarf): thus, if good befalls him, he is satisfied with Him; but if a trial assails him, he turns away utterly, losing [thereby both] this world and the life to come: [and] this, indeed, is a loss beyond compare!*﴿ (22:11). This means that among the two states (comfort and hardship), these people worship Allah only in one of them: that of comfort. As for comfort and hardship, each of them is a state or type (ḥarf) of the human condition.

Between these two basic views, there were additional ones with minor differences which some scholars considered to be separate views.

However, I will confine myself to the approach of Ibn al-Jazarī because it is the most precise, well-known, and comprehensive of them all. He states:

> I have studied all Qur'ān readings, including those that are sound, weak, anomalous (shādh)[44] and rejected, and have concluded that their variations come back to seven basic differences:

---

[36] He was the premier ḥadīth scholar and jurist of Makkah, born 107 and died 198. He performed Ḥajj seventy times, and countless people took ḥadīth from him.

[37] He was a great Egyptian scholar who was known for mastery of ḥadīth and fiqh along with great piety. He was among the best students of Malik, Sufyān b. ʿUyaynah, and Layth b. Sa'd.

[38] Muḥammad b. Jarīr b. Yazīd al-Ṭabarī was an early Qur'ānic commentator, historian, and author of numerous works.

[39] Abū Jaʿfar Aḥmad b. Muḥammad b. Salāmah al-Ṭaḥāwī hailed from Egypt and was a master of ḥadīth and fiqh, and author of a famous treatise on Muslim creed.

[40] He was a scholar and author of ḥadīth, fiqh, Arabic and poetry from Khurāsān.

[41] Abū Ḥātim Sahl b. Muḥammad b. ʿUthmān b. Yazīd was a great grammarian and Qur'ānic scholar from Baṣrah.

[42] Zarkashī, *al-Burhān*, vol 1, pg 219.

[43] Abū Muḥammad ʿAbdullah b. Muslim was a prolific scholar and author of a diverse range of works who was of Persian origin who hailed from Merv, became judge of Dīnavar and ultimately settled and in Baghdad, where he died.

[44] Shādh readings will be discussed extensively in a forthcoming section.

1. Variation in short-vowels without affecting the meaning or basic form of words. An example is the verse:

   الَّذِينَ يَبْخَلُونَ وَيَأْمُرُونَ النَّاسَ بِالْبُخْلِ

   ﴿*Those who are miserly and command others to be so.*﴾ (4:37)

   Here the word *bukhl* is read in two ways: the above rendition of ***bukhl*** (with a damma vowel on the letter bā and an unvowelled khā) or ***bakhal*** (with a fatḥa on both the bā and the khā):

   الَّذِينَ يَبْخَلُونَ وَيَأْمُرُونَ النَّاسَ بِالْبَخَلِ

2. Variation in short-vowels that affect the meanings but not the basic form of words. An example is in the verse:

   فَتَلَقَّىٰ آدَمُ مِن رَّبِّهِ كَلِمَاتٍ فَتَابَ عَلَيْهِ

   ﴿*And **Adam received words from his Lord** and repented.*﴾ (2:37)

   In this reading, the word *Ādamu* is read in the nominative case (ending with ḍamma) while the word *kalimātin* is read with kasrah indicating that it serves as the object of the sentence ('Adam received words'). The alternate reading flips the vowels of these same words and creates the meaning:

   فَتَلَقَّىٰ آدَمَ مِن رَّبِّهِ كَلِمَاتٌ فَتَابَ عَلَيْهِ

   *And **words came down to Adam** from his Lord and he repented.*[45]

3. Changes in letters (from dotting of consonants) which affect meanings but not the forms of words, as in the verse:

   هُنَالِكَ تَبْلُو كُلُّ نَفْسٍ مَّا أَسْلَفَتْ

   ﴿*There every single self **experiences** what it has previously done.*﴾ (10:30)

---

[45] The Bridges translation is: *Adam was received by words from his Lord.*

The word ***tablū*** is also read as a different word with bā replaced by tā (***tatlū***):

هُنَالِكَ تَتلُو كُلُّ نَفسٍ مَّا أَسلَفَت

*There every single self **reads** what it has previously done.*

4. Variations of letters which alter their form but not their meanings. An example is in the verse:

اهدِنَا الصِّرَاطَ المستَقِيمَ

﴿*Guide us to the straight path.*﴾ (1:6)

The word *ṣirāṭ* is also read with a sīn letter (***sirāṭ***):

السِّرَاط

5. Variations of letters in form as well as meaning. An example is in the verse:

كَانُوا هُم أَشَدَّ مِنهُم قُوَّةً

﴿*They were superior **to them** in strength.*﴾ (40:21)

The word ***minhum*** is also read as ***minkum***, meaning 'They were superior *to you* in strength':

كَانُوا هُم أَشَدَّ مِنكُم قُوَّةً

*They were superior **to you** in strength.*

6. Variations in word order. The following is an example:

يُقَاتِلُونَ فِي سَبِيلِ اللَّهِ فَيَقتُلُونَ وَيُقتَلُونَ

﴿*They fight in the way of Allah, so they **kill and get killed**.*﴾ (9:111)

The order of the last two words is switched to create the meaning:

يُقَاتِلُونَ فِي سَبِيلِ اللَّهِ فَيُقتَلُونَ وَيَقتُلُونَ

*They fight in the way of God, and **get killed and kill**.*

7. Variations of addition or omission. The word *wa waṣṣā* is read in two forms, one with an additional letter hamzah (*wa awṣā*):

وَوَصَّى بِهَا إِبْرَاهِيمُ بَنِيهِ

وَأَوصَى بِهَا إِبْرَاهِيمُ بَنِيهِ

﴾*And Ibrāhīm* ***enjoined*** *on his children to follow the same way.*﴿ (2:132)

There are many such examples of entire words that are added/ omitted from certain modes, such as preposition *min,* the conjunction *wāw,* the pronoun *huwa,* and others:

جَنَّاتٍ تَجْرِي تَحْتَهَا الْأَنْهَارُ

جَنَّاتٍ تَجْرِي مِن تَحْتِهَا الْأَنْهَارُ

﴾*Gardens* ***[from]*** *underneath which rivers flow.*﴿ (9:100)

فَإِنَّ اللَّهَ هُوَ الْغَنِيُّ الْحَمِيدُ

فَإِنَّ اللَّهَ الْغَنِيُّ الْحَمِيدُ

﴾*Allah* ***[He]*** *is Self-Sufficient, Immensely Praiseworthy.*﴿ (57:24)

وَسَارِعُوا إِلَىٰ مَغْفِرَةٍ مِّن رَّبِّكُمْ وَجَنَّةٍ

سَارِعُوا إِلَىٰ مَغْفِرَةٍ مِّن رَّبِّكُمْ وَجَنَّةٍ

﴾***[And]*** *hasten to the forgiveness of your Lord and to a Paradise.*﴿ (3:133)[46]

[46] Ibn al-Jazarī, *al-Nashr,* vol 1, pg 16-7. Dr. Yasin Dutton summarizes: 'In other words, Ibn al-Jazarī is saying that the seven aḥruf indicate seven types of linguistic variation, or we could say seven ways of modifying speech within the single framework of one language (the dialect of Quraysh) and while maintaining one meaning.'

The Relation between the Aḥruf and the Historical Readings

The seven modes of revelation are an entirely different entity than the seven, or ten, popular Qur'ānic readings, although they are related. We can say for certain that the Qur'ānic readings, at least a large portion of them, are part of the seven aḥruf.

These seven modes are a broader entity that includes within them the readings that have reached us as well as more than that. How so? The differences among the ten readings does not exceed these seven types of variation that were mentioned above, or the seven dialects, if we hold the opinion that they represent these dialects. Since the readings represent portions of the aḥruf, the aḥruf are naturally broader than the readings.

As for the complex issue of how the modes relate to the readings, there are two opposing views along with an intermediate one: that the current readings contain all of the seven aḥruf, only one of them, or some of them.

The Readings Contain All Seven Aḥruf

On one end, it was claimed that the readings corresponding to the 'Uthmānic codices are inclusive of all revealed modes of recitation. This was the view of a large group of jurists, Qur'ānic scholars and theologians. Their reasoning was that it would not have been allowed for the ummah to neglect the transmission of any of the modes through which the Qur'ān was revealed because that would be tantamount to neglecting the Qur'ān.

Proponents of this view are faced with a difficulty: how do you reconcile the existence of established Qur'ānic variants with sound isnāds which do not conform with 'Uthmānic codices? Having sound isnād to the Prophet shows that they were clearly part of the seven aḥruf, yet they contradicted the 'Uthmānic codex. For example, Abū al-Dardā' used to recite:

وَالذَّكَرِ وَالأُنثَىٰ

And by the male and female.

in place of:

وَمَا خَلَقَ الذَّكَرَ وَالأُنثَىٰ

﴿*And by the One who created male and female.*﴾ (92:3)

'Uthmān had sent a codex to Abū al-Dardā' in Syria to teach from. However, since it contained the latter reading, Abū al-Dardā' found it difficult because he had heard differently from the Prophet ﷺ, prompting him to look for corroboration:

> 'Alqamah reported: I came to Syria and offered a two-rak'ah prayer, after which I prayed, 'O Allah! Bless me with a good pious companion.' I then went to some people and sat with them. An old man came and

sat by my side. I asked, 'Who is he?' They replied, 'He is Abū al-Dardā'' I said to him, 'I prayed to Allah to bless me with a pious companion and He sent you to me.'

He asked me: To which country do you belong? I replied: I am one of the people of Iraq. He again asked: From where in Iraq? I replied: The city of Kūfah. He again asked: Do you recite according to the recitation of ʿAbdullah b. Masʿūd? I said: Yes. He said: Recite this verse ﴿*By the night when it covers*﴾. So I recited it: ﴿*By the night when it covers, and the day when it shines, and by the male and female*﴾. He smiled and said: I have heard the Messenger of Allah ﷺ reciting like this.[47]

This proves that both Ibn Masʿūd and Abū al-Dardā' were taught by the Prophet a reading which did not correspond to the ʿUthmānic compilation. This compilation was carried out by other Companions who had written them according to what they had also received from the Prophet ﷺ. Both variants had sound isnāds but only one of them corresponded to the ʿUthmānic codex. The non-ʿUthmānic codex variant, which happens to be related by Bukhārī and Muslim, is considered part of the shādh readings.

Another similar example is that Abū Bakr used to recite:

وَجَاءَت سَكرَةُ الحَقِّ بِالمَوتِ

in place of:

وَجَاءَت سَكرَةُ المَوتِ بِالحَقِّ

﴿*Lo, the agony of death has indeed come with the truth.*﴾ (50:19)[48]

Some scholars responded by pointing out that these variant readings with sound isnāds were originally part of the seven aḥruf but later abrogated. They based this on the Final Rehearsal[49] of the Prophet with Jibrīl in the last year of his life, which was witnessed by Zayd and later used by him to compile the muṣḥaf in accord with

---

[47] Ṣaḥīḥ Bukhārī: Kitāb faḍā'il al-ṣaḥābah—Bāb manāqib ʿAmmār wa Ḥudhayfah; Kitāb faḍā'il al-ṣaḥābah—Bāb manāqib ʿAbdullah b. Masʿūd; Kitāb tafsīr al-Qur'ān (sūrah wa al-layli idhā yaghshā)—Bāb wa al-nahāri idhā tajallā; Kitāb al-isti'dhān—Bāb man alqā lahu wisādah; Ṣaḥīḥ Muslim: Kitāb ṣalāh al-musāfirīn wa qaṣrihā—Bāb mā yataʿallaq bi al-qirāʿāt.

[48] Tafsīr Ṭabarī, vol 22, pg 346-7.

[49] According to sound reports, such as the sixth ḥadīth in the very beginning of Ṣaḥīḥ Bukhārī, the Prophet ﷺ would review the Qur'ān with Jibrīl each night during the month of Ramadan, but in the final year of his life, he reviewed the Qur'ān twice. Scholars termed this the Final Rehearsal (al-ʿarḍah al-akhīrah) and recognized its central role in many aspects of Qur'ānic sciences.

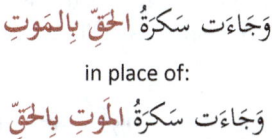

this final recital.[50] The ʿUthmānic codices, in their view, contain all of the seven aḥruf excluding the abrogated portions.

The Readings Contain Only One of the Aḥruf

On the other end, there is the view that all of the current Qur'ānic readings corresponding to the ʿUthmānic script are inclusive of only a single mode of the Qur'ān. This is the view of those who believe that the aḥruf represented dialects and that the ʿUthmānic codex was compiled in the single dialect (ḥarf) of Quraysh. This is the view of the likes of Ṭabarī, Abū al-Qāsim al-Shāṭibī (d. 590/1194),[51] Ibn Taymiyyah (d. 728/1328)[52] and others. Their reasoning was that the seven modes were never obligatory upon the ummah but merely a concession or allowance and that Muslims were free to choose from them what they wished. Each of the seven aḥruf was independently complete, as described in a Prophetic ḥadīth report.[53] When the Companions, however, saw that the nation was beginning to differ and fight due to not being under a single ḥarf, the Companions united behind one. This position was perfectly valid, and, as a community, they were protected from uniting on error. On their part, there was no abandoning of any obligation or engaging in any prohibited action. Abū Jaʿfar al-Ṭabarī elaborates:

> The ummah was ordered to preserve the Qur'ān and to choose for its recitation and memorization any of the seven modes, in the same way it has been ordered, when willfully breaking an oath to expiate, if

---

[50] The details of the Final Rehearsal remain murky, especially the witnessing of it by Companions. Shaykh Waleed admits: 'The matter of the Final Rehearsal is a thorny one and contains much that is unknown. We do know for certain that specific Companions 'witnessed' the Rehearsal but the exact details are disputed. One possibility is that these Companions were physically present during the Prophet's recital to Jibrīl. Another possibility is that what was meant was simply that, in the course of the six months since the Last Rehearsal and the death of the Prophet in Rabīʿ al-Awwal, these Companions learned the Qur'ān as affirmed in this Last Rehearsal, either by hearing it from the Prophet, reciting it to him, or hearing it from someone else who had recited the Final Rehearsal to the Prophet.'

Dr. Usāmah ʿAbd al-Wahhab Ḥamd concludes in a comprehensive analysis of the Final Rehearsal reports: 'There is no clear text that details the meaning of this witnessing, but they prove at a minimum that these Companions received the Qur'ān directly from the Prophet after his Last Rehearsal, not that they were physically present.'

[51] Abū al-Qāsim al-Qāsim b. Fīrruh b. Khalaf was a blind scholar of Andalus, from Xàtiva near Valencia, who was the greatest scholar of the Qur'ānic readings of his time as well as being a noted linguist. He authored the famous 1100-line poem *Ḥirz al-Amānī,* better known as *al-Shāṭibīyyah,* which remains the predominant way one learns the Seven Readings to this day.

[52] Abū al-ʿAbbās Taqī al-Dīn Aḥmad b. ʿAbd al-Ḥālim b. ʿAbd al-Salām b. Taymiyyah, who hailed from Ḥarrān near the Syria-Turkey border and settled in Damascus, was a Mamluk-era revivalist scholar who needs little introduction as his prolific pen and keen insights continues to enlighten nearly every Islamic discipline to this day.

[53] See footnote 31 on page 16.

> possessing means, through any one of three ways. If all of them were to agree on any one of the three expiations without prohibiting any of the others, they would have achieved the command of Allah and fulfilled His right upon them. Similarly, the ummah was ordered to preserve the Qur'ān and allowed to recite it in any mode it preferred. The nation then chose, for a valid reason, to confine themselves to one mode in their readings.[54]

Imām Abū 'Amr al-Dānī (d. 444)[55] stated:

> The reason for the variations in the readings is that the Messenger of Allah ﷺ used to review the Qur'ān with Jibrīl once each year, and twice in his final year. In these, Jibrīl used to teach the Prophet one mode and reading during each review, from the various modes and ways of reading. That is why the Prophet said, 'Indeed the Qur'ān was revealed in these modes, each of which is whole and sufficient.'[56] He allowed the ummah to recite whichever of these they wished while believing in and affirming all of them, as they were all revealed from God and taken from Him. He did not command the ummah to preserve all of them, nor recite by all of them. Rather, they were free to choose any of them in the same way that they were free to choose, in the case of the breaking of an oath, from any expiation [among the available choices].[57]

In fact, al-Dānī's claim that the Prophet in his annual review would recite one mode or reading has been contested by others. Others such as Ibn Ḥajar believe that the Prophet would review with Jibrīl all of the revealed modes every year. The Qur'ānic copies that were compiled in the era of Abū Bakr were written corresponding to all of these modes but as differences became numerous later on, Companions in the era of 'Uthmān compiled Qur'ānic copies corresponding to one mode only, which was the mode corresponding to the final Prophetic review.

The Readings Contain Some of the Seven Aḥruf

An intermediate view on this, and that of the majority of scholars, is that 'Uthmān intended for the codex to be compiled according to one aḥruf, but as the skeletal script was able to accommodate other readings, these were allowed and taught by the Companions.

---

[54] Ṭabarī, *Tafsīr al-Ṭabarī,* vol 1,pg 58.
[55] Abū 'Amr 'Uthmān b. Sa'īd al-Dānī of Cordoba was a great scholar, Qur'ānic expert and author of well-known works in the Qur'ānic sciences. He lived from 371 to 444.
[56] See footnotes 30 and 31 on page 16.
[57] Al-Dānī, *Jāmi' al-bayān fī al-qirā'āt al-sab',* pg 5.

In other words, the ʿUthmānic manuscripts encompassed from the readings all that the adopted script would allow, and these were those of the final Prophetic Rehearsal. These readings included much of the seven modes but not all of them. The ʿUthmānic codices did not include any canceled portions of the Qur'ān which were abrogated in the Final Rehearsal or before that. Evidence for that are the established readings of Companions which do not correspond to the ʿUthmānic script, such as the previously mentioned readings of Abū al-Dardā', Ibn Masʿūd, and Abū Bakr. These and other examples of readings which do not correspond to the ʿUthmānic script were clearly among the seven modes because these Companions had heard them from the Prophet ﷺ.

Alternately, it was claimed that the ʿUthmānic script incorporated all of the seven modes that were not abrogated, but this is not entirely precise. The codices were intended to exclude all abrogated portions of the Qur'ān and not necessarily to comprehensively include all of seven aḥruf. The ʿUthmānic codex project was intended to represent the Final Rehearsal, through a single mode and a single script (that of Quraysh), which was written in a manner that allowed the incorporation of some additional aḥruf.[58] More details on the ʿUthmānic codices are forthcoming in chapter 3.

Here, a problematic issue arises for some: why are differences among the readings, with their multiple transmissions and routes, seemingly much larger than the seven modes? The answer to that is historical.

---

[58] The information in this paragraph is taken from a direct exchange with Shaykh Waleed on 11/1/20.

History of the Qur'ānic Readings

The practice of the first three generations was that one simply followed the practice of their teacher in recitation, because recitation was a transmitted practice with no role for one's personal opinion.

The Prophet taught his Companions various readings and the Companions had their own students who in turn had their own students, all of them teaching Qur'ān with isnāds back to the Prophet.

As for those who read to more than one teacher, they could either confine themselves to one of them and leave the others or adopt for themselves a reading based upon a combination of what they read to their teachers. These personal selections were not confined to the seven popular Imāms or their transmitters. The proof for that is that Abū Ja'far al-Ṭabarī (d. 310/923) had his own personal adoption which he composed from 22 readings that he had read upon his teachers and in turn documented in his book *al-Qirā'āt*. Among the students of Ṭabarī who read his personal selection with him was Ibn Mujāhid (d. 324/936)[59] himself, the originator of the notion of the seven Imāms.

In the first generation there were various personal adoptions. Abū Ḥātim of Sijistān, for instance, narrated 24 readings, four from the seven known readings and twenty from outside of them. After these individuals, al-Hudhalī in his book *al-Kāmil* reported fifty readings. All of these readings were part of the seven modes.

Conceptually, the practice of these personal selections is like the notion of combinations and permutations in mathematics, which can almost become limitless. If a verse contains three words transmitted from the Prophet, each word with three possible ways of recitation, then this verse could potentially be read in 27 ways (3 x 3 x 3).

Over time, the teachers of the Qur'ān became extremely numerous until a 3rd century Qur'ānic scholar for the first time, based upon a wisdom known only to God, chose seven Qur'ānic teachers and documented their readings, giving rise to the notion of the Seven Readings. A student of Ṭabarī and teacher of Dāruquṭnī, Ibn Mujāhid was a master of Qur'ānic readings during his time who authored a book around the year 300 AH in which he confined himself to seven readings which he considered the dominant ones in his time. This was a significant year, destined to mark the end of the era of early scholars (*mutaqaddimīn*) of Qur'ānic readings, in the same way that it delineated the end of the early ḥadīth scholars. Ibn Mujāhid's students soon began to restrict themselves to his work alone as aspirations and ambitions dwindled over time. And so, the very same thing happened here which

[59] One of the most influential scholars of the Qur'ānic readings due to his selection of seven Imāms which bore a permanent imprint on the discipline of Qur'ānic sciences by establishing a seven-Imām canon. He authored his famous work, *Kitāb al-sab'ah fī al-qirā'āt,* in the year 300 AH. He lived from 245/859 to 324/936.

had happened with the restriction of jurisprudence to the four legal schools or the restriction of sunnah works to six canonical ḥadīth works. In ḥadīth, for example, after this era of documentation, it was no longer acceptable to mix the narration of one ḥadīth book with another and narration of ḥadīth was confined to the narrations found in these books.

Ibn Mujāhid in specifying these specific seven individuals from among their contemporaries wound up popularizing them, though in reality there existed more reading traditions beyond them. In fact, in the introduction to his famous book *Kitāb al-sab'*, which remains widely read and published to this day, Ibn Mujāhid wrote that he had chosen seven of the most popular and widely known Qur'ānic readers whose status, leadership in Qur'ānic scholarship, and soundness in narration was widely agreed upon. This was an admission that there were many others. He also mentioned the reason for choosing seven readers was simply to correspond to the number of aḥruf of Qur'ānic revelation for the purposes of blessing.

Scholars point out that Ibn Mujāhid selected readers from the five cities he believed an 'Uthmānic codex had been sent to: Makkah, Madīnah, Baṣrah, Kūfah and Damascus.

They also suggested that he should have selected two readers from Baṣrah, which had two great experts: Abū 'Amr and Ya'qūb. However, he had chosen Abū 'Amr and left out Ya'qūb simply because he did not possess an isnād to Ya'qūb's reading. For that reason, he substituted Ya'qūb with an additional reader from Kūfah to make three total readers from Kūfah: 'Āṣim, Ḥamzah and Kisā'ī. He himself admitted that Ya'qūb belonged on his list rather than Kisā'ī, but he was forced to make this adjustment.

Ibn Mujāhid's selection was a purely personal choice on his part based upon his own scholarly estimation (ijtihād). Many of his contemporaries had criticized him quite harshly foreseeing that it would lead to many individuals confusing these with the seven aḥruf. They suggested that he should have chosen a different number of readers to alleviate this confusion. Many of these peers of Ibn Mujāhid authored their own works on the readings, choosing six or eight, in opposition to Ibn Mujāhid. Ibn al-Khayyāṭ, for instance, authored *al-Kifāyah fī al-qirā'āt al-sitt* on six readings, and Ibn Ghalbūn authored *al-Tadhkirah fī al-qirā'āt al-thimān* on eight readings, adding Ya'qūb to the list. Others authored works on ten or thirteen readings, while al-Hudhalī authored *al-Kāmil* on fifty readings. Abū Ma'shar Ṭabarī authored *Sūq al-'arūs* on 350 transmissions of the Qur'ān from the Prophet.

How can we reconcile the seven aḥruf with such large numbers as 50 or 350 readings, or with earlier scholars such as Ṭabarī who had personally chosen twenty readings with isnād back to the Prophet, all of which were chosen from the readings at his disposal? The answer is that there is no single word found in all of the Qur'ānic readings which can be read in more than seven of these basic types of variations mentioned previously. Each variant was transmitted through isnād tracing back to the Prophet to a maximum of seven variants, but usually far less than that.[60] There was no role for reasoning or personal opinion here.

Abū ʿAmr, for instance, was an expert linguist and grammarian along with being a Qur'ānic reading expert. He used to say to his students on many occasions: 'Had the practice of Qur'ānic reading not been a transmitted phenomenon, I would have read this word as such.' These readers only taught based upon transmission from the Prophet, as numerous texts affirm. This obviously contradicts the claims of many Orientalists and those deceived by them who state that the rise of multiple readings was due to the ʿUthmānic codices being devoid of dotting, punctuation and alif letters, which allowed for multiple possibilities that were availed by the readers to recite each in their own way. This is blatantly false.

There has never been a single individual in the history of Islam who allowed freely reciting the Qur'ān in any manner that corresponded to Arabic and the ʿUthmānic codices without need for isnād, except for one individual from Baghdad in the fourth century named Ibn Miqsam (d. 354/965). However, his contemporaries opposed him greatly and asked him to repent lest he be deemed a disbeliever and executed for heresy. His case was brought before the Caliph in 322/934, who had him confined and asked him to repent in the presence of many jurists and scholars. He did so, expressing regret for his previous opinion, and officially recanted to the Muslim consensus.

Scholars subsequently issued a fatwā that whoever believes that it is allowed to recite the Qur'ān based upon one's own opinion has left the religion. On this issue, it is not enough to recite with conformity to Arabic language and an ʿUthmānic codex without having a sound isnād to the Prophet.

These Qur'ānic scholars learned various ways of reading from their teachers tracing back to the Prophet, with possibilities on a single word not exceeding seven. Each of these word variants was complete and sufficient, as the Prophet indicated. These scholars chose from the array of variants on each word that they had received from their teachers with isnād. For example, Imām Nāfiʿ, teacher of Warsh and Qālūn, was the primary Qur'ānic scholar of Madīnah who had read to seventy teachers from the Followers all of whom had read to Companions. Imām Nāfiʿ would invariably have read the Qur'ān in many different ways, having completed the Qur'ān seventy times with seventy teachers, each of them possessing an isnād in their particular reading. So Nāfiʿ would have had an array of variants he had learned, and he would have had to choose for each word one particular variant. He chose in sūrah al-Fātiḥah, for instance, *maliki* over *māliki*, *al-ṣirāṭ* rather than *al-sirāṭ*, and so on. The personal choices of one particular reader from the beginning of the Qur'ān to the end would become known as a reading that would be attributed to that individual.

---

[60] The majority of words in the Qur'ān in fact have no variants and are read uniformly in all of the readings.

Early scholars often used the term personal adoptions (ikthiyārāt) rather than readings (qirā'āt), so many second and third century works refer to the 'choices' of Nāfi', or the 'choices of the seven Imāms.' All of this points to the fact that these individuals were choosing to read from an array of allowable options they had learned with isnād from the Prophet ﷺ.

With analogy to the previously mentioned notion of combinations and permutations in mathematics, the potential differences can become nearly unlimited. Suppose a verse contains three words transmitted from the Prophet, with the first having two possible variants, the second with three, and the third with four: this verse could potentially be read in 24 ways (2 x 3 x 4). Similarly, the next verse could have twenty or thirty such ways of reading, and so on. From the beginning to the end of the Qur'ān, the total possibilities of reading would be enormous.

The current Qur'ānic readings represent the reading traditions of specific chosen Imāms (seven, ten, or fourteen), each with two student-transmitters, with each transmitter having many sub-students who related additional differences from them (known as *ṭuruq,* or paths of transmission). In each single path of transmission there might be a number of valid options in recitation (known as *wajh*).

As a practical illustration, Nāfi' of Madīnah had many students beyond his two transmitters Warsh and Qālūn. These students included Imām Mālik and Layth b. Sa'd, both of whom read to Nāfi'. In fact, among the readings whose isnād Ibn al-Jazarī documents is the reading of Layth from Nāfi', and that of Mālik from Nāfi' (here, it should be noted that Mālik's famous ḥadīth teacher Nāfi' was a different person than this Qur'ān teacher). From among many chains, those of Warsh and Qālūn were selected by Ibn Mujāhid. There are numerous differences between them, and among their own students there were differences among various paths, such as the transmission of al-Ḥalwānī or Abū Nashīṭ. Even within a single path of transmission, there are many equally valid options of reading. All of this added to the proliferation of Qur'ānic readings.

The Muslim convention developed that there are ten mutawātir readings, each with two major transmissions making for a total of twenty major ways of recitation. Each transmission has at least two to four major paths of transmission, each with some variation. The result is a staggering amount of differences, all of which, however, fall within the scope of the seven aḥruf of revelation and essentially represent personal choices.

It should be also noted here that scholars forbade inventing new readings by mixing these transmitted readings with one another. The real experts knew, however, that this could only be considered disliked (makrūh) at most, or not worthy for the position of a scholar. They were not strictly forbidden, on condition that the adoption does not corrupt the language or is not dishonest when intending to recite by narration (i.e. by attributing a recitation to a particular transmitter). Examples of potential corruptions of language would be to recite the verse, *'Adam received the words from His Lord'* (2:37)—where the verse structure includes *Adam* as the subject and *words* as the object—by reversing it such that both words are erroneously read as subjects or as objects.

Experts also stipulated that these adoptions not be done in the name of specific transmissions, so that one cannot read the word *maliki* (with a short vowel) in al-Fātiḥah while claiming the reading of Ḥafṣ from ʿĀṣim because that would be dishonest (the reading of Ḥafṣ is with a long vowel, as in *māliki*).

In sum, fourteen readings survived to our times with chains of transmission, ten of which are considered mass-transmitted while four are not. Each of these readings (*qirāʿāt*) has transmissions from two students (known as *riwāyāt*), which makes for a total of 28 transmissions. Each transmission has many independent paths, or chains. Each of the ten readings is based upon an Imām of Recitation (known as *qāri'*), whose two students of transmission are termed 'transmitters' (*rāwī*), while their own subsequent students are called *aṣḥāb al-ṭuruq* ('people of the paths of transmission'). All subsequent students at all links below are also called *aṣḥāb al-ṭuruq*.

As an example, ʿĀṣim is one of the ten Imāms of Recitation (qāri'), while the two students (rāwī) who transmitted from him are Ḥafṣ and Shuʿbah. Two further students narrated from Ḥafṣ: ʿAmr and ʿUbayd b. al-Ṣabāḥ. From ʿAmr were two further students: Fīl and Zarʿān.

So if you know that Ibn al-Jazarī in his book *al-Nashr* reported a reading with a chain from Shahrazūrī the author of *al-Miṣbāḥ*, who had a chain to al-Ḥammāmī from al-Walī from al-Fīl from ʿAmr from Ḥafṣ from ʿĀṣim, then you can call that transmission: *the Reading of ʿĀṣim with the Transmission of Ḥafṣ through the path of ʿAmr, or the path of Fīl, or the path of al-Walī, or the path of al-Ḥammāmī, or the path of al-Miṣbāḥ, or the path of Ibn al-Jazarī's al-Nashr.*

Ibn al-Jazarī included in his book *al-Nashr* hundreds of chains, or paths, for these ten readings. These must be kept distinct and not muddled up as if they were the same.

As for the notion that the Prophet ﷺ recited a complete recital in each of these readings, transmissions and paths, then that is not the case at all. Rather, the differences between these readings, transmissions and paths are of two broad types:

1. *Variants of specific words* (known as *farsh*): These are differences in words, through changes in either letters, vowels, or word order. For these cases, we say that the Prophet ﷺ did indeed read each variant wording, in all cases that have been authentically transmitted from him.
2. *Differences in principles of reading*: These include differences like the vowel-lengths (mudūd), the ghunnah nasalization, the imālah vowel, assimilation of letters and their likes. In these differences, the Prophet ﷺ either recited these variations in portions of the Qur'ān himself, or they were read to him by his Companions and he allowed them to do

> so thus affirming their usage. There are well-known general rules which govern all similar cases.

The important point is that even these principles were all taken from the Prophet ﷺ, though it is not necessarily the case that he read, for example, each instance of madd munfaṣil[61] with 2, 3, 4, 5 and 6 durations,[62] or portions with and without pausing (sakt).[63] We do know that the Prophet ﷺ would complete the reading to Jibrīl in the month of Ramadan of the entire revelation of the Qur'ān. This necessarily would have included all the revealed modes. Ibn Ḥajar mentioned that this necessitates that the Prophet would have read the Qur'ān in that setting by combining these readings in some way.

---

[61] A specific type of long-vowel that arises when the letter hamzah follows a madd letter in a different word.

[62] A *ḥarakah* is a basic unit of time duration in tajwīd.

[63] The brief pause without exhaling is a linguistic device that is part of some readings in specific cases.

Pillars of an Authentic Reading

The three pillars that have been deemed crucial to establishing an authentic Qur'ānic reading:

1. Broad consistency with the Arabic language
2. Broad uniformity with the 'Uthmānic codex in any possible way
3. Sound chain of narration

When all of these conditions are met in a reading, it would be considered sound and must be accepted, whether that reading originates with one of the seven Imāms, or the ten, or even from other accepted Imāms. When any condition is absent, then it is a weak or false reading which may not be relied upon, even if it were to be ascribed to one of the seven Imāms.[64]

Broad Conformity with Arabic

The first condition[65] is broad agreement with any of the possible forms of the Arabic language, irrespective of its degree of eloquence, or its unanimity or dispute.

It must be noted here is that the aim of including this condition by experts was to show that the readings cannot be inconsistent with the Arabic language, for Allah revealed His Book in the clear Arabic language.[66] The aim was not that a reading whose chain of transmission had been established could be rejected by a claim that it is inconsistent with some predominant usage of specific grammarians. The Arabic language is a vast ocean without shores. Linguists often affirm language usages by referring to verses of poetry or expressions, often from anonymous Arabic authors without any chains of transmission. Their isnāds are not even comparable to those of the Qur'ānic readings. Hence, it is more worthy that the authentic readings be used to support usages of Arabic language, and not vice versa.

In any event, there has never been a Qur'ānic reading that was disputed on linguistic grounds by any grammarian except that other experts of Arabic have defended it. In other words, you simply cannot find a sound Qur'ānic reading that does not correspond to the Arabic language in some manner, even if some linguists objected to specific variants based upon usages they were not familiar with, because for those same variants other scholars found evidences to establish their soundness.

---

[64] *Al-Nashr,* vol 1, pg 15.

[65] This section has been supplemented with content from *al-Qamar al-munīr,* pg 80.

[66] Qur'ān 16:103, 26:195.

Broad Conformity with ʿUthmānic Codex

The second condition is agreement with one of the ʿUthmānic Qur'ānic copies.[67] The reading of Ibn Kathīr for the following verse, for instance, corresponds to the Makkan copy:

جَنَّاتٍ تَجْرِي مِن تَحْتِهَا الأَنْهَارُ

﴾*Gardens **from** beneath which rivers flow.*﴿ (9:100)

whereas the other copies had the verse written without the preposition *min*:

جَنَّاتٍ تَجْرِي تَحْتَهَا الأَنْهَارُ

﴾*Gardens beneath which rivers flow.*﴿ (9:100)

It is sufficient for the codex to allow for a reading, as in the writing of 'q-l' (قل) as two unvowelled consonants, which may be read with multiple vowels as in *qul* or *qāla;* or the word ṣ-l-w-t (الصلوة) which may be read as *ṣalāh* or *ṣalawāt* (by adding a small alif); or the words *kabīran* and *kathīran,* both of which can be accommodated by the same skeletal script devoid of punctuation markings. The ʿUthmānic script of the Qur'ānic copies did not have punctuation or vowel markings. It also did not make frequent use of alif, which was often written with the waw or yā based upon its linguistic origins.

The Condition of Tawātur

The third condition[68] was the soundness of the chain of transmission (isnād), a condition which was unanimously agreed upon. However, whether this transmission needed to be one of mass-transmission (tawātur) was differed over.

A mutawātir ḥadīth is one that is reported by a large group of individuals from a large group of individuals in every link of transmission until it ends at a source-report that is based upon a sense-faculty, such as seeing or hearing something, and not on some reasoning or intellectual construct. The large group of individuals in each generation must be such that it would be impossible for their collusion on a combined lie to occur. To summarize, there are four specific conditions for a mutawātir report:

1. There must be a large number in each generation. Many early scholars did not stipulate any specific number. The large number imparts a sense of

---

[67] This will be discussed with more elaboration in chapter 3.
[68] This section contains significant content from *al-Qamar al-munīr,* pg 72-8.

knowledge and certainty. Other scholars did stipulate numbers, ranging from a minimum of ten in each generation, to more or less than that.

2. The numbers must be large enough to make their joint collusion on any lie impossible. A lie may be promoted by one or a few individuals, but it becomes more difficult and ultimately impossible as numbers increase.
3. These numbers must exist in every link of the isnād.
4. The source-report must concern something that is sensed, i.e. heard or seen. [69]

The correct view favored by experts is that tawātur was not a precondition for a reading to be considered sound simply because there is no strong evidence for that. The Prophet ﷺ would send single Companions to teach the Qur'ān. And people would learn verses from single Companions, act upon them and recite them in their prayers. Ibn al-Jazarī states:

> Some latter-day scholars stipulated tawātur as a condition here and believed that the Qur'ān is not established without mass-transmission, and that what comes through solitary channels cannot be considered Qur'ān. The [problems] in this view are not hidden, for if we were to stipulate mass-transmission for each difference, many of the differences which have been established from the seven Imāms would be invalidated. Even I used to incline towards this view until I realized its baselessness.[70]

Shawkānī (d. 1255/1839)[71] states:

> Tawātur has been claimed for each of the seven readings (the readings of Abū ʿAmr, Nāfiʿ, ʿĀṣim, Ḥamzah, Kisāʾī, Ibn Kathīr and Ibn ʿĀmir) as well as for the ten (which additionally include the readings of Yaʿqūb, Abū Jaʿfar and Khalaf), but there is in fact no semblance of knowledge in this view, for these readings are all transmitted in a solitary manner, as is well-known by those who know the isnāds of these Imāms in their respective readings. A group of Qur'ānic scholars have claimed consensus on the view that these readings collectively include portions which are mass-transmitted and portions which are not. None of them claimed that the seven were exclusively mass-transmitted, which is a view claimed by some scholars of Uṣūl, but the

[69] See *al-Khayr al-Kathīr,* pg 137.
[70] *Al-Nashr,* vol 1, pg 16.
[71] Muḥammad b. ʿAlī b. Muḥammad b. ʿAbdullah al-Shawkānī was a prolific scholar of Yemen who authored 150 works.

> experts of each discipline are more knowledgeable in their own field.'[72]

It can be claimed, however, concerning the chains of the ten readings that though they may be solitary, none of the ten Imāms were alone in their readings but shared their practice with their entire regions. However, most of these regional chains were interrupted and not continually transmitted onwards, as people sufficed themselves with the isnāds of the popular teachers. Ibn ʿĀmir, for instance, read upon Abū al-Dardā' who read upon the Prophet ﷺ, but Ibn ʿĀmir was not alone in transmitting Abū al-Dardā''s reading. In fact, at least 1,500 people had read upon Abū al-Dardā', though all of their chains did not reach us today. Similarly, Abū al-Dardā' did not exclusively transmit his reading from the Prophet ﷺ but other Companions had shared in teaching him. If this type of mass-transmission is meant by these claims, then it is justified. However, if it is claimed that each and every word of the seven or ten readings is transmitted by a massive amount of people in each generation until it reached the Prophet ﷺ, then there is no proof for that.

There were some scholars that considered only the seven readings to be mutawātir.[73] Other considered the three additional ones, with a total of ten, to be mutawātir. The three additional readings added by Ibn al-Jazarī are the readings of Abū Jaʿfar, Yaʿqūb and Khalaf. Among these three readings, many scholars of uṣūl al-fiqh and Qur'ānic readings did not consider the independent reading of Khalaf (not the narration by Khalaf of Ḥamzah's reading) to be mutawātir and some of them even considered it anomalous (shādh).

The majority position among scholars, however, is that the ten readings are all mutawātir. The view of Ibn al-Jazarī was that among the ten, there were elements that were transmitted by tawātur and elements otherwise, but he considered a sound isnād and not necessarily tawātur to be sufficient in establishing the soundness of a reading. Initially, he had stipulated tawātur as an essential condition to establishing a sound reading, as mentioned in his *Munjid al-muqri'īn,* but he subsequently recanted that position in his chronologically later book *al-Nashr*:

> Every reading that concords with any form of Arabic usage, conforms to an ʿUthmānic codex in any possible way, and possesses a sound isnād, is considered a sound and correct reading which cannot be rejected or denied. It would be part of the seven modes of revelation which are obligatory for all people to accept, whether these are from the seven Imāms, or the ten, or even from other than them. If any of these conditions, however, are not present in a reading, then it would be considered weak, anomalous or false, even if it be from the seven Imāms or someone even greater than them. This is the correct

[72] Shawkānī, *Irshād al-fuḥūl,* pg 63.
[73] This section is taken from *al-Qamar al-munīr,* pg 72-8.

> position of discerning experts of past and present, as made clear by Imām Abū ʿAmr ʿUthmān b. Saʿīd al-Dānī, Makkī b. Abī Ṭālib in several contexts, Abū al-ʿAbbās Aḥmad b. ʿAmmār al-Mahdawī, and Abū al-Qāsim ʿAbd al-Raḥmān b. Ismāʿīl, better known as Abū Shāmah. This is also the position of the predecessors and no difference is known from them on this.[74]
>
> By our stipulation of 'sound isnād' we mean that the reading is reported by trustworthy and accurate individuals at every level of its isnād. In addition, they should be known to the experts of this discipline, accurate in their readings, and not associated with mistakes or anomalies.
>
> Some latter-day scholars stipulated tawātur as a condition here and did not deem a sound isnād alone to be sufficient. They believed that the Qur'ān is not established without mass-transmission and that all that comes through solitary channels cannot be considered to be Qur'ān. The [problems] in this view are not hidden, for, if tawātur is really achieved, then there would be no need for the other two conditions. If a variant were to be mass-transmitted from the Prophet, it would be binding to accept it and consider it Qur'ān, irrespective of whether it conformed to an ʿUthmānic codex. And if we were to stipulate tawātur for each variant, many of the differences which have been established from the seven Imāms would be invalidated. Even I used to incline towards this view until I realized its baselessness and saw the agreement on this point of past and present experts.[75]

There exists an intermediate view: that only the word variants (farsh) within readings are mutawātir and not the broader principles of reading and tajwīd such as rules pertaining to madd vowels, assimilation of letters, heaviness/lightness of letters, and rules of hamzah. This was the view of Ibn al-Ḥājib (646/1249)[76] and close to Ibn Taymiyyah's position, who expressed in a letter answering questions pertaining to the readings that every word variant, such as an additional or omitted alif, was transmitted from the Prophet ﷺ whereas the rules of reading such as rules of hamzah articulation, madd vowels, imālah vowels and others, were not necessarily

---

[74] *Al-Nashr,* vol 1, pg 9.

[75] *Al-Nashr,* vol 1, pg 13.

[76] Jamāl al-Dīn Abū ʿAmr ʿUthmān b. ʿUmar b. Abī Bakr al-Dūnī (from a village in Nahawand where his ancestors came from) was a Mālikī jurist, born and raised near Cairo, Egypt, who went on to become the most famous grammarian of his time. He was called Ibn al-Ḥājib, 'son of the gatekeeper,' because his father was the gatekeeper for ʿIzz al-Dīn, the maternal uncle of Ṣalāḥ al-Dīn al-Ayyūbī. His teachers included Shāṭibī, the author of *Ḥirz al-Amānī*. His students included the ḥadīth expert al-Mundhirī (d. 656 AH), Nāṣir al-Dīn b. al-Munayyar (d. 683 AH), Shihāb al-Dīn al-Qarāfī (d. 684 AH). He lived from 570/1174 —646/1249.

transmitted from the Prophet in their entirety. Experts maintain that these rules of reading are derived from language and dialects.

The summary of Ibn al-Jazarī's view is that the ten readings are all either mutawātir in the sense of containing elements that have been transmitted by massive numbers in each generation or widely transmitted (mashhūr mustafīḍ) with numbers that do not reach technical tawātur. In either case, it is all firmly established beyond doubt.

It must also be pointed out that the usage of tawātur does not necessitate that it refer to technical tawātur of a massive group at each level of the isnād until the end. It has become convention in latter times to refer to the ten readings as mutawātir readings, in light of the fact that the readings contain elements that are mutawātir and elements that are less than that but still widespread. The elements of tawātur within the readings allow the ten readings as a whole to be referred to as mutawātir. Similarly, shādh has become a term that is now customarily used for all readings outside of the ten.

In conclusion, these seven readings, plus the additional three, are generally deemed mutawātir and accepted for the purposes of deriving rulings.

Shādh Readings

As for those readings apart from these ten, when they function as tafsīr of Qur'ān, then they are also acted upon. This includes the tafsīr readings of many Companions[77] like Ibn Mas'ūd's reading of 4:12:

Original verse:

وَإِن كَانَ رَجُلٌ يُورَثُ كَلَالَةً أَوِ امْرَأَةٌ وَلَهُ أَخٌ أَوْ أُخْتٌ

﴿*And if a man or a woman has no heir in the direct line, but has a brother or a sister, . . .*﴾ (4:12)

Ibn Mas'ūd's reading:

وَإِن كَانَ رَجُلٌ يُورَثُ كَلَالَةً أَوِ امْرَأَةٌ وَلَهُ أَخٌ أَوْ أُخْتٌ مِن أُمٍّ

And if a man or a woman has no heir in the direct line, but has a brother or a sister ***from his mother****, . . .* [78]

There are two scholarly views on when these non-mutawātir readings contradict Prophetic ḥadīth: one, that they are acted upon even when they do, and two, that the ḥadīth is acted upon instead.

The shādh readings are those which were read by Followers but either failed to be widely transmitted or were transmitted with weak isnāds. They were recorded, documented, and utilized by scholars, however, mostly for the purposes of tafsīr. They include various types of readings, the strongest of which are those which possess sound isnāds and correspond to the 'Uthmānic codex. There are also some that possessed sound isnāds but did not correspond to the 'Uthmānic codex. Many scholars deemed them to be readings which were once allowed but later abrogated by the Prophet's Final Rehearsal. Other scholars believed that since Companions compiled the muṣḥaf in the era of 'Uthmān and unanimously abandoned these other readings, they are now considered extremely weak even if they possessed sound isnāds. An example is found in the previously mentioned ḥadīth of 'Alqamah who related the reading of Abū al-Dardā' and Ibn Mas'ūd. In this case, the Prophet had recited and taught this particular reading, which is part of the legacy of readings

[77] *Qirā'āt tafsīrīyah* is a term used for explanatory reports of Companions concerning Qur'ān passages that were transmitted alongside the verses and referred in a loose manner as a reading. Of course, these are not really Qur'ānic readings but explanatory remarks, though many have been confused by the terminology.

[78] This reading-explanation has been transmitted from more than one Companion including Sa'd b. Abī Waqqāṣ; see *al-Tamhīd,* vol 5, pg 199; Muṣannaf Ibn Abī Shaybah, vol 6, pg 298; Ṭabarī, vol 6, pg 483.

transmitted by Companions with sound isnāds. Despite that, they are considered shādh readings. (Shādh readings will be further discussed in chapter 5).

Differences Complementary not Contradictory

Variations and differences when they arise generally are of two types: those that are complementary and those that contradict one another.

Complementary variations are those where both or multiple variants are equally correct, like in the example of the various opening supplications of prayer that have been established in the sunnah, the modes of tashahhud (what is recited in the sitting portion of the prayer), the call to prayer, the exact manner of the prayer for fear, and other examples which represent what the Prophet ﷺ did in multiple manners. One who adopts any of these ways would be correct in doing so.

Contradictory differences, on the other hand, are those where only one option could logically be correct while the other must necessarily be false.

The variant readings represent complementary variations not contradictory one. Al-Jaṣṣāṣ (d. 370/981)[79] states: 'Contradictory differences do not appear in the Qur'ān at all, and all potential cases actually agree in meaning, wisdom and evidence-value.'[80] Ibn al-Jazarī says: 'The reality of the variation among these seven which are established from the Prophet ﷺ is that they are complementary in nature and not contradictory nor incompatible.[81] In fact, Ibn Taymiyyah has claimed consensus on this:

> There is no dispute among Muslims over the belief that the seven modes in which the Qur'ān was revealed do not contain anything contradictory or incompatible, but their meanings are uniform and close to one another, as 'Abdullah b. Mas'ūd stated, 'It is like your saying *aqbil,* or *halumma,* or *ta'āl* (all synonyms for 'come').' The meaning of each word might not be exactly identical but they are all correct, for these are variations that are complementary in nature, not contradictory or incompatible.
>
> These readings in which the meanings vary all represent the truth, for each reading here is like the different verses of the Qur'ān. We must believe in all of them and follow what they contain in terms of knowledge and practice. It is not allowed to leave what one mandates for the sake of another believing that they are contradictory, for it is as Ibn Mas'ūd said: 'Whoever rejects one mode has rejected all of them.' In addition, those differences which agree in wording and meaning can differ in exact articulation, such as hamza letters, long-vowels, imālah vowel, alteration of vowels, iẓhār

[79] Abū Bakr Aḥmad b. 'Alī al-Rāzī al-Jaṣṣāṣ hailed from Rayy and was the senior Ḥanafī scholar of his time who authored an important jurisprudential tafsīr work entitled *Aḥkām al-Qur'ān.*
[80] Jaṣṣāṣ , *al-fuṣūl fī al-uṣūl,* vol 1, pg 378.
[81] *Al-Nashr,* vol 1, pg 49.

> (manifest articulation of letters), partial vowels, heaviness of rā, and their likes. None of these contradict in any way, but only represent varying articulations of the same word.[82]

These insightful words of Ibn Taymiyyah reveal that differences among the readings are three types:

1. Variant words with same meanings
2. Alternate meanings which are also true
3. Alternative articulations while the words and meanings remain the same

Ibn Taymiyyah has clarified that these three types of differences are complementary and not contradictory:

> It is also asked how these differences can be complementary when some of the early Muslims were known to reject some of these readings and consider them mistakes. We respond by saying that they were excused because these variants were not properly established by transmission in their eyes. These would even include ʿUmar's initial rejection of Hishām b. Ḥakīm's recitation of Sūrah al-Furqān and many other examples, all of which represent mistaken reasoning on their part, which is forgiven.[83]

[82] Ibn Taymiyyah, *Majmūʿ al-fatāwā*, vol 13, pg 391-2.
[83] *Majmūʿ al-fatāwā*, vol 20, pg 34-5.

Chapter 2: History and Chains of the Fourteen Qur’ānic Readings

القراءات الأربعة عشر وأسانيدهم

Importance and Value of Isnād

Isnād comes from the fourth form of the verbal root s-n-d and literally means *reliance* or *support* because a text (*matn*) relies on that for support or referencing. In the realm of ḥadīth, isnād connects the statement to its speaker.[1] In the Islamic sciences, isnād is the chain of narrators that connects to the source-text, which lies at the end of the isnād chain and represents the speech or report.

Among the world's nations, the Muḥammadan ummah is the only one to have been distinguished and honored by this system of isnād. For that reason, scriptures of other faith traditions were corrupted and the sound reports of their prophets lost, ultimately being replaced by falsehoods and distortions. Concern for isnād is really a defining symbol of this nation. 'Abdullah b. al-Mubārak (d. 181/797)[2] said, 'Isnād is part of religion. Had it not been so, whoever wanted could have said whatever they wished.'[3] Sufyān al-al-Thawrī (d. 161/778)[4] said: 'The isnād is the weapon of a believer.'[5]

For this reason, leading Muslim scholars have devoted their efforts to meticulously documenting the transmitters of the Qur'ān and Sunnah. From one perspective, they researched the moral uprightness ('adālah) and academic accuracy (ḍabṭ) of narrators in order to distinguish those who were reliable from those who were weak. From another angle, they scrutinized their biographical details—such as birth-death chronologies, detailed studies, travels and native regions—in order to distinguish contiguous chains of transmission from disconnected ones with major gaps.

Some people have presumed that concern for isnād is limited to ḥadīth scholars who worked on Prophetic reports but the reality is that Qur'ānic scholars also exerted themselves similarly in preserving isnāds for Qur'ānic readings and applied the same methodologies in scrutinizing isnāds that were used by ḥadīth scholars. For this reason, one of the pillars of a sound Qur'ānic reading was deemed to be a sound isnād. There were a great number of experts of ḥadīth who were at the same time scholars of Qur'ān, who researched the biographies of Qur'ānic teachers and identified the sources, i.e. isnāds, of their readings. These included the likes of Abū 'Amr al-Dānī,[6] author of *Tārīkh al-qurrā'* (*'History of the Reciters'*), Abū al-'Ālā' al-

---

[1] Al-Fayrūzābādī, *Al-Qāmūs al-muḥīṭ*, vol 1, pg 314.

[2] A noble scholar of ḥadīth and fiqh from the early generations, author of numerous beneficial works, known for great piety, worship, and courage. He died after returning from battle with the Byzantines in 181.

[3] Ṣaḥīḥ Muslim: Muqaddimah.

[4] Sufyān b. Sa'īd b. Masrūq al-Thawrī was a great Kūfan jurist known also for his mastery of ḥadīth sciences, earning him the title 'Amīr al-mu'minīn fī al-ḥadīth.'

[5] Suyūṭī, *Tadrīb al-rāwī*, vol 2, pg 94.

[6] See footnote 55 in chapter 1.

Hamadhānī (d. 569/1173),[7] author of *Ṭabaqāt al-qurrāʾ* (*'Ranks of the Reciters'*), Imam Dhahabī (d. 748/1348),[8] author of *Maʿrifat al-qurrāʾ al-kibār* (*'Knowing the Great Reciters'*), and Imām Ibn al-Jazarī, author of *Ghāyat al-nihāyah fī ṭabaqāt al-qurrāʾ* (*'The End Result Concerning the Ranks of the Reciters'*).

It should be noted that this science was quite layered and sophisticated, as it was often the case that some narrators were considered reliable in transmission of Qur'ān while being weak in transmitting ḥadīth, and vice versa. Also, others were reliable only in the reports of certain regions, or from specific teachers, while being weak in their other reports.

Highest Qur'ānic Isnāds[9]

An elevated isnād is one with the least number of intermediaries to the Prophet ﷺ (known as *'uluww al-muṭlaq,* 'absolute elevation'), or one with the least intermediaries to another well-known scholar within the chain (*'uluww al-muqayyad,* 'particular elevation'), such as the ten Imāms, Abū ʿAmr al-Dānī, Shāṭibī, or Ibn al-Jazarī. Elevated isnāds were a sought-after feature for the Companions and those that followed them, and many of them often traveled widely in search of these chains. Muḥammad b. Aslam (d. 242/857)[10] said: 'Closeness in chain (to the Prophet) is closeness to God.' Aḥmad b. Ḥanbal (d. 241/855)[11] said:' Seeking an elevated isnād is a practice of those that preceded us.'[12] Just as ḥadīth scholars actively sought out elevated isnads, so too the scholars of Qur'ān, either in total length to the Prophet ﷺ or to one of the great Imāms of the readings, such as Dānī, Shāṭibī, Ibn al-Jazarī or Mutawallī (d. 1313/1895-6).[13]

Since the highest Qur'ān isnāds in the Islamic world today necessarily go through Ibn al-Jazarī, then the highest such chains today are easily measured by searching for the least intermediaries to him. He himself mentioned that his most elevated isnāds were the following: the isnād of Ḥafṣ from ʿĀṣim through the book

---

[7] Abū al-ʿĀlāʾ Al-Ḥasan b. Aḥmad al-Hamadhānī was a great scholar of Hamedan (also known as Hamadhān, in current day Iran) who divided his days equally between teaching Qur'ān and ḥadīth.

[8] Muḥammad b. Aḥmad b. 'Uthmān a-Dahabi was a great ḥadīth scholar and historian of Damascus, a student of Ibn Taymiyyah, who wrote some of the most widely read and referenced works in Islam, like *Siyar aʿlām al-nubalāʾ*.

[9] This section is appended with information from Shaykh Waleed's *al-Qamar al-munīr fī sharḥ al-zamzamīyah.*

[10] Muḥammad b. Aslam al-Ṭūsī was a great scholar known for his piety, worship and adherence to the sunnah.

[11] He was the great ḥadīth scholar who was the author of the *Musnad,* one of the largest ḥadīth works in our tradition, and great jurist-founder of the fourth Sunnī school of jurisprudence.

[12] Suyūṭī, *Tadrīb al-rāwī*, vol 2, pg 90-4.

[13] Muḥammad b. Aḥmad al-Mutawallī was the leading Qur'ānic scholar of his time, blind, author of over forty works on the readings, and a reference-point for this science.

al-Kifāyah authored by the grandson of Khayyāṭ, and the isnād of the transmission of Ibn Dhakwān from Ibn ʿĀmir, both of which consist of thirteen intermediaries, all of them great and reliable Imāms.

After great research in comparing the current Qur'ānic isnāds and ijāzahs in the Muslim world—from Arabia to Egypt, Syria, Iraq, Morocco, India and Pakistan—as well as mutual correspondence with a number of contemporary Qur'ānic scholars who are involved in this, it has become apparent to me that the highest Qur'ānic isnād in our times belonged to Shaykh Bakrī b. ʿAbd al-Majīd al-Ṭarābīshī of Damascus (d. 1433/2012).[14] Equivalent to his level are also some living students—at the time of publication—of Shaykh al-Fāḍilī Abū Laylah al-Dasūqī (d. 1385/1965), such as my two teachers Shaykh Miṣbāḥ Ibrāhīm Wadn al-Dasūqī of Egypt (born 1362/1943) and Shaykh Muḥammad Yūnus Ghalbān of Egypt (born 1365/1946), as well as Shaykh Muḥammad Ibrāhīm al-Badawī. Between all these individuals and Ibn al-Jazarī in the seven readings exist only eleven individuals, all of them well-known and reliable scholars. These scholars represent the twenty-eighth link in the isnād from the Prophet ﷺ, for between them and the Prophet exist only twenty seven individuals, all of whom recited the complete Qur'ān to their teachers.

The Great Practice of Memorizing the Qurʾān

Muslim scholars have considered it obligatory to memorize the Qur'ān—and deemed it a communal obligation (farḍ kifāyah)—in order to maintain it as evidence, argument and witness over mankind, and in order to follow in the footsteps of the Prophet ﷺ.[15] Committing the Qur'ān to memory by at least a portion of the ummah of Muḥammad becomes a great means to this end.

Not being able to write, the Prophet ﷺ had preserved the Qur'ān instead in his blessed heart and memory. A large group of Companions followed his example and also memorized the Qur'ān by heart. They were people of intelligence, acumen and wisdom. There were those who memorized the Qur'ān but did not transmit it and those who both preserved and transmitted it.

Memorizing the Qur'ān is considered by scholars to be a communal obligation upon Muslims in every age. That is, there must exist individuals who have memorized the entire Qur'ān in every time. In addition, there is a minimum portion of the Qur'ān whose memorization is obligatory upon each individual Muslim: namely, sūrah al-Fātiḥah which must be recited in every prayer.

[14] He was a great contemporary Qur'ānic scholar from Damascus who was the last living student of eminent Qur'ānic scholar of Syra Muḥammad Salīm al-Ḥulwānī (d. 1363/1944).

[15] This entire section is taken from *al-Qamar al-munīr*, pg 87-9, and *al-Khayr al-kathīr*, pg 111-2.

Allah praised those who memorize His Book: ﴿*But it is a set of clear revelations preserved in the hearts of those gifted with knowledge.*﴾ [16] Here, Allah indicates that the Qur'ān is protected within the hearts of scholars, and not merely written on pages.

The Prophet ﷺ, while delivering a sermon one day, said:

> Behold, my Lord commanded me that I should teach you what you do not know and which He has taught me today. . . . And said: I have revealed the Book to you *which cannot be washed away by water*, so that you may recite it while in the state of wakefulness or sleep.[17]
>
> أَلَا إِنَّ رَبِّي أَمَرَنِي أَنْ أُعَلِّمَكُمْ مَا جَهِلْتُمْ مِمَّا عَلَّمَنِي يَوْمِي هَذَا . . . وَأَنْزَلْتُ عَلَيْكَ كِتَابًا لَا يَغْسِلُهُ الْمَاءُ ، تَقْرَؤُهُ نَائِمًا وَيَقْظَانَ .

'*Which cannot be washed away by water*' is a reference to preservation in the hearts, because a book written on paper can be washed away with water while a book that is memorized cannot. Reciting in a state of wakefulness and sleep is another reference to the same notion because someone who has memorized the Qur'ān will be able to recite it most of the time, including when he is reclining on his bed in order to sleep.

The Prophet ﷺ also stated:

> *The one who recites the Qur'ān and is proficient in it will be with noble and upright scribes, while the one who struggles with it and finds it difficult will have two rewards.*[18]
>
> الْمَاهِرُ بِالْقُرْآنِ مَعَ السَّفَرَةِ الْكِرَامِ الْبَرَرَةِ ، وَالَّذِي يَقْرَأُ الْقُرْآنَ وَيَتَتَعْتَعُ فِيهِ وَهُوَ عَلَيْهِ شَاقٌّ لَهُ أَجْرَانِ .

Many experts point out in their commentaries that the difference between the two levels is one of memorization and not, as commonly explained, concerning the rules of tajwīd. In fact, the version of the report that is utilized in Ṣaḥīḥ Bukhārī contains the wording: *The one who recites the Qur'ān and has memorized it (wa huwa ḥāfiẓun lahu) . . .*[19] That is, the proficient ones are the ones who have memorized the Qur'ān and are able to recite it smoothly from memory, without hesitating, stopping, or

---

[16] Qur'ān 29:49.

[17] Ṣaḥīḥ Muslim: Kitāb al-jannah wa ṣifat na'īmihā wa ahlihā—Bāb al-ṣifāt allatī yu'raf bihā fī al-dunyā ahl al-jannah wa ahl al-nār.

[18] Ṣaḥīḥ Bukhārī: Kitāb tafsīr al-Qur'ān—Bāb sūrah 'abasa. Ṣaḥīḥ Muslim: Kitāb ṣalāh al-musāfirīn wa qaṣrihā—Bāb faḍl al-māhir bi al-Qur'ān walladhī yatata'ta'u fīhī.

[19] Ṣaḥīḥ Bukhārī: Kitāb tafsīr al-Qur'ān—Bāb sūrah 'abasa. The report in Bukhārī includes *'wa huwa ḥāfiẓun lahu'* ('and has memorized it'), while the report in Muslim contains: *'wa huwa mhfirun bihi'* ('and is proficient in it').

repeating. As for the ones who struggle, they are the ones who haven't memorized and thus are not able to recite smoothly, though they might be proficient in tajwīd. If these persons exert their best efforts and struggle with their memory, they will earn both the reward of reciting and the reward of the struggle.

The Prophet ﷺ also said:

> *It will be said to the reciter of the Qur'ān: 'Recite and ascend! Recite measuredly just as you used to do so in the world, and your final station will be at the final verse you recite!'*[20]

> يُقَالُ - يَعْنِي لِصَاحِبِ الْقُرْآنِ - اقْرَأْ وَارْتَقِ وَرَتِّلْ كَمَا كُنْتَ تُرَتِّلُ فِي الدُّنْيَا فَإِنَّ مَنْزِلَتَكَ عِنْدَ آخِرِ آيَةٍ تَقْرَأُ بِهَا.

Scholars clarify that this ḥadīth is also about the one who has memorized the Qur'ān and that every person's position in Paradise will be according to the last verse they used to recite from memory. Had this ḥadīth been about reciting from the muṣḥaf, then every Muslim would have recited and reached the same level. However, each person will recite from memory until they stop at various verses, and their position will be determined by that. The more one has memorized, the higher will be that person's position.

The Issue of Memorization and Comprehension

The methodology of the Companions in memorizing the Qur'ān was that they would take a portion of the Qur'ān at a time—usually consisting of ten verses—and learn their meanings, memorize them and practice their teachings in their lives before moving on. In that, they were memorizers as well as full scholars of the Qur'ān. Abū 'Abd al-Raḥmān al-Sulamī, one of the best Qur'ānic students of the Companions, states the following:

> Those who taught us the Qur'ān, like 'Uthmān b. 'Affān, Ibn Mas'ūd and others, reported to us that whenever they learned ten verses from the Prophet ﷺ they would not move on until they learned what they

[20] Tirmidhī: Kitāb faḍā'il al-Qur'ān; Abū Dāwūd : Kitāb al-ṣalāh—Bāb layfa yustaḥabb al-tartīl fī al-qirā'ah; Nasā'ī (Sunan al-Kubrā): Kitāb faḍā'il al-Qur'ān—Bāb al-tartīl; Musnad Aḥmad Musnad 'Abdullah b. 'Amr b. al-'Āṣ. It was deemed ḥasan ṣaḥīḥ by Tirmidhī, and ṣaḥīḥ by Ibn Ḥibbān, Ḥākim, and Ibn Ḥajar. Contemporary scholars who deemed it ṣaḥīḥ include 'Abd al-Qādir Arnā'ūṭ and al-Albānī.

> could in terms of knowledge and practice. They said: 'We learned the Qur'ān, knowledge and practice all together.'[21]

At the same time, however, Ibn Mas'ūd and others made a distinction between the one who memorized (qāri') and the scholar (faqīh):

> You are living in a time when men of understanding (fuqahā') are many and Qur'ānic memorizers (qurrā') are few, when the limits of behavior defined in the Qur'ān are guarded well while its letters are lost, when few people ask and many give, when they make the prayer long and the khuṭbah short, and put their actions before their desires.
>
> But soon a time will come upon people when their scholars will be few while their Qur'ānic memorizers many, when the letters of the Qur'ān will be guarded carefully but its limits lost, when many ask but few give, when they make the khuṭbah long but the prayer short, and put their desires before their actions.[22]

Also, the ḥadīth about the one who should lead prayers reinforces this distinction:

> The Prophet ﷺ said: *The imām for the people should be the one who knows more of Allah's Book, and if they are alike in its recitation, then the one who is more knowledgeable of the sunnah. If they are alike in the sunnah, then the one who made the hijrah first, and if that is the same, then the one who came to Islam first.*[23]

> قَالَ رَسُولُ اللهِ صَلَّى اللهُ عَلَيْهِ وَسَلَّمَ : يَؤُمُّ الْقَوْمَ أَقْرَؤُهُمْ لِكِتَابِ اللهِ فَإِنْ كَانُوا فِي الْقِرَاءَةِ سَوَاءً فَأَعْلَمُهُمْ بِالسُّنَّةِ ، فَإِنْ كَانُوا فِي السُّنَّةِ سَوَاءً فَأَقْدَمُهُمْ هِجْرَةً ، فَإِنْ كَانُوا فِي الْهِجْرَةِ سَوَاءً فَأَقْدَمُهُمْ سِلْمًا .

This demonstrates that the one who is more versed (*aqra*' in the Qur'ān, i.e. the one who has memorized more Qur'ān, takes precedence in leading prayers over the one who is more knowledgeable. This Prophetic instruction was practically demonstrated in his lifetime, as shown by the following reports:

---

[21] Reported by Aḥmad in his Musnad, 'Abd al-Razzāq in his Muṣannaf, Ibn Abī Shaybah, Ṭabarī in his tafsīr, Ḥākim in his Mustadrak, Bayhaqī in al-Sunan al-Ka'bīr, and Ṭaḥāwī in Sharḥ Mushkil al-Āthār. Ḥākim deemed it ṣaḥīḥ on the conditions of Bukhārī and Muslim, and Dhahabī agreed with him.

[22] Muwaṭṭa' Mālik: Kitāb al-ṣalāh—Bāb jāmi' al-ṣalāh. Also related by Ḥākim in al-Mustadrak, where he deems it ṣaḥīḥ on the conditions of Bukhārī and Muslim, and others such as Bazzār, 'Abd al-Razzāq, Bayhaqī, Ibn Abī Shaybah, and Ṭabarānī.

[23] Ṣaḥīḥ Muslim: Kitāb al-masājid wa mawāḍi' al-ṣalāh—Bāb man aḥaqq bi al-imāmah.

ʿAbdullah b. ʿUmar reported: When the earliest emigrants came to ʿUṣbah, a place in Qubā', before the arrival of the Prophet ﷺ, Sālim, the freed slave of Abū Ḥudhayfah, who knew more Qur'ān than the others, used to lead them in prayer, and in their ranks were ʿUmar, Abū Salamah, Zayd and ʿĀmir b. Rabīʿah.[24]

عَنْ عَبْدِ اللهِ بْنِ عُمَرَ قَالَ: لَمَّا قَدِمَ الْمُهَاجِرُونَ الْأَوَّلُونَ الْعُصْبَةَ، مَوْضِعٌ بِقُبَاءَ، قَبْلَ مَقْدَمِ رَسُولِ اللهِ صَلَّى اللهُ عَلَيْهِ وَسَلَّمَ، كَانَ يَؤُمُّهُمْ سَالِمٌ ، مَوْلَى أَبِي حُذَيْفَةَ، وَكَانَ أَكْثَرَهُمْ قُرْآنًا.

وفي رواية: فِيهِمْ أَبُو بَكْرٍ وَعُمَرُ وَأَبُو سَلَمَةَ وَزَيْدٌ وَعَامِرُ بْنُ رَبِيعَةَ.

ʿAmr b. Salamah reported: When my father returned to his tribe, he said, 'By Allah, I have indeed come to you from the Prophet ﷺ, who has said: 'Offer such-and-such prayer at such-and-such a time, and when the time for the prayer comes, then one of you should pronounce the adhān, and let the one who knows the most Qur'ān lead the prayer." So they looked around for such a person and found none who knew more Qur'ān than I, because of what I used to learn from the caravans.[25] They put me forward ahead of them (to lead the prayers), and I was only six or seven years of age at the time. I was wearing a cloak such that when I prostrated it would reveal my body. A lady from the tribe said, 'Why don't you cover the rear-end of your reciter for us?' So they bought (a piece of cloth) and made a shirt for me. I had never been so happy with

عَنْ عَمْرِو بْنِ سَلِمَةَ قَالَ: وَبَدَرَ أَبِي قَوْمِي بِإِسْلَامِهِمْ، فَلَمَّا قَدِمَ قَالَ: جِئْتُكُمْ وَاللهِ مِنْ عِنْدِ النَّبِيِّ صَلَّى اللهُ عَلَيْهِ وَسَلَّمَ حَقًّا، فَقَالَ: صَلُّوا صَلَاةَ كَذَا فِي حِينِ كَذَا، وَصَلُّوا كَذَا فِي حِينِ كَذَا، فَإِذَا حَضَرَتِ الصَّلَاةُ فَلْيُؤَذِّنْ أَحَدُكُمْ، وَلْيَؤُمَّكُمْ أَكْثَرُكُمْ قُرْآنًا . فَنَظَرُوا فَلَمْ يَكُنْ أَحَدٌ أَكْثَرَ قُرْآنًا مِنِّي، لِمَا كُنْتُ أَتَلَقَّى مِنَ الرُّكْبَانِ، فَقَدَّمُونِي بَيْنَ أَيْدِيهِمْ، وَأَنَا ابْنُ سِتٍّ أَوْ سَبْعِ سِنِينَ، وَكَانَتْ عَلَيَّ بُرْدَةٌ، كُنْتُ إِذَا سَجَدْتُ تَقَلَّصَتْ عَنِّي، فَقَالَتِ امْرَأَةٌ مِنَ الْحَيِّ: أَلَا تُغَطُّوا عَنَّا اسْتَ قَارِئِكُمْ ؟ فَاشْتَرَوْا فَقَطَعُوا لِي قَمِيصًا، فَمَا فَرِحْتُ بِشَيْءٍ فَرَحِي بِذَلِكَ الْقَمِيصِ.

---

[24] Ṣaḥīḥ Bukhārī: Kitāb al-adhān—Bāb imāmah al-ʿabd wa al-mawlā; Kitāb al-aḥkām—Bāb istiqḍā' al-mawālī wa istiʿmālihim.

[25] The tribe was situated in a crossroads of caravans, where travelers would speak about the Prophet and various verses that came down. ʿAmr as a young boy learned portions of the Qur'ān in this manner.

> anything before as I was with that
> shirt.[26]

There are many related ḥadīth reports which refer to the notion of memorizing the Qur'ān through various terms used in the Prophetic era: *qāri', ḥāfīẓ,* 'gathering (*jama'a*) the Qur'ān', 'holding (wa'ā) the Qur'ān',[27] or being 'a person of the Qur'ān' (*ahl al-Qur'ān, ṣāḥib al-Qur'ān*). All of these terms have to do with memorizing the Qur'ān by heart irrespective of the element of comprehension and understanding (*fahm*).

Finally, Ibn al-Jazarī in al-Nashr reports with his isnād to Imām Aḥmad of a dream in which Imām Aḥmad saw Allah and asked him how one gets closer to Him. Allah replied: 'Through my words.' Imām Aḥmad asked: 'With or without understanding?' He replied: 'With or without understanding.'[28]

---

[26] Ṣaḥīḥ Bukhārī: Kitāb al-maghāzī—Bāb wa qāla al-Layth ḥaddathanī Yūnus.

[27] Sunan al-Dārimī: Kitāb faḍā'il al-Qur'ān—Bāb faḍl man qara'a al-Qur'ān.

[28] Reported by Ibn al-Jawzī in *Manāqib al-Imām Aḥmad,* Abū Ya'lā al-Farrā' (d. 457) in *Ibṭāl al-ta'wīlāt*, Nawawī in *al-Tibyān fī ādāb ḥamalat al-Qur'ān*, Dhahabī in *Siyar,* and Ghazālī in Iḥyā' 'ulūm al-dīn among others. Its authenticity is subject to some dispute. Shaykh Salman al-'Awdah expressed that he was not aware of any critical analysis of the report, and Shaykh Ibn Baz and 'Uthaymīn expressed similar opinions. Others doubted its authenticity to the point of deeming it fabricated due to the reporter Aḥmad b. Muḥammad b. Miqsam.

Qur'ān Memorizers Among the Companions

As for those who memorized the Qur'ān in the Prophet's lifetime, they were numerous. But the Companions that appear in the chains of the Qur'ān are only eight in number: 'Umar, 'Uthmān, 'Alī, Ubayy, Zayd b. Thābit, Abū al-Dardā', Abū Mūsā al-Ash'arī, and Ibn Mas'ūd. Furthermore, these Companions who transmitted the Qur'ān and appeared in Qur'ānic isnāds are two levels: those who took directly from the Prophet and those who took from other Companions.

Eight Companions in Qur'ān Isnāds

The ḥadīth expert Dhahabī stated:

> Those who reviewed the Qur'ān with the Messenger of Allah ﷺ included 'Uthmān b. 'Affān, 'Alī b. Abū Ṭālib, Ubayy b. Ka'b, 'Abdullah b. Mas'ūd, Zayd b. Thābit, Abū Mūsā al-Ash'arī, and Abū al-Dardā', may Allah be pleased with them all. These are the ones about whom it has reached us that they had memorized the Qur'ān in the lifetime of the Prophet ﷺ and that the Qur'ān was taken from them by succeeding generations. The Qur'ānic isnads of the ten Imāms goes through them. There were other Companions who also had preserved the Qur'ān, like Mu'ādh b. Jabal, Abū Yazīd, Sālim the freed-slave of Abū Ḥudhayfah, 'Abdullah b. 'Āmr, and 'Uqbah b. 'Āmir, but their readings did not reach us.[29]

Dhahabī fails to mention, perhaps forgetfully, the name of 'Umar b. al-Khaṭṭāb, although some isnāds of Nāfi', Ibn Kathīr, Abū 'Āmr, Ḥamzah, and Kisā'ī do go back through him—as shall be mentioned later. Similarly, Hishām b. 'Ammār and 'Abdullah b. Dhakwān both recited to Ayyūb b. Tamīm who recited to Yaḥyā al-Dhimārī who recited to Ibn 'Āmir and Wāthilah b. al-Athqa' who learned from the Prophet ﷺ. Dhahabī's statement also suggests that those who recited the entire Qur'ān to the Prophet ﷺ were not confined to four [as some believe].

Abū Sulaymān al-Khaṭṭābī (d. 388/988)[30] says: 'Every scholar of the readings from Arabia, Syria, and Iraq attributed their readings to a Companion who had recited the entire Qur'ān upon the Messenger of Allah ﷺ not leaving out anything. Thus, 'Āṣim and Abū 'Āmr b. al-'Ulā' referenced their reading to Ubayy while 'Abdullah b. 'Āmir referenced his reading to 'Uthmān. Since all of these Companions

---

[29] Dhahabī, *Ma'rifat al-qurrā' al-kibār,* vol 1, pg 42.
[30] Noted ḥadīth scholar, author and Shāfi'ī jurist who was born in Lashkargāh (also known as Bost), capital of Helmand Province, Afghanistan.

explicitly stated that they recited to the Prophet ﷺ, the isnād of these particular readings is fully connected and its transmitters all reliable.'[31]

Four Qur'ānic Companions in Ḥadīth Reports[32]

On the other hand, we have two ḥadīth reports, both of them from Anas b. Mālik, that seem to restrict the Companions who preserved the Qur'ān to four. In one report, Qatādah reports from Anas: 'Four individuals, all of them from the Anṣār, gathered[33] the Qur'ān in the lifetime of the Prophet ﷺ: Ubayy, Mu'ādh b. Jabal, Abū Zayd, and Zayd b. Thābit.'[34] In another report, Thābit al-Bunānī reports from Anas: 'The Prophet ﷺ died and only four had gathered the entire Qur'ān: Abū al-Dardā', Mu'ādh b. Jabal, Zayd b. Thābit and Abū Zayd.'[35]

It appears that Anas intended his statement in a non-exclusive sense, since he substituted Ubayy b. Ka'b in place of Abū al-Dardā' in one of the reports and reported the other version with a more non-exclusive wording ('Four individuals, all of them from the Anṣār, preserved the Qur'ān . . .').

In fact, the version with the exclusive wording does not even include Ubayy b. Ka'b, who was known to be the single most versed Companion in the Qur'ān by the testimony of the Prophet ﷺ: 'The most versed of my nation in the Qur'ān is Ubayy b. Ka'b.'[36] After the Prophet once said to him: 'Allah has commanded me to recite Qur'ān to you'; he asked: 'Did Allah really mention me to you?' The Prophet replied: 'Yes,' and Ubayy burst into tears.[37]

There were individuals that erroneously claimed, based upon these reports, that these were the only four individuals who had memorized the Qur'ān. This was obviously problematic since there are more than four individuals in these two reports of Anas. This view was also criticized heavily by many scholars, even to the point of deeming it heretical. The senior Mālikī jurist al-Mādhirī (d. 536/1141)[38] said:

---

[31] Tafsīr Qurṭubī, vol 1, pg 59.

[32] This entire section is reorganized and reconstructed from a combination of all four of Shaykh Waleed's works, especially: *al-Qamar al-munīr*, pg 90-96; and *al-Khayr al-kathīr*, pg 112-8.

[33] The Arabic word in the report is *jam'*, which conveys the sense of preserving, protecting and memorizing.

[34] Ṣaḥīḥ Bukhārī: Kitāb manāqib al-Anṣār—Bāb manāqib Zayd b. Thābit; Kitāb faḍā'il al-Qur'ān—Bāb al-qurrā' min aṣḥāb al-nabī; Ṣaḥīḥ Muslim: Kitāb faḍā'il al-ṣaḥābah—Bāb min faḍā'il Ubayy b. Ka'b.

[35] Ṣaḥīḥ Bukhārī: Kitāb faḍā'il al-Qur'ān—Bāb al-qurrā' min aṣḥāb al-nabīyy.

[36] Ṭabarānī, al-Mu'jam al-ṣaghīr: Bāb al-'ayn—Man ismuhū 'Alī.

[37] Ṣaḥīḥ Bukhārī: Kitāb manāqib al-Anṣār—Bāb manāqib Ubayy; Kitāb tafsīr al-Qur'ān—Bāb sūrah lam yakun—ḥadīth inna Allaha amaranī an uqri'aka al-Qur'ān; Ṣaḥīḥ Muslim: Kitāb ṣalāt al-musāfirīn wa qaṣrihā—Bāb istiḥbāb qirā'at al-Qur'ān 'alā ahl al-faḍl wa al-ḥudhdhāq fīhi.

[38] Abū 'Abdullah Muḥammad b. 'Alī al-Tamīmī al-Mādhirī of Tunisia was the leader of the Mālikī jurists of his time whose students included Ibn al-'Arabī of Spain, Qāḍī 'Iyāḍ, and Muḥammad b. Tūmurt, founder of the Muwaḥidūn (Almohads) movement of North Africa.

'Some heretics took this report of Mālik and claimed that only four or five Companions had memorized the Qur'ān.' In the end, most scholars rejected this erroneous view quite strongly and gave a series of arguments (in addition to what was mentioned) for why the reports are not at all meant to be exclusive to these individuals.

First, the words were simply never meant to be exclusive and never precluded the existence of other memorizers. Some pointed to the existence of the implied preposition *min* ('from') in these reports, a common linguistic device in Arabic. In other words, the report is understood to say: '*From those* who had memorized the Qur'ān were four.' This also explains many reports such as: 'The best of deeds is . . .' or 'The most beloved of deeds to Allah is . . .' All of these are understood in the same way, with an implicit *min*: '*From* the best deeds is . . .' and '*From* the most beloved deeds to Allah is . . .'

Another explanation given is that Anas simply intended by his statements that he wasn't aware of anyone else who had memorized the Qur'ān other than these individuals, which does not preclude others from knowing of such individuals.

Another possibility is that these four had preserved the Qur'ān through all of its reading variants while others had preserved the Qur'ān in only some, not all, of them. Yet another explanation is that these four were the only ones who heard the entire Qur'ān directly from the mouth of the Prophet ﷺ whereas others had learned only portions from the Prophet and the rest through other Companions. It is well known that Companions would teach one another. Some older Companions were even known to learn from younger ones. This idea is supported by the report of Ibn Mas'ūd: 'I memorized from the mouth of Allah's Messenger seventy sūrahs of the Qur'ān.'[39] At face value, this proves that he had not learned all the sūrahs from the Prophet ﷺ. In other words, he had learned seventy directly and the rest through an intermediary. Also, Ibn Mas'ūd stated: 'By Him besides Whom there is no god, there is no chapter in the Book of Allah about which I do not know as to where it was revealed; and there is no verse about which I do not know in what context it was revealed; and if I were to know of one having a better understanding of the Book of Allah than I (and I could reach him) on the back of the mule, I would have definitely gone to him on camel's back.'[40] This shows how keen they were to learn from one another, and that Ibn Mas'ūd had surely memorized the entire Qur'ān during the Prophet's lifetime, learning a good portion from him directly.

Another explanation is that these were the only four or five Companions who had preserved the entire Qur'ān *in writing* during the Prophetic era and not only by memory. The verb used in the ḥadīth (*jama'a*) is the same one that was used for work of Abū Bakr and 'Uthmān in compiling written copies of the Qur'ān (e.g. '*jama'a*

[39] Ṣaḥīḥ Bukhārī: Kitāb faḍā'il al-ṣaḥābah—Bāb al-qurrā' min aṣḥāb al-nabī.

[40] Ṣaḥīḥ Bukhārī: Kitāb faḍā'il al-ṣaḥābah—Bāb al-qurrā' min aṣḥāb al-nabī. Ṣaḥīḥ Muslim: Kitāb faḍā'il al-ṣaḥābah—Bāb min faḍā'il Abdillāh b. Mas'ūd.

'Uthmān al-muṣḥaf'). These individuals had written copies of the entire Qur'ān in their possession whereas others had memorized it without necessarily having it in written form.

Finally, it may be that Anas had intended by his words that these individuals were the ones who had preserved the entire Qur'ān, including the final verses that were revealed shortly before the demise of the Prophet ﷺ, whereas others may have preserved all of the Qur'ān but did not have the chance to hear the final verses or recite them to the Prophet ﷺ due to his passing. Of course, they would have gone on to complete the verses afterwards by reciting them to other Companions. Seventy Qur'ānic reciters were mentioned to have been martyred in the Battle of Yamāmah[41] during the reign of Abū Bakr, while a similar number were martyred in the life of the Prophet ﷺ during the incident of the well of Ma'ūnah,[42] all of which allude to the great number of Qur'ān readers among the Companions.[43]

It was also claimed that these were the individuals who were actively teaching the Qur'ān and not the only ones who had memorized, but this is a weaker claim.

Ibn Ḥajar discusses these possible explanations and considers most of them to be far-fetched. He is among those who considered the ḥadīth to apply simply to those who had memorized the Qur'ān from the clan of Khazraj alone. Khazraj was the clan of Anas b. Mālik, the reporter of the ḥadīth.

In one of the versions of the report, Qatādah had asked Anas: 'Who had memorized the Qur'ān in the Prophet's lifetime?' Anas responded: 'Four people, all from the Anṣār: Ubayy b. Ka'b, Mu'ādh b. Jabal, Zayd b. Thābit, and Abū Zayd.' Qatādah asked: 'Who was Abū Zayd?' Anas replied: 'One of my uncles.'[44] Qatādah had asked Anas as he was not familiar with the fourth individual, whose full name was Qays b. al-Sakan.

After a study of all the isnāds of this ḥadīth, Ibn Ḥajar came to the conclusion that these statements were uttered in the context of the rivalry between Aws and Khazraj. He provides the historical context for the ḥadīth of Anas:

> Ṭabarī reports through Sa'īd b. Abī 'Arūbah from Qatādah from Anas, who said: 'The clans of Aws and Khazraj were perpetual rivals. The Aws clan once said: We have four individuals: the one for whom the Divine Throne shook (Sa'd b. Mu'ādh),[45] the one whose testimony was

[41] The first major battle fought in the post-Prophetic era between the armies of Abū Bakr and the false prophet Musaylimah, which occurred in the year 11/632.

[42] A tragic incident that occurred four months after the Battle of Uḥud in 4/625 in which a large group of Muslims sent by the Prophet were massacred near a well. This prompted the Prophet to pray against the perpetrators in his prayers for many days.

[43] *Al-Itqān,* vol 1, pg 80-2.

[44] See footnote 34.

[45] He was a loyal Companion of the Prophet ﷺ who faithfully fought alongside him in his battles, about him the Prophet ﷺ stated: *The throne of the All-Merciful shook at the death of Sa'd b. Mu'ādh.* Ṣaḥīḥ Bukhārī: Kitāb manāqib al-Anṣār—Bāb manāqib Sa'd b. Mu'ādh.

> deemed to be equivalent to two men (Khuzaymah b. Thābit),[46] the one whom the angels themselves washed (Ḥanẓalah b. Abī ʿĀmir),[47] and the one protected by wasps (ʿĀṣim b. Thābit).[48] The Khazraj responded by boasting that they had four men who had preserved the entire Qur'ān and that no one else had done so.
>
> I am inclined to the explanation that the intent [of the ḥadīth of Anas] was simply to affirm these virtues for the Khazraj clan to the exclusion of the Aws only, and that it did not at all preclude individuals from other clans from having preserved the Qur'ān.[49]

So these words were uttered in the context of mutual rivalry between two clans, a context which makes clear that the words were not meant in an exclusive sense but merely to highlight and boast of four individual who had memorized the Qur'ān among them.

Additional Qur'ān Memorizers Among Companions

There were clearly others who had memorized the Qur'ān, such as ʿAbdullah b. ʿAmr b. al-ʿĀṣ, who said: 'I had memorized the Qur'an and used to recite it all in one night.' The Messenger of Allah ﷺ said: 'I am afraid that you may live a long life and get tired [of this practice], so recite it over the period of one month.' I said: 'Let me benefit from my strength in my youth.' He said: 'Recite it in ten days.' I said: 'Let me benefit from my strength and my youth.' He said: 'Recite it in seven days.' I said: 'Let me benefit from my strength and my youth,' but the Prophet refused (to alter it any further).[50]

There is also another report from ʿAbdullah b. ʿAmr, who said, when ʿAbdullah b. Masʿūd was mentioned before him: This is a man I cannot stop loving, for I heard the Prophet ﷺ said: *'Learn the Qur'ān from four: ʿAbdullah b. Masʿūd—he started*

---

[46] See section: "Writing the Qur'ān" in chapter 3 for his story.

[47] Ḥanẓalah b. Abī ʿĀmir was a loyal Companion whose wedding night coincided with the Battle of Uḥud. Having gotten permission to remain in Madīnah and get married, he did so but in the morning left hastily for the battle without performing the obligatory ghusl. He was martyred while attacking Abū Sufyān and the Prophet ﷺ reported seeing him being given the bath by angels, earning him the title *Ghasīl al-malā'ikah.*

[48] ʿĀṣim b. Thābit al-Anṣārī was the father-in-law of ʿUmar who was sent by the Prophet as the head of an expedition of ten people which resulted in his martyrdom at the hands of the Liḥyān clan in 4 AH. When they tried to sever his head in order to sell it, Allah sent a swarm of bees to protect his corpse. See Ṣaḥīḥ Bukhārī: Kitāb al-maghāzī—Bāb ḥaddathanī ʿAbdullah b. Muḥammad al-Juʿfī.

[49] *Fatḥ,* Dār al-Maʿrifah, vol 9, pg 51.

[50] Ṣaḥīḥ Bukhārī:Kitāb faḍā'il al-Qur'ān—Bāb fī kam yaqra'a al-Qur'ān; Ṣaḥīḥ Muslim: Kitāb al-ṣiyām—Bāb al-nahy ʿan ṣawm al-dahr liman taḍarrara bihī; Sunan Ibn Mājah: Kitāb iqāmat al-ṣalāh wa al-sunnah fīhā—Bāb fī kam yustaḥabb yakhtim al-Qur'ān; al-Nasā'ī: Sunan al-Kubrā: Kitāb faḍā'il al-Qur'ān—Bāb fī kam yaqra'a al-Qur'ān.

with him—Sālim the freed slave of Abū Ḥudhayfah, Mu'ādh b. Jabal, and Ubayy b. Ka'b.'[51]

These four include two Muhājirīn (Sālim and Ibn Mas'ūd) and two from the Anṣār (Mu'ādh b. Jabal and Ubayy). About this ḥadīth, some scholars have claimed that this could be considered the first Qur'ānic ijāzah from the Prophet ﷺ, because ijāzah is basically permission to teach the Qur'ān (iqrā').[52]

Sālim b. Ma'qal was the freed slave of Abū Ḥudhayfah and one of the most senior and learned of all Companions. He did not live long, having been killed as a martyr. As a result, he was not able to transmit as much knowledge as others who managed to live longer. However, his great standing is indicated by the statement of 'Umar on his own deathbed: 'Had Sālim the freed slave of Abū Ḥudhayfah been alive, I would have appointed him as Caliph after me.'[53]

Also, during the military expedition of Bi'r Ma'ūnah in the Prophet's lifetime, seventy Qur'ānic Companions (qurrā') were killed.[54] This term was customarily used in a broader sense not only for memorizing the Qur'ān but also for its understanding and implementation. A large number of such individuals having been killed in one battle points to the abundance of Qur'ān memorizers among the Companions. Also, there was the martyrdom of many such individuals in the wars of apostasy in the reign of Abū Bakr, which was so close to the era of the Prophet that these individuals surely must have memorized the Qur'ān in the lifetime of the Prophet just months earlier. This was in fact the very incentive that drove Abū Bakr to compile the Qur'ān into one binding in the first place.

Another example was a report of a female Companion that had memorized the Qur'ān. Ibn Sa'd in his *Ṭabaqāt* relates with his isnād to Umm Waraqah bint 'Abdullah b. al-Ḥārith that the Prophet used to visit her, named her *al-Shahīdah* (' martyr'), and ordered her to lead her household in prayer because she had memorized the Qur'ān. Prior to the battle of Badr, she had sought the Prophet's permission to accompany them in battle so she could tend to the wounded and become a martyr. He asked her to remain home and said to her: 'Allah will grant you martyrdom.' Later during the reign of 'Umar, she was strangled to death in her own home by a cloth by her

---

[51] Ṣaḥīḥ Bukhārī: Kitāb manāqib al-anṣār—Bāb manāqib Ubayy; Kitāb faḍā'il al-Qur'ān—Bāb al-qurrā' min aṣḥāb al-nabī; Ṣaḥīḥ Muslim: Kitāb faḍā'il al-ṣaḥābah—Bāb min faḍā'il 'Abdullah b. Mas'ūd.

[52] *Al-Qamar al-munīr fī sharḥ al-Zamzamī,* pg 90.

[53] Musnad Aḥmad: Musnad 'Umar b. al-Khaṭṭāb.

[54] Ṣaḥīḥ Bukhārī: Kitāb al-witr—Bāb al-qunūt qabla al-rukū'; Kitāb al-janā'iz—Bāb man jalasa 'inda al-muṣībah ya'rifu fīhī al-ḥuzn; Kitāb al-jihād wa al-sayr—Bāb al-'awn bi al-madad; Kitāb al-jizyah—Bāb du'ā' al-imām 'alā man nakatha 'ahdan; Kitāb al-maghāzī—Bāb ghazwat al-Rajī' wa Dhakwān wa Bi'r Ma'ūnah; Kitāb al-da'awāt—Bāb al-du'ā' 'alā al-mushrikīn; Ṣaḥīḥ Muslim: Kitāb al-masājid wa mawāḍi'u al-ṣalāh—Bāb istiḥbāb al-qunūt fī jamī' al-ṣalāh idhā nazalat bi al-muslimīna nāzilah. See footnote 42 on page 55.

two slaves, concerning whom she had previously announced that they would be manumitted upon her death.[55]

Abū 'Ubayd al-Qāsim b. al-Sallām in his book on the readings listed all the qurrā' among the Companions, starting with the four Rightly-Guided Caliphs. He reasoned that since Abū Bakr was ordered by the Prophet to lead the prayers, he was among the most learned of them in Qur'ān as the Prophetic command was to have the most versed individual in Qur'ān lead prayers.

'Umar used to lead Fajr prayer daily with about seven rub' of the Qur'ān.[56] In other words, he would recite from his memory lengthy sūrahs of the likes of sūrah Yūnus and Hūd. Many Qur'ānic isnāds ultimately go back to 'Umar, 'Uthmān or 'Alī, as will be discussed in more detail later.

The First Tier: Those Who Learned from the Prophet

To summarize, those who memorized the Qur'ān in the Prophet's lifetime were numerous. They included the four Rightly-Guided Caliphs, Ṭalḥah, Sa'd b. Abī Waqqāṣ, 'Abdullah b. Mas'ūd, Ḥudhayfah b. al-Yamān, Abū Mūsā al-Ash'arī, Mu'ādh b. Jabal, Abū Zayd al-Anṣārī, Sālim the freed slave of Abī Ḥudhayfah, 'Abdullah b. 'Umar, 'Uqbah b. 'Āmir, Abū Ayyūb al-Anṣārī, 'Ubādah b. al-Ṣāmit, Mujammi' b. Jāriyah, Faḍālah b. 'Ubayd, Maslamah b. Makhlad, Umm Waraqah bint 'Abdullah b. al-Ḥārith al-Anṣārī, 'Abdullah b. 'Abbās, Abū Hurayrah, 'Abdullah b. al-Sā'ib b. Abī al-Sā'ib al-Makhzūmī, and 'Abdullah b. 'Ayyāsh b. Abī Rabī'ah.[57]

As for the Companions that appeared in the chains of the Qur'ān, they were only eight in number: 'Umar, 'Uthmān, 'Alī, Ubayy, Zayd b. Thābit, Abū al-Dardā', Abū Mūsā al-Ash'arī, and Ibn Mas'ūd.

'Umar b. al-Khaṭṭāb (d. 23/644)

'Umar b. al-Khaṭṭāb was the close Companion of the Prophet, 'Commander of the Faithful,' second of the Rightly-Guided Caliphs, and Allah's answer to the Prophetic supplication: 'Oh Allah, strengthen Islam with one of the two 'Umars.' He embraced Islam five years prior to the Hijrah, after which the Muslims began to practice their faith openly. Thereafter, he closely associated himself with the Prophet ﷺ, accompanied him on all missions, and was one of his two ministers. He became the second Caliph by the choice of the Muslim ummah, and expanded the lands of Islam, spread the faith and established the Hijrī calendar and state treasury. He was assassinated by the Zoroastrian Abū Lu'lu' while leading Fajr prayer in Dhū al-Ḥijjah in the year 23 AH.

---

[55] Abū Dāwūd: Kitāb al-ṣalāh—Bāb imāmat al-nisā'.

[56] The rub' is a set portion of the Qur'ān, eight of which comprise one juz'.

[57] *Fath*, vol 8, pg 668; *al-Itqān*, vol 1, pg 199-204

'Uthmān b. 'Affān (d. 35/656)

'Uthmān b. 'Affān was the third of the Rightly-Guided Caliphs, one of the ten promised Paradise, and among the earliest Companions. Ibn 'Abd al-Barr (d. 463/1071)[58] said: 'He was referred to by the kunyā Abū 'Abdullah and Abū 'Amr, but Abū 'Amr was the more famous of the two. His wife Ruqayyah, daughter of the Prophet ﷺ bore him a son named 'Abdullah giving rise to the first kunyā. 'Abdullah soon died and he had another son named 'Amr, giving rise to his second kunyā, which he kept until his death.'[59] He was noble and wealthy before Islam, and as a Muslim he spent it in defense of his faith. He first married the daughter of the Prophet ﷺ Ruqayyah, and upon her death, married her sister Umm Kulthūm, thereby earning the title *Dhū al-Nūrayn* ('possessor of two lights').

He was a scribe of the Prophet tasked with recording revelation. Al-Dānī states that he used to read the Qur'ān to the Prophet ﷺ. He was given the role of Caliph after 'Umar, after which he expanded the borders of Islam and compiled the Qur'ān into standardized copies. He was unjustly killed in his own home at the age of 82.

His students included his sons Abān, Sa'īd, and 'Amr; his freed slave Ḥumrān; 'Abdullah b. Mas'ūd, 'Abdullah b. 'Abbās, 'Abdullah b. 'Umar, 'Abdullah b. al-Zubayr, 'Abdullah b. Ja'far b. Abī Ṭālib, Zayd b. Thābit, 'Imrān b. Ḥuṣayn, Anas b. Mālik, Abū Hurayrah, and many others.

'Alī b. Abī Ṭālib (d. 40/661)

'Alī b. Abī Ṭālib was the cousin of the Prophet ﷺ, fourth of the Rightly-Guided Caliphs, one of the ten promised Paradise, and son-in-law of the Prophet who married his daughter Fāṭimah. Known by the kunyā Abū Turab, he was among the earliest Muslims and closest to the Prophet, having witnessed all his battles and major events. He related much information from the Prophet and read the Qur'ān with him. He had numerous students, which were documented by Mizzī in *Tahdhīb al-Kamāl*.

Ubayy b. Ka'b (d. 30/649)

Ubayy b. Ka'b was known by the kunyā Abū al-Mundhir, and 'Umar gave him the title Abū al-Ṭufayl. He was the leader of all Qur'ānic experts and the most learned Companion. He had many merits and witnessed all battles and major events of the Prophet ﷺ. He read the Qur'ān to the Prophet ﷺ. Those who learned Qur'ān from him included Ibn 'Abbās, Abū Hurayrah, 'Abdullah b. al-Sā'ib, 'Abdullah b. 'Ayyāsh

---

[58] Abū 'Umar Yūsuf b. 'Abdullah of Cordoba, better known as Ibn 'Abd al-Barr, was a great ḥadīth expert, judge, Mālikī jurist, historian and man of letters who was born in Cordoba in 368/978 and died in Xàtiva (Shāṭibah) in 463/1071.

[59] Ibn 'Abd al-Barr, *al-Istī'āb fī ma'rifat al-aṣḥāb,* vol 3, pg 1037.

and Abū ʿAbd al-Raḥmān al-Sulamī. Suwayd b. Ghafalah, ʿAbd al-Raḥmān b. Abzā, Abū al-Muhallab and others.

He was one of the four whom the Prophet ﷺ advised learning the Qur'ān from: 'Learn the reading of the Qur'ān from four individuals: Ibn Masʿūd, Sālim the freed slave of Abū Ḥudhayfah, Ubayy and Muʿādh b. Jabal.'[60] ʿUmar used to say: 'Ubayy is the most learned of us in the Qur'ān, and ʿAlī is the best judge.'[61] Once the Prophet ﷺ informed Ubayy that he was ordered to recite the Qur'ān to him. When he asked if Allah had mentioned his name, the Prophet replied: 'Yes.' Then Ubayy began to weep.[62] The Prophet also said to Ubayy: 'May knowledge be pleasant for you, Oh Abū al-Mundhir.'[63] Dhahabī even stated that Ubayy was more learned in the Qur'ān than Abū Bakr and ʿUmar. Ibn ʿAbbās related that Ubayy said to ʿUmar: 'I have received the Qur'ān from the one who received it fresh from Jibrīl.'[64]

His date of death was disputed, and Dhahabī preferred the opinion that it was in 30 AH.

Zayd b. Thābit (d. 45/665)

Zayd b. Thābit was a young boy of eleven years when the Prophet ﷺ arrived in Madīnah. Extremely clever and intelligent, he learned Arabic orthography and the Hebrew language, and became one of the scribes of revelation. He was among those who recited the Qur'ān to the Prophet ﷺ, and he also recited to Abū Bakr and ʿUmar. His students included his son Khārijah, Ibn ʿAbbās, Ibn ʿUmar, Marwān b. al-Ḥakam, ʿUbayd b. al-Sabbāq, ʿAṭā' b. Yasār, Busr b. Saʿīd, ʿUrwah b. al-Zubayr, Ṭāwūs, and many others. Abū ʿAmr al-Dānī stated: Ibn ʿAbbās, Abū al-ʿĀliyah, and Abū ʿAbd al-Raḥmān al-Sulamī read the Qur'ān with him. He witnessed the Battle of the Trench and all subsequent ones. ʿUmar placed him in charge of Madīnah when he went for Ḥajj. He was the one placed in charge of compiling the muṣḥaf in the time of ʿUthmān. He was the one charged with distributing the spoils from Yarmūk.'[65] Zayd states: 'When revelation would come down, the Prophet ﷺ would send for me to write it down.'[66]

---

[60] Ṣaḥīḥ Bukhārī: Kitāb faḍā'il al-ṣaḥābah—Bāb manāqib Sālim; Bāb manāqib ʿAbdullah b. Masʿūd; Kitāb manāqib al-anṣār—Bāb manāqib Muʿādh; Bāb manāqib Ubayy; Kitāb faḍā'il al-Qur'ān—Bāb al-qurrā' min aṣḥāb al-nabī; Ṣaḥīḥ Muslim: Kitāb faḍā'il al-ṣaḥābah—Bāb min faḍā'il ʿAbdullah b. Masʿūd.

[61] Ṣaḥīḥ Bukhārī: Kitāb tafsīr al-Qur'ān—Bāb qawluhū mā nansakh min āyatin; Kitāb faḍā'il al-Qur'ān—Bāb al-qurrā' min aṣḥāb al-nabī.

[62] Ṣaḥīḥ Bukhārī: Kitāb manāqib al-anṣār—Bāb manāqib Ubayy; Kitāb tafsīr al-Qur'ān—Bāb sūrah lam yakun; Ṣaḥīḥ Muslim: Kitāb ṣalāh al-musāfirīn wa qaṣrihā—Bāb istiḥbāb qirā'at al-Qur'ān ʿalā ahl al-faḍl wa al-ḥudhdhāq fīhi.

[63] Ṣaḥīḥ Muslim: Kitāb ṣalāh al-musāfirīn wa qaṣrihā—Bāb faḍl sūrah al-Kahf wa āyat al-kursī.

[64] Musnad Aḥmad: Musnad al-Anṣār—Ḥadīth Abī al-Mundhir Ubayy b. Kaʿb.

[65] Dhahabī, *Tārīkh al-Islām*, vol 2, pg 407.

[66] Tirmidhī: Kitāb al-Shamā'il—Bāb mā jā'a fī khalq rasūlillāh.

Zayd reported: Abū Bakr said to me: 'You are a wise young man and we do not have any suspicion about you. You used to write the revelation for Allah's Messenger. So search for (the fragmentary scripts of) the Qur'an and collect it in one book.' I said to him: 'How will you do something which Allah's Messenger did not do?' He replied: 'By Allah, it is a good project.' Abū Bakr kept on urging me to accept his idea until Allah opened my chest.[67]

'Abdullah b. Mas'ūd (d. 32/653)

'Abdullah b. Mas'ūd was one of the early Companions of the Prophet and among those who made the first migration to Abyssinia. He witnessed all the battles of the Prophet ﷺ. The Prophet used to confide his secrets in him. He was among the most learned of all Companions in the Qur'ān, having memorized it in the lifetime of the Prophet ﷺ. He once confessed: 'I learned seventy sūrahs directly from the mouth of the Prophet ﷺ'.[68] Among those who read Qur'ān to him were 'Alqamah, Masrūq, Aswad, Zirr b. Ḥubaysh, Abū 'Abd al-Raḥmān al-Sulamī and others. The Prophet ﷺ stated: 'Whoever desires to hear the Qur'ān as fresh as it was revealed should listen to the recitation of Ibn Umm 'Abd.'[69] Abū Mas'ūd, another Companion, said while pointing to him: 'I do not know of anyone that was left by the Prophet ﷺ who was more knowledgeable about Allah's Book than the man who is standing.'[70] Ibn Sīrīn related that Ibn Mas'ūd said: 'If I knew of anyone within travelable distance that was more knowledge about the last rehearsal of the Prophet than me, I would surely travel to him.'[71] Masrūq relates that Ibn Mas'ūd said: 'There is no single verse that was revealed except that I know concerning what it was revealed, and if I were to know of anyone who knew the Qur'ān more than myself within travelable distance, I would surely travel to them.'[72]

Abū al-Dardā' (d. 32/652)

Abū al-Dardā' was also among those who recited to the Prophet, and Dhahabī remarks that it was not known that he ever recited to anyone other than the Prophet ﷺ. Suwayd b. 'Abd al-'Azīz states that after Fajr prayer, people would gather in the

[67] Ṣaḥīḥ Bukhārī: Kitāb tafsīr al-Qur'ān (sūrah al-Barā'ah)—Bāb qawluhū laqad jā'akum rasūlun min anfusikum; Kitāb faḍā'il al-Qur'ān—Bāb jam' al-Qur'ān; Kitāb al-aḥkām—Bāb yustaḥabb lil-kātib an yakūna amīnan 'āqilan.

[68] Ṣaḥīḥ Bukhārī: Kitāb faḍā'il al-Qur'ān—Bāb al-qurrā' min aṣḥāb al-nabī.

[69] Ḥadīth of Abū Bakr and 'Umar related by Aḥmad and Ibn Mājah, and authenticated by al-Albānī in Ṣaḥīḥ al-Jāmi' (5961).

[70] Ṣaḥīḥ Muslim: Kitāb faḍā'il al-ṣaḥābah—Bāb min faḍā'il 'Abdullah b. Mas'ūd.

[71] Al-Qāsim b. Sallām, *Faḍā'il al-Qur'ān,* vol 1, pg 102. Ibn al-Jawzī in *Ṣifat ṣafwah,* vol 1, pg 402.

[72] Ṣaḥīḥ Bukhārī: Kitāb faḍā'il al-Qur'ān—Bāb al-qurrā' min aṣḥāb al-nabī; Ṣaḥīḥ Muslim: Kitāb faḍā'il al-ṣaḥābah—Bāb min faḍā'il 'Abdullah b. Mas'ūd.

Damascus Mosque to read Qur'ān with him. He divided people into groups of ten and designated one of his teachers with each group, while he stood in the mimbar overlooking the whole process (more details forthcoming).

Abū Mūsā al-Ash'arī (d. 44/665)

Abū Mūsā al-Ash'arī (d. 44/665) was among those who recited to the Prophet ﷺ and was the single most learned person of Baṣrah in the Qur'ān according to Dhahabī. He was the noble one concerning whose recitation the Prophet ﷺ remarked: 'Oh Abū Mūsā, you have been given one of the flutes of the family of Dāwūd.'[73] The Prophet prayed for his forgiveness himself, and made him in charge of Zabīd and 'Adan. 'Umar placed him in charge of Kūfah and Baṣrah. Those who related from him included his sons Abū Bakr, Abū Burdah, Mūsā, and Ibrāhīm; as well as others such as Rib'ī b. Ḥirāsh, Zahdam al-Jarmī, Sa'īd b. al-Musayyab[74] and others.

[73] Ṣaḥīḥ Bukhārī: Kitāb faḍā'il al-Qur'ān—Bāb ḥusn al-ṣawt bi al-qirā'ah li al-Qur'ān; Ṣaḥīḥ Muslim: Kitāb ṣalāh al-musāfirīn wa qaṣrihā—Bāb istiḥbāb taḥsīn al-ṣawt bi al-Qur'ān.
[74] He was a great scholar and jurist of Madīnah, and son-in-law of Abū Hurayrah. Imām Aḥmad considered him to the single-best person from entire generation of Followers. He died in 94 AH.

The Second Tier: Those Who Learned from Other Companions

From these eight Companions, a large group of other Companions learned the Qur'ān. Surely, they must have also heard portions of the Qur'ān from the Prophet ﷺ, but their learning of the Qur'ān in a complete manner was from these eight Companions and not from the Prophet ﷺ.

Those who took the Qur'ān from 'Umar included 'Abdullah b. al-Sā'ib, and Abū al-'Āliyah al-Riyāḥī Rafī' b. Mahrān of Baṣrah. Those who took from 'Uthmān included al-Mughīrah b. Abī Shihāb and Abū 'Abd al-Raḥmān al-Sulamī. Those who took from 'Alī included Abū 'Abd al-Raḥmān al-Sulamī and Abū al-Aswad al-Du'alī. Those who took from Ubayy were Abū Hurayrah, Ibn 'Abbās, 'Abdullah b. al-Sā'ib, Abū 'Abd al-Raḥmān al-Sulamī, 'Abdullah b. 'Ayyāsh, Abū al-'Āliyah. Those who took from Zayd were Abū 'Abd al-Raḥmān al-Sulamī and Abū al-'Āliyah. Those who took from Ibn Mas'ūd were Aswad, 'Alqamah, and Abū 'Abd al-Raḥmān al-Sulamī. Those who took from Abū al-Dardā' included Ibn 'Āmir, one of the ten Imāms. Those who took from Abū Mūsā were Ḥaṭṭān b. 'Abdullah al-Raqqāshī and Abū Rajā' al-'Uṭāridī 'Imrān b. Taym of Baṣrah.

In sum, these are the individuals that connect the chains of the mass-transmitted readings. There were other Companions that were part of Qur'ānic isnāds that comprised the shādh readings. For instance, the reading of Mu'ādh b. Jabal through his student Abū Baḥriyyah al-Ḥimṣī is preserved in some of the books documented in *al-Nashr* and counted among the shādh readings.

However, the most important Qur'ānic students of the first-rank Companions were the following:

Abū Hurayrah (d. 58/678)

Abū Hurayrah, whose name was 'Abd al-Raḥmān b. Ṣakhr according to the dominant opinion, was from the clan of Daws and was the single-most prolific narrator of ḥadīth. Though he embraced Islam in the year 7 AH, he devoted himself to accompanying the Prophet and learning from him, ultimately relating from him more than five thousand ḥadīth reports. He was placed as the governor of Baḥrayn by the Caliph 'Umar and later removed because of his lenient disposition. He was the governor of Madīnah for a number of years during the reign of Mu'āwiyah. He recited the Qur'ān to Ubayy b. Ka'b. Those who read Qur'ān to him included 'Abd al-Raḥmān b. Hurmuz al-A'raj, Imām Abū Ja'far Yazīd b. Qa'qā' of Madīnah, and Ṣāliḥ b. Khawwāt al-Anṣārī.

ʿAbdullah b. ʿAbbās (d. 68/687)

ʿAbdullah b. ʿAbbās was the prolific scholar and cousin of the Prophet ﷺ. ʿAṭā b. Abī Rabāḥ'[75] used to say: 'I have never seen the moon without being reminded of the face of Ibn ʿAbbās.'[76] He was the one about whom the Prophet ﷺ prayed: 'Oh Allah, teach him the understanding of Qur'ān and the religion.'[77] He became blind later in life and died in Ṭā'if in 68. He recited the Qur'ān upon Ubayy b. Kaab. Those who read to him included Mujāhid, Saʿīd b. Jubayr,[78] Aʿraj, ʿIkrimah b. Khālid, Sulaymān b. Qattah, Abū Jaʿfar, and Saʿīd b. al-Musayyab.

ʿAbdullah b. al-Sā'ib (d. ~70/690)

ʿAbdullah b. al-Sā'ib b. Abī al-Sā'ib was among the junior Companions who read to Ubayy, and from whom Mujāhid and ʿAbdullah b. Kathīr took the Qur'ān.

Al-Mughīrah b. Abī Shihāb al-Makhzūmī (d. 91/710)

Al-Mughīrah b. Abī Shihāb al-Makhzūmī read the Qur'ān to ʿUthmān, and from him, Ibn ʿĀmir took the Qur'ān.

Ḥiṭṭān b. ʿAbdullah al-Raqqāshī (d. ~70/689)

Ḥiṭṭān b. ʿAbdullah al-Raqqāshī read to Abū Mūsā al-Ashʿarī, and Ḥasan al-Baṣrī read to him.

Al-Aswad b. Yazīd (d. 75/694)

Al-Aswad b. Yazīd al-Nakhaʿī read to Ibn Masʿūd and was counted among his most senior students. Yaḥyā b. Waththāb, Ibrāhīm al-Nakhaʿī, and Abū Isḥāq al-Sabīʿī read to him.

---

[75] He was a prolific scholar and muftī of Makkah, of African descent, known for his courage, piety, humility and deep knowledge. Imām Abū Ḥanīfah's said about him: 'Of all the people I have met, there was none better than he.' He died in 114 AH.

[76] Dhahabī, *Maʿrifat al-qurrā' al-kibār,* vol 1, pg 23.

[77] Related by Aḥmad in his Musnad: Musnad Banī Hāshi —Musnad Ibn ʿAbbās. Imām Muslim related the wording: Oh Allah grant him understanding (Kitāb faḍā'il al-ṣaḥābah—Bāb faḍā'il ʿAbdullah b. ʿAbbās), while Bukhārī related the wording: 'Oh Allah grant him understanding in religion.' (Kitāb al-wuḍū'—Bāb waḍʿ al-mā' ʿinda al-khalā')

[78] Saʿīd b. Jubayr was a client of the Asad clan, great Follower, and student of Ibn ʿAbbās, who was killed Ḥajjāj in 95/714.

'Alqamah b. Qays (d. 62/681)

'Alqamah b. Qays b. 'Abdullah b. Mālik al-Nakha'ī was born in the lifetime of the Prophet ﷺ and recited the Qur'ān upon Ibn Mas'ūd. He was the closest of Ibn Mas'ūd's students to his teacher in characteristics, manners, and knowledge. Those who recited to him included Yaḥyā b. Waththāb, 'Ubayd b. Naḍīlah, Abū Isḥāq, and others.

Abū 'Abd al-Raḥmān al-Sulamī (d. 74/693)

Abū 'Abd al-Raḥmān al-Sulamī (d. 74/693) read to 'Uthmān, 'Alī, Ibn Mas'ūd, Zayd b. Thābit, and Ubayy b. Ka'b. From him, 'Āṣim (one of the ten Imāms), Yaḥyā b. Waththāb, 'Aṭā' b, al-Sā'ib, 'Abdullah b. 'Īsā b. Abī Laylah, Muḥammad b. Ayyūb, al-Thaqafī, Sha'bī, and Ismā'īl b. Abī Khālid. In addition, Ḥasan and Ḥusayn, the grandsons of the Prophet ﷺ read to him as well.

'Abdullah b. 'Ayyāsh (d. ~74/693)

'Abdullah b. 'Ayyāsh was born in Abyssinia and read the Qur'ān to Ubayy. It is said that he saw the Prophet ﷺ.

Abū Rajā' al-'Uṭāridī 'Imrān b. Taym of Baṣrah (d. 105/723)

Abū Rajā' al-'Uṭāridī 'Imrān b. Taym of Baṣrah (d. 105/723) read the Qur'ān with Ibn 'Abbās and reviewed it with Abū Mūsā. He also met Abū Bakr. Abū al-Ash-hab al-'Uṭāridī read upon him.

Abū al-Aswad al-Du'alī (d. 69/688)

Abū al-Aswad al-Du'alī, whose name was Ẓālim b. 'Amr, embraced Islam in the lifetime of the Prophet ﷺ but did not see him. He read the Qur'ān with 'Alī. He was the one who first laid down principles of grammar at the insistence of 'Alī. When 'Alī reviewed those principles, he remarked: 'What an excellent method (*naḥw*) you have pursued (*naḥauta*),' which is why grammar earned the name *'naḥw'* ('pursuit'). He died during the plaque of Jārif in Baṣrah. From him, his son Abū Ḥarb, Yaḥyā b. Ya mar, and 'Abdullah b. Buraydah took the Qur'ān.

Abū al-'Āliyah al-Riyāḥī (d. 90/708)

Abū al-'Āliyah al-Riyāḥī Rafī' b. Mahrān of Baṣrah embraced Islam in the time of Abū Bakr and read the Qur'ān to Ubayy, Zayd b. Thābit, and Ibn 'Abbās. It is even reported that he recited to 'Umar the entire Qur'ān three of four times. Those who recited to him included Shuʿayb b. Ḥabḥāb, Rabīʿ b. Anas, Aʿmash, and, according to some, Abū ʿAmr.

CHAPTER TWO

Qur'ānic Teaching Circles of Companions

It is important to review the era of the Companions in terms of their Qur'ānic teaching circles, their locations, the amount of recitation, means of teaching, and exact ways of learning and teaching Qur'ān.[79] My review of this time period reveals that the Companions had a particular methodology of Qur'ānic teaching that had a number of distinctive features.

Humility

First, there was a particular humility during this period that allowed older individuals to learn from younger ones. Ibn 'Abbās said: 'I used to teach the Qur'ān to men from the Emigrants, including 'Abd al-Raḥmān b. 'Awf.'[80] Ibn 'Abbās also said: I used to teach Qur'ān to 'Abd al-Raḥmān b. 'Awf during the era of 'Umar, and I never saw a man tremble more during recitation.'[81] Ibn Baṭṭāl comments that this proves that knowledge can be attained from younger individuals, for Ibn 'Abbās was not among the Emigrants due to his young age.[82]

Forming Circles

Second, these teachings sessions took on the form of circles. Abū Sa'īd al-Khuḍrī relates the following:

> I was once sitting in a circle of the Anṣār. Some of them were sitting behind others because of lack of clothing, while a reader was reciting to us, with the rest of us listening. The Prophet ﷺ came and stood beside us. The reader stopped and greeted him. The Prophet asked: 'What were you doing?' We replied: O Messenger of Allah, we had a reader who was reciting to us the Book of Allah while we were listening. The Prophet then said: 'Praise be to Allah Who has placed among my people those with whom I have been ordered to endure.' He then sat among us as if her were one of us and signaled with his hand to have us sit in a circle with our faces turned towards him.
>
> I don't think that the Prophet ﷺ recognized anyone there except me. He said: 'Rejoice, Oh group of poor emigrants, in the perfect light

---

[79] This section is taken from *al-Iqrā' 'inda al-ṣaḥābah*, pg 45-52.

[80] Ṣaḥīḥ Bukhārī: Kitāb al-ḥudūd—Bāb rajm al-ḥublā min al-zinā; Kitāb al-i'tiṣām bi al-kitāb wa al-sunnah—Bāb mā dhakara al-nabī wa ḥaḍḍa 'alā ittifāq ahl al-'ilm.

[81] Ṣaḥīḥ Ibn Ḥibbān: Kitāb al-birr wa al-iḥsān—Bāb ḥaqq al-wālidayn.

[82] Ibn Baṭṭāl, *Sharḥ Ṣaḥīḥ al-Bukhārī*, vol 8, pg 457.

> you will have on the Day of Judgement. You will enter Paradise before the rich by half a day, and that is five hundred years.[83]

This shows the intense passion of the Companions to learn the Qur'ān and stick to these Qur'ānic circles despite their extreme poverty that resulted in some of them not having sufficient clothes to cover themselves.

Abū al-Dardā', for instance, used to teach after praying Fajr in the Umayyad Mosque. He would divide people into groups of ten, with one teacher leading each group. He had as many as 150 groups at one time. He would sit in the miḥrāb and oversee the entire congregation, correcting when necessary. Generally, he would teach ten verses to each of the 150 group-leaders, and they would in turn teach their own groups. He would also walk through the groups listening to all of them, and on occasions he would gather them all and recite to them.[84]

Suwayd b. 'Abd al-'Azīz mentioned that Ibn 'Āmir was one of these teachers under Abū al-Dardā'. When his teacher died, Ibn 'Āmir took his place as the primary teacher. Sallām b. Mishkam relates that when Abū al-Dardā' once asked him to gather students of Qur'ān for him, he gathered over 1600 students, whom he divided into groups of ten. When students in each group mastered their reading, they would then come to Abū al-Dardā' to recite to him.[85]

From this, we learn the following key features: timing of the circles after Fajr prayer, ten participants in each circle, a sub-teacher over each circle, Abū Dardā' presiding over all of them, and students graduating from circles to move on to Abū al-Dardā' to recite to him.

Unity

A third key feature was their lack of discord and disunity. Jābir relates: The Prophet ﷺ came to us while we were reciting the Qur'an, and there were among us Bedouins and non-Arabs. He ﷺ said: *'Recite, for all is well. In the near future there will appear people who will straighten it (the Qur'an) like an arrow, reciting it quickly.'*[86] Sahl b. Sa'd al-Sā'idī relates: The Prophet came to us one day while we were reciting the Qur'ān. He ﷺ said: *'Praise by to Allah. The Book of Allah is one and among you are the red, white and black. Recite it before there appears a people who will recite it,*

---

[83] Musnad Aḥmad: Musnad Abī Sa'īd al-Khuḍrī; Sunan Abī Dāwūd: Kitāb al-'ilm—Bāb fī al-qiṣaṣ. The report of Abū Dāwūd mentions the same story with the detail that the circle consisted of the Anṣār.

[84] See *al-Khayr al-Kathīr,* pg 177.

[85] Dhahabī, *Ma 'rifat al-qurrā',* vol 1, pg 20.

[86] Sunan Abī Dāwūd: Kitāb al-ṣalāh—Bāb mā yujzi' al-ummī wa al-a'jamī min al-qirā'ah.

straightening it like an arrow. They will get their reward for it in this world but not the next.'[87]

Learning Gradually

A fourth feature was that they would learn the verses in a gradual manner. ʿUthmān, Ibn Masʿūd and Ubayy relate that the Prophet would teach them ten verses at a time, and they would not move on to other verses until they learned them and practiced them.[88] Khāqānī in his ode on tajwīd stated: 'The ruling for you if you want to take [Qur'ān] with taḥqīq[89] from a teacher, is not to exceed ten [verses].' Dānī in explaining this stated: 'Those reciters who wish to read to a teacher in the manner of taḥqīq in order to master tajwīd must know that ten verses are sufficient. This is enough to perfect each principle in all its dimensions. This method is light on the tongue and more conducive to becoming habitual and natural for the person. When this level is achieved, then the person is worthy of moving on to more amounts with the teacher.'[90] As the student's level of recitation increases, the teacher can choose to increase the amount as desired. Ṣafāqisī (d. 1118/1706)[91] stated:

> People of expertise did not exceed ten verses for their students, as Khāqānī in his ode on tajwīd stated: 'The ruling for you if you want to take [Qur'ān] with taḥqīq from a teacher, is not to exceed ten [verses].' There were some later scholars who did not confine themselves to this but advocated considering the state of the student to determine how much they would be able to handle. ʿAlam al-Dīn Sakhāwī (d. 643/1245)[92] chose this opinion, relying on the practice of Ibn Masʿūd, who recited to the Prophet in one sitting from the beginning of Sūrah al-Nisā' (4:1) through (4:41). Ibn al-Jazarī also approved of this view and stated in *al-Nashr*:
>
>> This was the practice of many early scholars and many of the experts whom we met. Imām Yaʿqūb said: 'I read the

---

[87] Ibid. According to many scholars, this ḥadīth refers to those who only seek worldly rewards for reciting the Qur'ān, making it a profession or career and even reciting as proficiently as the shooting of arrows. These individuals would have corrupted the worship-oriented nature of recitation and will be deprived of the reward in the next life.

[88] Abū ʿAmr al-Dānī, *Kitāb al-bayān.*

[89] As part of a range of recitation speeds, taḥqīq lies at one end of the spectrum and refers to a slow pace—without excess or exaggeration—that allows one to focus on precision and accuracy.

[90] Dānī, *Sharḥ qaṣīdah Abī Muzāḥim,* pg 171.

[91] Abū al-Ḥasan ʿAlī al-Nūrī was a Mālikī jurist and Qur'ānic scholar of the city of Sfax, Tunisia.

[92] ʿAlam al-Dīn Abū al-Ḥasan ʿAlī b. Muḥammad was a Shāfiʿī scholar, Qur'ān commentator and linguist who served as Shaykh al-Qurā' of Damascus. His teachers included Shāṭibī and Ibn ʿAsākir.

> Qur'ān in one and a half years upon Sallām, and upon Shihāb al-Dīn b. Sharīfah in five days. Shihāb al-Dīn read the Qur'ān upon Maslamah b. Maḥārib in nine days. . . . When Ibn Mu'min traveled to Ṣā'igh, he read to him the readings in a combined manner from a number of books in seventeen days.'
>
> When I first traveled to Egypt, I had, in my combined readings to Shaykh Ibn al-Ṣā'igh, reached to Sūrah al-Ḥijr. I began with him from the beginning of al-Ḥijr on Saturday and finished the Qur'ān on Thursday. I had remaining portions from the beginning of Sūrah al-Wāqi'ah, which I completed to him in one sitting.[93]

Hierarchy of Teachers

A fifth feature was a stepwise approach to teachers. In other words, the Qur'ānic students would read to junior teachers before moving on to senior ones, as the practice of Abū Dharr in the Umayyad Mosque showed. Dhahabī mentioned the following in the biography of his own teacher Yaḥyā b. Aḥmad al-Ṣawwāf: 'I traveled to him to learn Qur'ān and found that he was [nearly] blind and deaf, 87 years of age, but still possessing vigor and intelligence. I read one juz' of Qur'ān to him by raising my voice so he could hear. I expressed to him that I wanted to read the seven readings to him. He asked me to read sūrah al-Fātiḥah and some beginning verses of al-Baqarah, while he taught me the variants therein, including those of Ya'qūb and others (i.e. beyond the seven). I replied that I only wanted to learn the seven. He must have understood then that I was only a beginner, for he then asked me to read to one of his students first, before reading to him.'[94]

Individual Recitation

A sixth and final characteristic was that they would read to teachers individually one-by-one. Dānī says: 'When one starts reading teaching Qur'ān to students, they would do one student at a time. This is the Prophetic practice, as he asked 'Umar and Hishām b. Ḥakīm to recite one at a time.'[95] Dhahabī comments during his discussion of the biography of Sakhāwī that he used to allow two or more students to recite to him, each one reciting one sūrah, but comments that this is opposed to the sunnah

---

[93] Ṣafāqisī, *Ghayth al-naf' fī al-qirā'āt al-sab'*, pg 22. *Al-nashr,* vol 2, pg 198.
[94] Dhahabī, *Ma'rifat al-qurrā',* vol 2, pg 697.
[95] Dānī, *Sharḥ qaṣīdah Abī Muzāḥim,* pg 181.

because we have been ordered to be silent when another recites so that we may understand and reflect.[96] He also states:

> I do not know of any scholar of the readings who allowed two or more students to recite at a time other than Shaykh ʿAlam al-Dīn, but there is something unnatural in the soul concerning this practice, for *Allah has never put two hearts in one person's body*.[97] There is no doubt that this is against the sunnah, for Allah has said: ﴿*So when the Qur'an is recited, listen carefully to it, and keep silent so that you may, be shown mercy.*﴾ [98]
>
> If one student were to recite one sūrah while another one recites another and so on, this would entail many harms, including decreasing the splendor of the Qur'ān among listeners, confusing the other reciters, and opposing the command to listen. Furthermore, these students could not claim that they recited the entire Qur'ān to their teachers while they were listening, nor can the teachers claim that the student recited the entire Qur'ān to them while they listened, for this is not humanly possible. ʿĀ'ishah stated: 'Glory be to the One Whose Hearing Hears all voices.' The ijāzah of such teachers is valid, but the transmission would be considered one of ijāzah (permission) and not direct audition (samāʿ).[99]

---

[96] *Siyar,* vol 23, pg 124.
[97] Qur'ān 33:4.
[98] Qur'ān 7:204.
[99] *Maʿrifat al-qurrā',* vol 2, pg 632.

Specific Readings Attributed to the Prophet

The basic principle is that all readings are ultimately transmitted from the Prophet in some way, although not every variant is transmitted in books of ḥadīth.[100] We simply don't need ḥadīth reports to establish Qur'ānic readings because they were transmitted by their own experts, whose readings gained the consensus of the ummah.

For this reason, it is a major mistake to consider, as some have done, the takbīr associated with Ibn Kathīr's reading to be a weak practice simply because the isnād of their reports in ḥadīth works was weak. Bazzī was the one who reported the practice of takbīr from Ibn Kathīr, and he is the same one who transmitted the mutawātir reading of Ibn Kathīr which is recited in prayer and enjoys the consensus of all scholars. Therefore, his practice of takbīr in the ending sūrahs should also be accepted.

Moreover, an individual deemed reliable by ḥadīth experts does not equate to him being reliable for Qur'ānic scholars, and vice versa. Bazzī and Ḥafṣ were both weak by standards of ḥadīth scholars, as were many other Qur'ān transmitters, because they were not ḥadīth specialists. But at the same time, scholars were unanimous in accepting their expertise in Qur'ānic reading. A Qur'ānic reader could make mistakes in transmitting ḥadīth, reporting them by meaning and dropping some words due to not being a specialist in this field, yet still retain mastery and expertise in the Qur'ān and its variants. The converse is also true. Some senior ḥadīth experts were known to be weak in their preserving of the Qur'ān and its readings, making mistakes. Their expertise in ḥadīth did not necessarily translate into expertise in Qur'ān. At the same time, there were also individuals that did master both Qur'ān and ḥadīth.

In the end, we do not evaluate the Qur'ānic readings by the standards of ḥadīth. For this reason, we find some specific verse variants transmitted in Bukhārī and Muslim that were deemed shādh by Qur'ānic experts.

---

[100] Despite that, most ḥadīth works included reports pertaining to specific variants attributed to the Prophet. Ḥākim, for instance, dedicated a chapter in his Mustadrak (Kitāb al-tafsīr—Bāb qirā'āt al-nabī mimmā lam yukharrijāhu wa qad ṣaḥḥa sanaduhu) to document about 112 such reports. This section is taken entirely from *al-Qamar al-munīr,* pg 81-2.

Attribution of a Reading to an Individual

It became customary to ascribe the Qur'ānic readings to its teachers from among the great experts, by referring, for example, to the 'reading of Nāfi'' or the 'reading of 'Āṣim.' The meaning of these terms is simply that these individuals were the most devoted to reciting, teaching and preserving these ways of readings, which they had ultimately received from their own teachers. It does not mean in any way that they invented or came up with these readings on their own accord.

In other words, these Imāms simply chose these particular linguistic variants of recitation and preferred to recite in that manner until they became popularized through their practice. Ultimately, people began to learn and transmit these readings from them. These readings were ascribed to them simply in the sense of choice, habit or preference, and not in the sense of invention, personal opinion or interpretation.[101]

As an example, the Prophet ﷺ ascribed a reading to an individual in the following report: 'Whoever desires to hear the Qur'ān as fresh as it was revealed should listen to the recitation of Ibn Umm 'Abd.'[102] He was referring to 'Abdullah b. Mas'ūd who had learned the Qur'ān from the Prophet and narrated it from him. On the other hand, Ibrāhīm al-Nakha'ī (d. 95)[103] did say, 'They would dislike referring to a reading by ascribing it to a person.' However, Nawawī (d. 677)[104] ascribed the consensus of early and later scholars on the permissibility of doing such,[105] and the aforementioned ḥadīth is proof of that.

---

[101] *Al-Nashr,* vol 1, pg 25.
[102] Ḥadīth of Abū Bakr and 'Umar related by Aḥmad and Ibn Mājah, and authenticated by al-Albānī in Ṣaḥīḥ al-Jāmi' (5961).
[103] Great jurist of Iraq who saw 'Ā'ishah when he was young and inherited the fiqh of Ibn Mas'ūd from his students. He became one of the sources for the Ḥanafī school of jurisprudence.
[104] Famed Shāfi'ī scholar of Damascus and author of some of the most popular and widely-read works in our tradition.
[105] Nawawī, *al-Tibyān*, pg 266.

The Fourteen Imāms and their Isnāds

1. Imām Nāfi' of Madīnah (d. 169/785)

His name was Abū Ruwaym Nāfi' b. 'Abd al Raḥmān b. Abī Nu'aym and his family was originally from Isfahan in Persia. He was a client of the clan of Layth of Madīnah. He was the undisputed expert of Qur'ān in Madīnah during his time. He was described as having black skin. He was the most versed person in the reading of Madīnah and actively taught people in the blessed city for more than seventy years. He had noble manners and was kind towards his students. He had a good sense of humor and would often give unique nicknames to his students, which they would in turn honor. He is the one, for instance, who gave the title Qālūn to his famous student, which meant 'excellent' in a Roman language, and the title Warsh to his other student, because of his resemblance to the intensely white dove known as *warshān,* as he was extremely white in complexion.

Nāfi' was born in 70 AH and died in 169 AH at the age of 99. There is an interesting observation I have noted about experts of Qur'ānic readings in the past and present: that Allah granted them lengthy lives and enabled them to enjoy their minds and Qur'ānic knowledge until the ends of their days. This is perhaps due to the fact that Allah uses them for His obedience and designated them to be one of the means to preserve His Book.

Imām Nāfi' learned the Qur'ān from seventy Followers, but his five most prominent teachers were Abū Ja'far Yazīd b. al-Qa'qā', 'Abd al-Raḥmān b. Hurmuz al-A'raj, Ibn Shihāb al-Zuhrī, Shaybah b. Niṣāḥ, and Yazīd b. Rūmān. He related ḥadīth from the likes of Nāfi' the freed slave of Ibn 'Umar and A'raj the student of Abū Hurayrah.

His students in Qur'ān included Imām Mālik, who said about his teacher's reading, 'the reading of Nāfi' is the sunnah.' Other students included Layth b. Sa'd and Abū 'Amr (another one of the seven Imāms), but his two most famous students were Qālūn (d. 220/835)[106] and Warsh (d. 197/812).[107]

After the era of the Followers, the people of Madīnah were unanimous in choosing his reading, as attested to by Mālik's statement above. 'Abdullah the son

---

[106] Abū Mūsā 'Īsā b. Mīnā b. Wardān b. 'Īsā al-Zarqī was a descendent of Byzantine captives during the reign of 'Umar. He spent more than twenty years with Nāfi'. Nāfi' loved his recitation, gave him the title Qālūn due to his excellent reading, and even referred people to learn from him. He was described as being deaf to a great degree but could only hear the Qur'ān, and would be able to discern mistakes from the lips of his students. He died in Madīnah in the year 220.

[107] Abū Sa'īd 'Uthmān b. Sa'īd was born in in 110 AH in the town of Qifṭ in Egypt who traveled to Madīnah in 155 AH to learn from Nāfi', reading the Qur'ān with him several times, and returned to teach in Egypt until his death in 197 AH. His reading became widespread throughout Andalus and north Africa.

of Imām Aḥmad asked his father which of the readings was dearest to him, and he replied, 'the reading of the people of Madīnah.'

Today, Libya, Morocco and great parts of Western Africa continue to hold on to this reading. In Libya and Tunisia, the transmission of Qālūn is predominantly recited whereas in Morocco, Algeria and Mauritania, it is the Warsh transmission.

He had a number of extraordinary feats related about him. When Nāfiʿ used to recite the Qur'ān, the smell of musk would emanate from his mouth. When asked if he perfumed his mouth, he replied no, but explained that this started happening after he saw a dream that the Prophet ﷺ was reciting into his mouth. Shāṭibī versified this extraordinary quality in line 25 of his poem:

فَأَمَّا الكَرِيمُ السِّرِّ فِي الطِّيبِ نَافِعٌ / فَذاكَ الَّذِي اخْتَارَ المَدِينَةَ مَنزِلَا

The noble secret of the scent was about Nāfiʿ
He was the one chosen by Madīnah for his position

On his deathbed, his children asked him for advice and he recited the verse: ﴿*So fear Allah, and set things right between you, and obey Allah and His Messenger if you are true believers.*﴾ (8:1)

Isnāds

Nāfiʿ recited to Imām Abū Jaʿfar Yazīd b. Qaʿqāʿ and Aʿraj—both of whom recited to Ibn ʿAbbās—who recited to Ubayy and Zayd—both of whom recited to the Prophet.

Nāfiʿ also recited to Abū Jaʿfar, Aʿraj, and Ṣāliḥ b. Khawwāt: all of whom recited to Abū Hurayrah—who recited to Ubayy—who recited to the Prophet.

Nāfiʿ also recited to Imām Abū Jaʿfar and Aʿraj—both of whom recited to ʿAbdullah b. ʿAyyāsh—who recited to Ubayy—who recited to the Prophet.

Nāfiʿ also recited to Yazīd b. Rūmān, Muslim b. Jundub, and Shaybah b. Niṣāḥ—all of whom recited to ʿAbdullah b. ʿAyyāsh—who recited to Ubayy—who recited to the Prophet.

Nāfiʿ also recited to Shaybah b. Niṣāḥ—who recited to ʿUmar b. al-Khaṭṭāb—who recited to the Prophet.

Nāfiʿ also recited to Ibn Shihāb al-Zuhrī—who recited to Saʿīd b. al-Musayyab—who recited to Ibn ʿAbbās and Abū Hurayrah—all of whom recited to Ubayy—who recited to the Prophet.

Nāfiʿ also recited to Zuhrī—who recited to Saʿīd b. al-Musayyab—who recited to Ibn ʿAbbās—who recited to Zayd—who recited to the Prophet.

2. Imām Ibn Kathīr of Makkah (d. 120/737)

His name was Abū Ma'bad 'Abdullah b. Kathīr al-'Aṭṭār al-Dārī and he was a noble Follower who hailed from Makkah. He was brown-skinned, with white hair that was usually dyed with henna, and massively tall. He was extremely eloquent and impressive in speech and an expert in Arabic language. He had an aura of dignity and calmness. He was of Persian descent and inherited the leadership of Qur'ānic reading in Makkah in the time of the Followers. He was born in 45 AH and died in 120 AH at the age of 75.

He recited the Qur'ān upon Abū al-Sā'ib 'Abdullah b. al-Sā'ib al-Makhzūmī, Mujāhid b. Jabr and Darbās, the freed slave of Ibn 'Abbās. He related ḥadīth from Abū Ayyūb al-Anṣārī, Anas and 'Abdullah b. al-Zubayr.

His students in Qur'ān included many leading scholars such as Sufyān b. 'Uyaynah, Ḥammād b. Zayd, Ḥammād b. Salamah, al-Khalīl b. Aḥmad, and Abū 'Amr b. al-'Ulā'. His two famous transmitters, al-Bazzī (d. 250/864)[108] and Qunbul (d. 291/904),[109] were not direct students but related from him through intermediaries.

Ibn Mujāhid said: He continued to be the undisputed expert of Qur'ān in Makkah until he passed. Aṣma'ī[110] asked Abū 'Amr about his reading with Ibn Kathīr, and he replied: I completed the reading of Qur'ān with Ibn Kathīr after I completed it with Mujāhid b. Jabr, and he was more versed in Arabic than Mujāhid. Imām Shāfi'ī used to recite by Ibn Kathīr's reading, as he had learned Qur'ān from 'Abdullah b. Qusṭanṭīn, a student of Ibn Kathīr.

Isnāds

Ibn Kathīr recited to 'Abdullah b. al-Sā'ib—who recited to 'Umar and Ubayy—both of whom recited to the Prophet.

Ibn Kathīr also recited to Mujāhid b. Jabr and Darbās—both of whom recited to Ibn 'Abbās—who recited to Ubayy and Zayd b. Thābit—both of whom recited to the Prophet.

---

[108] Abū al-Ḥasan Aḥmad b. Muḥammad b. Abdullah b. al-Qāsim b. Nāfi' b. Abū Bazzah al-Makkī was born in 170H of Persian descent and was the mu'adhdhin of Masjid al-Ḥaram in Makkah and the leading rector of Makkah during his time. His teachers included his father among many others. He was the narrator of the ḥadīth that mentions the practice of reciting takbīr (Allah akbar) in the ending chapters of the Qur'ān beginning with al-Ḍuḥā. He died in Makkah at the age of eighty in the year 250H.

[109] Abū 'Amr Muḥammad b. 'Abd al-Raḥmān b. Khālid al-Makhzumī al-Makkī was born in 195H and became known as a leading reciter of the Ḥijāz and was among the teachers of Ibn Mujāhid (d 324H). He stopped teaching seven years before his death due to old age and illness. He died at the age of 96 in the year 291H in Makkah.

[110] 'Abd al-Malik b. Qurayb b. 'Abd al-Malik b. Aṣma' was a trustworthy scholar and linguist of Baṣrah who died in 216/828.

3. Imām Abū ʿAmr of Baṣrah (d. 154/770)

His name was Abū ʿAmr Zabān b. al-ʿUlā' al-Māzinī and he was a noble Follower from Baṣrah. He was of pure Arab lineage[111] from the Māzin clan who settled in Baṣrah and became the undisputed expert of Qur'ān and Arabic there. He was known to be truthful and trustworthy. He was born in 68 AH and died in 154 AH at the age of 86.

Among the seven Imāms, he was one of the two of pure Arab descent, a fact Shāṭibī versified in line 41:

أَبُو عَمْرِهِمْ وَالْيَحْصَبِيُّ ابْنُ عَامِرٍ / صَرِيحٌ وَبَاقِيهِمْ أَحَاطَ بِهِ الْوَلَا

Abū ʿAmr and Yaḥṣabī Ibn ʿĀmir both
Were pure [Arabs] while the rest were clients (freed slaves)

Among the Imāms, he traveled the most and had the most teachers. In fact, he read the Qur'ān with another three of the ten Imāms (and five of the fourteen): Ibn Kathīr, ʿĀṣim and Abū Jaʿfar. He also read with Ḥasan al-Baṣrī, Ibn Muḥayṣin, Mujāhid b. Jabr, Saʿīd b. Jubayr, Abū al-ʿĀliyah, ʿAṭā', ʿIkrimah,[112] and Yaḥyā b. Yaʿmar. He related ḥadīth from Anas, making him from the ranks of the Followers.

Many great scholars learned Qur'ān from him, including Sībawayh the famous grammarian, Aṣmaʿī, and Yaḥyā al-Yazīdī. His two transmitters Dūrī (d. 246/860)[113] and Sūsī (d. 261/874)[114] relate from Yaḥyā b. al-Mubārak al-Yazīdī from him.

Once Ḥasan al-Baṣrī passed by his teaching circle and said: 'Every great honor if not strengthened by knowledge returns to humiliation.' Shuʿbah b. al-Ḥajjāj once advised: 'You should hold on to the reading of Abū ʿAmr for he is going to be an Imām of the people one day.'

Sufyān b. ʿUyaynah related that he asked the Prophet in a dream as to which reading he should recite by and was told, 'the reading of Abū ʿAmr.' Sufyān being Makkan previously used to recite by the reading of Ibn Kathīr.

---

[111] Among the seven Imāms, two were ethnically Arabs while the remaining five were non-Arabs.

[112] ʿIkrimah was a Berber slave of Ibn ʿAbbās who lived in Madīnah and learned from his master, from ʿAlī and many other Companions, until he began teaching and issuing rulings in the lifetime of Ibn ʿAbbās. He died in 107.

[113] Abū ʿAmr Ḥafṣ b. ʿUmar b. ʿAbd al-ʿAzīz al-Dūrī (derived from a place near Baghdād) was born in 195H and despite being blind, excelled in the knowledge of Qur'ān. He learned from Ismāʿīl b. Jaʿfar, a student of Nāfiʿ; Ismāʿīl's brother Yaʿqūb b. Jaʿfar, a student of Ibn Jammāz who in turn was a student of Imām Abū Jaʿfar; Abū Bakr al-Shuʿbah, the student of Imām ʿĀṣim; and others. He is a transmitter of the reading of Abū ʿAmr through his student Yaḥyā b. al-Mubārak al-Yazīdī. He is also a transmitter of the reading of Kisā'ī.

[114] Abū Shuʿayb Ṣāliḥ b. Ziyād b. ʿAbdullah al-Sūsī was born in 171H and was among the teachers of Imām al-Nasā'ī. He died close to seventy years of age in 261H. He is a transmitter of the reading of Abū ʿAmr through his student Yaḥyā b. al-Mubārak al-Yazīdī.

Imām Aḥmad was asked as to which reading one should read by, and he advised, 'Hold on to the way of Abū ʿAmr, the language of Quraysh and the most eloquent of the Arabs.'

After seeing that the bulk of the Muslim world in the 9th and 10th centuries were devoted to the transmission of Dūrī, Ibn al-Jazarī commented: 'I realized the insight of Shuʿbah.' The reading of Abū ʿAmr through the transmission of Dūrī was the predominant reading in the entire Muslim world at one point, but today, parts of Sudan, Somalia and Eastern Africa continue to read it.

Isnāds

Abū ʿAmr recited to Saʿīd b. Jubayr and Mujāhid b. Jabr—both of whom recited to Ibn ʿAbbās—who recited to Ubayy and Zayd—both of whom recited to the Prophet.

Abū ʿAmr also recited to Mujāhid—who recited to ʿAbdullah b. al-Sā'ib—who recited to ʿUmar and Ubayy—both of whom recited to the Prophet.

Abū ʿAmr also recited to ʿIkrimah the freed slave of Ibn ʿAbbās and ʿIkrimah b. Khālid al-Makhzūmī—both of whom recited to Ibn ʿAbbās—who recited to Ubayy and Zayd—both of whom recited to the Prophet.

Abū ʿAmr also recited to ʿAṭā' b. Abī Rabāḥ—who recited to Abū Hurayrah—who recited to Ubayy—who recited to the Prophet.

Abū ʿAmr also recited to ʿAbdullah b. Abī Isḥāq—who recited to Yaḥyā b. Yaʿmar al-ʿAdwānī—who recited to Ibn ʿAbbās—who recited to Ubayy and Zayd—both of whom recited to the Prophet.

Abū ʿAmr also recited to ʿAbdullah b. Abī Isḥāq—who recited to Yaḥyā b. Yaʿmar al-ʿAdwānī and Naṣr b. ʿĀṣim al-Laythī—both of whom recited to Abū al-Aswad al-Du'alī—who recited to ʿUthmān and Ali—both of whom recited to the Prophet.

Abū ʿAmr also recited to Ḥasan al-Baṣrī—who recited to Abū al-ʿĀliyah al-Riyāḥī—who recited to ʿUmar, Ubayy, and Zayd—all of whom recited to the Prophet.

Abū ʿAmr also recited to Ḥasan al-Baṣrī—who recited to Abū al-ʿĀliyah al-Riyāḥī—who recited to Ibn ʿAbbās—who recited to Ubayy and Zayd—both of whom recited to the Prophet.

Abū ʿAmr also recited to Ḥasan al-Baṣrī—who recited to Ḥaṭṭān b. ʿAbdullah al-Raqqāshī—who recited to Abū Mūsā al-Ashʿarī—who recited to the Prophet.

Abū ʿAmr also recited to Ibn Kathīr through his isnāds.

4. Imām Ibn ʿĀmir of Damascus (d. 118/736)

His name was ʿAbdullah b. ʿĀmir b. Zayd b. Tamīm al-Yaḥṣabī[115] of Damascus, and he was a notable Follower. He was of pure Arab lineage from the clan of Yaḥṣab who

[115] Also pronounced *Yaḥṣubī*.

settled in Damascus where he became the undisputed leader of Qur'ānic reading in the era of the Followers. He was known to be extremely eloquent, possessed a dignified aura and was held in high esteem. He was born in Damascus in the 8th year after the Hijrah, 2 years before the passing of the Prophet ﷺ (though he did not see him) and died in 188 AH at the age of 110.

He recited the Qur'ān to Abū al-Dardā' and al-Mughīrah b. Shihāb al-Makhzūmī. Abū al-Dardā' had a particular methodology of teaching Qur'ān in the Umayyad Masjid of Damascus (see previous section) utilizing group leaders to teach a large group of over 1,000. The best of these group leaders was Ibn 'Āmir, and he took over the position of Abū al-Dardā' after him.

He related ḥadīth from Mu'āwiyah b. Abī Sufyān, Wāthilah b. al-Asqa', Nu'mān b. Bashīr, and Abū al-Dardā'.

His two transmitters Hishām b. 'Ammār (d. 245/859)[116] and 'Abdullah b. Dhakwān (d. 242/856)[117] were not direct students but related from him through an intermediary: Yaḥyā b. al-Ḥārith al-Dhimārī.

He was the Imām of the Umayyad Masjid in Damascus during the reign of 'Umar b. 'Abd al-'Azīz, who used to pray behind him and designated him the chief Imām, Qur'ānic teacher and judge in the city which served as the capital of the Caliphate and the meeting point for global scholars. The people of Syria united behind his reading where it continued to be the dominant one until the year 500 AH.

Among the ten Imāms, he has the highest chain in the Qur'ān, with only one intermediary to the Prophet ﷺ.

Isnāds

Ibn 'Āmir recited to Abū al-Dardā'—who recited to the Prophet.

Ibn 'Āmir also recited to al-Mughīrah b. Abī Shihāb—who recited to 'Uthmān—who recited to the Prophet.

5. Imām 'Āṣim of Kūfah (d. 127/745)

His name was Abū Bakr 'Āṣim b. Bahdalah b. Abī al-Najūd, and he was a seller of wheat in Kūfah, client of the Asad clan, and a notable Follower.

---

[116] Abū al-Walīd Hishām b. 'Ammār b. Naṣīr b. Maysarah al-Sulamī was born in 153H and was a notable scholar of Qur'ān, ḥadīth and fiqh in Damascus, Syria. He had many notable teachers and narrated ḥadīth from Imām Mālik and Sufyān b. 'Uyaynah among others. His students included Abū 'Ubayd al-Qāsim b. al-Sallām and al-Tirmidhī among others. His narrations are accepted by Bukhārī and most authors of the canonical texts of ḥadīth. He died in Damascus in 245H.

[117] Abū 'Amr 'Abdullah b. Aḥmad b. Bishr b. Dhakwān al-Qurashī al-Fahrī was born in 173H and was the Imām of the Umayyad Mosque in his time. His teachers included Imām al-Kisā'ī and his students who transmitted his reading included his son Aḥmad among others. He died in Damascus in 242H.

He was blind, a resident of Kūfah, extremely eloquent and precise, with one of the best voices of Qur'ānic recitation. He was the one who inherited the teaching position of Abū 'Abd al-Raḥmān al-Sulamī, the teacher of Ḥasan and Ḥusayn and the one who sat in the Masjid of Kūfah for forty years teaching Qur'ān from the reign of 'Uthmān to the governorship of Ḥajjāj.

It is not known for certain when he was born but it is known that he met some Companions. He died in the year 172 AH of advanced age.

He recited the Qur'ān to three Followers: Abū 'Abd al-Raḥmān al-Sulamī, Zirr b. Ḥubaysh, and Sa'd b. Ilyās al-Shaybānī. He related ḥadīth from Anas b. Mālik, Abū Ramthah al-Tamīmī, and al-Ḥārith b. Ḥassān.

Many great scholars learned Qur'ān from him, including Ḥammād b. Zayd, Ḥammād b. Salamah, Khalīl b. Aḥmad, and two of the seven Imāms: Abū 'Amr and Ḥamzah. His two transmitters were Abū Bakr b. 'Ayyāsh, better known as Shu'bah (d. 193/809),[118] and Ḥafṣ b. Sulaymān (d. 180/796).[119]

His ḥadīth reports are found among the six books. Whenever Abū Wā'il used to visit him, he would kiss his hand. Imām Aḥmad described him as 'a pious man, trustworthy and good.' When asked about his preferred reading, Imām Aḥmad replied that it was the reading of Madīnah, and then the reading of 'Āṣim. Shu'bah stated: I could not count how many times Abū Isḥāq al-Sabī'ī said, 'I have not seen one more versed in the Qur'ān than 'Āṣim.'

The reading of 'Āṣim is the dominant one in the entire world today, which is a tremendous honor for him, testimony to his status, and means of reward for him.

Shu'bah stated that he visited 'Āṣim on his deathbed and found him repeating the verse: ﴾*Then all are restored to Allah, their true protector.*﴿ [120] He was reciting it as if he were in prayer.

Isnāds

'Āṣim read to Abū 'Abd al-Raḥmān al-Sulamī—who read to Ibn Mas'ūd, Zayd, 'Uthmān, 'Alī, and Ubayy—all of whom read to the Prophet.

---

[118] Abū Bakr b. 'Ayyāsh b. Sālim al-Asadī al-Kūfī was born in 95H and also was a seller of wheat by trade. He was a devoted student of Imām 'Āṣim, reciting to him a total of three times. Those who narrated ḥadīth from him included Abū Dāwūd and Imām Aḥmad b. Ḥanbal. He was an avid worshipper known to devote himself to the Qur'ān nightly for much of his life. On his deathbed, he consoled his weeping sister, 'Do not grieve, for in this room I have finished the Qur'ān 18,000 times.' He stopped teaching Qur'ān seven years before he died in 193H in Kūfah.

[119] Abū 'Amr Ḥafṣ b. Sulaymān b. al-Mughīrah al-Asadī al-Kūfī was the main student of Imām 'Āṣim (who happened to be his stepfather) and taught mostly in Kūfah but also in Makkah. He taught for a long period of his life and had numerous students, including 'Amr b. al-Ṣabāḥ and 'Ubayd b. al-Ṣabāḥ. He died close to 90 years old.

[120] Qur'ān 6:62.

ʿĀṣim also read to Zirr b. Ḥubaysh—who read to ʿUthmān, ʿAlī and Ibn Masʿūd—all of whom read to the Prophet.

ʿĀṣim also read to Sa'd b. Iyās al-Shaybānī—who read to Ibn Masʿūd—who read to the Prophet.

6. Imām Ḥamzah of Kūfah (d. 156/773)

His name was Abū 'Amārah Ḥamzah b. Ḥabīb al-Zayyāt al-Kūfī al-Taymī. He was a merchant of oil in Kūfah (hence the title *al-Zayyāt*) and client of the clan of Taym. He was the leading scholar of the readings in Kūfah after Aʿmash and ʿĀṣim. He used to earn from his own work, trading oil between Kūfah and Ḥalwān in Iraq. He was extremely scrupulous and on principle never accepted any compensation for his Qur'ānic teaching. Once, he even rejected cold water from a student while teaching on an extremely hot day, saying, 'I do not take compensation for the Qur'ān.' He was known for his worship and otherworldliness. Shāṭibī mentioned him in line 37:

وَحَمْزَةُ مَا أَزْكَاهُ مِن مُتَوَرِّعٍ / إِمَامًا صَبُورًا لِلقُرَانِ مُرَتِّلَا

How pure and pious was Ḥamzah!
A leader, full of patience, ever reciting the Qur'ān.

He was born in 80 AH and died in 156 AH. He read Qur'ān with Abū Isḥāq al-Sabīʿī, Ḥumrān b. A'yun, Aʿmash and Jaʿfar al-Ṣādiq. Jaʿfar al-Ṣādiq read to his father Muḥammad al-Bāqir, who read to his father Zayn al-ʿĀbidīn, who read to his father Ḥusayn, who read to his father ʿAlī, who read to the Prophet, peace be upon him. Ḥusayn also read to Abū ʿAbd al-Raḥmān al-Sulamī who read to ʿUthmān and ʿAlī. This is a chain that pure consists of the family of the Prophet ﷺ.

Ḥamzah also met some Companions (but did not report ḥadīth from them), and related ḥadīth from Aʿmash, Abū Isḥāq and others. His students included Sulaym b. ʿĪsā, Kisāʾī, Farrā', and Yazīdī. His two transmitters were Khalaf (d. 229/844)[121] and Khallād (d. 220/835)[122] who related the Qur'ān through Sulaym from him.

His teacher Aʿmash upon seeing him would refer to him as a 'scholar of the Qur'ān' and recite the verse ﴿*glad tidings to those that humble themselves.*﴾ [123] Sufyān al-Thawrī used to say: Ḥamzah did not recite a single letter except with precedence. Abū Ḥanīfah said to him once: 'There are two things you have overpowered us in: Qur'ān and knowledge of rulings of inheritance (farā'iḍ).'[124]

[121] See subsequent entry on Imām Khalaf.
[122] Abū ʿĪsā Khallād b. Khālid al-Shaybānī al-Kūfī was a noted scholar of the Qur'ān who had many teachers and even more students. He died in Kūfah in 220H.
[123] Qur'ān 22:34.
[124] *Siyar,* vol 7, pg 9.

Dislike of Ḥamzah's Reading

There are reports from a number of jurists, such as Imām Aḥmad, that they disliked the readings of Ḥamzah and Kisā'ī for prayer. Imām Aḥmad admitted it was due to 'widespread imālah vowels.' He was not correct in that, for experts reported consensus on the validity of reciting with the reading of Ḥamzah in prayer. Even Imām Aḥmad himself, when asked if someone must repeat their prayer behind an imām who read with the reading of Ḥamzah, answered that they did not, saying: 'It does not reach that level.' This simply indicates a personal dislike or preference on his part.

It is also quite possible that some of those who read with Ḥamzah's reading in Aḥmad's time may have read with mistakes or exaggerated vowels, having not perfected it in practice. This reading does contain some intense features, such as frequent pauses before hamzah letters, long vowels, and frequent imālah. For these reasons, he may not have appreciated this reading. It is further reported that other people also complained of some readers of Ḥamzah who were pausing for so long, that 'one could even button their shirt during those pauses!'[125] So in the end, it is possible that individual readers were exaggerating in their pauses, either in their length or in their forcefulness or abruptness, causing others to criticize this reading. In any event, scholars from past to present were unanimous, according to Dhahabī, in the belief that Ḥamzah's reading was among the mutawātir ones, being definitively part of the Qur'ān, and fully acceptable for recitation in prayer. Dhahabī even went on to comment: 'Whoever in our times disputes this should be reprimanded, and evidence established against him.'

Isnāds

Ḥamzah read to A'mash—who read to Abū al-'Āliyah—who read to 'Umar, Ubayy, and Zayd—all of whom read to the Prophet.

Ḥamzah also read to A'mash—who read to Zirr b. Ḥubaysh—who read to 'Uthmān, 'Alī and Ibn Mas'ūd—all of whom read to the Prophet.

Ḥamzah also read to A'mash—who read to Zayd b. Wahb al-Juhanī—who read to Ibn Mas'ūd—who read to the Prophet.

Ḥamzah also read to Abū Isḥāq al-Sabī'ī—who read to Abū 'Abd al-Raḥmān al-Sulamī—who read to 'Uthmān, 'Alī, Zayd, Ubayy, and Ibn Mas'ūd—all of whom read to the Prophet.

Ḥamzah also read to Abū Isḥāq al-Sabī'ī—who read to Zirr b. Ḥubaysh—who read to 'Uthmān, 'Alī, and Ibn Mas'ūd—all of whom read to the Prophet.

---

[125] Al-Dānī, *al-Taḥdīd fī al-itqān wa al-tajwīd,* vol 1, pg 91.

Ḥamzah also read to Abū Isḥāq al-Sabīʿī—who read to ʿAmr b. Maymūn, ʿUbaydah b. ʿAmr, ʿAmr b. Shuraḥbīl, ʿAlqamah, Aswad—all of whom read to Ibn Masʿūd—who read to the Prophet.

Ḥamzah also read to Abū Isḥāq al-Sabīʿī—who read to ʿĀṣim b. Ḍamrah—who read to ʿAlī—who read to the Prophet.

Ḥamzah also read to Abū Isḥāq al-Sabīʿī—who read to al-Ḥārith b. ʿAbdullah al-Hamadānī—who read to ʿAlī and Ibn Masʿūd—both of whom read to the Prophet.

Ḥamzah also read to Ḥumrān b. Aʿyun al-Kūfī—who read to ʿUbayd b. Naḍlah al-Khuzāʿī—who read to Ibn Masʿūd—who read to the Prophet.

Ḥamzah also read to Ḥumrān b. Aʿyun al-Kūfī—who read to ʿUbayd b. Naḍlah al-Khuzāʿī—who read to ʿAlqamah—who read to Ibn Masʿūd—who read to the Prophet.

Ḥamzah also read to Ḥumrān b. Aʿyun al-Kūfī—who read to Abū al-Aswad al-Duʾalī—who read to ʿUthmān and ʿAlī—both of whom read to the Prophet.

Ḥamzah also read to Muḥammad b. ʿAbd al-Raḥmān b. Abī Laylah—who read to his brother ʿĪsā b. ʿAbd al-Raḥmān—who read to his father ʿAbd al-Raḥmān b. Abī Laylah—who read to ʿAlī— who read to the Prophet.

Ḥamzah also read to Jaʿfar al-Ṣādiq—who read to his father Muḥammad al-Bāqir—who read to his father Zayn al-ʿĀbidīn—who read to his father Ḥusayn—who read to his father ʿAlī—who read to the Prophet ﷺ.

7. Imām Kisāʾī of Kūfah (d. 189/804)

His name was Abū al-Ḥasan ʿAlī b. Ḥamzah, and he was of Persian descendent from Kūfah, client of the Asad clan. He earned his name because he once entered the state of iḥrām[126] for Ḥajj or ʿUmrah and kept his outer garment (known as *kisāʾ*) on in error. Shāṭibī mentioned him in line 39:

وأمّا عَلِيٌّ فالكِسائِيُّ نَعْتُهُ / لِما كانَ في الإحْرامِ فِيهِ تَسَرْبَلا

As for ʿAlī, Kisāʾī was his description
Because in iḥrām he happened to be clothed

He was the chief expert of all grammarians in Kūfah during the same time Sībawayh was the foremost expert of grammar in Baṣrah. They had a long-standing association and rivalry, and their exchanges are well-documented in books of Arabic language.

He became the undisputed leader of Qurʾānic readings in Kūfah after Ḥamzah. Since he had a large number of students, he would often sit on a chair and recite the entire Qurʾān to the audience. They would listen to him and note all the details of

[126] Iḥrām is the sacred state one enters during the pilgrimage of Ḥajj or ʿUmrah which enjoys certain restrictions such as not wearing any garment other than a simple unsewn upper and lower garment.

reading. He would also have students recite Qur'ān to him until they became too numerous and he was forced to switch to reading to them instead.

He was born in 119 AH and died in 189 AH. He read the Qur'ān with Ḥamzah, Muḥammad b. 'Abd al-Raḥmān b. Abī Laylā, 'Alī b. 'Īsā al-Hamadhānī and others. He related ḥadīth from Ḥamzah, Abū Bakr b. 'Ayyash and others. His most famous students in Qur'ān were Ḥafṣ al-Dūrī (d. 246/860),[127] Abū al-Ḥārith al-Layth b. Khālid (d. 240/854),[128] Khalaf, Ya'qūb al-Ḥaḍramī, Abū 'Ubayd al-Qāsim b. Sallām, Farrā' and Yaḥyā b. Ādam. His two transmitters were Ḥafṣ al-Dūrī and Abū al-Ḥārith Layth b. Khālid.

The likes of Imām Aḥmad and Yaḥyā b. Ma'īn related from him. Yaḥyā used to say: 'I have not seen with these eyes of mine someone with better articulation than Kisā'ī.' Shāfi'ī used to say: 'One who wants to delve deep into grammar is indebted to Kisā'ī.' Ibn al-Anbārī said: 'Kisā'ī was unique in the Qur'ān and its rare words.' When Kisā'ī died, Hārūn remarked: 'Today we buried grammar itself.'

Isnāds

Kisā'ī read to Muḥammad b. 'Abd al-Raḥmān b. Abī Laylah—who read to his brother 'Īsā b. 'Abd al-Raḥmān—who read to his father 'Abd al-Raḥmān b. Abī Laylah—who read to 'Alī— who read to the Prophet.

Kisā'ī also read with Ismā'īl the son of Ja'far al-Ṣādiq—who read to Shaybah b. Niṣāḥ—who read to 'Abdullah b. 'Ayyāsh—who read to Ubayy—who read to the Prophet.

Kisā'ī also read to Mufaḍḍal b. Muḥammad al-Ḍabbī, Zā'idah b. Qudāmah al-Thaqafī, and 'Īsā b. 'Umar al-Hamadānī—all of whom read to A'mash—who read to Abū al-'Āliyah—who read to 'Umar—who read to the Prophet.

Kisā'ī also read to Mufaḍḍal b. Muḥammad al-Ḍabbī, Zā'idah b. Qudāmah al-Thaqafī, and 'Īsā b. 'Umar al-Hamadānī—all of whom read to A'mash—who read to Zirr b. Ḥubaysh—who read to 'Uthmān, 'Alī, and Ibn Mas'ūd—all of whom read to the Prophet.

Kisā'ī also read to Mufaḍḍal b. Muḥammad al-Ḍabbī, Zā'idah b. Qudāmah al-Thaqafī, and 'Īsā b. 'Umar al-Hamadānī—all of whom read to A'mash—who read to Zayd b. Wahab—who read to Ibn Mas'ūd—who read to the Prophet.

Kisā'ī also read to Imām Ḥamzah

Kisā'ī also read to 'Īsā b. 'Umar al-Hamadānī and Shu'bah—both of whom read to 'Āṣim—who read to Abū 'Abd al-Raḥmān al-Sulamī—who read to 'Uthmān, 'Alī, Zayd, Ubayy, and Ibn Mas'ūd—all of whom read to the Prophet.

---

[127] See previous footnote 113.

[128] Abū al-Ḥārith al-Layth b. Khālid al-Baghdādī was the primary student of Imām al-Kisā'ī.

Kisā'ī also read to 'Īsā b. 'Umar al-Hamadānī and Shu'bah—both of whom read to 'Āṣim—who read to Zirr b. Ḥubaysh—who read to 'Uthmān, 'Alī, and Ibn Mas'ūd—all of whom read to the Prophet.

8. Imām Abū Ja'far of Madīnah (d. 130/738)

His name was Abū Ja'far Yazīd b. al-Qa'qā' of Madīnah, and he was a noble Follower, client of the Makhzūm clan. He was a leader of Qur'ānic reading in Madīnah. As a child he was brought to Umm Salamah, who touched his forehead and prayed for him. He used to continually fast on alternate days. We do not know exactly when he was born but he was described as an active teacher of Qur'ān in Madīnah during the battle of Ḥarrah[129] in the year 63 and died in 130 AH. He must have lived a long life.

He read the Qur'ān with his client 'Abdullah b. 'Ayyash al-Makhzūmī and with Ibn 'Abbās and Abū Hurayrah. He related ḥadīth from Jābir, Ibn 'Abbās, Ibn 'Umar, and Abū Hurayrah, but has very few ḥadīth reports.

His most famous students were 'Īsā b. Wardān (d. circa 160/777)[130] and Sulaymān b. Jammāz (d. circa 170/786).[131] Nāfi', one of the ten Imāms, also read with him.

Ibn 'Umar used to advance him to lead and prayed behind him. Imām Mālik referred to him as a righteous man. Yaḥyā b. Ma'īn said: 'Abū Ja'far was the Imām of Madīnah in Qur'ān and was trustworthy.' Imām Nāfi' stated that when he was washed after his death, a page of the muṣḥaf was seen to appear on his chest, and many witnesses saw the same.

Isnāds

Abū Ja'far read to Abū Hurayrah and 'Abdullah b. 'Ayyāsh—both of whom read to Ubayy and heard from 'Umar—both of whom read to the Prophet.

Abū Ja'far read to Ibn 'Abbās—who read to Ubayy and Zayd—both of whom read to the Prophet ﷺ.

9. Imām Ya'qūb of Baṣrah (d. 205/821)

His name was Abū Muḥammad Ya'qūb b. Isḥāq b. Zayd b. 'Abdullah of Baṣrah, and he was a client of the Ḥaḍramī clan. After Abū 'Amr, he was the leader of the Qur'ānic readings in Baṣrah. He was the imām of the main masjid of Baṣrah. He was known

---

[129] A battle between the Umayyad ruler Yazīd and people of Madīnah who had rebelled against his unjust rule under the Companion 'Abdullah b. al-Zubayr.

[130] Abū al-Ḥārith 'Īsā b. Wardān was a reciter of Madīnah, student of Nāfi' and Abū Ja'far, who died close to 160. He was also a teacher Qālūn.

[131] Abū al-Rabī' Sulaymān b. Muslim b. Jammāz al-Zahrī al-Madanī, another student of Abū Ja'far and Nāfi' who died in Madīnah after 170H.

for his piety and scrupulousness, and was learned in fiqh, ḥadīth and Arabic. He had great status in Baṣrah as if he were a prince. He was born in 117 AH and died 205 AH.

He read Qur'ān with Sallām b. Sulaymān al-Ṭawīl, Mahdī b. Maymūn, and Abū al-Ashhab Ja'far b. Ḥayyān al-'Uṭāridī. He related ḥadīth from his grandfather and from Zā'idah b. Qudāmah. His two transmitters were Muḥammad b. Mutawakkil al-Lu'lu'ī, better known as Ruways (d. 238/852),[132] and Rawḥ b. 'Abd al-Mu'min (d. 234/848).[133]

Abū Ḥātim of Sijistān stated: 'Ya'qūb was the most knowledgeable of those I met in the variant readings, the schools of grammar and the ḥadīth reports of the jurists.' Abū 'Amr al-Dānī said: 'After Abū 'Amr, most of the people of Baṣrah followed his selections in reading, to the point that I heard Ṭāhir b. Ghalbūn say, 'The imām of the grand masjid of Baṣrah only recites with the reading of Ya'qūb.''[134] The likes of Abū Qilābah and Abū 'Amr al-Fallās related from him.

Isnāds

Ya'qūb read with Ja'far Ḥayyān—who read with 'Imrān b. Taym—who read with Abū Mūsā al-Ash'arī—who read with the Prophet. Ibn al-Jazarī comments that this isnād is one of the highest in elevation and soundness, and Ya'qūb had other chains as well.

Ya'qūb also read with Mahdī b. Maymūn—who read with Shu'ayb b. al-Ḥabḥāb—who read with Abū al-'Āliyah—who read with Ibn 'Abbās—who read with Ubayy and Zayd—both of whom read with the Prophet.

Ya'qūb also read to Shihāb b. Shurnufah al-Mujāshi'ī—who read with Hārūn b. Mūsā al-A'war—who read with 'Abdullah b. Abī Isḥāq—who recited to Yaḥyā b. Ya'mar al-'Adwānī and Naṣr b. 'Āṣim al-Laythī—both of whom recited to Abū al-Aswad al-Du'alī—who recited to 'Uthmān and Ali—both of whom recited to the Prophet ﷺ.

10. Imām Khalaf of Baghdad (d. 229/844)

His name was Abū Muḥammad Khalaf b. Hishām b. Tha'lab al-Bazzār of Baghdad. He was the leading expert of Qur'ān and ḥadīth in Kūfah. He would prioritize the students of Qur'ān and then those of ḥadīth, sitting first in the day to teach his Qur'ān students and after that moving on to his ḥadīth students. He was trustworthy, pious,

---

[132] Abū 'Abdullah Muḥammad b. al-Mutawakkil al-Lu'lu'ī al-Baṣrī was one of the primary students of Imām Ya'qūb, completing the Qur'ān with him a number of times. He died in Baṣrah in 238 AH.

[133] Abū al-Ḥasan Rūḥ b. 'Abd al-Mu'min al-Hadhlī al-Baṣrī was a noted scholar of Qur'ān and Arabic who was among the main students of Imām Ya'qūb as well as learning from some of the students of Imām Abū 'Amr. He had many students, including Bukhārī. He died in 234 AH.

[134] *Al-Nashr,* vol 1, pg 149.

worshipful, and devoted to the sunnah. He memorized Qur'ān at the age of ten and began learning other sciences at the age of thirteen. He was wealthy and spent it in his pursuit of knowledge. It is said that he inherited great wealth from his father and spent it all on his studies and travels throughout the world to learn ḥadīth. He was born in 150 AH and died in 229 AH.

He read Qur'ān with Sulaym the student of Ḥamzah and with Ya'qūb b. Khalīfah al-A'shā, student of Shu'bah, the transmitter from 'Āṣim. He also related some modes of reading from Kisā'ī. He related ḥadīth from Mālik and Ḥammād b. Zayd among others. His most famous students were Idrīs b. 'Abd al-Karīm al-Ḥaddād (d. 292/904)[135] and Isḥāq b. Ibrāhīm b. 'Uthmān al-Marwazī (d. 286/899).[136]

The likes of Imām Muslim, Abū Dāwūd and 'Abdullah the son of Imām Aḥmad related ḥadīth from him. Imām Aḥmad said about him: 'By Allah, he is in our eyes trustworthy and reliable.' When he left Baghdad at the age of nineteen to pursue learning in other lands, his teacher Sulaym wrote: 'He did not leave anyone in Baghdad as learned in Qur'ān as him.' At the time, he was nineteen years in age!

Khalaf related the reading of Ḥamzah through Sulaym and also made his own personal reading from a combination of what he learned from his teachers. His personal reading, though, did not depart from the readings of Shu'bah from 'Āṣim, Ḥamzah and Kisā'ī in any significant way. That is, on those verses with variants, he would choose from the variants of one of the above. For this reason, Ibn al-Jazarī mentioned him as follows in *al-Ṭayyibah*:

.... ولاَ رَمْزَ يَرِدْ / عَنْ خَلَفٍ لِأَنَّهُ لَمْ يَنْفَرِدْ

There is no symbol [in this poem] that goes back
To Khalaf for he was not unique [in any variant]

Ibn al-Jazarī had assigned an individual code to each reader except for Khalaf because there was no need as he did not bring any unique variant. He is part of the compounded codes that represent more than one reading.

Isnāds

Khalaf read to Isḥāq b. Muḥammad al-Musayyabī—who read to Imām Nāfi' (see his previous chains).

Khalaf also read to 'Ubayd b. 'Uqayl al-Hilālī—who read to Shibl b. 'Abbād al-Makkī, Muslim b. Khālid al-Zanjī, 'Īsā b. 'Umar al-Thaqafī, and Hārūn b. Mūsā al-'Atakī—all of whom read to Imām Ibn Kathīr.

---

[135] Abū al-Ḥasan Idrīs b. 'Abd al-Karīm al-Ḥaddād al-Baghdādī was a student of Khalaf and a teacher of many, including Ibn Mujāhid. He related ḥadīth from Aḥmad. He died on the greatest day of the year 'Īd al-Aḍḥā, in 292 AH.

[136] Abū Ya'qūb Isḥāq b. Ibrāhīm b. 'Abdullah al-Marwazī al-Baghdādī was one of the scribes as well as students of Imām Khalaf.

Khalaf also read to ʿAbd al-Wahhāb b. ʿAṭāʾ al-Khaffāf—who read to Ismāʿīl b. Muslim al-Makkī—who read to Imām Ibn Kathīr.

Khalaf also read to ʿAbd al-Wahhāb b. ʿAṭāʾ al-Khaffāf, Saʿīd b. Aws al-Anṣārī, and ʿUbayd b. ʿUqayl—all of whom read to Imām Abū ʿAmr.

Khalaf also read to Yaʿqūb b. Muḥammad al-Aʿshā and Yaḥyā b. Ādam al-Ṣulḥī—both of whom read to Shuʿbah—who read to Imām ʿĀṣim.

Khalaf also read to ʿUbayd b. ʿUqayl—who read to Hārūn b. Mūsā—who read to Imām ʿĀṣim.

Khalaf also read to Saʿīd b. Aws al-Anṣārī—who read to Mufaḍḍal al-Ḍabbī—who read to Imām ʿĀṣim.

Khalaf also read to Sulaym b. ʿĪsā al-Kūfī—who read to Imām Ḥamzah.

Khalaf also read to Imām Kisāʾī.

11. Imām Ibn Muḥayṣin of Makkah (d. 123/740)

His name was Abū Ḥafṣ Muḥammad (it is also said his name was ʿUmar) b. ʿAbd al-Raḥmān b. Muḥayṣin of Makkah, client of the Sahmī clan.

He was a Qurʾānic teacher in Makkah along with Ibn Kathīr, well versed in Arabic, and trustworthy. It is not known when he was born but he died in Makkah in 123 AH.

He read Qurʾān with Saʿīd b. Jubayr, Mujāhid b. Jabr, and Darbās the freed slave of Ibn ʿAbbās. He related ḥadīth from his father and from Muḥammad b. Qays and Ṣafiyyah bint Shaybah. His students in Qurʾān included Abū ʿAmr b. al-ʿUlāʾ and Shibl b. ʿAbbād.

He was a reliable reporter whom Muslim accepted in his Ṣaḥīḥ. Those who related ḥadīth directly from him included Ibn Jurayj, Hushaym, Sufyān b. ʿUyaynah, and Sufyān al-Thawrī. He was a contemporary of Ibn Kathīr of Makkah and shared the same teachers. But the people of Makkah preferred the reading of Ibn Kathīr due to its conformity with the ʿUthmānic codex whereas Ibn Muḥayṣin's reading did not.

Isnāds

Ibn Muḥayṣin read to Saʿīd b. Jubayr, Mujāhid, and Darbās—all three of whom read to Ibn ʿAbbās—who read to Ubayy and Zayd b. Thābit—who read to the Prophet ﷺ.

12. Imām Yazīdī of Baṣrah (d. 202/817)

His name was Abū Muḥammad Yahya b. al-Mubārak b. al-Mughīrah al-ʿAdawī of Baṣrah, better known as Yazīdī. He was the personal tutor of the Caliph al-Maʾmūn and for the children of Yazīd b. Manṣūr the uncle of the Caliph al-Mahdī (this is how he earned his title). He was a senior scholar of Baghdad in the Qurʾānic readings,

Arabic language, literature, and history. He authored a number of works including *al-Nawādir fī al-Lughah.* He was born in 128 AH and died in 202 AH.

He read Qur'ān with Ḥamzah and Abū 'Amr al-'Ulā', and was a narrator of one of his transmissions. He related ḥadīth from 'Abd al-Malik b. Jurayj and Abū 'Amr, but he was not an expert of this field. His students included Dūrī and Sūsī, both of whom were transmitters of the reading of Abū 'Amr from him. In addition, Dūrī and Sulaymān b. al-Ḥakam related from him his own reading which was considered shādh.

His own reading did not differ from the accepted reading of Abū 'Amr except in ten words. Of these ten words, all of them correspond to one of the other ten mass-transmitted readings except for two: he read *khāfiḍatun rāfi'atun* (56:3) and *'āmilatun nāṣibatun* (88:3) in the accusative case (with fatḥah at the end of each word in place of ḍammah).

Dhahabī praised him such: 'He was reliable and an authority in the readings. He was an erudite scholar, extremely eloquent, and excelled in language and literature. It is said that he had dictated 10,000 pages of knowledge from Abū 'Amr, Khalīl and others.'

Isnāds

Yazīdī read to Imām Abū 'Amr.

13. Ḥasan al-Baṣrī (d. 110/728)

His name was Abū Sa'īd Ḥasan b. Yasār of Baṣrah, client of Zayd b. Thābit, and he was a well-known Follower. He was a leading expert of his time in knowledge, practice, worship, eloquence, piety, and courage. He was known for his tremendous reverence for Allah and frequent weeping. He would enjoin good and forbid wrong, not concerning himself with any blame. He would not be afraid to advise even the likes of Ḥajjāj b. Yūsuf, to the point that Ḥajjāj even threatened to kill him. He was full-bodied, strong, and handsome-faced. He participated in the conquests in Khurāsān and was the companion of brave warriors like Qaṭarī b. al-Fujā'ah and Muhallib b. Abī Ṣufrah. Commanders would put him in the frontline of battles due to his courage. He was born in 21 AH and died in 110 AH.

He read the Qur'ān with Abū al-'Āliyah and Ḥiṭṭān b. 'Abdullah al-Raqāshī. He related ḥadīth from 'Imrān b. Ḥuṣayn, al-Mughīrah b. Shu'bah, Abū Bakr al-Thaqafī, and al-Nu'mān b. Bashīr. He was raised in the home of Umm Salamah, who breastfed him. He saw 'Uthmān, Ṭalḥah and senior Companions.

His students in Qur'ān included Abū 'Amr, Sallām al-Ṭawīl, 'Īsā al-Thaqafī and others.

His praises from others were innumerable, but sufficient to note is that Umm Salamah would pray for him and take him around as a child to various Companions.

Anas b. Mālik used to say: 'Ask Ḥasan for he remembers when we forget.' Qatādah used to say: 'I have never sat with a jurist except that I felt the superiority of Ḥasan.' Shāfi'ī said: 'If I could, I would say that the Qur'ān was revealed in the language of Ḥasan, due to his supreme eloquence.'

Isnāds

Ḥasan read to Ḥaṭṭān b. 'Abdullah al-Raqqāshī—who read to Abū Mūsā al-Ash'arī—who read to the Prophet.

Ḥasan also read to Abū al-'Āliyah—who read with 'Umar, Ubayy, Ibn 'Abbās and Zayd b. Thābit—all of whom read to the Prophet ﷺ.

14. A'mash (d. 147/764)

His name was Sulaymān b. Mahrān, client of the Asad clan and resident of Kūfah. He was a leading scholar of Kūfah in knowledge, practice, piety, and worship. He was a proficient expert and had broad-ranging knowledge. He avoided rulers. His sight became weak and he eventually became blind.

He was cheerful with his Qur'ān students and slightly harsh with the ḥadīth students, with many interesting anecdotes related from him in this regard. He was born in 60 AH and died in 148 AH.

He read Qur'ān with Zirr b. Ḥubaysh, Mujāhid, Ibrāhīm al-Nakha'ī, 'Āṣim, Abū al-'Āliyah, and Yaḥyā b. Waththāb. He related ḥadīth from Anas, 'Abdullah b. Abī Awfā, Sa'īd b. Jubayr, Mujāhid and many others.

His Qur'ān students included Ḥamzah, Muḥammad b. 'Abd al-Raḥmān b. Abī Laylā, Zā'idah b. Qudāmah, Abū Bakr Shu'bah b. 'Ayyāsh and others.

Sufyān b. 'Uyaynah said: 'A'mash was the most knowledge of people in Qur'ān, ḥadīth and fiqh.' Wakī' said: 'A'mash has not missed the opening takbīr of the prayer in over seventy years.' Yaḥyā al-Qaṭṭān used to say: 'He was a supreme scholar of Islam.'

Isnāds

A'mash read to to Abū al-'Āliyah—who read with 'Umar, Ubayy, Ibn 'Abbās and Zayd b. Thābit—all of whom read to the Prophet.

A'mash also read to Ibrāhīm al-Nakha'ī—who read with 'Alqamah and Aswad—both of whom read to Ibn Mas'ūd—who read to the Prophet.

A'mash also read to Zirr b. Ḥubaysh—who read to Ibn Mas'ūd—who read to the Prophet.

A'mash also read to Imām 'Āṣim.

CHAPTER TWO

Examples of Contemporary Isnāds

Allah has blessed me with connected isnāds in the Qur'ān through these fourteen Imāms whose names and isnāds to the Prophet ﷺ have just been mentioned. I will list a few illustrations of these connected chains in the Qur'ānic readings.

Isnād of Ḥafṣ from ʿĀṣim

I have recited the Qur'ān to multiple teachers through this reading, separately as well as in a combined manner with other readings, but I will mention one isnād:

I have completed the recitation of the entire Qur'ān in the transmission of Ḥafṣ from Imām ʿĀṣim through the path of Shāṭibīyyah upon the eminent Shaykh Dr. ʿAbbās b. Muṣṭafā Anwar of Egypt[137] who recited to the scholar with the highest isnād the noble Shaykh Bakrī Ṭarābishī, who read with the leader of the reciters of Syria Muḥammad Salīm al-Ḥulwānī (d. 1363 AH),[138] who read with his father the leader of the reciters of Syria Aḥmad al-Ḥulwānī al-Kabīr (d. 1307),[139] who read with the leader of the reciters of Ḥijāz Aḥmad al-Marzūqī (d. 1262),[140] who read with the leader of the reciters of the Egyptian lands Shaykh Ibrāhīm al-ʿUbaydī (d. 1237),[141] who recited with the Shaykh of Azhar Muḥammad b. Ḥasan al-Samanūdī al-Munayyar (d. 1199),[142] who recited with ʿAlī al-Rumaylī (d. after 1130),[143] who read with the leader of the reciters of his time Muḥammad b. Qāsim al-Baqarī (d. 1111),[144] who recited with leader of the reciters of Egypt ʿAbd al-Raḥmān b. Shaḥādhah al-Yamanī (d. 1050),[145] who read with his father as well as ʿAlī b. Ghānim al-Maqdisī (d. 1004), who read with Muḥammad b. Ibrāhīm al-Samadīsī (d. 932), who read with al-

---

[137] He is a professor at Cairo University and an eminent scholar of the Qur'ānic readings who has traveled widely for elevated isnāds.

[138] He was the leading scholar of Qur'ān in Syria who read with his father Aḥmad al-Ḥalwānī, who lived from 1285—1363.

[139] Aḥmad b. Muḥammad ʿAlī al-Ḥulwānī al-Kabīr (1228—1307) was the leader of the reciters of Syria and Ḥijāz during his time. His students included the Syrian reformist scholar Jamāl al-Dīn al-Qāsimī (1866—1914).

[140] Aḥmad b. Muḥammad b. Ramaḍān al-Marzūqī (1205—1262) was of Egyptian origin and settled in Makkah, where he became its leading Qur'ānic scholar.

[141] He was a Mālikī scholar who inherited the leadership of the reciters in Egypt.

[142] He was the grand Shaykh of Azhar, and historically the first Shāfiʿī scholar to hold that position, previously always held by Mālikī scholars. He was known for his worship and fasting. He lived from 1099 to 1199.

[143] Abū al-Ṣalāḥ ʿAlī b. Muḥsin al-Ṣaʿīdī al-Wafāʾī al-Rumaylī was a notable Mālikī scholar and author of *Nayl al-marām fī waqf Ḥamzah wa Hishām.*

[144] Muḥammad b. Qāsim b. Ismāʿīl al-Shannāwī al-Baqarī (1018—1111) hailed from al-Baqar, an Egyptian town, who authored *al-Qawāʿid al-Baqariyyah.*

[145] A great scholar who learned fiqh from al-Shams al-Ramlī. He lived from 975 to 1050. He was wealthy and known to spend his wealth on students. Most of the reciters of Syria, Egypt and Ḥijāz had read with him.

Shihāb Aḥmad b. Asad al-Umyūṭī (d. 872), who read with the Imām and expert Muḥammad b. Muḥammad b. Muḥammad b. al-Jazarī al-Shāfiʿī (d. 833) author of *al-Nashr*, *al-Ṭayyibah* and other blessed works. Ibn al-Jazarī read with ʿAbd al-Raḥmān b. Aḥmad of Baghdad (d. 781), who read with the leader of the reciters of Egypt Muḥammad b. Aḥmad al-Ṣā'igh (d. 725), who recited with ʿAlī b. Shujāʿ al-Kamāl (d. 661) who was blind and the son-in-law of Imām Shāṭibī. He recited with Imām Abū al-Qāsim al-Shāṭibī (d. 590), who recited with Imām ʿAlī b. Muḥammad b. Hudhayl al-Balansī (d. 564), who recited with Abū Dāwūd Sulaymān b. Najāḥ (d. 496), who read with Imām Abū ʿAmr al-Dānī (d. 444), who read the transmission of Ḥafṣ with Ṭāhir b. Ghalbūn (d. 399),[146] who read with ʿAlī b. Muḥammad al-Hāshimī (d. 368), who read with Aḥmad b. Sahl al-Ushnānī (d. 307), who read with Abū Muḥammad ʿUbayd b. al-Ṣabāḥ (d. 235), who read with Ḥafṣ b. Sulaymān (d. 180), who read with ʿĀṣim b. Bahdalah b. Abī al-Nujūd (d. 127), who read with Abū ʿAbd al-Raḥmān al-Sulamī (d. 74), who received the Qur'ān from five Companions: ʿUthmān, ʿAlī, Ibn Masʿūd, Ubayy b. Ka'b and Zayd b. Thābit; all of whom received the Qur'ān from the Prophet ﷺ who received the Qur'ān from Jibrīl from his Lord.

Dr. ʿAbbās also read the entire Qur'ān with the eminent scholar Shaykh Aḥmad ʿAbd al-ʿAzīz al-Zayyāt,[147] who read with the ten major readings (al-ʿashr al-kubrā) with Shaykh ʿAbd al-Fattāḥ al-Hunaydī,[148] who read with the leader of the reciters of Egypt Muḥammad b. Aḥmad al-Mutawallī (d. 1313/1895),[149] who read with Sayyid Aḥmad al-Durrī al-Tihāmī (d. ~1284),[150] who read with the leader of the reciters of Egypt Aḥmad Salāmūnah (d. 1265),[151] who read with Ibrāhīm al-ʿUbaydī (whose chain is mentioned previously).

My Isnād of the Ten Readings

As for the ten readings through the Shāṭibīyyah and Durrah texts, I have read them completely with my esteemed Shaykh Dr. Īhāb b. Aḥmad Fikry Ḥaydar.[152] I have recited the ten readings through the Ṭayyibah text with my esteemed Shaykh Dr.

---

[146] Scholar of Aleppo who settled in Egypt.

[147] He was a prolific Azharī scholar who became the leading expert of the Qur'ānic readings in his era. Born in Cairo in 1325/1907, he possessed the highest chain in the Qur'ān in our times. He died in 1424/2003.

[148] A prolific scholar, speaker and poet who happened to be the last remaining student of Mutawallī. His last remaining student was al-Zayyāt. He was teacher in the College of Arabic of Azhar University, and later in the College of Qur'ān in Madīnah University.

[149] Great Qur'ānic scholar of Egypt who lived from 1248/1832 to 1313/1895.

[150] Mālikī scholar of Egypt who was also an expert in the readings.

[151] He was a Mālikī scholar who became the leader of the reciters of Egypt after Ibrāhīm al-ʿUbaydī.

[152] He is a great scholar known for his knowledge and piety, born in 1374, who learned fiqh from Najīb al-Muṭīʿī and ʿAbdullah al-Ghadayān, and recited with Shaykh al-Zayyāt.

Muḥammad Sāmir b. Muḥammad Mamdūḥ al-Naṣ.[153] Both teachers read the ten major readings (al-ʿashr al-kubrā) with the great scholar and researcher Aḥmad b. Aḥmad Muṣṭafā Abū Ḥasan,[154] who read these with Shaykh Aḥmad ʿAbd al-ʿAzīz al-Zayyāt whose chain was mentioned previously to Ibn al-Jazarī, who had his own connected chains to each of the ten Imāms, who had their own chains back to the Prophet, peace be upon him. Ibn al-Jazarī's isnāds are well-known and mentioned in his book al-Nashr fī al-Qirāʿāt al-ʿAshr.

My Isnād of the Four Shādh Readings

I have received these reading through the text al-Fawā'id al-Muʿtabarah from my esteemed teacher Shaykh ʿAbdullah b. Ṣāliḥ al-ʿUbayd, when I read to him in Riyad. He read them with the great scholar Ibrāhīm b. Shaḥātah al-Samanūdī[155] in his hometown of Samanoud. He in turn read them with Ḥanafī al-Siqā, who read them with Khalīl al-Janāyīnī, who read them with Muḥammad b. Aḥmad al-Mutawallī, who had his chains back to Ibn al-Jazarī and Muḥammad b. Khalīl al-Qabāqibī,[156] both of whom had their own chains back to the Prophet, peace be upon him.

The only purpose in mentioning these chains was to show the historical continuity, through recitation, of the chains of these various readings to our times throughout the Muslim world, and that this is part of the manner through which Allah preserved His Book.

---

[153] He is a Ḥanafī jurist and proficient scholar of the readings. He read the Qur'ān with senior scholars of Syria and Egypt. He learned fiqh with Abū al-Yusr ʿĀbidīn the muftī of Syria on the authority of his grandfather on the authority of his brother Ibn ʿĀbidīn, the author of the famous *Ḥāshiyah*.

[154] He was an Egyptian Azharī scholar who later studied and lived in Riyad. Many senior scholars of today read Qur'ān with him. He was born in 1341 and died in 1429/2008.

[155] He was a great Azharī scholar and one of the greatest contemporary scholars of the readings. He died in 1429/2008 at the age of 96.

[156] He was a great scholar and author of the readings who was from Damascus, who lived from 777 to 849 AH.

Historical Survey of the Qur'ānic Readings

I have reached the following conclusions regarding the historical spread of these readings in the Muslim lands.

Worldwide Readings in the Time of Ibn Mujāhid

Up until the time of Ibn Mujāhid (245/859—324/936), who was known as the 'delineator of the seven readings' and who authored his book in the year 300 AH, his chosen seven readings plus a few others were widespread throughout the Muslim lands. However, they exhibited regional predominance in the following manner: in Madīnah the predominant reading was that of Nāfi', in Makkah Ibn Kathīr, in Syria Ibn 'Āmir, in Baṣrah Abū 'Amr and Ya'qūb, and in Kūfah 'Āṣim and Ḥamzah. Makkī b. Abū Ṭālib[157] says:

> In the beginning of the 200s, the people of Baṣrah were upon the readings of Abū 'Amr and Ya'qūb, Kūfah upon the readings of Ḥamzah and 'Āṣim, Syria on the reading of Ibn 'Āmir, Makkah on the reading of Ibn Kathīr, and Madīnah on the reading of Nāfi'. This persisted until the beginning of the 300s when Ibn Mujāhid replaced the name of Ya'qūb with Kisā'ī.[158]

The reason Ibn Mujāhid did not include the reading of Ya'qūb in his book though it was the dominant one in Baṣrah during his time was simply because he did not possess an isnād in it. In its place, he substituted instead the Kūfan reading of Kisā'ī, despite the fact that he had already included two other Kūfan readings—that of 'Āṣim and Ḥamzah—which happened to be more widespread.

Shu'bah dominated Ḥafṣ, and Ḥamzah over 'Āṣim, in Kūfah

In Kūfah during the time of Ibn Mujāhid, the transmission of Shu'bah from 'Āṣim was much more predominant than that of Ḥafṣ, and the reading of Ḥamzah was more predominant overall than that of 'Āṣim. This is supported by Ibn Mujāhid's testimony himself:

> The reading of 'Āṣim was relied upon by a portion of the people of Kūfah but not the majority of them, for the following reason: Abū

[157] Abū Muḥammad Makkī b. Abī Ṭālib Ḥammūsh b. Muḥammad al-Qaysī was one of the ummah's greatest scholars of the Qur'ānic readings. He hailed from Qayrawān, traveled to Egypt and settled in Cordoba where he taught in the Grand Mosque. He authored about 80 works. He was born in 355 AH and died in 437/1045.
[158] Ibn Ḥajar, *Fatḥ al-Bārī*, Maktabat al-Malik Fahd, vol 8, pg 660.

> Bakr b. ʿAyyāsh, as it is said, was the more accurate student of ʿĀṣim, for he had learned the Qur'ān from him five verses at a time every day. So the Kūfans did not trust any of the students of ʿĀṣim except for Abū Bakr. Abū Bakr, however, rarely accepted students and did so only for those who were extremely proficient. As a result, this reading became scarce and difficult to master it. For this reason, the predominant reading in Kūfah until our times is the reading of Ḥamzah b. Ḥabīb al-Zayyāt.[159]

Post-Ibn Mujāhid Yaʿqūb Predominance in Baṣrah

In the 5th century, the reading of Ya'qūb remained predominant in Baṣrah (despite not being included in Ibn Mujāhid's seven), as can be gleamed from the words of the expert Abū ʿAmr al-Dānī (d. 444): After Abū ʿAmr, most of the people of Baṣrah followed his selections in reading, to the point that I heard Ṭāhir b. Ghalbūn say, 'The imām of the grand masjid of Baṣrah only recites with the reading of Yaʿqūb.'[160]

Syrian Reading of Ibn ʿĀmir Replaced by Abū ʿAmr in 500 AH

The inhabitants of Syria continued following the reading of Ibn ʿĀmir until the end of the 5th century, until the arrival in their midst of a great Qur'ānic scholar named Ibn Ṭāwūs (d. 536/1141),[161] who began to teach the transmission of Dūrī from Abū ʿAmr, which gradually began to spread in the region until it replaced the reading of Ibn ʿĀmir. This is supported by Ibn al-Jazarī's words: 'Syria continued to be entirely upon the reading of Ibn ʿĀmir in terms of recitation, prayer and teaching until approximately the year 500, and the first one to teach the reading Abū ʿAmr, as is reported, was Ibn Ṭāwūs.'[162]

Warsh and Qālūn Dominate North Africa

Imām Warsh was the leader of the Qur'ānic scholars in Egypt who had traveled to Nāfiʿ of Madīnah, where he completed four complete recitals, before returning to Egypt to disseminate the reading of his teacher Nafi. From him, Nāfiʿ's reading spread to the far reaches of northwest Africa (al-Maghrib) and a great number of African

---

[159] Ibn Mujāhid, *Kitāb al-Sabʿah,* pg 71.
[160] *Al-Nashr,* vol 1, pg 149.
[161] Hibatullāh b. Aḥmad b. ʿAbdullah b. ʿAlī b.Ṭāwūs, also known as Imām Abū Muḥammad al-Baghdādī, was a great Qur'ānic scholar from Baghdad who settled in Damascus, where he became the imam of the Grand Mosque and taught Qur'ān to thousands of students for a number of years. He is the author of work on the readings entitled *al-Hidāyah fī al-ʿAshrah.* He lived from 461/1068 through 536/1141.
[162] Ibn al-Jazarī, *Ghāyat al-niyāyah,* vol 1, pg 381.

lands.[163] There was another important factor that helped this spread in this region: this happened to be the preferred reading of Imām Mālik. So just as the people northwest Africa adopted the fiqh of Madīnah, so too they adopted the reading of Madīnah. The far reaches of north Africa (current day Libya, Tunisia and Chad), however, adopted the reading of Nāfiʿ through the transmission of his other student Qālūn, due to it being easier than the transmission of Warsh, which contained very lengthy vowels and difficult imālah declensions.

Rise of Abū ʿAmr in the Heartland

The reading of Dūrī from Abū ʿAmr remained predominant among Iraq, Arabia, Yemen, Syria, Egypt, Sudan, and eastern Africa until the 10th century. Ibn al-Jazarī states:

> Ibn Mujāhid stated: And they related to us from Wahb b. Jarīr who said: Shuʿbah said to me: Hold fast to the reading of Abū ʿAmr, because it will become relied upon by people.
>
> He also said: Muḥammad b. ʿĪsā b. Ḥayyān related to me: Naṣr b. ʿAlī related to us: My father said to me: Shuʿbah said: Pay attention to what Abū ʿAmr chooses to recite for himself, for it will one day be relied upon by people. Naṣr said: I asked my father: How do you recite? He replied: I recite upon the reading of Abū ʿAmr. I asked al-Aṣmaʿī: How do you recite? He replied: I recite upon the reading of Abū ʿAmr.
>
> What Shuʿbah claimed was indeed correct, for the predominant reading of people today in Syria, Arabia, Yemen and Egypt is the reading of Abū ʿAmr. You will not find any teacher today except that he is teaching this reading, especially in its wordings, though they may make mistakes in its general methodology. Syria used to read by the reading of Ibn ʿĀmir until the end of the 500s, when they abandoned it after an individual came from Iraq[164] and began teaching people in the Umayyad Mosque the reading of Abū ʿAmr. He gained many students, and stayed many years, until this reading became widespread. This is what has reached me, for I know of no other reason for these people abandoning their reading of Abū ʿĀmir in favor of this one. I count this has one of the miracles of Shuʿbah.[165]

---

[163] From North Africa it also spread to Andalus, where it was the predominant reading for the same reasons.
[164] Ibn Ṭāwūs, see above.
[165] *Ghāyat al-nihāyah,* pg 445.

Ḥafṣ Rises in the East to Eclipse All Others

At the same time that the transmission of Dūrī from Abū ʿAmr began to spread in the aforementioned regions (Iraq, Arabia, Yemen, Syria, Egypt, Sudan and eastern Africa), the transmission of Ḥafṣ began to spread among the Turks. As the Ottoman state began to extend its authority over most reaches of the Islamic world, the transmission of Ḥafṣ spread throughout the world through their hands. It was also disseminated through the many copies of the Qur'ān which were produced and printed by the Ottomans in the Ḥafṣ transmission. The Ḥafṣ reading began to gradually replace the reading of Dūrī from Abū ʿAmr, which ultimately became confined to Yemen, Sudan and the horn of Africa. I have personally come across tajweed works of Yemeni scholars authored around the year 1370/1951 which correspond to the Dūrī from Abū ʿAmr reading and indicate that this reading was followed in Ḥaḍramawt and many regions of Yemen during that time. Keeping in mind the weakened control of the Ottomans over north Africa, where extreme love for Imām Mālik was widespread, the reading of Nāfiʿ remained predominant there until our day. Ibn ʿĀshūr (d. 1394/1973)[166] mentioned in his tafsīr *al-Taḥrīr wa al-Tanwīr*:

> The readings which are read in the Muslim world today are: the reading of Nāfiʿ through the transmission of Qālūn in some regions of Tunisia, Egypt, and Libya; the transmission of Warsh in some regions of Tunisia, Egypt, all of Algeria and Morocco and what borders those regions such as Sudan; and the reading of ʿĀṣim through the transmission of Ḥafṣ which is predominant in the entire eastern world, most of Egypt, India, Pakistan, Turkey and Afghanistan. I have also learned that the reading of Abū ʿAmr of Baṣrah is still recited in regions of Sudan bordering Egypt.[167]

In our current times, it is well known that contemporary media resources, including audio and video, have had a great role in spreading the transmission of Ḥafṣ throughout the world, including in those regions where the transmissions of Dūrī, Qālūn or Warsh continued to be recited. In addition, the publication of copies of the Qur'ān in various formats has contributed to this. The end-result has been a near

---

[166] Great scholar and Qur'ānic commentator of Tunisia, born in 1296/1879, educated in the renowned al-Zaytūnah University, died in 1394/1973 at the age of 94. He is famous for his courageous commitment to the truth: when the President of Tunisia desired a fatwa to justify abandoning the fast of Ramadhan because it decreased productivity, he responded by Reciting: ﴿*Prescribed for you is fasting. . .*﴾, and saying: 'Surely Allah has spoken the truth while Habib Bourgiba (the president) lies.'

[167] Ibn ʿĀshūr, *Tafsīr al-taḥrīr wa al-tanwīr,* vol 1, pg 63.

extinction of other readings. Of course, this is all from God's decree, and His decrees are governed by His ultimate and deep wisdom.

Nevertheless, there has been in the last few years the beginnings of a great revival of knowledge and learning, particularly with respect to the Qur'ānic readings, in many parts of the world, such that the young generations have begun to learn and teach the ten readings, which is a healthy thing that bodes well for the future, and all praise is for Allah.

Chapter 3: The ʿUthmānic Codex and the Qurʾānic Readings

المصحف العثماني وعلاقته بالقراءات

Writing the Qurʾān in the Prophetic Era

The fact is that the entire Qur'ān was written down during the lifetime of the Prophet ﷺ with his permission, under his directive, and through his own dictation.[1] He had numerous designated scribes tasked with writing down the ongoing revelation. However, the entire Qur'ān was not bound together in one book but scattered among various pages, bone fragments, leather parchments, stones, palm fronds and their likes. The Prophet had up to 26 such scribes—it was even said that there were 42—whose ranks included the four Rightly-Guided Caliphs, Zubayr b. al-ʿAwwām, al-Mughīrah b. Shuʿbah, Zayd b. Thābit, Ubayy b. Kaʿb, Ibn Masʿūd, Muʿādh b. Jabal, Ḥanẓalah b. al-Rabīʿ, Khālid b. Walīd, Muʿāwiyah b. Abī Sufyān, ʿĀmir b. Fuhayrah, Yazīd b. Abī Sufyān, ʿAmr b. al-ʿĀṣ, and Thābit b. Qays.[2]

Compared to previous scriptures, this is a unique distinction for the Qur'ān: that it was completely written down from beginning to end during the Prophet's own lifetime and under his full direction.

The reason that the entire Qur'ān was not compiled into one binding in the lifetime of the Prophet ﷺ was simply due to the anticipation of ongoing revelation or abrogation of specific portions, a process which continued until the death of the Prophet ﷺ. Jibrīl would bring verses of revelation and direct the Prophet to add them in various sequences and portions to what was already revealed. This process quite obviously prevented the Prophet ﷺ from having the Qur'ān written down in its entirety and in its proper sequence.

After his demise, Abū Bakr and the Companions were spared these concerns, and the welfare of the community now necessitated its compilation into a single binding. That compilation was done in the era of Abū Bakr, in its proper sequence.

From here we understand the principle that an action would only be considered a (blameworthy) innovation in the religious sense (bidʿah) if the motive or demands for it were present in the Prophetic era and he abstained from the act, or, conversely, there existed some obstacles that prevented the Prophet from doing something he had originally wanted. As for new demands and motives that arose after the Prophetic era which were not present before, or hindering factors that were no longer there, then such actions that arise from these would not be considered religious innovations in the technical sense. The compilation of the muṣḥaf is one such example. It fulfilled a pressing need for the Muslim community. The Prophet ﷺ did not do it simply because the motive was not there during his time (the fear for the loss of Qur'ān due to the demise of Qur'ān memorizers) and there existed the hindrance of ongoing revelation.

---

[1] This section is heavily supplemented with content from *al-Khayr al-kathīr,* pg 124-34.

[2] See *Manāhil al-ʿUrfān*, vol 1, pg 248-9. Also see *al-Khayr al-kathīr,* pg 122-3.

CHAPTER 3

The First Compilation of the Qur'ān

The immediate reason for the first compilation of the muṣḥaf (al-jam'at al-ūlā) was the martyrdom of many Qur'ān reciters in the Battle of Yamāmah,[3] which prompted 'Umar to suggest this task to Abū Bakr. The first compilation took place in the era of Abū Bakr upon the advice of 'Umar, while the second compilation took place in the era of 'Uthmān upon the advice of Ḥudhayfah.

Abū Bakr entrusted the project to Zayd b. Thābit, who happened to be one of the Prophet's scribes who had memorized the Qur'ān and witnessed the last recital of the Prophet ﷺ with Jibrīl. Discussions ensued between Abū Bakr and 'Umar, and then between Abū Bakr and Zayd, until all of them agreed to compile the Qur'ān. The full account is related by Bukhārī in his Ṣaḥīḥ:

> Mūsā b. Ismā'īl reported to me: from Ibrāhīm b. Sa'd: from Ibn Shihāb: from 'Ubayd b. al-Sabbāq: Zayd b. Thābit said:
>
> Abū Bakr sent for me when the people of Yamāmah had been killed. I found 'Umar b. al-Khaṭṭāb sitting with him.
>
> Abū Bakr said to me: 'Umar has come to me and said: Casualties were heavy among the memorizers (qurrā') of the Qur'ān on the day of the Battle of Yamāmah and I am afraid that more heavy casualties may take place among the qurrā' of other lands, causing a large part of the Qur'ān to be lost. So I see that you should order that the Qur'ān be collected. I said to 'Umar: How can you do something which Allah's Messenger did not do? 'Umar replied: By Allah, this would be a good thing. 'Umar kept on insisting until Allah opened my heart and I began to incline to the view of 'Umar.
>
> Then Abū Bakr said to me: You are a wise young man and we do not have any suspicion about you, and you used to write the revelation for Allah's Messenger ﷺ. So search for (the fragmentary scripts of) the Qur'ān and collect it [in one book].
>
> By Allah, had they had ordered me to move one of the mountains, it would not have been heavier for me than ordering me to collect the Qur'ān. I said to Abū Bakr: How will you do something which Allah's Messenger ﷺ did not do? Abū Bakr replied, By Allah, it would be a good thing. Abū Bakr kept on insisting until Allah opened my heart in the same way he had opened the hearts of Abū Bakr and 'Umar.
>
> So I began searching for the Qur'ān and collecting it from palm fronds, cloth, shoulder bone, stones and from the men who knew it by

[3] See footnote 41 in chapter 2.

> heart,[4] until I found the last verse of sūrah at-Tawbah with Abū Khuzaymah al-Anṣārī, and I did not find it with anybody else: ﴿*Verily there has come unto you a Messenger from among yourselves. It grieves him that you should receive any injury or difficulty . . .*﴾ (9:128-9)
>
> Then these complete pages [of the Qur'ān] remained with Abū Bakr until his passing, then with 'Umar for the remainder of his life, and then with Ḥafṣah, the daughter of 'Umar.[5]

The methodology used by Zayd, under the authority of Abū Bakr and 'Umar, was not to rely on memorization alone but to confirm each verse with a written record from a minimum of two Companions who had written the verses down in the presence of the Prophet ﷺ through his dictation. This was done along with relying on the memory of those who had memorized the Qur'ān, which included Zayd himself.

Among the reasons Zayd was selected for leading this project was the fact that he had witnessed the Final Rehearsal of the Prophet with Jibrīl.[6] As such, Zayd was fully aware of the final order of the Qur'ān that the Prophet had followed as well as the verses that were abrogated by the final recital. There was a clear wisdom in the Prophet's selection of Zayd for this.

During the project, Zayd began to match his memory of the Qur'ān—and that of others—with the written records compiled in the Prophet's lifetime, requiring two records for each verse. He was able to find every single verse with at least two written documents, except for the last two verses of sūrah al-Tawbah, which were found to be in written form in the presence of a single Companion: Khuzaymah b. Thābit of the Anṣār.[7] However, the Prophet himself had previously deemed his testimony to be equivalent to two individuals.[8] This was a great virtue ascribed to Khuzaymah, and for this reason his single record was accepted.

In addition to that, other transmissions of the ḥadīth indicate that Zayd required two just witnesses to testify that each written record was part of the Qur'ān and compiled in the lifetime of the Prophet ﷺ. In that, Zayd was following the direction

---

[4] The translation of these various materials are taken from a composite of the reports of Bukhārī of this ḥadīth.

[5] Ṣaḥīḥ Bukhārī: Kitāb faḍā'il al-Qur'ān—Bāb jam' al-Qur'ān. Also related by Bukhārī from Abū al-Yamān from Shu'ayb from Zuhrī in Kitāb tafsīr al-Qur'ān (sūrah al-Barā'ah)—Bāb qawluhū la qad jā'akum rasūlun min anfusikum; and from Yaḥyā b. Bukayr from Layth from Yūnus from Zuhrī in Kitāb faḍā'il al-Qur'ān—Bāb kātib al-nabī; and from Muḥammad b. 'Ubaydullah Abū Thābit from Ibrāhīm b. Sa'd in Kitāb al-aḥkām—Bāb yustaḥabb li al-kātib an yakūna amīnan 'āqilan; and with the same isnād in Kitāb al-Tawḥīd—Bāb wa kāna 'arshuhū 'alā al-mā'.

[6] See footnotes 49 and 50 in chapter 1.

[7] He was a well-known Companion and native of Madīnah who had participated in the battle of Badr and was martyred fighting on the side of 'Alī in the Battle of Ṣiffīn in 37/657.

[8] See Ṣaḥīḥ Bukhārī: Kitāb al-jihād wa al-sayr—Bāb qawl Allāh min al-mu'minīna rijālan; Kitāb tafsīr al-Qur'ān (sūrah al-Aḥzāb)—Bāb faminhum man qaḍā naḥbahu.

of Abū Bakr, who had instructed 'Umar and Zayd: 'Sit at the door of the masjid and whoever comes with two witnesses for any writing of the Qur'ān, write it down.'[9]

The details of what was meant by these two witnesses was subject to dispute. Some scholars believed that two witnesses meant two individuals who could testify that these written verses were part of the Qur'ān and that they had witnessed its revelation in the Prophetic era. This process was meant for a greater degree of certainty in verification, and the Companions were pursuing extreme caution and care in preserving the Qur'ān. For each portion, they had required actual memorization, the presence of two written copies, and two witnesses for each written copy. This was the view of Sakhāwī.

Others such as Ibn Ḥajar were of the view that the term 'two witnesses' simply referred to the memorization and writing of each verse, and that these two means had to correspond for a verse to be accepted.[10] There is no major contradiction in these views, for all of it falls under greater caution in verification and preservation of the Qur'ān.

The resultant copy of the Qur'ān was preserved with great care in the house of Abū Bakr, consisting of fragments of bone, sheets, wood, palm fronds and leather parchment. These were later transcribed to sheets in the lifetime of Abū Bakr—some said in the era of 'Umar[11]—and this manuscript was kept in the house of 'Umar throughout his rule, and then transferred after his death, upon his wishes, to the house of his daughter and mother of the believers, Ḥafṣah. It was then kept in her possession until it was borrowed, and later returned, by 'Uthmān in order to produce an official copy. After her death, her brother 'Abdullah b. 'Umar sent the pages to Marwān, the governor of Madīnah, who had them destroyed—either by washing, tearing or burning—since there was no longer any need for it due to the official 'Uthmānic compilations that now existed.

---

[9] Related though a disconnected chain by Ibn Abī Dāwūd in Kitāb al-maṣāḥif.

[10] *Al-Itqān,* vol 1, pg 58.

[11] *Al-Itqān,* vol 1, pg 59.

The ʿUthmānic Codex Project

The specific cause for the ʿUthmānic compilation originated with the Companion Ḥudhayfah b. al-Yamān. After participating in the conquests of Armenia and Azerbaijan, he was deeply disturbed by the differences in recitation among people and the resultant disputes concerning those differences.

Mūsā b. Ismāʿīl reported to us: Ibrāhīm reported to us: Ibn Shihāb reported to us: Anas bin Malik related that Ḥudhayafah b. al-Yamān came to ʿUthmān at the time when the people of Syria and Iraq were engaged in the wars in Armenia and Azerbaijan. Ḥudhayfah was greatly fearful over their differences in the recitation of the Qur'ān, so he said to ʿUthmān: O commander of the believer, save this nation before they differ over their scripture as Jews and the Christians had done before. So ʿUthmān sent a message to Ḥafṣah saying: Send us the pages of the Qur'ān so that we may compile copies from them and return them back to you.

After she sent them, ʿUthmān ordered Zayd b. Thābit, ʿAbdullah b. al-Zubayr, Saʿīd b. al-ʿĀṣ and ʿAbd al-Raḥmān b. al-Ḥārith b. Hishām to transcribe them into copies. ʿUthmān said to the three men from Quraysh: If you differ from Zayd on any matter of the Qur'ān, then write it in the script of Quraysh, for it was revealed in their tongue.

They did so, and when they had compiled several copies, ʿUthmān returned the original manuscripts to Hafsah and sent to every Muslim province one of the copies they had compiled, with orders that all the other Qur'ānic materials, on pages or whole copies, to be burnt.[12]

حَدَّثَنَا مُوسَى، حَدَّثَنَا إِبْرَاهِيمُ، حَدَّثَنَا ابْنُ شِهَابٍ أَنَّ أَنَسَ بْنَ مَالِكٍ حَدَّثَهُ: أَنَّ حُذَيْفَةَ بْنَ الْيَمَانِ قَدِمَ عَلَى عُثْمَانَ، وَكَانَ يُغَازِي أَهْلَ الشَّأْمِ فِي فَتْحِ إِرْمِينِيَةَ وَأَذْرَبِيجَانَ مَعَ أَهْلِ الْعِرَاقِ، فَأَفْزَعَ حُذَيْفَةَ اخْتِلَافُهُمْ فِي الْقِرَاءَةِ، فَقَالَ حُذَيْفَةُ لِعُثْمَانَ: يَا أَمِيرَ الْمُؤْمِنِينَ، أَدْرِكْ هَذِهِ الأُمَّةَ قَبْلَ أَنْ يَخْتَلِفُوا فِي الْكِتَابِ، اخْتِلَافَ الْيَهُودِ وَالنَّصَارَى، فَأَرْسَلَ عُثْمَانُ إِلَى حَفْصَةَ : أَنْ أَرْسِلِي إِلَيْنَا بِالصُّحُفِ نَنْسَخُهَا فِي الْمَصَاحِفِ ثُمَّ نَرُدُّهَا إِلَيْكِ، فَأَرْسَلَتْ بِهَا حَفْصَةُ إِلَى عُثْمَانَ ، فَأَمَرَ زَيْدَ بْنَ ثَابِتٍ، وَعَبْدَ اللهِ بْنَ الزُّبَيْرِ، وَسَعِيدَ بْنَ الْعَاصِ، وَعَبْدَ الرَّحْمَنِ بْنَ الْحَارِثِ بْنِ هِشَامٍ، فَنَسَخُوهَا فِي الْمَصَاحِفِ، وَقَالَ عُثْمَانُ لِلرَّهْطِ الْقُرَشِيِّينَ الثَّلَاثَةِ: إِذَا اخْتَلَفْتُمْ أَنْتُمْ وَزَيْدُ بْنُ ثَابِتٍ فِي شَيْءٍ مِنَ الْقُرْآنِ فَاكْتُبُوهُ بِلِسَانِ قُرَيْشٍ، فَإِنَّمَا نَزَلَ بِلِسَانِهِمْ، فَفَعَلُوا، حَتَّى إِذَا نَسَخُوا الصُّحُفَ فِي الْمَصَاحِفِ رَدَّ عُثْمَانُ الصُّحُفَ إِلَى حَفْصَةَ، وَأَرْسَلَ إِلَى كُلِّ أُفُقٍ بِمُصْحَفٍ مِمَّا نَسَخُوا، وَأَمَرَ بِمَا سِوَاهُ مِنَ الْقُرْآنِ فِي كُلِّ صَحِيفَةٍ أَوْ مُصْحَفٍ أَنْ يُحْرَقَ.

[12] Ṣaḥīḥ Bukhārī: Kitāb faḍā'il al-Qur'ān—Bāb jamʿ al-Qur'ān.

The committee tasked with writing the Qur'ān was composed of four senior and learned Qur'ānic experts from the Companions. Three were from Quraysh and the fourth, Zayd b. Thābit, was the same one who had presided over the first compilation.

They fulfilled the project in the masjid of the Prophet ﷺ and did so with meticulous care observing Qurayshī rules of orthography—even as they may have differed in exact articulation. They would actively search for those individuals who were known to have learned directly from the Prophet ﷺ—even a verse—sometimes summoning a single person living as far as a three-night journey from Madīnah in order to ask him how the Prophet had taught them a particular verse.

Other reports provide further details and inform us that they did not differ in orthography (exact lettering and writing) with Zayd except in one word. ʿUthmān had ordered them in the event of any difference to give preference to the language of Quraysh. The only difference the members had with Zayd was in one particular word—*tābūt* ('Ark') in sūrah al-Baqarah:

وَقَالَ لَهُمْ نَبِيُّهُمْ إِنَّ آيَةَ مُلْكِهِ أَن يَأْتِيَكُمُ **التَّابُوتُ** فِيهِ سَكِينَةٌ مِّن رَّبِّكُمْ
وَبَقِيَّةٌ مِّمَّا تَرَكَ آلُ مُوسَىٰ وَآلُ هَارُونَ تَحْمِلُهُ الْمَلَائِكَةُ

﴿*Their Prophet further informed them: The sign of his appointment as king from Allah is that during his reign you will get back the Ark [of the Covenant], wherein are the means of your peace of mind from your Lord, and which contains the sacred relics of the family of Mūsā and Hārūn.*﴾ (2:248)

The difference was over whether the ending letter of tābūt should be written with a tā or hā. For Zayd, the language of the Anṣār dictated that it be written with hā since it represented a tā marbūṭah which is pronounced on stopping with hā. The other Qurayshī delegates considered it a full tā and so, in compliance with the orders to follow the Quraysh, they wrote it with tā. This was the only reported difference.

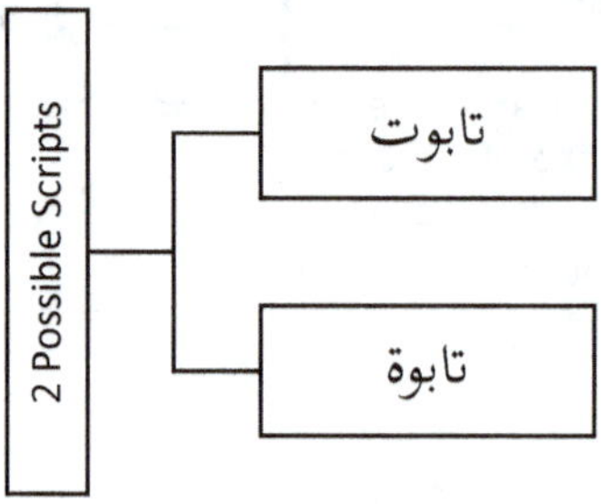

When they were done transcribing pages from this manuscript, ʿUthmān returned it to Ḥafṣah and sent copies to each major city while ordering the other copies of the Qur'ān to be burned.

Some versions of this ḥadīth reveal that the same Khuzaymah b. Thābit had another role in this second compilation. There was a single verse of sūrah al-Aḥzāb for which they could not find the written record, although they had memorized it and were certain that it was part of the Qur'ān:

مِّنَ الْمُؤْمِنِينَ رِجَالٌ صَدَقُوا مَا عَاهَدُوا اللَّهَ عَلَيْهِ ۖ فَمِنْهُم مَّن قَضَىٰ نَحْبَهُ
وَمِنْهُم مَّن يَنتَظِرُ ۖ وَمَا بَدَّلُوا تَبْدِيلًا

﴾*Among the believers there are those who have remained true to the covenant they made with Allah. Among those some of them have fulfilled their vow and others await the appointed time. They have not changed in the least.*﴿ (33:23)

They searched for it far and wide until they found it with Khuzaymah and then included it in their transcribing.[13]

Ibn Ḥajar states that the ʿUthmānic compilation took place in the year 25 AH.[14] The stimulus for the ʿUthmānic project were the great differences that arose in Qur'ānic reading among the people of Syria and Iraq, which had become contentious to the point of accusations of disbelief. Scholars maintained that the likely reason for these great differences were the memorization of abrogated portions—verses or entire sūrahs—by some individuals unaware of their later abrogation. These included sūrah al-Khalʿ and sūrah al-Ḥafd, which were recited as supplications in the qunūt duʿā' of prayer.[15] Since these were major differences involving entire portions that were recited by some individuals as part of the Qur'ān, and entirely missing from the Qur'ānic copies of others, individuals began to dispute among themselves even to the point of nearly accusing each other of disbelief. For this reason, ʿUthmān resolved to provide a standard transcript for these Qur'ānic copies and to burn others that did not conform to it. He wanted there to remain one standardized

---

[13] Ṣaḥīḥ Bukhārī: Kitāb faḍā'il al-Qur'ān—Bāb jamʿ al-Qur'ān.

[14] The reign of ʿUthmān was from 23/644 — 35/656, so this was relatively early in his Caliphate.

[15] These refer to the qunūt supplication of the Witr prayer which is recited in the Ḥanafī school, with sūrah al-Khalʿ referring to the first half and sūrah al-Ḥafd referring to the second half: *Allāhumma innā nastaʿīnuka wa nastaghfiruka wa nuthnī ʿalayka al-khayra kullahu wa nashkuruka wa lā nakfuruk wa nakhlaʿu wa natruku man yafjuruk / Allāhumma iyyāka naʿbudu wa laka nuṣallī wa nasjudu wa ilayka nasʿā wa naḥfadu narjū raḥmatak wa nakhshā ʿadhābaka, inna ʿadhābaka bi al-kuffāri mulḥiq.* Suyūṭī in al-Durar al-manthūr maintains that these were revealed sūrahs which were later abrogated.

decisive muṣḥaf which was compiled directly from the pages which were written in the Prophet's own lifetime. This ʿUthmānic codex had a number of other key distinctions: it corresponded to the memorization of senior Companions, bore the testimony of multiple Companions, and corresponded to the Final Rehearsal of the Prophet with Jibrīl. Moreover, it was free of abrogated portions and corresponded to the proper Qur'ānic sequence (many pre-ʿUthmānic codices had a different order).

In the end, the ʿUthmān codex was a masterful accomplishment. The first compilation had been motivated by fear of losing the Qur'ān's preservers, while the second compilation was intended to mitigate the differences that were leading to disputes and disunity.

The Number of ʿUthmānic Copies

Imām Mālik stated:

> They compiled the Qur'ānic copies in accord with what they had heard from the recitation of Allah's Messenger ﷺ. It was the practice of the Companions when there were multiple ways of reading a word traced back to the Prophet to write those words with a script that could accommodate these readings. If that were not possible, then they would compile some copies in one reading and some on others.[16]

The exact number of ʿUthmānic codices compiled was subject to scholarly dispute. Some scholars believed there were four, based on the number of delegates in the committee, each of which compiled one codex. Abū ʿAmr al-Dānī states:

> Most scholars are of the view that ʿUthmān compiled four official copies, which he sent to various corners of the Muslim world: one to each of Kūfah, Baṣrah, and Syria, while keeping one for himself in Madīnah, which was referred to as the primary copy (*al-muṣḥaf al-imām*). It is also said that there was a fifth copy which was sent to Makkah. It was also claimed that there were seven in total, one of them being sent to Baḥrayn. However, the first view is more correct and in line with the majority of the ummah.[17]

Others believed there were six in total, with an extra one compiled for Makkah and second one for Madīnah, in addition to the previously mentioned four. ʿUthmān had kept one copy for himself in his home in Madīnah and left one in the Masjid.

Other scholars believed there were seven, including an extra one that was sent to Baḥrayn. Suyūṭī (d. 911/1505)[18] states:

> The number of copies that ʿUthmān sent to various quarters is differed upon but the widespread view is that they were five. And Ibn Abī Dāwūd (d. 316/929)[19] narrates through Ḥamzah al-Zayyāt who said, "Uthmān sent four copies.'

---

[16] Al-Dānī, *al-Muqniʿ*, pg 8-9; *al-Itqān*, vol 1, pg 60.

[17] *Al-Muqniʿ*, pg 10.

[18] Jalāl al-Dīn ʿAbd al-Raḥmān b. Abī Bakr b. Muḥammad al-Khuḍayrī, better known as Imām al-Suyūṭī, was one of the most prolific Muslim scholars and authors who has left no field untouched. He lived from 849 to 911.

[19] ʿAbdullah was the son of Abū Dāwūd of Sijistān author of the famous Sunan work of ḥadīth. He authored a famous work on the readings entitled *Kitāb al-Maṣāḥif*. He died in 316/929. There is some dispute on his status, and his father is reported to have called him a liar when he was young, but this was before his maturing as a scholar of ḥadīth.

> Ibn Abī Dāwūd states: And I have heard Abū Ḥātim of Sijistān say, 'There were five copies, one of each sent to Makkah, Syria, Yemen, Baḥrayn, Baṣrah and Kūfah, and one was kept in Madīnah.'[20]

Perhaps what is correct is that ʿUthmān began by compiling four copies, and then added a fifth, sixth or seventh to cover all regions. It could also be that those who claimed there were four meant so in addition to the one kept by ʿUthmān for himself in Madīnah, while those who counted five included that one.

What is worthy of mention is that ʿUthmān in sending these copies to various quarters was keen on sending along with each a teacher who had memorized the Qur'ān in accordance with the reading of that particular codex. This was done so that the Muslims would receive the Book of God from human beings directly—whether it was by hearing from the person or reciting to him—and not rely on written copies. This is proof for the tradition that the Qur'ān is taken by instruction from a teacher before it is taken from a written copy. Zayd b. Thābit was the teacher of the Madīnan codex, while ʿAbdullah b. Sā'ib was the teacher in Makkah, Mughīrah b. Shihāb in Syria, Abū ʿAbd al-Raḥmān al-Sulamī in Kūfah and ʿĀmir b. ʿAbd al-Qays in Baṣrah.

In the end these codices in each location were used by these teachers to transmit the Qur'ān to their students and have individuals transcribe their own copies from them. This led to the proliferation of these ʿUthmānic codices. The singular term ʿUthmānic codex (muṣḥaf ʿUthmānī) is a general term that encompasses any of the official codices that were compiled at the bequest of ʿUthmān. These ʿUthmānic codices were distinguished by several features:

1. They left out what was abrogated in recitation and not confirmed in the Last Rehearsal.
2. They observed the order of the verses as well as sūrahs, whereas the compilation of Abū Bakr had only preserved the verse order and not that of sūrahs.
3. They were compiled with a script that accommodated the multiple readings and modes that the Qur'ān was revealed in. It was devoid of dots, punctuation, vowel markings and the letter alif.
4. These copies were stripped of any material other than the Qur'ān, as many Companions had included in their personal copies such additional material as explanatory remarks, clarifications, notes on abrogation, and their likes.[21]

It should be noted that the current printings of the Qur'ān in various parts of the Muslim world follow the transmissions of the ʿUthmānic codices in their own locales. For instance, the muṣḥafs that are printed in the Ḥafṣ reading follow the ʿUthmānic

---

[20] Suyūṭī, *al-Itqān,* vol 1, pg 62.
[21] Al-Zarqānī, *Manāhil al-ʿUrfān*, vol 1, pg 260-1.

codex that was sent to Kūfah. The readings of the region of Kūfah such as ʿĀṣim correspond to the Kūfan codex and all copies of the Qur'ān in that region were historically transcribed from that codex. Many of these early copies are still present today. Scholars of orthography have passed on details of the Kūfan codex from those who had seen it.

The Qur'ānic copies printed in Morocco correspond to the reading of Warsh from Nāfiʿ or Qālūn from Nāfiʿ, both of which corresponded to the Madīnan codex. In these you will find the verses written in a way reflecting the Madīnan variants, such as:

فَإِنَّ اللَّهَ الْغَنِيُّ الْحَمِيدُ

rather than

فَإِنَّ اللَّهَ هُوَ الْغَنِيُّ الْحَمِيدُ

﴿*Allah* ***[He]*** *is Self-Sufficient, Immensely Praiseworthy.*﴾ (57:24)

سَارِعُوا إِلَىٰ مَغْفِرَةٍ مِّن رَّبِّكُمْ وَجَنَّةٍ

rather than

وَسَارِعُوا إِلَىٰ مَغْفِرَةٍ مِّن رَّبِّكُمْ وَجَنَّةٍ

﴿***[And]*** *hasten to the forgiveness of your Lord and to a Paradise.*﴾ (3:133)

فَلَا يَخَافُ عُقْبَاهَا

rather than

وَلَا يَخَافُ عُقْبَاهَا

﴿*So he does not fear its outcome.*﴾ (91:15)

The Qur'ānic copies found in Sudan and Somalia correspond to the transmission of Dūrī from Abū ʿAmr, which corresponded to the Baṣran codex which influenced Eastern Africa, Sudan and Somalia.

CHAPTER 3

Abrogation in the Qur'ān

Abrogation of Qur'ān took place in either Qur'ānic words (and hence, its recitation was removed) or in the rulings of verses (while they continued to be recited). Those Qur'ānic verses which were abrogated were not written down in these codices. However, these abrogated verses were still found in some of the personal Qur'ānic copies of some Companions. 'Uthmān was well aware of this and instructed the committee members to specifically exclude all abrogated portions and only write down what was confirmed in the Final Rehearsal. In addition, those verses whose ruling was abrogated but not their recitation were included in these codices.

Abrogation in the Qur'ān took place in three forms: abrogation of a ruling but not the physical verse, abrogation of verses but not their rulings, and abrogation of both verse and ruling.

The first type includes a verse that was recited which is no longer part of the Qur'ān but its ruling persisted: that five sucklings of breastfeeding make marriage unlawful.[22]

خَمسُ رَضَعَاتٍ مَعلُومَاتٍ يُحَرِّمنَ

Five known sucklings deem marriage unlawful.[23]

Another example is found in Ṣaḥīḥ Bukhārī:

> 'Abdullah b. 'Abbās reported that 'Umar b. al-Khaṭṭāb sat on the pulpit of Allah's Messenger ﷺ and said: 'Verily Allah sent Muhammad ﷺ with truth and sent down the Book upon him, and the verse of stoning was included in what was sent down to him. We recited it, retained it in our memory and understood it. Allah's Messenger ﷺ awarded the punishment of stoning to death (to the married adulterer and adulteress) and, after him, we also awarded the punishment of stoning, I am afraid that with time, people will forget and say: 'We do not find the punishment of stoning in the Book of Allah,' and thus go astray by abandoning this duty prescribed by Allah. Stoning is a duty laid down in Allah's Book for married men and women who commit

---

[22] In Islamic jurisprudence, breastfeeding through a wetnurse established family bonds which affected rules of marriage. For instance, a male and female child breastfed by the same wetnurse would become siblings and hence would never be able to marry one another.
[23] For ḥadīth reference see below.

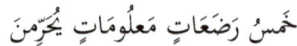

adultery when proof is established, or if there is pregnancy, or a confession.[24]

Here, ʿUmar was clarifying that this verse about stoning was abrogated in recitation but its ruling persisted and was implemented by the Prophet ﷺ even after its abrogation of recitation. The verse was as follows:

وَالشَّيخُ وَالشَّيخَةُ إِذَا زَنَيَا فَارجُمُوهُمَا أَلبَتَّةَ نَكَالًا مِنَ اللهِ وَرَسُولِهِ

The old man or woman who commits zinā, you should stone them absolutely as a punishment prescribed by Allah and His Messenger.

An example of a verse whose words and ruling were both abrogated is a verse that stipulated that ten sucklings deemed marriage unlawful, as revealed in the following ḥadīth:

حَدَّثَنَا يَحْيَى بْنُ يَحْيَى قَالَ: قَرَأْتُ عَلَى مَالِكٍ، عَنْ عَبْدِ اللهِ بْنِ أَبِي بَكْرٍ، عَنْ عَمْرَةَ، عَنْ عَائِشَةَ، أَنَّهَا قَالَتْ : كَانَ فِيمَا أُنْزِلَ مِنَ الْقُرْآنِ عَشْرُ رَضَعَاتٍ مَعْلُومَاتٍ يُحَرِّمْنَ ، ثُمَّ نُسِخْنَ بِخَمْسٍ مَعْلُومَاتٍ، فَتُوُفِّيَ رَسُولُ اللهِ صَلَّى اللهُ عَلَيْهِ وَسَلَّمَ، وَهُنَّ فِيمَا يُقْرَأُ مِنَ الْقُرْآنِ.

ʿĀʾishah reported that it had been revealed in the Qurʾān that ten clear sucklings make marriage unlawful, and then it was abrogated (and substituted) by five sucklings. Then Allah's Messenger ﷺ died and it was before that time recited as the Qurʾān.[25]

Here the original verse was abrogated in wording and ruling and replaced by the second verse whose words were abrogated but its ruling persisted:

عَشرُ رَضَعَاتٍ مَعلُومَاتٍ يُحَرِّمنَ

Ten known sucklings deem marriage unlawful.

خَمسُ رَضَعَاتٍ مَعلُومَاتٍ يُحَرِّمنَ

Five known sucklings deem marriage unlawful.

Examples of the final type of abrogation (ruling but not recitation) include the following verses:

[24] Ṣaḥīḥ Bukhārī: Kitāb al-ḥudūd wa mā yaḥdhar min al-ḥudūd—Bāb rajm al-ḥublā min al-zinā idhā aḥṣanat; Kitāb al-Iʿtiṣām bi al-kitāb wa al-sunnah—Bāb mā dhakara al-nabī wa ḥaḍḍa ʿalā ittifāq ahl al-ʿilm; Ṣaḥīḥ Muslim: Kitāb al-ḥudūd—Bāb rajm al-thayyib fī al-zinā.

[25] Ṣaḥīḥ Muslim: Kitāb al-raḍāʿ—Bāb al-taḥrīm bi khams raḍaʿāt. Muwaṭṭaʾ Mālik: Kitāb al-raḍāʿah—Bāb jāmiʿ mā jāʾa fī al-raḍāʿah.

CHAPTER 3

وَعَلَى الَّذِينَ يُطِيقُونَهُ فِدْيَةٌ طَعَامُ مِسْكِينٍ

﴿*As for those who can fast (but do not), the expiation of this shall be the feeding of one needy person for one fast day.*﴾ (2:184)

According to a large group of Companions, this verse presented a free choice to those were able to fast between fasting or feeding another person. This ruling was lifted but the verse continues to be recited.

Another example is the following verse:

يَا أَيُّهَا النَّبِيُّ حَرِّضِ الْمُؤْمِنِينَ عَلَى الْقِتَالِ ۚ إِن يَكُن مِّنكُمْ عِشْرُونَ صَابِرُونَ يَغْلِبُوا مِائَتَيْنِ ۚ وَإِن يَكُن مِّنكُم مِّائَةٌ يَغْلِبُوا أَلْفًا مِّنَ الَّذِينَ كَفَرُوا بِأَنَّهُمْ قَوْمٌ لَّا يَفْقَهُونَ

﴿*O Prophet! Rouse the believers to fighting. If they be twenty of you who persevere they shall vanquish two hundred; and if there be of you a hundred, they shall vanquish a thousand of those who disbelieve, for they are a people who lack understanding.*﴾ (8:65)

This verse obligated resisting the enemy as large as ten times your own numbers, with no possibility of retreat or surrender, but this ruling was replaced by the next verse which obligated resisting if the enemy numbers were double the Muslim army:

الْآنَ خَفَّفَ اللَّهُ عَنكُمْ وَعَلِمَ أَنَّ فِيكُمْ ضَعْفًا ۚ فَإِن يَكُن مِّنكُم مِّائَةٌ صَابِرَةٌ يَغْلِبُوا مِائَتَيْنِ ۚ وَإِن يَكُن مِّنكُمْ أَلْفٌ يَغْلِبُوا أَلْفَيْنِ بِإِذْنِ اللَّهِ ۗ وَاللَّهُ مَعَ الصَّابِرِينَ

﴿*Allah has now lightened your burden for He found weakness in you. So if there be hundred of you who persevere, they shall vanquish two hundred; and if there be a thousand of you they shall, by the leave of Allah, vanquish two thousand. Allah is with those who persevere.*﴾ (8:66)

Another example is the following verse:

وَإِن تُبْدُوا مَا فِي أَنفُسِكُمْ أَوْ تُخْفُوهُ يُحَاسِبْكُم بِهِ اللَّهُ

﴾*Allah will call you to account for what is in your minds whether you disclose it or hide it.*﴿ (2:284)

This verse vexed the Companions greatly who feared punishment for their inner thoughts. They responded, with words that were quoted in the next verse:

وَقَالُوا سَمِعْنَا وَأَطَعْنَا ۖ غُفْرَانَكَ رَبَّنَا وَإِلَيْكَ الْمَصِيرُ

﴾*We have heard the Message and submitted to it. Our Lord, we look up to You for forgiveness, for to You we shall all return.*﴿ (2:285)

Allah then revealed the following verse, which abrogated the first one:

لَا يُكَلِّفُ اللَّهُ نَفْسًا إِلَّا وُسْعَهَا ۚ لَهَا مَا كَسَبَتْ وَعَلَيْهَا مَا اكْتَسَبَتْ

﴾*Allah does not burden any human being with a responsibility heavier than he can bear. Everyone will enjoy the fruit of the good that one has earned and shall suffer for the evil that one has committed.*﴿ (2:286)[26]

The Prophet clarified this same point by saying: *Allah forgives my followers those (evil deeds) their souls may whisper or suggest to them as long as they do not act (on it) or speak.*[27]

Another example is the following:

كُتِبَ عَلَيْكُمْ إِذَا حَضَرَ أَحَدَكُمُ الْمَوْتُ إِن تَرَكَ خَيْرًا الْوَصِيَّةُ لِلْوَالِدَيْنِ وَالْأَقْرَبِينَ بِالْمَعْرُوفِ ۖ حَقًّا عَلَى الْمُتَّقِينَ

﴾*It has been prescribed for you that when death approaches one of you and he is leaving some property behind him, he should bequeath it equitably for his parents and relatives: it is an obligation on those who fear Allah.*﴿ (2:180)

Though this verse is still recited, the ruling is abrogated and it is not considered permissible to bequeath to an heir such as one's parents or other close relatives.

---

[26] See Tafsīr Ṭabarī, vol 6, pg 101-146.

[27] Ṣaḥīḥ Bukhārī: Kitāb al-ʿitq—Bāb al-khaṭaʾ wa al-nisyān fī al-ʿatāqah wa al-ṭalāq; Kitāb al-aymān wa al-nudhūr—Bāb idhā ḥanitha nāsiyan fī al-aymān; Ṣaḥīḥ Muslim: Kitāb al-īmān—Bāb tajāwaza Allahu ʿan ḥadīth al-nafs wa al-khawāṭir bi al-qalb idh lam tastaqirr.

CHAPTER 3

Skeletal Script of the ʿUthmānic Codices

A unique feature of the ʿUthmānic codices was the use of a bare skeletal script that accommodated a range of variant readings and modes.

For instance, the *maliki/māliki* variants were accommodated by writing the word with three letters: m-l-k, which could be read the way it is written to produce *maliki* or with an additional alif after mīm to produce *māliki.*

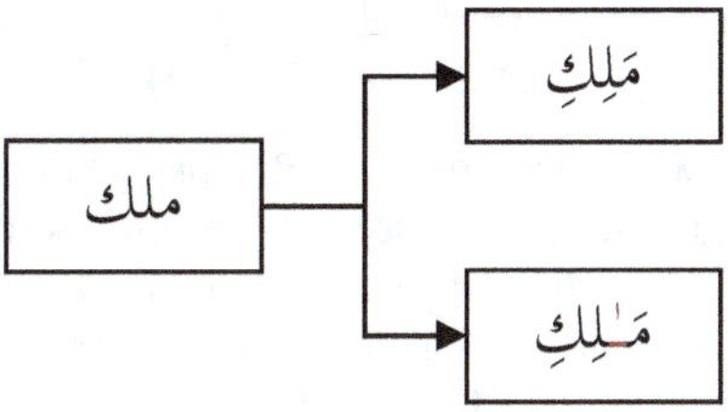

The *Ibrāhīm/Ibrāhām* variants were accommodated by writing the word devoid of vowels with the base letters *alif-b-r-h-m* which could be read both ways by adding an additional alif or yā vowel after hā. However, this only applied to specific verses and not every instance of Ibrāhīm in the Qur'ān. For those instances in which the Prophet only recited the word with yā, it was written with yā in the ʿUthmānic codices:

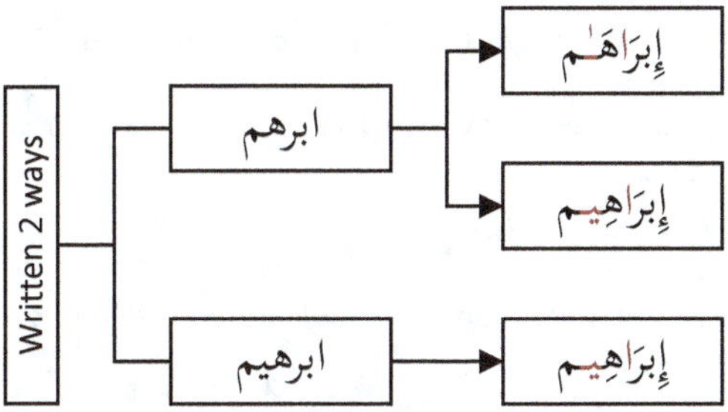

They did the same with the *qul/qāla* variants, writing q-l without alif where it was read both ways, and with alif where it was read only with alif. Sometimes they wrote the same word in different ways across different codices in order to accommodate variant readings.

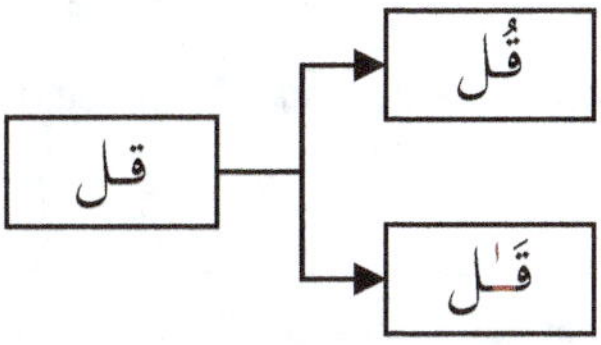

Also, the alif vowels which can also be read with imālah vowels[28] were sometimes written with yā to allow it to be read in both ways:

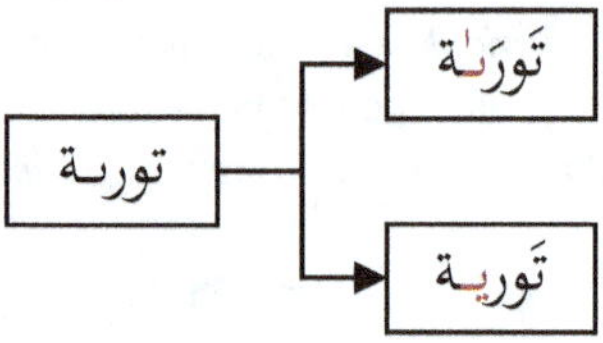

These variant readings were learned by the Companions from the Prophet ﷺ and directed into the orthography of the codices. If they could accommodate the variants within a single orthography, they left it as one script. Occasionally, when a single script was not able to accommodate multiple variants, they placed differing scripts into the additional copies of the ʿUthmānic codices.

As an example, the following two verses with a variant of the letter wāw/ fā could not be accommodated within one script, so one codex was written in each way:

وَلَا يَخَافُ عُقْبَاهَا

﴿*And he does not fear its outcome.*﴾

فَلَا يَخَافُ عُقْبَاهَا

﴿*So he does not fear its outcome.*﴾ (91:15)

Other examples include the following variant verses, each of which was written differently into a codex:

وَسَارِعُوا إِلَىٰ مَغْفِرَةٍ مِّن رَّبِّكُمْ وَجَنَّةٍ

﴿***And** hasten to the forgiveness of your Lord and to a Paradise.*﴾

سَارِعُوا إِلَىٰ مَغْفِرَةٍ مِّن رَّبِّكُمْ وَجَنَّةٍ

﴿*Hasten to the forgiveness of your Lord and to a Paradise.*﴾ (3:133)

وَالَّذِينَ اتَّخَذُوا مَسْجِدًا ضِرَارًا وَكُفْرًا

﴿***And** the ones who took a mosque to cause harm and disbelief. . .*﴾

[28] Imālah is the articulation of alif closer to yā. See footnote 27 on page 14.

الَّذِينَ اتَّخَذُوا مَسْجِدًا ضِرَارًا وَكُفْرًا

﴿*The ones who took a mosque to cause harm and disbelief. . .*﴾
(9:107)

جَنَّاتٍ تَجْرِي مِن تَحْتِهَا الأَنْهَارُ

﴿*Gardens **from** beneath which rivers flow.*﴾

جَنَّاتٍ تَجْرِي تَحْتَهَا الأَنْهَارُ

﴿*Gardens beneath which rivers flow.*﴾ (9:100)

فَإِنَّ اللَّهَ هُوَ الْغَنِيُّ الْحَمِيدُ

﴿*Allah **[He]** is Self-Sufficient, Immensely Praiseworthy.*﴾

فَإِنَّ اللَّهَ الْغَنِيُّ الْحَمِيدُ

﴿*Allah is Self-Sufficient, Immensely Praiseworthy.*﴾ (57:24)

CHAPTER 3

Conformity of the ʿUthmānic Orthography with the Readings

What has preceded has clearly established that it was the Qur'ānic readings that the Companions directed into the codices, for they would compose the script of a codex according to the readings with which the Qur'ān was revealed.

The matter, however, is not as presumed by many Orientalists: that it was the existence of these multiple codices along with the primordial Arabic script they contained which allowed multiple ways of reading due to the absence of punctuation and vowel markings that led to the rise of multiple readings. This assertion was first popularized by the Hungarian Jewish Orientalist Goldziher and later followed by Arthur Jeffery, and even some Muslim researchers such as Dr. ʿAlī ʿAbd al-Wāḥid Wāfī.[29]

The obvious danger of these presumptions is that it equates the Qur'ānic readings with human views and opinions, which would contain the possibility of being correct or mistaken. This ultimately can lead to the notion that the Qur'ān is not the word of God revealed unto His Prophet ﷺ.

It also opens the door for those who wish to invent new readings based upon these codices alone without having any connected chains to the Prophet ﷺ, and the falsehood of that is apparent. We respond to these doubts in a number of ways.

The Companions wrote the word *qāla* (قال) without the alif (قل), for instance, in those places where there were multiple ways of reading that word so that this way of spelling could accommodate these variants.[30] When the readings concurred on articulating the verse in one way, for instance as *qāla,* then they would write it with the alif. There are many such examples which show that the script followed the readings, and not vice versa.

Moreover, there was scholarly consensus that it is not allowed to recite with a reading that might correspond to the rules of Arabic and the ʿUthmānic orthography without having a sound and connected chain back to the Prophet ﷺ. Ibn al-Jazarī states on this matter:

> There is another type of rejected reading: that which corresponds to Arabic as well as orthography but is not historically transmitted in any way at all. The rejection of this type is far more pressing and its danger far graver. The perpetrator of such engages in a major sin. The

[29] He professed these views in his work *Fiqh al-Lughah* and later recanted them in a subsequent edition.

[30] There are two ways of reading this word: *qāla* and *qul.* Writing the word without the alif can accommodate both since alif is a non-essential letter in Arabic writing which can always be added while reading, whereas an added alif in the script is more difficult to ignore or remove.

> allowance for such a practice was first attributed to the grammarian and reciter Abū Bakr Muḥammad b. al-Ḥasan b. Miqsam of Baghdād, which was after 300 AH.[31]

Imām Abū Ṭāhir b. Abū Hāshim states in his book *al-Bayān:* 'A person in our times originated the claim that any reading which corresponds to an aspect of Arabic and the ʿUthmānic codex can be recited in prayer or other rituals. He started an innovation which strayed people from the right path.'[32]

Because of his claim, an assembly was convened for him in Baghdad attended by many Qur'ānic scholars and jurists who were unanimous on the need to refute and discipline him. He subsequently repented and recanted his view. These proceedings were published against him, as mentioned by al-Khaṭīb in his *Tārīkh Baghdād.* As a result, reciting by one's own interpretation not supported by any of the readings in any way was deemed forbidden. The following statement was narrated from ʿUmar b. al-Khaṭṭāb and Zayd b. Thābit from the Companions; and from Ibn al-Munkadir, ʿUrwah b. Zubayr, ʿUmar b. ʿAbd al-ʿAzīz, and ʿĀmir al-Shaʿbī from the Followers: 'Recitation of Qur'ān is a followed practice taken by one generation from the preceding one, so recite according to the way you have been taught.' Because of this, many Imāms of the readings such as Nāfiʿ and Abū ʿAmr used to say, 'Were it not for the fact that I only recite according to what I was taught, I would have recited this verse in this particular way and that verse in that way.'[33]

Abū ʿAmr al-Dānī states in his book *Jāmiʿ al-Bayān* after mentioning the sukūn (unvowelled state) of the words *bāriʾkum* and *yaʾmurkum* in the reading of Abū ʿAmr which was rejected by the grammarian Sībawayh: 'The sukūn is more correct from the perspective of transmission, more widely read, and what I have personally adopted from my learning.' And when he mentioned the texts concerning its transmitters: 'The Imāms of the readings did not adopt any readings according to widespread linguistic usage or by what they deemed more correct Arabic, but they did so only based on stronger precedence and transmission. When a transmission was soundly established, it could not be opposed by stronger Arabic or more widespread linguistic usage because recitation is a practice established by precedence which must necessarily be followed.'[34]

---

[31] *Al-Nashr,* vol 1, pg 17.
[32] Al-Zarqānī, *Manāhil al-ʿUrfān*, vol 1, pg 346.
[33] Al-Dānī, *al-Muqniʿ,* pg 10-1; Suyūṭī, *al-Itqān*, vol 2, pg 167.
[34] *Al-Nashr,* vol 1, pg 21.

CHAPTER 3

Necessity of Following ʿUthmānic Orthography

To reiterate,[35] the three pillars that have been deemed crucial to establishing an authentic Qur'ānic reading are the following:

1. Broad consistency with the Arabic language
2. Broad uniformity with the ʿUthmānic codex in any possible way
3. Sound chain of narration

Scholars stipulated conformity to an ʿUthmānic codex with the qualifier *'in any possible way'* because the mutawātir readings sometimes differ from the ʿUthmānic orthography in the letters wāw, alif, yā, or hā, which were considered to be minor elements like vowel endings (tahskīlāt) and dottings, and not true differences. They do not represent a difference in the form or structure of words. For instance, the word ṣalāh is written with wāw though pronounced with alif (صلوة). This would not be an example of non-conformity. Similarly, adding or dropping vowel letters within words, like *māliki/maliki* or *akun/akūna*, are not considered to be significant and can be read from the same codex.

Scholars have three basic views concerning the necessity of following the ʿUthmānic orthography.

The first view is that the orthography of the ʿUthmānic codices is a textual matter which cannot be differed upon. This was the view of the majority of scholars of past and present. They based their view on the fact that ʿUthmān had based his codices on the codex of Abū Bakr, which was compiled by Zayd from what was written in the lifetime of the Prophet ﷺ in the script written by the designated scribes of revelation. Moreover, it was the ʿUthmānic orthography which preserved the established readings. Imām Aḥmad b. Ḥanbal said, 'It is forbidden to differ from the script of the ʿUthmānic codex in any letter, including the *wāw, yā, alif* or any other.' Imām Mālik was asked concerning writing a copy of the Qur'ān in any new alphabet and replied, 'I don't allow that, but it should be written according to the first writing.' Abū ʿAmr al-Dānī said, 'No scholar differed on this.'[36]

The evidence for this position includes the consensus of Companions as well as that of the entire Muslim nation in all regions. In addition, preserving all the readings is not possible without this script, nor is the knowledge of stopping, such as stopping with the letter *tā* on the words *rahmat* and *imra'at*. Also, words that are written together in a combined manner in these codices are not meant to be separated when stopping on them.

---

[35] This section is supplemented with content from *al-Qamar al-munīr,* pg 79.
[36] *Al-Nashr,* vol 1, pg 16.

Putting a stop to any potential avenues for distorting the Qur'ān is a strong consideration here. Since orthography is based upon technical rules that change from place to place, opening the door to allowing changes in script every time customary usages change would multiply the ways of writing the Qur'ān and lead to confusion and potential mistakes. Had this door been opened, there could exist Qur'ānic copies which are not able to be recited properly because their particular system, or school, of orthography might not be known anymore.

A counterargument can be made that the approval of the Prophet ﷺ and consensus of Companions proves the permissibility, not obligation, of the ʿUthmānic orthography. I would respond that the Qur'ānic script is a matter connected to worship as it is a means to recite the Qur'ān, an obvious act of worship. Here, means carry the same rulings as aims. Based on this, the evidence would indicate obligation in light of the fact that all the benefits mentioned previously could not be realized without the ʿUthmānic script nor can the harms be warded off without it.

The second view is that the ʿUthmānic orthography is a technical matter which is neither obligatory upon the ummah nor forbidden to differ from. This was the view of Ibn Khaldūn (d. 808/1406)[37] and Bāqillānī (d. 403/1013)[38], but is rejected based upon the preceding discussion.

The third view is an intermediary one: that it is allowed to compile the Qur'ān in a script that incorporates the latest orthographic conventions of people in order to make it easier for them to recite the Qur'ān, all while preserving copies containing the ʿUthmānic orthography for reference purposes as needed. This was the view of ʿIzz b. ʿAbd al-Salām (d. 660/1262)[39] and Zarkashī.[40]

The first view is the strongest one in my opinion.

What about the difficulty that the ʿUthmānic orthography potentially posed for people in terms of containing letters which are written and not recited, and vice versa?[41] The simple answer is that there is no language in the world whose writing corresponds exactly to its verbal expression. The ease of recitation or reading comes with learning and practice, not necessarily from changing the way of writing.

---

[37] ʿAbd al-Raḥmān b. Muḥammad b. Khaldūn al-Ḥaḍramī was brilliant North African scholar of Andalusian descent who authored seminal works in numerous disciplines including a multi-volume work on history, the first volume of which is known as the Muqaddimah and remains widely read today as a progenitor of the fields of sociology, anthropology and political science.

[38] Muḥammad b. Ṭayyib Abū Bakr al-Bāqillānī was a famous judge and Ashʿarī theologian who authored a number of works. He died in 403 AH.

[39] ʿIzz al-Dīn ʿAbd al-ʿAzīz v, ʿAbd al-Salām b. al-Qāsim al-Sulamī was a Shāfiʿī scholar of Damascus, later settling in Egypt as its chief qāḍī, known as the 'Sultan of the Scholars' due to his prolific scholarship and numerous written works. He lived from 577 through 660.

[40] *Al-Burhān*, vol 1, pg 379.

[41] It should be noted that this is a historical discussion as all copies of the Qur'ān in modern times are derivatives of the ʿUthmānic orthography and now written with full vowels and markings in accordance with particular readings.

In the end, the Qur'ān should always be written in the same script that was utilized by the Companions. The impermissibility of opposing the 'Uthmānic script, however, is for those who are compiling the entire Qur'ān, not portions of it. If you are quoting the Qur'ān in an article, for instance, through a verse or part of a verse, then there is no problem with using any conventional script. For compiling the entire Qur'ān, then the 'Uthmānic orthography must be used.

Chapter 4: The Influence of Variant Readings on Theology

المصحف العثماني وعلاقته بالقراءات

ʿAqīdah and the Qurʾānic Readings

The theology and creed (ʿaqīdah) of Islam has a firm connection with the Qur'ānic readings. The term *ʿaqīdah* comes from the root *ʿa-q-d* which means to tie or bind something. However, few scholars have ventured to define it in its technical meaning, not even someone like Jurjānī (d. 816/1414)[1] who had a knack for defining terms that had never been defined before him. This could be explained, at least partially, by the fact that the discipline of ʿaqīdah was previously known as the science of the 'foundations of religion' (*uṣūl al-dīn*), theology (*kalām*), or God's oneness (*tawḥīd*). Some scholars even called it *sunnah,* and Abū Ḥanīfah referred to it as the 'greatest understanding' (*al-fiqh al-akbar*).

A latter-day definition was given by ʿAbd al-Raḥmān b. Muḥammad b. Qāsim al-ʿĀṣimī of Najd (d. 1392/1972):[2] '*I'tiqād*[3] means to affirm something in a general sense and is used for the beliefs in matters of religion.'[4] It is also said that it refers to tying the heart with the reports and rulings of the Qur'ān and Sunnah. This employs a linguistic usage of the term and includes affirming the rulings themselves and the belief that they are fully established.

Here, it is important to distinguish the usage of ʿaqīdah for the specific tenets of belief as opposed to referring to the discipline as a whole. As a science, it includes certain branches of other sciences like fiqh, such as the affirmation of the validity of wiping over leather socks in ablution which has found its way into some works of ʿaqīdah. But ʿaqīdah does not include the entirety of rulings that are established from Allah and His Messenger ﷺ, which would be the domain of fiqh. Nor does it include the details of reports that are found throughout the Qur'ān and Sunnah. Some defined it as 'firm belief that leaves no room for doubt.'[5]

Moreover, many of these definitions of ʿaqīdah are circular in nature, by including within the definition certain derivatives of the original term. This, unfortunately, is a common defect of defining things.

Islam's creed is firmly connected with the Qur'ānic readings. One of the great proofs for that is the readiness of some heterodox[6] groups from past to present to reject established Qur'ānic readings. At the same time, some of these groups invented certain readings to correspond with their aberrant views. However, we

---

[1] ʿAlī b. Muḥammad b. ʿAlī al-Jurjānī was a Persian theologian and grammarian who authored about 50 works, including *Taʿrīfāt* ('Definitions').

[2] He was a contemporary Saudi scholar and editor who was responsible for reviving many of Ibn Taymiyyah's works in the modern period.

[3] A related word.

[4] Al-Najdī, *Ḥāshiyah al-Durrah,* pg 17.

[5] Al-ʿAql, *Mujmal uṣūl,* pg 5.

[6] I have translated *bidʿah* (literally 'innovation') as heterodoxy since that conveys a better sense of the term bidʿah, which in essence is to branch out from the mainstream, trodden path.

believe that Allah has guaranteed the preservation of His Book and prepared individuals that could protect it from the distortions of others.

As an example, an early follower of the Muʿtazilī creed once read the verse: ﴿*And Allah spoke to Mūsā*﴾ (4:164) in an alternate way. He read the word for God in the accusative case (i.e. by reading with a fatḥah vowel ending instead of ḍammah) which produced the meaning: *'And Mūsā spoke to Allah.'* Someone responded to him by asking what he would then do for the verse: ﴿*And when Mūsā came at Our appointment and his Lord spoke to him.*﴾ (7:142)? He had no response.[7]

In another incident of this variant, a person of the same affiliation in his reading to his teacher Shuʿbah, the transmitter from ʿĀṣim, read the same verse (4:164) with the word for God with the accusative case ending (fatḥah), to which Shuʿbah objected: 'No one reads this way except a disbeliever, for I read with Aʿmash, who read with Yaḥyā b. Waththāb, who read with Abū ʿAbd al-Raḥmān al-Sulamī, who read with ʿAlī, who read with the Prophet ﷺ, who read the word for God with ḍammah (in the nominative case ending).[8] Similar incidents are recorded from Abū ʿAmr b. al-ʿUlā'. In fact, Jahm b. Ṣafwān even said once about the verse—﴿*The Most Compassionate Lord is settled on the Throne.*﴾ (20:5): 'If I could do so, I would erase the word *'settled'* (*istawā*) and replace it with the word *'overpowered'* (*istawlā*).'

In this chapter, I will explore the influence and impact that the variant readings have exerted upon our understandings in the realm of ʿaqīdah. I am relieved to point out that major creedal differences do not stem from these variant readings and that the creed of the mainstream Muslim body that follows the pious predecessors (ahl al-sunnah wa al-jamāʿah) is basically one and the same. However, these readings can serve to affirm specific valid tenets of belief, clarify them further, and provide additional proofs for them.

---

[7] Al-Ḥakamī, *Maʿārij al-qubūl,* vol 1, pg 357.
[8] Ibn Kathīr, *Tafsīr,* vol 1, pg 601.

Part 1: The Fourteen Readings and Belief in God

Establishing Allah's Beautiful Names and Their Variants

The variant readings have specified and delineated a range of Allah's beautiful names. The great importance of this issue stems from the fact that these names are textual (tawqīfī)[9] in nature with no room for any alteration, even by a single letter. We have observed some individuals so keen to preserve these names that they would reprimand others for pronouncing the name *'Abd al-Bārī,* for instance, by reading it with an ending hamzah: *'Abd al-Bāri',* unaware that both readings of Allah's name are established by the readings. For that reason, I would like to first explore how the fourteen readings differ in the articulation of these names and whether those differences affect the meanings in certain cases.

Al-Bārī

Al-Bārī' means creator or originator from nothingness.[10] It is also said that *khāliq* is the one who wills the existence of something while *bāri'* is the one who brings forth the destined object to existence, making it arise out of non-existence.[11]

Ḥamzah and Hishām read this word by converting the hamzah to yā when stopping on it, while Ibn Muḥayṣin read it with yā in all circumstances, with some differences reported from him **[al-Bārī]**. Dūrī from Kisā'ī read the word with an imālah of the alif after bā **[al-Bayrī]**. All other readings articulate it with a normal alif and an ending hamzah **[al-Bāri']**.[12]

There is no change of meaning with these variants.

Al-Ra'ūf

Al-Ra'ūf means extremely and enormously merciful.[13] Abū 'Amr, Ḥamzah, Kisā'ī, Shu'bah, Ya'qūb, Khalaf, Yazīdī and Muṭṭawi'ī[14] read the word with hamzah vowelled with short-vowel ḍammah after rā **[al-Ra'uf]**. In addition, Ḥamzah upon stopping on the word reads the hamzah with tas-hīl.[15]

---

[9] *Ma'ārij al-qubūl*, vol 1, pg 118; *al-Qawā'id al-muthlā*, pg 34.
[10] Tafsīr al-Jalālayn, pg 734.
[11] *Ma'ārij al-qubūl*, vol 1, pg 132.
[12] *al-Ittiḥāf*, pg 414; *al-Budūr*, pg 318; *al-Qirā'āt al-shādhdha*, pg 87.
[13] *Al-I'tiqād,* vol 2, pg 64.
[14] Abū al-'Abbās Ḥasan b. Sa'īd b. Ja'far was an expert of the qirā'āt from Istakhar, Iran who died in 371.
[15] Tas-hīl is a softening of the normally sharp hamzah sound.

Warsh from Nāfiʿ through path of Azraq reads the word with hamzah vowelled with a long-vowel ḍammah after rā. This long-vowel is potentially read with 2, 4 or 6 vowel durations. **[al-Raʾūf, al-Raʾūūf, al-Raʾūūūf]**

All other readings read the word with hamzah vowelled with a long-vowel ḍammah (of the normal 2 durations) after rā **[al-Raʾūf]**. It is also reported from Ibn Wardān from Abū Jaʿfar that he read the hamzah with tas-hīl.[16]

There is no meaning change with these variants.

Al-Qayyūm

Al-Qayyūm refers to the one who subsists and persists without perishing. Its meaning is based on the notion of perpetuity and everlastingness, which is one of the attributes of essence. It is also said that it means the manager and director of all that occurs in the world. In this meaning, it would be an attribute of action.[17]

Qayyūm denotes self-subsistence for Allah Himself by agreement of Qurʾānic commentators and linguists, which is a matter that is compellingly and necessarily known. But does it also denote His subsistence for others along with His self-subsistence?

The sounder view on this is that it does impart both meanings. It denotes the eternal and complete nature of God's subsistence, due to the form of the verb that denotes exaggerated and superlative meanings. Indeed, the Lord neither perishes nor ceases.[18]

Al-Muṭṭawiʿī in his narration from Aʿmash read the word as *qayyām* with an alif **[al-Qayyām]**, while everyone else reads it with waw **[al-Qayyūm]**.[19]

As for the difference in meaning, Ibn Abī al-ʿIzz[20] comments: The meaning of *qayyūm* is deeper than *qayyām,* since the letter wāw is stronger than alif.[21]

Al-Mutaʿālī

Al-Mutaʿālī highlights the loftiness and highness of Allah in all of its meanings: the highness of His Self, the highness of His affairs, and the highness of His power. Bayhaqī (d. 458/1066),[22] however, defines it in a more limited way: '*Mutaʿālī* means transcendence from the attributes of creation, and this attribute belongs to His

---

[16] *al-Ittiḥāf*, pg 149; *al-Budūr*, pg 141.

[17] *Al-Iʿtiqād,* vol 2, pg 62.

[18] Ibn Abī al-ʿIzz , *Sharḥ al-Ṭaḥāwīyyah,* vol 1, pg 91.

[19] *al-Ittiḥāf*, pg 161.

[20] ʿAlī b. Yūsuf b. Muḥammad b. Abī al-ʿIzz was a Ḥanafī jurist and judge of Damascus who was a student of Ibn Kathīr. He died in Cairo in 737.

[21] *Sharḥ Ṭaḥāwīyyah*, vol 1, pg 91.

[22] Aḥmad b. al-Ḥusayn b. ʿAlī Abū Bakr al-Bayhaqī was a great ḥadīth expert and author.

essence and means His highness above all His creation in power.'[23] 'Abd al-Razzāq al-'Afīfī[24] counters: 'This is actually fleeing from affirming the attribute of highness.'[25]

Ibn Kathīr and Ya'qūb read the word with an ending yā **[Muta'ālī]**. The rest read the word without an ending yā **[Muta'āl]**.[26] Both forms are valid and proper from a linguistic perspective, though the affirmation of yā is more predominant. However, the majority of readers dropped it in conformity with the 'Uthmānic codex.[27] There is no difference of meaning here.

---

[23] *Al-I'tiqād*, vol 2, pg 64.

[24] 'Abd al-Razzāq b. 'Afīfī b. 'Aṭīyyah al-Nūbī al-Shanshūrī was a Mālikī scholar and jurist and one of the ummah's greatest contemporary scholars. He was born in Egypt in 1322 and died in Riyad in 1415. He was one of this author's greatest and closest teachers.

[25] Al-'Afīfī, *Fatāwā wa rasā'il,* vol 1, pg 86.

[26] *al-Ittiḥāf*, pg 270; *al-Budūr*, pg 169.

[27] *Al-Kashf,* vol 2, pg 24.

CHAPTER 4

Establishing Additional Names of Allah

Some of the variant readings establish additional names of Allah not found in others. It is obligatory to believe in all of God's names affirmed in any sound reading.

Al-Ḥāfiẓ

Allah says the following in sūrah Yūsuf:

فَاللَّهُ خَيْرٌ حَافِظًا

﴾*Allah is the* ***Best Protector.***﴿ (12:64)

Ḥafṣ, Ḥamzah, Kisāʾī, Ibn Muḥayṣin (with differences reported from him), and Abū al-Faraj al-Shannabūdhī[28] read it in the above way **[khayrun ḥāfiẓan]**.

Muṭṭawiʿī in his transmission from Aʿmash read this portion of the verse as a possessive (muḍāf) construct **[khayru ḥāfiẓin]**:

فَاللَّهُ خَيْرُ حَافِظٍ

﴾*Allah is the* ***best of Protectors.***﴿

The rest read it in the following way **[khayrun ḥifẓan]**:[29]

فَاللَّهُ خَيْرٌ حِفظًا

﴾*Allah is the* ***best in protection.***﴿

The third reading as a simple verbal noun (*ḥifẓ*: 'protection') is justified by the following context: Yūsuf had refused to provide the food to his brothers, who had not yet recognized him, until they brought their other brother back to Egypt. In the verse in question (12:64), their father objects: ﴾*The father said: 'Shall I trust you with regard to him as I had trusted you earlier with regard to his brother? Allah is the best in protection and is the Most Merciful.'*﴿ In the next verse, the brothers, after finding their goods restored, promised to protect their brother, utilizing the same basic verb:

وَنَحفَظُ أَخَانَا

---

[28] Abū al-Faraj Muḥammad b. Aḥmad b. Ibrāhīm b. Yūsuf, known as Shannabūdhī from his infamous teacher Ibn Shannābūdh, was a prolific scholar of the readings and Qur'ānic tafsīr who was known to have memorized 50,000 verses of poetry to support meanings of the Qur'ān. He lived from 300 to 388.

[29] *al-Ittiḥāf*, pg 266.

﴾*We will **protect** our brother.*﴿ (12:65).

The other two readings of the word (*ḥāfīẓ*) as an active participle (ism fā'il) is justified by (12:12), where the brothers promised to protect Yūsuf using the same active participle form:

وَإِنَّا لَهُ لَحَافِظُونَ

﴾*We are **protectors** over him.*﴿ (12:12).

In addition, the codex of Ibn Mas'ūd had the variant **[khayr al-ḥāfiẓīn]**:[30]

فَاللَّهُ خَيرُ الحَافِظِينَ

﴾*Allah is the **best of the protectors.***﴿

Two of the three variants establish Allah's name *al-Ḥāfīẓ*, which is further supported by another verse:

وَكُنَّا لَهُم حَافِظِينَ

﴾*And it was We Who **guarded** them.*﴿ (21:82).

Another related name of Allah is also supported in the Qur'ān **[*al-Ḥafīẓ*]** by the following verse:

إِنَّ رَبِّي عَلَىٰ كُلِّ شَيءٍ حَفِيظٌ

﴾*Surely, my Lord is a **Guardian** over all things.*﴿ (11:57).

Bayhaqī comments: '*Al-Ḥāfiẓ* means He is a protector over all things and all persons whom He wills to protect. It is also said that it means that He never forgets what He knows, so its meaning is in the sense of knowledge.'[31]

Al-Muṣawwir

Al-Muṣawwir is the one who brings forth His creation in various forms,[32] and this name is established by the following verse **[al-Muṣawwir]**:

هُوَ اللَّهُ الخَالِقُ البَارِئُ المُصَوِّرُ

﴾*He is Allah, the Creator, the Originator, the **Shaper.***﴿ (59:24)

---

[30] *Al-Kashf,* vol 2, pg 13.
[31] *al-I'tiqād,* vol 2, pg 59.
[32] *al-I'tiqād,* vol 2, pg 56; *Ma'ārij al-qubūl,* vol 1, pg 132.

This is the uniform readings of all reciters except for Ḥasan al-Baṣrī, who read the word in the passive tense as an object (*al-muṣawwara*) in the following way **[al-Muṣawwar]**:

هُوَ اللَّهُ الخَالِقُ البَارِئُ المُصَوَّرَ

﴾*He is Allah, the Creator,* ***the Originator of all Designed Things.***﴿

In this form, it would mean that Allah is the originator and inventor of all things that He fashions and assembles in their various forms and structures. The word is referring to all fashioned creation as a single group, as if to say that God is the creator of all fashioned things.

In this passive participle reading, al-Samīn al-Ḥalabī[33] cautions: 'It is forbidden to stop at this word but rather, it must be read in continuity with the next verse so that the ending vowel (of fatḥah) would become apparent lest a misunderstanding (in meaning) arise.'[34] However, it can be countered that Ibn Muḥayṣin read the word as an active participle in the accusative case (*al-Muṣawwira*) as well as the word before it **[*al-Bārīya al-Muṣawwira*]**:[35]

هُوَ اللَّهُ الخَالِقُ البَارِيَ المُصَوِّرَ

﴾*He is Allah, the Creator, who is* ***the Real Originator of all Designed Things!***﴿

As for the meaning of that, the use of naṣb (accusative case) here (which sets this adjective apart from the rest which are the nominative case) highlights the praise of that attribute more emphatically than the rest.

This potential misunderstanding alluded to by al-Samīn in the passive participle reading of Ḥasan (al-muṣawwar) could be one of two things: that someone else fashioned Allah—and exalted He is above that—or that Allah has a form like the forms of creation.

---

[33] Aḥmad b. Yūsuf b. Muḥammad of Aleppo, better known as al-Samīn, was a grammarian and Qur'ānic commentator who died in 756.

[34] Since the ending fatḥah vowel is the only thing that indicates that the word is an object ('Inventor *of fashioned things*'), and without it, one might understand the passive word 'fashioned' to refer to Allah himself. See *al-Ittiḥāf,* pg 414; *al-Qirā'āt al-shādhdhah,* pg 87.

[35] *al-Ittiḥāf,* pg 414.

Al-Razzāq

Al-Razzāq is the one who is responsible for establishing the sustenance of a person and enabling him to benefit from that.[36] Razzāq is the exaggerated form of the basic word *rāziq*, which simply means 'provider.' *Al-Razzāq* appears in the following verse **[al-Razzāq]**:

إِنَّ اللَّهَ هُوَ الرَّزَّاقُ ذُو الْقُوَّةِ الْمَتِينُ

﴿*Indeed, it is Allah who is* ***the [continual] Provider****, the Possessor of strength, the All-Firm.*﴾ (51:58)

Ibn Muḥayṣin, in some of his transmissions, reads the name as the basic-form participle **[al-Rāziq]**:

إِنَّ اللَّهَ هُوَ الرَّازِقُ ذُو الْقُوَّةِ الْمَتِينُ

Indeed, it is Allah who is ***the Provider****, the Possessor of strength, the All-Firm.*

In addition, Ibn Muḥayṣin, in some of his transmissions, reads this same word *al-Rāziq* into the following verse **[rāziqkum]**:

وَفِي السَّمَاءِ رَازِقُكُمْ وَمَا تُوعَدُونَ

And in the heaven is ***your Provider*** *and whatever you are promised.* (51:22)

This reading of this verse supports the highness of Allah, which will be discussed later. The normative reading of this verse in the other readings is as follows **[rizqakum]**:[37]

وَفِي السَّمَاءِ رِزْقُكُمْ وَمَا تُوعَدُونَ

﴿*And in the heaven is* ***your provision*** *and whatever you are promised.*﴾ (51:22)

---

[36] *al-I'tiqād,* vol 2, pg 58.

[37] *al-Ittiḥāf,* pg 399, 499; *al-Qirā'āt al-shādhdhah,* pg 84.

CHAPTER 4

Al-Matīn

Al-Matīn refers to extreme strength which does not diminish or become affected by fatigue.[38] This name appears in the following verse **[al-Matīnu]**:

إِنَّ اللَّهَ هُوَ الرَّزَّاقُ ذُو الْقُوَّةِ الْمَتِينُ

﴾*Indeed, it is Allah who is the Continual Provider, the Possessor of strength,* ***the All-Firm.***﴿ (51:58)

Aʿmash reads the word in the genitive case **[al-Matīni]** as an adjective of strength, meaning 'possessor of firm strength':

إِنَّ اللَّهَ هُوَ الرَّزَّاقُ ذُو الْقُوَّةِ الْمَتِينِ

Indeed, it is Allah who is the Continual Provider, the Possessor of ***firm*** *strength.*

The adjective remains in the masculine form even though the noun ('strength') is feminine and various explanations have been given for that. One is that even though the noun is feminine, it is not an actual one. It was also held that strength carries the meaning of 'hands' or 'power' which are actually masculine words. It was also said that the noun is a verbal noun which can accept both genders.

In any case, the reading of Aʿmash ostensibly fails to support *al-Matīn* as a proper name for Allah. However, the word, though it ends with the kasrah vowel, can still be considered to be in the nominative case with an approximated and understood ḍammah-ending that was prevented from manifesting due to the neighboring word. With this possibility, the name is still affirmed in the reading of Aʿmash.[39] All other readings, however, explicitly support the name.

---

[38] *Al-Iʿtiqād,* vol 2, pg 58.
[39] *Al-Ittiḥāf,* pg 399.

Al-Khallāq

Al-Khallāq is the exaggerated form of the simple active participle *al-Khāliq* ('Creator') and this name appears in the following verse **[al-Khallāq]**:

وَهُوَ الخَلَّاقُ العَلِيمُ

﴾*He is the* ***All-Creating****, All-Knowing.*﴿ (36:81)

This is the reading of all readers except for Ḥasan al-Baṣrī, who read the name as the simple active participle **[al-Khāliq]**:[40]

وَهُوَ الخَالِقُ العَلِيمُ

He is the ***Creator****, All-Knowing*

Both variants establish Allah's names, all of which are true.

Dhū al-Jalāl wa al-Ikrām

Dhū al-Jalāl wa al-Ikrām is the one who is truly majestic and full of splendor without dispute. In that, it is an intrinsic attribute. The meaning of *ikrām* can also be to honor those who deserve it in this world by remembering them and in the next life with His Paradise. In this, it would be an attribute of action.[41] The name appears in the following two verses of the same sūrah **[Dhū al-lalāl wa al-ikrām]**:

وَيَبْقَىٰ وَجهُ رَبِّكَ ذُو الجَلَالِ وَالإِكرَامِ

﴾*Only the* ***Face*** *of your Lord,* ***which is full of majesty and splendor,*** *will endure.*﴿ (55:27)

In this verse, all reciters read the word *dhū* (meaning 'person of . . .'; 'the one full of . . .') in the nominative case (with a wāw letter: *dhū*) as an adjective for *wajh* ('Face'), except for Ibn Mas'ūd who read the word in the genitive case (with a yā: *dhī*) as an adjective for *rabbik* ('your Lord' **[Dhī al-lalāl wa al-ikrām]**:

وَيَبْقَىٰ وَجهُ رَبِّكَ ذِي الجَلَالِ وَالإِكرَامِ

Only the Face of your ***Lord, who is full of majesty and splendor****, will endure.*

[40] *Al-Qirā'āt al-shādhdhah,* pg 76.
[41] *Al-I'tiqād,* vol 2, pg 65.

In the first reading, the Face of the Lord is being described as being full of majesty and splendor. In the second reading, the Lord is being described as such.

The second verse where this word appears is the following:

تَبَارَكَ اسمُ رَبِّكَ ذِي الجَلَالِ وَالإِكرَامِ

﴿*Blessed be the name of your* ***Lord, who is full of Majesty and Splendor.***﴾ (55:78)

In this verse, all readers read the word in the genitive case (with a yā: *dhī*) as an adjective for *rabbik* ('your Lord'), while Ibn ʿĀmir read the word *dhū* in the nominative case (with a wāw letter: *dhū*) as an adjective for *ismu rabbik* ('the name of your Lord'):

تَبَارَكَ اسمُ رَبِّكَ ذِي الجَلَالِ وَالإِكرَامِ

﴿*Blessed be the* ***name*** *of your Lord,* ***which is full of Majesty and Splendor.***﴾ (55:78)

The Syrian ʿUthmānic codex was written with wāw.[42]

In all readings, this expression can be counted as a Divine Name whereas in the reading of Ibn ʿĀmir it is even more explicit (since the expression is an adjective to the 'name' of the Lord). Makkī b. Abī Ṭālib comments: 'Whoever makes it an adjective to the word *ism* intends by it to refer to the Lord, so the two cases go back the same meaning.'[43]

---

[42] *Al-Ittiḥāf,* pg 407.

[43] *Al-Kashf,* vol 2, pg 303.

Al-Ilāh

The variant readings read the following verse, which appears twice, in various ways:

قُلْنَ حَاشَ لِلَّهِ

﴿***Allah*** *save us!*﴾ (12:31, 12:51)

Azmīrī states: Ḥasan al-Baṣrī read this verse by substituting the word 'god' for Allah:[44]

قُلْنَ حَاشَ الإِلَهُ

May the ***God*** *save us!*

This reading establishes *al-Ilāh* a one of God's names. In meaning, it refers to one who is an object of worship and obedience, the one towards whom hearts turn in love, reverence, humility, fear, and other aspects of worship.

This name also appears in the Prophetic sunnah during the incident of the martyrdom of the Companion Khubayb, who prayed two rakʿahs before his execution and recited some verses which included the line:

وَذَلِكَ فِي ذَاتِ الإِلَهِ

And that is all for the sake of ***God***[45]

There are a number of examples of various weaker opinions about readings of particular Qur'ānic words being names of God. They include the following:

---

[44] Al-Azmīrī, *Nūr al-iʿlām bi infirādāt al-arbaʿat al-aʿlām,* pg 13.

[45] Ṣaḥīḥ Bukhārī: Kitāb al-jihād wa al-sayr—Bāb hal yasta'sir al-rajul wa man lam yasta'sir; Kitāb al-Maghāzī—Bāb ḥaddathanī ʿAbdullah b. Muḥammad al-Juʿfī; Kitāb al-Maghāzī—Bāb ghazwat al-Rajīʿ wa Riʿlin wa Dhakwān wa Bi'r Maʿūnah; Kitāb al-Tawḥīd—Bāb mā yudhkaru fī al-dhāt wa al-nuʿūt wa asāmī Allāh.

CHAPTER 4

Al-Qudus

The expression 'Holy Spirit' (*rūḥ al-qudus*) refers to the angel Jibrīl and the word *al-qudus* ('holy') is simply an adjective for 'spirit' according to most readers. It appears in the following verses **[al-Qudus]**:

بِرُوحِ الْقُدُسِ

﴿*With the **holy spirit***﴾ (2:87, 2:253, 5:110)

رُوحُ الْقُدُسِ

﴿*The **holy spirit***﴾ (16:102)

On the other hands, it is reported from Mujāhid, Ḥasan al-Baṣrī, and al-Rabīʿ b. Anas that the word is one of Allah's names.[46] This can be supported by the above reading or the variant with an unvowelled dāl by Ibn Kathīr and Ibn Muḥayṣin **[al-Quds]**:

بِرُوحِ الْقُدْسِ

﴿*With the spirit **of the Holy One***﴾ (2:87, 2:253, 5:110)

رُوحُ الْقُدْسِ

﴿*The spirit **of the Holy One***﴾ (16:102)

The Disjointed Letters

It is reported from Ibn ʿAbbās, Suddī,[47] Sālim b. ʿAbdullah, and Shaʿbī that the disjointed letters that begin some chapters of the Qur'ān are actually the names of Allah.[48]

There are many more examples from the variant readings of words that were considered names of Allah by some but I have left these for the sake of brevity.[49]

---

[46] Tafsīr Ibn Kathīr, vol 1, pg 173.
[47] Abū Muḥammad Ismāʿīl b. ʿAbd al-Raḥmān b. Abī Karīmah was a great authority and scholar of tafsīr from Arabia who settled in Kūfah. He was a student of Anas and Ibn ʿAbbās, and teacher of Shuʿbah and Sufyān al-al-Thawrī. He died in 127 AH.
[48] Tafsīr Ibn Kathīr, vol 1, pg 62.
[49] For more of these examples, refer to *Al-Ittiḥāf*, pg 59, 90, 125, 303.

Establishing Allah's Attributes of Action

Some of the attributes of Allah are related to His Being, His Essence, and His Self (Dhāt). These include Allah's attributes of Life and Knowledge. These are not dependent upon His willing them, and so it would not be correct to say that He has life so long as He wills it or knowledge of something so long as He wills so. Allah never ceases to be Ever-Living or All-Knowledgeable at all times.

Other attributes are linked to His will, including His ascension over the Throne, His descent to the lower part of the heavens, and His anger. These are linked to His actions, and He performs them at specific times. Allah says about His ascension:

خَلَقَ السَّمَاوَاتِ وَالأَرضَ فِي سِتَّةِ أَيَّامٍ ثُمَّ استَوَىٰ عَلَى العَرشِ

﴿*He created the heavens and the earth in six days, and then ascended His Throne.*﴾ (7:54)

The Prophet ﷺ states in a report: 'Today my Lord has become angry in a way that He never did so before and will never do so again.'[50]

Ibn Taymiyyah writes: 'Allah's becoming close to some of His servants, His coming on the Day of Judgment, and His ascending over the Throne, are all affirmed by those who acknowledge Allah's actions of choice for Himself. This is the way of the leaders among the predecessors, the most famous scholars of Islam and the people of ḥadīth and transmission who related them through mass-transmission.'[51]

Both types of attributes—those relating to His essence and those relating to His actions—can only be established textually through the Qur'ān or Sunnah. On this, Imām Aḥmad stated: 'Do not describe Allah except through how He was described by Himself or by the Prophet ﷺ and never exceed the Qur'ān and ḥadīth.'[52]

These attributes appear in the texts either as verbal nouns ('power'; 'might') or as active verbs ('created the heavens'; 'ascended the throne'). They are also established through the meanings of His names. For instance, the name *al-Samī'* (the All-Hearing') establishes the attribute of His Hearing. Many attributes are established through more than one way or even through all of them. This should make clear the obvious importance of the variant readings on this issue since these readings serve as evidence for Allah's attributes and actions. Just as Allah possesses many names—some of which He has used Himself, some of which He has taught to some of His creation, some revealed through His Book, and others He has kept hidden in the

---

[50] Ṣaḥīḥ Bukhārī: Kitāb aḥādīth al-anbiyā'—Bāb qawl Allah innā arsalnā Nūḥan ilā qawmihī; Kitāb tafsīr al-Qur'ān—Sūrah Banī Isrā'īl—Bāb dhurriyata man ḥamalnā ma'a Nūḥ.
[51] *Majmū' al-fatāwā*, vol 5, pg 466.
[52] Al-'Uthaymīn, *Al-Qawā'id al-muhtlā*, pg 68.

knowledge of the unseen—this also applies to His attributes, because every name contains one or more attribute.

The way of the predecessors is to affirm that both Allah and His creation possess actions. Those actions of people which are ascribed to Allah in the texts are so ascribed in the sense that Allah is the ultimate creator of those actions not that He has done them Himself.

Some theological schools, on the other hand, hold the position that all actions belong to God and not to human beings, for Allah is the sole Doer and Originator of all actions. The actions of human beings are ascribed to God in the sense that He (God) carries them out. The ascription of actions to human beings is only in the sense that they *acquire* those actions. As for the difference between actions *done* by human beings (which they deny) and actions *acquired* by them (which they affirm), then that is a problematic issue about which they have differed so greatly that one of their experts stated that the notion of acquiring (kasb) has no reality to it. Abū Isḥāq al-Shāṭibī (d. 790/1388)[53] writes: 'Causes and means are not real effectors but the effect arises next to them, not through them. When the subject acts, Allah is the creator of the cause while the subject merely acquires the action.'[54]

Ibn Taymiyyah clarified the approach of the predecessors on this matter: 'The majority of the people of Sunnah everywhere, who affirm the doctrine of predestination, state that human subjects act in real ways, with actual power and ability. They do not deny the existence of natural means and causes but affirm them fully as they are proven by the Sharīʿah and the intellect. Indeed, Allah gives rise to clouds through wind, sends down rain through clouds, and gives rise to vegetation from water. They do not deny the effect or power of the natural powers and elements found in creation but affirm that they have real effects.'[55]

---

[53] Abū Isḥāq Ibrāhīm b. Mūsā b. Muḥammad al-Lakhmī was a great Andalusian jurist, ḥadīth scholar and linguist who authored a number of widely read works such as *al-Iʿtiṣām* on religious innovations and *al-Muwāfaqāt* on legal theory.

[54] Shāṭibī, *al-Muwāfaqāt,* vol 1, pg 314.

[55] *Minhāj al-sunnah,* vol 3, pg 12.

Allah's Promising (Wa'd/Muwā'adah)

From Allah's actions are that He promised Mūsā and the Israelites, as many verses attested to:

وَإِذْ وَاعَدْنَا مُوسَىٰ أَرْبَعِينَ لَيْلَةً

﴿*And recall when We* ***made an appointment with*** *Mūsā for forty nights.*﴾ (2:51)

وَوَاعَدْنَا مُوسَىٰ ثَلَاثِينَ لَيْلَةً

﴿*And We* ***made an appointment with*** *Mūsā for thirty nights.*﴾ (7:142)

يَا بَنِي إِسْرَائِيلَ قَدْ أَنجَيْنَاكُم مِّنْ عَدُوِّكُمْ وَوَاعَدْنَاكُمْ جَانِبَ الطُّورِ الْأَيْمَنَ

﴿*Children of Israel! We saved you from your enemy and* ***made a covenant with you*** *on the right side of the Mount.*﴾ (20:80)

All reciters read the word as a derived-form verb **[*wā'adnā*]** except for Abū 'Amr, Abū Ja'far, Ya'qūb, Yazīdī and Ibn Muḥayṣin, who read the verb as a simple primary form verb **[wa'adnā]**:

وَإِذْ وَعَدْنَا مُوسَىٰ أَرْبَعِينَ لَيْلَةً

﴿*And recall when We* ***appointed*** *for Mūsā forty nights.*﴾ (2:51)

The primary form verb carries the single-action meaning 'to promise' or 'appoint' whereas the derivative verb usually carries a reflexive meaning (i.e. action coming from both parties), here meaning 'make an appointment with.' Baghawī (d. 516/1122)[56] comments:

> The word *wā'adnā* is the reflexive derived form but it denotes an action coming from one side, as in the expression *'āfākallāhu* ('May God cure you'). Zajjāj[57] states: In this expression, the command was from God while the acceptance was from Mūsā, and hence, the reflexive form. The reciters of Baṣrah, however, read the word in the simple primary form, meaning simply 'to promise.'[58]

---

[56] Abū Muḥammad Ḥusayn b. Maḥmūd al-Baghawī was a great Persian-origin ḥadīth scholar, Shāfi'ī jurist and author of a noted Qur'ānic commentary entitled *Ma'ālim al-tanzīl* among many other works.
[57] Abū Isḥāq Ibrāhīm b. Muḥammad b. al-Sarīyy al-Zajjāj was a famous linguist of Baghdad who authored a book on the meanings of the Qur'ān. He died in 311/923.
[58] Baghawī, *Ma'ālim al-tanzīl*, vol 1, pg 93.

CHAPTER 4

Allah's Causing to Forget or Postpone (Nasa'/Insā')

From Allah's actions are that He causes to forget, as the following verse attests **[nunsihā]**:

مَا نَنسَخ مِن آيَةٍ أَو نُنسِهَا نَأتِ بِخَيرٍ مِّنهَا أَو مِثلِهَا

﴿*We do not abrogate a verse nor **cause it to be forgotten** except that We bring forth [one] better than it or similar to it.*﴾ (2:106)

Ibn Kathīr, Abū ʿAmr, Ibn Muḥayṣin and Yazīdī read this word in a different form **[nansaʾhā]** derived from the root *nasaʾa* ('to postpone, defer, or delay'):

مَا نَنسَخ مِن آيَةٍ أَو نَنسَأهَا نَأتِ بِخَيرٍ مِّنهَا أَو مِثلِهَا

﴿*We do not write/reveal a verse nor **defer it** except that We bring forth [one] better than it or similar to it.*﴾

This means to defer its writing (another meaning of *naskh*), referring to revelation here. In other words, we erase its words and its rulings.

Ḥasan al-Baṣrī read this word from the root word *nasiya* ('to forget') in the second person addressed to the Prophet ﷺ **[tansaʾhā]**:

مَا نَنسَخ مِن آيَةٍ أَو تَنسَأهَا نَأتِ بِخَيرٍ مِّنهَا أَو مِثلِهَا

*We do not abrogate a verse nor **is there one that you forget** except that We bring forth [one] better than it or similar to it.*

The reading of Ḥasan al-Baṣrī attributes the act of forgetting to the Prophet whereas the rest attribute the causing of the act of forgetting to Allah.[59] More details will come on this matter in the discussion on the Prophet's infallibility. Baghawī comments:

> The term *nunsihā* means to command the leaving of something and involves replacing the original with something new in its place. The term *nansaʾhā* involves the same abrogation without putting something else in its place.
>
> Ibn Kathīr and Abū ʿAmr read the word as *nansaʾhā* which means to defer the verse without replacing it. It is similar to the expression *ansaʾallāhu ajalakum* ('God prolong your life.'). There are two views as to its meaning in the verse.

---

[59] *al-Ittiḥāf*, pg 145; *al-Qirāʿāt al-shādhdhah*, pg 32.

The first opinion is that it means that Allah removes its recitation and continues its ruling, as was the case in the verses of stoning [as a punishment for adultery]. In this view, the meaning of abrogation (*naskh*) in the verse would be to lift both the recitation as well as its ruling, whereas the meaning of deferring (*insā'*) would be to lift its recitation but not its ruling.

The second opinion is that of Sa'īd b. al-Musayyab and 'Aṭā', that *naskh* in the verse means to write (from *nuskhah:* 'copy'), i.e. what was revealed in the Qur'ān, whereas the meaning of deferring (*insā'*) is to defer its revelation, i.e. to leave the verses in the Preserved Tablets[60] and not reveal them.[61]

Allah's Ability (Istiṭā'ah)

From Allah's actions is His ability as attested to by the majority reading of the following verse **[yastaṭī'u]**:

هَل يَستَطِيعُ رَبُّكَ أَن يُنَزِّلَ عَلَينَا مَائِدَةً مِّنَ السَّمَاءِ

﴿*Can* ***your Lord send down*** *to us a table [spread with food] from the heaven?*﴾ (5:112)

In this verse, only Kisā'ī reads the word in the second person **[tastaṭī'u]**:[62]

هَل تَستَطِيعُ رَبَّكَ أَن يُنَزِّلَ عَلَينَا مَائِدَةً مِّنَ السَّمَاءِ

﴿*Can* ***you [ask] your Lord*** *to send down to us a table [spread with food] from the heaven?*﴾

In the majority reading **[yastaṭī'u]**, the meaning would be: 'Can your Lord do so or fulfill your request?' In Kisā'ī's reading **[tastaṭī'u]**, the meaning would be: 'Can you, 'Īsā, ask your Lord?' In this latter reading, the ability is that of 'Īsā. Baghawī comments on this:

> Kisā'ī's reading is also that of 'Alī, 'Ā'ishah, Ibn 'Abbās and Mujāhid, and means: 'Are you able to supplicate and ask your Lord?' In the other reading, the questioners did not doubt Allah's ability, but asked: 'Will your Lord send the table down or not?' It is similar to a man

---

[60] The Preserved Tablets (*al-lawḥ al-maḥfūẓ*) are the repository of God's revelation, commands and decree which is in the highest heavens guarded by angels and from which Allah reveals His specific revelation and Divine decrees to the earth at various times.

[61] *Ma'ālim al-tanzīl*, vol 1, pg 133.

[62] *al-Ittiḥāf,* pg 204; *al-Nashr,* vol 2, pg 256.

saying to another: 'Can you help me get up?' That man is not doubting the other person's ability to do so, but is simply requesting his help. It is like saying, 'Will you do so or not?'

It is also claimed that the word carries the meaning of obeying or following, meaning: 'Will your Lord listen to you?'

Others followed the overt meaning and believed that those people as human beings had fallen into doubts [about God's ability and power to do so] before the matter was clarified to them, to which 'Īsā responded in the same verse, 'Fear Allah if you are believers' (i.e. do not doubt his ability).[63]

Allah's Raising Up and Reviving of Bones

From Allah's attributes is His raising up and reviving bones based upon the following verse:

وَانظُرْ إِلَى العِظَامِ كَيفَ نُنشِزُهَا ثُمَّ نَكسُوهَا لَحمًا

﴾*And look at the bones [of this donkey] - how We **raise them** and then We cover them with flesh.*﴿ (2:259)

The above reading with the letter zā **[nunshizuhā]** is that of Ibn 'Āmir, 'Āṣim, Kisā'ī, Khalaf and A'mash, whereas the one with the letter rā **[nunshiruhā]** is that of the rest:

وَانظُرْ إِلَى العِظَامِ كَيفَ نُنشِرُهَا ثُمَّ نَكسُوهَا لَحمًا

﴾*And look at the bones [of this donkey] - how We **resurrect** them and then cover them with flesh.*﴿

Ḥasan read the word with another change: *nanshuruhā,* as a simple primary verb **[nanshuruhā]**:[64]

وَانظُرْ إِلَى العِظَامِ كَيفَ نَنشُرُهَا ثُمَّ نَكسُوهَا لَحمًا

*And look at the bones [of this donkey] - how We **scatter** them and then We cover them with flesh.*

Baghawī states: 'The reciters of Ḥijāz and Baṣrah read the verb as *nunshiruhā,* which means to revive or bring back to life. Allah says, using the same verb: ﴾*And then, if it be His will, He shall raise him again to life*﴿ (80:22). The other reciters read the verb

[63] *Ma'ālim al-tanzīl*, vol 3, pg 117.
[64] *al-Ittiḥāf,* pg 162.

as *nunshizuhā,* which means to raise them up from the ground, return them to their position in the body and reassemble them. The word *inshāz* means to stand up something or disturb it.'[65]

Allah's Relating and Decreeing (Qaṣaṣ/Qaḍā')

The following verse has two readings. Abū Ja'far, Nāfi', Ibn Kathīr, and 'Āṣim read the following verse with a verb form related to *qaṣaṣ* ('story, account') **[yaquṣu]**:

$$قُل إِنِّي عَلَىٰ بَيِّنَةٍ مِّن رَّبِّي وَكَذَّبْتُم بِهِ ۚ مَا عِندِي مَا تَسْتَعْجِلُونَ بِهِ ۚ إِنِ الْحُكْمُ إِلَّا لِلَّهِ ۖ يَقُصُّ الْحَقَّ ۖ وَهُوَ خَيْرُ الْفَاصِلِينَ$$

❴*Say: I take stand upon a clear evidence from my Lord and it is that which you have given the lie to. That which you desire to be hastened is not within my power. Judgement lies with Allah alone. He **declares** the Truth, and He is the best of judges.*❵ (6:57)

The rest of the readers along with Ḥasan, A'mash and Yazīdī read the following variant, utilizing a verb related to the word *qaḍā'* ('decree') **[yaqḍī]**:[66]

$$يَقْضِ الْحَقَّ$$

❴*He **decrees** the Truth, and He is the best of judges.*❵

This latter reading is supported contextually by the rest of the verse '*And He is the best of judges.*' The former reading is supported by many other verses that affirm Allah's relating of information, including:

$$نَحْنُ نَقُصُّ عَلَيْكَ أَحْسَنَ الْقَصَصِ بِمَا أَوْحَيْنَا إِلَيْكَ هَٰذَا الْقُرْآنَ وَإِن كُنتَ مِن قَبْلِهِ لَمِنَ الْغَافِلِينَ$$

❴ *We **narrate** to you in the best manner the **stories** of the past although before this narration you were utterly unaware of them.*❵ (12:3)

---

[65] *Ma'ālim al-tanzīl,* vol 1, pg 316.
[66] *al-Ittiḥāf,* pg 209; *al-Nashr,* vol 2, pg 258.

CHAPTER 4

Allah's Commanding (Amr)

The following verse has two readings:

وَإِذَا أَرَدنَا أَن نُّهلِكَ قَريَةً **أَمَرنَا** مُترَفِيهَا فَفَسَقُوا فِيهَا فَحَقَّ عَلَيهَا القَولُ

فَدَمَّرنَاهَا تَدمِيرًا

> ﴿*When We decide to destroy a town, We* ***command*** *the affluent among them, whereupon they commit sins in it, then the decree (of chastisement) becomes due against them and thereafter We destroy that town utterly.*﴾ (17:16)

All readers follow this reading as a simple verb **[amarnā]** except for Yaʿqūb and Ḥasan who read the verb with an initial long vowel **[āmarnā]**:[67]

وَإِذَا أَرَدنَا أَن نُّهلِكَ قَريَةً **آمَرنَا** مُترَفِيهَا فَفَسَقُوا فِيهَا فَحَقَّ عَلَيهَا القَولُ

فَدَمَّرنَاهَا تَدمِيرًا

> ﴿*When We decide to destroy a town, We* ***make its affluent ones in command****, whereupon they commit sins in it, then the decree (of chastisement) becomes due against them and thereafter We destroy that town utterly.*﴾

The first reading has three possible meanings:

1. The object of the verb could be implicit, with the verse meaning: 'We commanded them [to obey us], but they commit sins.' This is the view of Saʿīd b. Jubayr.
2. The second meaning could be to 'make abundant its affluent ones . . .'
3. The third meaning can be that 'We made the affluent ones in charge.'[68]

The latter reading follows the pattern of the verb (fāʿala) which usually carries a reflexive meaning, but here means: 'We made abundant its affluent ones . . .'[69]

---

[67] *al-Ittiḥāf,* pg 282; *al-Nashr,* vol 2, pg 306.
[68] *Zād al-muyassar,* vol 5, pg 18-9.
[69] *Al-Baḥr al-muḥīṭ,* vol 6, pg 20; *al-Qirā'āt wa athruhā,* vol 2, pg 588-9.

Allah's Marveling ('Ajab)

The following verse has multiple readings:

فَاسْتَفْتِهِمْ أَهُمْ أَشَدُّ خَلْقًا أَم مَّنْ خَلَقْنَا ۚ إِنَّا خَلَقْنَاهُم مِّن طِينٍ لَّازِبٍ ﴿١١﴾ بَلْ عَجِبْتَ وَيَسْخَرُونَ ﴿١٢﴾ وَإِذَا ذُكِّرُوا لَا يَذْكُرُونَ ﴿١٣﴾

﴾*So ask them (that is, human beings): "Were they harder to create than the objects We created?" We created them from sticky clay. (11)* ***You marvel*** *(at the wondrous creations of Allah) and they scoff at it, (12) and when they are admonished, they pay no heed.*﴿ (37:11-3)

All readers recite it in the second person as above **['ajibta]** except for Ḥamzah, Kisā'ī, Khalaf and A'mash, who read the verb in the first person **['ajibtu]**:[70]

بَلْ عَجِبْتُ وَيَسْخَرُونَ

﴾***I marvel*** *(at the wondrous creation) while they scoff at it.*﴿

The word means to marvel, be amazed, or well-pleased with something. In the first person reading, Allah is marveling at the disbelief of these people. This action is ascribed to God in a manner that befits Him, without any sense of anthropomorphism, assigning modality or negating the action entirely. This reading affirms this attribute for Allah.

Zajjāj states: 'Some read this word in the first person ascribing the action to Allah, while others objected to that as inappropriate to Allah. This objection is not correct, as many readings and transmissions affirm it. However, this marveling by Allah is different from that of human beings, in the same way that He says: ﴾*They plot and Allah plots*﴿ (8:30); ﴾*Allah pokes fun at them*﴿ (9:79); and ﴾*It is He who deceives them*﴿ (4:142). Here, Allah's plotting, poking fun, and deceiving is different from that of human beings.'[71]

There are also a number of ḥadīth reports that also affirm this attribute of Allah.

عَنْ أَبِي هُرَيْرَةَ رَضِيَ اللهُ عَنْهُ: عَنِ النَّبِيِّ صَلَّى اللهُ عَلَيْهِ وَسَلَّمَ قَالَ: عَجِبَ اللهُ مِنْ قَوْمٍ يَدْخُلُونَ الْجَنَّةَ فِي السَّلَاسِلِ.

Abū Hurayrah relates that he heard the Prophet ﷺ say: 'Allah marvels at those people who will enter Paradise in chains.'[72]

---

[70] *al-Ittiḥāf,* pg 368.

[71] Al-Zajjāj, *Ma'ānī al-Qur'ān,* vol 4, pg 300.

[72] Bukhārī: Kitāb al-jihād wal-sayr—Bāb al-usārā fī al-salāsil; Abū Dāwūd: Kitāb al-jihād—Bāb fī al-asīr yūthaq. According to Ibn Ḥajar, this refers to those who were prisoners or slaves in this life who managed to retain their faith until death.

Ibn Mas'ūd relates that the Prophet ﷺ said: Our Lord marvels at a man who fights in the path of Allah, where his companions fled (retreated) but he knew that it was a sin, so he continued until his blood was shed. Then Allah says to His angels: Look at My servant; he returned seeking what I have in store for him and fearing my punishment, until his blood was shed.[73]

عَنْ عَبْدِ اللهِ بْنِ مَسْعُودٍ قَالَ: قَالَ رَسُولُ اللهِ صَلَّى اللهُ عَلَيْهِ وَسَلَّمَ: عَجِبَ رَبُّنَا عَزَّ وَجَلَّ مِنْ رَجُلٍ غَزَا فِي سَبِيلِ اللهِ عَزَّ وَجَلَّ فَانْهَزَمَ يَعْنِي أَصْحَابَهُ فَعَلِمَ مَا عَلَيْهِ فَرَجَعَ حَتَّى أُهَرِيقَ دَمُهُ فَيَقُولُ اللهُ عَزَّ وَجَلَّ لِمَلَائِكَتِهِ: انْظُرُوا إِلَى عَبْدِي رَجَعَ رَغْبَةً فِيمَا عِنْدِي، وَشَفَقَةً مِمَّا عِنْدِي حَتَّى أُهَرِيقَ دَمُهُ.

'Uqbah b. 'Āmir relates that he heard the Prophet ﷺ say: Your Lord is pleased with a shepherd high in the mountains who announces the call to prayer and prays. Allah says: Look at this slave of Mine, who calls to prayer and establishes it, fearing Me. I have forgiven My slave and admitted him to Paradise.[74]

عَنْ عُقْبَةَ بْنِ عَامِرٍ، قَالَ: سَمِعْتُ رَسُولَ اللهِ صَلَّى اللهُ عَلَيْهِ وَسَلَّمَ يَقُولُ: يَعْجَبُ رَبُّكَ عَزَّ وَجَلَّ مِنْ رَاعِي غَنَمٍ فِي رَأْسِ شَظِيَّةٍ بِجَبَلٍ يُؤَذِّنُ لِلصَّلَاةِ وَيُصَلِّي، فَيَقُولُ اللهُ عَزَّ وَجَلَّ: انْظُرُوا إِلَى عَبْدِي هَذَا يُؤَذِّنُ وَيُقِيمُ لِلصَّلَاةِ، يَخَافُ مِنِّي، قَدْ غَفَرْتُ لِعَبْدِي، وَأَدْخَلْتُهُ الْجَنَّةَ.

Allah's Hiding (Ikhfā')

The following verse has multiple readings:

فَلَا تعلَمُ نَفسٌ مَّا أُخفِيَ لَهُم مِّن قُرَّةِ أَعيُنٍ جَزَاءً بِمَا كَانُوا يَعمَلُونَ

﴾*No person knows what is **kept concealed** for them of joy as a reward for what they used to do.*﴿ (32:17)

Most readers read the word in the passive tense **[ukhfiya]** above, while Ḥamzah and Ya'qūb read the word as an active first-person verb going back to Allah **[ukhfī]**:

فَلَا تعلَمُ نَفسٌ مَّا أُخفِي لَهُم مِّن قُرَّةِ أَعيُنٍ جَزَاءً بِمَا كَانُوا يَعمَلُونَ

﴾*No person knows what is **I am concealing** for them of joy as a reward for what they used to do.*﴿

[73] Abū Dāwūd: Kitāb al-jihād—Bāb fī al-rajul alladhī yahsrī nafsahu. Authenticated by al-Albānī as ḥasan in *Ṣaḥīḥ al-Jāmi'*, vol 4, pg 27.

[74] Abū Dāwūd: Kitāb al-ṣalāh—Bāb al-adhān fī al-safr; al-Nasā'ī: Kitāb al-masājid—Abwāb al-adhān. Authenticated by al-Albānī as ṣaḥīḥ in *al-Silsilah al-Ṣaḥīḥah'*, vol 1, pg 65.

Ibn Muḥayṣin and Aʿmash through the transmission of Shannabūdhī read the verb in the past tense [akhfā]:

فَلَا تَعْلَمُ نَفْسٌ مَّا أَخْفِي لَهُم مِّن قُرَّةِ أَعْيُنٍ جَزَاءً بِمَا كَانُوا يَعْمَلُونَ

❮*No person knows what **He has kept hidden** for them of joy as a reward for what they used to do.*❯

Aʿmash through the transmission of Muṭawwiʿī reads it in the first-person past tense [akhfaytu]:[75]

فَلَا تَعْلَمُ نَفْسٌ مَّا أَخْفَيْتُ لَهُم مِّن قُرَّةِ أَعْيُنٍ جَزَاءً بِمَا كَانُوا يَعْمَلُونَ

❮*No person knows what **I have kept hidden** for them of joy as a reward for what they used to do.*❯

All of these readings ascribe the action of concealment back to Allah, as He Himself says in another verse:

أَكَادُ أُخْفِيهَا

❮*I almost conceal it.*❯ (20:15)

---

[75] *al-Ittiḥāf*, pg 352; *al-Qirāʾāt al-shādhdhah*, pg 74.

CHAPTER 4

Allah's Sending Down Angels (Inzāl al-Malā'ikah)

The following verse has multiple readings:

مَا نُنَزِّلُ الْمَلَائِكَةَ إِلَّا بِالْحَقِّ وَمَا كَانُوا إِذًا مُّنظَرِينَ

﴿***We do not send down the angels*** *except with truth; and the disbelievers would not then be reprieved.*﴾ (15:8)

Ḥafṣ from ʿĀṣim, Ḥamzah, Kisāʾī, Khalaf and Aʿmash read the word in the derived form **[nunazzilu al-malāʾikata]**, meaning: 'We do not send down the angels'; while Shuʿbah reads it in the third person passive tense with *angels* as the subject **[tunazzalu al-malāʾikatu]**:

مَا تُنَزَّلُ الْمَلَائِكَةُ إِلَّا بِالْحَقِّ وَمَا كَانُوا إِذًا مُّنظَرِينَ

﴿***The angels are not sent down*** *except with truth; and the disbelievers would not then be reprieved.*﴾

The other readers recite it in the active tense with *angels* as the subject **[tanazzala al-malāʾikatu]**:

مَا تَنَزَّلُ الْمَلَائِكَةُ إِلَّا بِالْحَقِّ وَمَا كَانُوا إِذًا مُّنظَرِينَ

﴿***The angels do not descend*** *except with truth; and the disbelievers would not then be reprieved.*﴾

Ibn Muḥayṣin reads it as a simple verb in the first-person plural with *angels* as the object **[nunzilu al-malāʾikata]**:

مَا نُنزِلُ الْمَلَائِكَةُ إِلَّا بِالْحَقِّ وَمَا كَانُوا إِذًا مُّنظَرِينَ

﴿***We do not send down the angels*** *except with truth; and the disbelievers would not then be reprieved.*﴾

Bazzī reads, in some of his transmissions from Ibn Kathīr, reads the verb with a shaddah when it is joined with the previous word:[76]

مَا تَّنَزَّلُ الْمَلَائِكَةُ

[76] *Ḥujjat al-qirāʾāt*, pg 318; *al-Kashf*, vol 2, pg 29.

The following related verse also has multiple readings:

نَزَلَ بِهِ الرُّوحُ الأَمِينُ

﴿*The Trustworthy Spirit* ***has brought it down.***﴾ (26:193)

Nāfi', Ibn Kathīr, Abū 'Amr, Ḥafṣ, Abū Ja'far and Ibn Muḥayṣin read it as above with a simple verb whose subject is the *Trustworthy Spirit,* i.e. Jibrīl **[nazala]**. The other readers recite the word in a derived verb form with *the Trustworthy Spirit* as the object and *Allah* as the subject **[nazzala]**:[77]

نَزَّلَ بِهِ الرُّوحَ الأَمِينَ

﴿***He sent down the Trustworthy Spirit with it.***﴾

It should be noted that the first reading ('The Trustworthy Spirit brought it down') was used by some theologians to prove their belief that the meanings of the Qur'ān are from God while the words are from Jibrīl. The variant reading here, however, removes this doubt and proves that the one who sends Jibrīl is Allah. Jibrīl is merely the messenger of the Qur'ān, whose words and meanings are from Allah.

Allah's Defending (Daf'/Difā')

The following verse has multiple readings and establishes Allah's defense of the believers:

إِنَّ اللَّهَ يُدَافِعُ عَنِ الَّذِينَ آمَنُوا

﴿*Indeed, Allah* ***firmly defends*** *those who have believed.*﴾ (22:38)

All readers recite this word as a present-tense derived word form **[yudāfi'u]**, which represents an intensive and stronger meaning of the verb, highlighting Allah's powerful defense of the believers. Ibn Kathīr, Abū 'Amr, Ya'qūb, Ibn Muḥayṣin and Yazīdī read it as a simple present-tense verb **[yadfa'u]**, meaning simply defend or repel:[78]

إِنَّ اللَّهَ يَدفَعُ عَنِ الَّذِينَ آمَنُوا

﴿*Indeed, Allah* ***defends/repels harm from*** *those who have believed.*﴾ [79]

---

[77] *al-Ittiḥāf,* pg 334.

[78] *al-Ittiḥāf,* pg 315.

[79] I have presented two potential translations of this verse, with the latter from the Bridges' translation of the ten Qira'at of the Holy Qur'ān.

Allah's Rolling Up the Heavens (Ṭayy al-Samā')

The following verse has multiple readings and establishes Allah's rolling up the heavens:

$$يَوْمَ نَطْوِي السَّمَاءَ كَطَيِّ السِّجِلِّ لِلْكُتُبِ$$

❮On that Day We shall **roll up** the skies as written scrolls are rolled up.❯ (21:104)

All reciters read the word [naṭwī] as above except for Abū Jaʿfar who read the word in the passive tense [tuṭwā]:[80]

$$يَوْمَ تُطْوَى السَّمَاءُ كَطَيِّ السِّجِلِّ لِلْكُتُبِ$$

❮On that Day when **the heavens will be rolled up** as written scrolls are rolled up.❯

The dominant reading establishes Allah's action directly, while the latter one does so implicitly.

Allah's Giving Time (al-Imlā')

Many verses establish Allah's giving time or respite to disbelievers and unjust persons while not punishing them immediately:

$$وَأُمْلِي لَهُمْ ۚ إِنَّ كَيْدِي مَتِينٌ$$

❮And I will **give them time**. Indeed, my plan is firm.❯ (7:183)

$$فَأَمْلَيْتُ لِلْكَافِرِينَ$$

❮**I granted respite** to the unbelievers for a while.❯ (22:44)

The following verse has variant readings on the relevant word:

$$الشَّيْطَانُ سَوَّلَ لَهُمْ وَأَمْلَى لَهُمْ$$

❮Satan enticed them and **prolonged hope** for them.❯ (47:25)

---

[80] al-Ittiḥāf, pg 312.

In this last verse, all reciters read the word as above **[amlā]** with the subject being Shayṭān (it could also be understood that the subject is Allah), except for Abū ʿAmr who read the word in the passive tense **[umliya]**:

الشَّيطَانُ سَوَّلَ لَهُم وَأُملِيَ لَهُم

﴾*Satan enticed them, and thus* ***they were filled with prolonged hope.***﴿

Also, Yaʿqūb read the verb in the active first-person **[umlī]**:

الشَّيطَانُ سَوَّلَ لَهُم وَأُملِي لَهُم

﴾*Satan enticed them and thus* ***I filled them with prolonged hope.***﴿

The meaning of Shayṭān prolonging their hope is his whispering into their ears and filling them with false hopes until their deaths upon disbelief. Abū ʿAmr disagreed, asserting that Shayṭān cannot prolong anything for anyone.[81]

---

[81] *Ḥujjat al-qirāʿāt,* pg 667-8; *al-Kashf*, vol 2, pg 227, 278.

Allah's Protecting from Violence (al-Iḥṣān min al-Ba's)

The following verse has multiple readings and establishes Allah's giving time or respite to disbelievers and unjust persons and does not punish them immediately:

وَعَلَّمنَاهُ صَنعَةَ لَبُوسٍ لَّكُم لِتُحصِنَكُم مِّن بَأسِكُم

﴿*It was We Who taught him the art of making armor* ***so that it may protect you*** *from each other's violence.*﴾ (21:80)

In this verse, Ibn 'Āmir, Ḥafṣ and Ḥasan al-Baṣrī read the word as above **[lituhşinakum]**, meaning 'the art of making coats of mail will protect you.' Here the subject could either be the making of armor, the wearing of armor or the armor itself. Shu'bah and Ruways read the verb in the first-person plural **[linuhşinakum]**, meaning 'Allah will protect you:

وَعَلَّمنَاهُ صَنعَةَ لَبُوسٍ لَّكُم لِنُحصِنَكُم مِّن بَأسِكُم

﴿*It was We Who taught him the art of making* ***armor so that We may protect you*** *from each other's violence.*﴾

The rest read the verb in the third person **[liyuhşinakum]**, whose subject can either be Allah, Dāwūd, the teaching, or the armor:[82]

وَعَلَّمنَاهُ صَنعَةَ لَبُوسٍ لَّكُم لِيُحصِنَكُم مِّن بَأسِكُم

﴿*It was We Who taught him the art of making armor* ***so that He/it may protect you*** *from each other's violence.*﴾

[82] *al-Ittiḥāf,* pg 311.

Allah's Separating (Faṣl/Tafṣīl)

From Allah's attributes is that He separates His slaves. The meaning of the simple verb (*faṣala/yafṣilu*) is either to judge, decide, or to separate a union, i.e. by entering believers to Paradise and disbelievers to Hellfire. The derived verb (*faṣṣala/yufaṣṣilu*) means to separate. This attribute is found in the following verse with variant readings:

يَومَ القِيَامَةِ **يَفصِلُ** بَينَكُم

﴾*On the Day of Judgment, He will* ***decide*** *between all of you.*﴿ (60:3)

ʿĀṣim, Yaʿqūb and Ḥasan al-Baṣrī read this word as above, as a simple present-tense verb **[yafṣilu]**, whose subject goes back to Allah (see verse 1 of the same sūrah). On the other hand, Nāfiʿ, Ibn Kathīr, Abū ʿAmr, Abū Jaʿfar, Hishām in some of his transmission, Ibn Muḥayṣin and Yazīdī read the verb in the simple passive tense **[yufṣalu]**:

يَومَ القِيَامَةِ **يُفصَلُ** بَينَكُم

﴾*On the Day of Judgment,* ***a decision will be made*** *between all of you.*﴿

Ibn Dhakwān and Hsiham in some of his transmissions reads the verb in its derived form and passive tense **[yufaṣṣalu]**:

يَومَ القِيَامَةِ **يُفَصَّلُ** بَينَكُم

﴾*On the Day of Judgment,* ***you will be separated*** *among yourselves.*﴿

Ḥamzah, Kisāʾī, Khalaf and Aʿmash read the word as a derived form verb in the active present-tense **[yufaṣṣilu]**:[83]

يَومَ القِيَامَةِ **يُفَصِّلُ** بَينَكُم

﴾*On the Day of Judgment,* ***He will be separate*** *all of you.*﴿

[83] *al-Ittiḥāf,* pg 414; *Ḥujjat al-qirāʾāt,* pg 706; *al-Kashf,* vol 2, pg 318.

CHAPTER 4

Allah's Writing (Kitābah)

Writing and recording is an established attribute of Allah in a manner that befits His perfection. This attribute is found in the following verse among others:

سَنَكْتُبُ مَا قَالُوا وَقَتْلَهُمُ الْأَنبِيَاءَ بِغَيْرِ حَقٍّ وَنَقُولُ ذُوقُوا عَذَابَ الْحَرِيقِ

﴾***We will record*** *what they said and their killing of the prophets without right and will say: Taste the punishment of the burning Fire.*﴿ (3:181)

This dominant reading is in the first person plural present tense **[sanaktubu]**. Ḥamzah read the verb in the third-person passive tense **[sayuktabu]**:[84]

سَيُكْتَبُ مَا قَالُوا وَقَتْلَهُمُ الْأَنبِيَاءَ بِغَيْرِ حَقٍّ وَنَقُولُ ذُوقُوا عَذَابَ الْحَرِيقِ

﴾*What they said* ***will be written down*** *and their killing of the prophets without right and will say, "Taste the punishment of the Burning Fire.*﴿

The dominant reading establishes explicitly Allah's recording and writing down. This attribute is also established in many other verses and Prophetic ḥadīth reports:

وَكَتَبْنَا لَهُ فِي الْأَلْوَاحِ

﴾*And We wrote for him on the Tablets.*﴿ (7:145)

وَإِنَّا لَهُ كَاتِبُونَ

﴾*Verily! We record it in his Book of deeds.*﴿ (21:94)

In the discussion between Adam and Mūsā, Adam stated: 'You are the one for whom Allah wrote the Torah with His hand.'[85]

---

[84] *al-Ittiḥāf,* pg 183.

[85] Ṣaḥīḥ Bukhārī: Kitāb al-qadr—Bāb taḥāj Ādam wa Mūsā ʿind Allāh; Ṣaḥīḥ Muslim: Kitāb al-qadr—Bāb ḥijāj Ādam wa Mūsā.

Allah's Saddening of Faces (Sū' al-Wujūh)

The following verse has variant readings:

فَإِذَا جَاءَ وَعْدُ الآخِرَةِ لِيَسُوءُوا وُجُوهَكُمْ

﴿*Then when the final promise came, [We sent your enemies]* ***to sadden*** *your faces.*﴾ (17:7)

This dominant reading is in the third person plural **[liyasū'ū]**, and the subject is 'the enemies.' Kisā'ī read the verb in the first-person plural **[linasū'a]** which makes the subject of the verb *Allah*:

فَإِذَا جَاءَ وَعْدُ الآخِرَةِ لِنَسُوءَ وُجُوهَكُم

﴿*Then when the final promise came,* ***We saddened*** *your faces.*﴾

Ibn 'Āmir, Shu'bah, Ḥamzah, Khalaf and A'mash read the verb in the third person singular **[liyasū'a]** making the subject either Allah or the promise:[86]

فَإِذَا جَاءَ وَعْدُ الآخِرَةِ لِيَسُوءَ وُجُوهَكُم

﴿*Then when the final promise came,* ***He/it saddened*** *your faces.*﴾

[86] *al-Ittiḥāf,* pg 282.

CHAPTER 4

Allah's Effecting Natural Disasters

The following verses have variant readings:

أَفَأَمِنتُم أَن يَخسِفَ بِكُم جَانِبَ البَرِّ أَو يُرسِلَ عَلَيكُم حَاصِبًا ثُمَّ لَا تَجِدُوا
لَكُم وَكِيلًا ﴿٦٨﴾ أَم أَمِنتُم أَن يُعِيدَكُم فِيهِ تَارَةً أُخرَىٰ فَيُرسِلَ عَلَيكُم
قَاصِفًا مِّنَ الرِّيحِ فَيُغرِقَكُم بِمَا كَفَرتُم ثُمَّ لَا تَجِدُوا لَكُم عَلَينَا بِهِ تَبِيعًا ﴿٦٩﴾

﴾*Can you, then, ever feel sure that* ***He will not cause a tract of dry land to swallow you up****, or* ***let loose upon you*** *a deadly storm-wind, whereupon you would find none to be your protector? Or can you, perchance, feel sure that* ***He will not*** **make you put back** *to sea once again, and then* ***let loose upon you*** *a raging tempest and* ***cause you to drown*** *in requital of your ingratitude - whereupon you would find none to uphold you against Us?*﴿ (17:68-9)

This dominant reading of the highlighted verbs in these verses is in the third person singular **[yakhisfa/yursila/yuʿīdakum/fayursila/fayughriqakum]**, with Allah being the subject of each action. On the other hand, Ibn Kathīr, Abū ʿAmr, and Ibn Muḥayṣin read all of these same verbs consistently in the first-person plural **[nakhisfa/nursila/nuʿīdakum/fanursila/fanughriqakum]**, all of which also go back to Allah:

أَفَأَمِنتُم أَن نَخسِفَ بِكُم جَانِبَ البَرِّ أَو نُرسِلَ عَلَيكُم حَاصِبًا ثُمَّ لَا تَجِدُوا
لَكُم وَكِيلًا ﴿٦٨﴾ أَم أَمِنتُم أَن نُعِيدَكُم فِيهِ تَارَةً أُخرَىٰ فَنُرسِلَ عَلَيكُم
قَاصِفًا مِّنَ الرِّيحِ فَنُغرِقَكُم بِمَا كَفَرتُم ثُمَّ لَا تَجِدُوا لَكُم عَلَينَا بِهِ تَبِيعًا
﴿٦٩﴾

﴾*Can you, then, ever feel sure that* ***We will not cause a tract of dry land to swallow you up****, or* ***let loose upon you*** *a deadly storm-wind, whereupon you would find none to be your protector? Or can you, perchance, feel sure that* ***We will not*** **make you put back** *to sea once again, and then* ***let loose upon you*** *a raging tempest and* ***cause you to drown*** *in requital of your ingratitude - whereupon you would find none to uphold you against Us?*﴿

In addition, Abū Ja'far and Ruways read one of the verbs in the feminine third-person **[fatughriqakum]**, where the subject would be 'the wind' or 'raging tempest':[87]

فَنُرسِلَ عَلَيكُم قَاصِفًا مِّنَ الرِّيحِ **فَتُغرِقَكُم** بِمَا كَفَرتُم

﴿. . .*and then* ***let loose upon you*** *a raging tempest* ***which will cause you to drown*** *in requital of your ingratitude - whereupon you would find none to uphold you against Us?*﴾

[87] *al-Ittiḥāf,* pg 285.

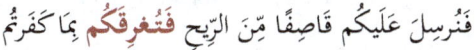

CHAPTER 4

Allah's Sailing and Anchoring (Ijrā'/Irsā')

There are a number of variant readings in the following verse:

وَقَالَ ارْكَبُوا فِيهَا بِسْمِ اللَّهِ مَجْرَاهَا وَمُرْسَاهَا ۚ إِنَّ رَبِّي لَغَفُورٌ رَّحِيمٌ

﴿*Noah said: ' Embark in it. In the name of Allah* ***is its sailing and its anchoring****. My Lord is Ever Forgiving, Most Merciful.*﴾ (11:41)

Ḥamzah, Kisā'ī, and Ḥafṣ read the first word with fatḥah of the mīm **[majrāhā]**, while the rest read it with ḍammah, and all read the second word with ḍammah of mīm **[mursāhā]**:

وَقَالَ ارْكَبُوا فِيهَا بِسْمِ اللَّهِ مُجْرَاهَا وَمُرْسَاهَا

Ḥasan al-Baṣrī read these two verbs as active participles **[mujrīhā wa mursīhā]**, with Allah being the subject and these verbs being His attributes. In addition, this reading was related from Ibn Mujāhid, al-Jaḥdarī and others:

وَقَالَ ارْكَبُوا فِيهَا بِسْمِ اللَّهِ مُجْرِيهَا وَمُرْسِيهَا ۚ إِنَّ رَبِّي لَغَفُورٌ رَّحِيمٌ

﴿*Noah said: ' Embark in it. In the name of Allah* ***who is responsible for its sailing and its anchoring****. My Lord is Ever Forgiving, Most Merciful.*﴾

Dimyāṭī comments on this verse:

> There was a difference over this word (majrāhā). Ḥafṣ, Ḥamzah, Kisā'ī and Khalaf read it with a fatḥah on the mīm and imālah vowel on the rā **[majrayhā]**—and this is the only example of imālah in the reading of Ḥafṣ—while the rest, namely, Abū 'Amr, Ibn Dhakwān from the path of Ṣūrī, and Shannabūdhī, read the verb with ḍamma on the mīm and imālah of the rā **[mujrayhā]**. Azraq, a transmitter from Warsh, read the verb with a lighter imālah. Ḥamzah, Kisā'ī, Khalaf read the second word (mursāhā) with imālah of sīn **[mursayhā]**, and Azraq in some of his transmissions with lesser imālah. Muṭawi'ī reads the two words with a fatḥah of mīm along with imālah rā **[majrayhā wa marsayhā]**. Ḥasan al-Baṣrī read the two verbs with an unvowelled yā rather than alif **[mujrīhā wa mursīhā]**, and this would make both verbs going back to Allah.[88]

---

[88] *al-Ittiḥāf,* vol 1, pg 320.

Scholars of Arabic point out that the terms *mujrīhā* and *mursīhā* can be considered descriptions of Allah, or that He is the one that causes these actions. Zamksharī stated:

> Mujāhid read these two words in the genitive case as descriptions of Allah.' Wāḥidī stated that these words are verbal nouns like others in the Qur'ān. Those who advocate this reading of *mujrīhā* as referring to Allah reference the next verse and point out that had the verb been attributed to the ark rather than Allah, it would have been used in this way:
>
> وَهِيَ تَجْرِي بِهِم
>
> ﴿*It (i.e. the Ark) sailed along with them.*﴾ (11:42)
>
> Others say both usages are close enough to be used interchangeably. The reading of *irsāhā* as a verbal noun is supported by other verses such as the following:
>
> وَالجِبَالَ أَرسَاهَا
>
> ﴿*And [Allah] anchored in it mountains.*﴾ (79:32)
>
> Ibn 'Abbās mentioned that the meaning is that the ark sailed with Allah's Name and Power and anchored with Allah's Name and Power.[89]

---

[89] *Al-Tafsīr al-Kabīr,* vol 5, pg 150.

CHAPTER 4

The Vision of Allah (Ru'yat Allah)

From Allah's attributes is that He will be seen in the Hereafter. The following verse has one variant reading:

وَإِذَا رَأَيْتَ ثَمَّ رَأَيْتَ نَعِيمًا وَمُلْكًا كَبِيرًا

﴿*Wherever you look around, you will see an abundance of bliss and the glories of a great* ***kingdom.***﴾ (76:20)

Ya'lā b. Ḥākim al-Thaqafī, a trustworthy scholar and transmitter from Ibn Kathīr of Makkah, read the word as a different noun meaning 'king' **[malikan]**:[90]

وَإِذَا رَأَيْتَ ثَمَّ رَأَيْتَ نَعِيمًا وَمَلِكًا كَبِيرًا

﴿*Wherever you look around, you will see an abundance of bliss and the glories of a great* ***King.***﴾

This reading, which is one of the shādh ones, establishes the seeing of Allah in the Hereafter, which is a tenet of belief that is universally agreed upon by Sunnī Muslims and whose evidences are abundant in the Qur'ān and Sunnah. Some of these verses include the following:

وُجُوهٌ يَوْمَئِذٍ نَّاضِرَةٌ ﴿٢٢﴾ إِلَىٰ رَبِّهَا نَاظِرَةٌ ﴿٢٣﴾

﴿*Some faces on that Day will be fresh and resplendent, and will be looking towards their Lord.*﴾ (75:22-3)

لِّلَّذِينَ أَحْسَنُوا الْحُسْنَىٰ وَزِيَادَةٌ

﴿ *For those who do good there is good reward and more besides*[91]*.*﴾ (10:26)

---

[90] *Ghāyat al-nihāyah,* vol 2, pg 319.

[91] This promise of something more has been interpreted by commentators as the seeing of Allah in the next life.

The Highness of Allah ('Uluww)

The approach of the pious predecessors is to affirm that Allah is High in His essence, in His Power, and in His Affairs; that He has ascended over the Throne above the seventh heaven; that He is High above His creation and separate from them; that He is with His creation through His knowledge; that He hears all and sees all; and that nothing escapes Him. The evidence for these beliefs are too numerous to mention here. Dhahabī in his work *al-'Uluww* lists many of these. Among the fourteen readings there are two further pieces of evidence that support the Highness of Allah. The first is the following verse:

وَفِي السَّمَاءِ **رِزْقُكُمْ** وَمَا تُوعَدُونَ

﴿*And in heaven is* ***your provision*** *and also what you are being promised.*﴾ (51:22)

The majority read the verb above as 'your provision' **[rizqukum]**, except for Ibn Muḥayṣin who read this word in two ways, as 'your Provider' **[rāziqkum]** and as 'your provisions' **[arzāqkum]**:

وَفِي السَّمَاءِ **رَازِقُكُمْ** وَمَا تُوعَدُونَ

And in heaven is ***your Provider*** *and also what you are being promised.*

وَفِي السَّمَاءِ **أَرزَاقُكُمْ** وَمَا تُوعَدُونَ

And in heaven is ***your provisions*** *and also what you are being promised.*

The reading of Ibn Muḥayṣin establishes the highness of Allah above His creation and the fact that He is in the heavens. This meaning also comes from the following verses:

أَأَمِنتُم مَّن فِي السَّمَاءِ

﴿*Do you feel secure that He Who is in the heaven will not . . .*﴾ (67:16)

أَم أَمِنتُم مَّن فِي السَّمَاءِ

﴿*Do you feel secure that He Who is in the heaven will not . . .*﴾ (67:17)

In addition, the Prophet ﷺ stated: 'Will you not trust me, whereas I am a trustee of Him Who is in the heaven?'[92]

There is another verse which potentially supports the notion that Allah is in heavens and the earth:

وَهُوَ اللَّهُ فِي السَّمَاوَاتِ وَفِي الْأَرْضِ ۖ يَعْلَمُ سِرَّكُمْ وَجَهْرَكُمْ

﴿*And He it is Who is One True God in the heavens and in the earth. He knows your deeds, both secret and open.*﴾ (6:3)

This has been explained in various ways. Firstly, that the verse is actually two separate sentences:

وَهُوَ اللَّهُ فِي السَّمَاوَاتِ / وَفِي الْأَرْضِ يَعْلَمُ سِرَّكُمْ وَجَهْرَكُمْ

And He it is Who is One True God in the heavens. / And in the earth, He knows your deeds, both secret and open.

The second explanation is that both prepositional phrases are descriptions of the latter portion of the verse:

وَهُوَ اللَّهُ / فِي السَّمَاوَاتِ وَفِي الْأَرْضِ يَعْلَمُ سِرَّكُمْ وَجَهْرَكُمْ

And He it is Who is One True God. / In the heavens and in the earth, He knows your deeds, both secret and open.

Another explanation is that Allah here is being used to describe the One who is worshipped, i.e. the One True God in the heavens and the earth.[93] This meaning is supported by the following verse:

وَهُوَ الَّذِي فِي السَّمَاءِ إِلَٰهٌ وَفِي الْأَرْضِ إِلَٰهٌ

﴿*He it is Who is God in the heavens and the earth.*﴾ (43:84)

There is a second verse with variant readings that establishes Allah's Highness:

وَجَعَلُوا الْمَلَائِكَةَ الَّذِينَ هُمْ عِبَادُ الرَّحْمَٰنِ إِنَاثًا ۚ أَشَهِدُوا خَلْقَهُمْ ۚ سَتُكْتَبُ شَهَادَتُهُمْ وَيُسْأَلُونَ

[92] Ṣaḥīḥ Bukhārī: Kitāb al-maghāzī—Bāb bu'itha 'Alī wa Khālid; Ṣaḥīḥ Muslim: Kitāb al-zakāh—Bāb dhikr al-khawārij wa ṣifātuhum

[93] This is the preferred translation of Abū al-A'lā Mawdūdī in his *Tafhīm al-Qur'ān,* and Muṣṭafā Khaṭṭāb in his *The Clear Qur'ān*.

﴿*They claim that angels,* ***who are the chosen servants of the All-Merciful One****, are females. Did they witness how their body is constituted? Their testimony shall be written and they shall be called to account.*﴾ (43:19)

The dominant reading is that of Abū 'Amr, 'Āṣim, Ḥamzah, Kisā'ī, and Khalaf and reads the highlighted word as the plural of *'abd* **['ibād al-Raḥmān]**. The others read it as an entirely different word **['inda al-Raḥmān]**:[94]

وَجَعَلُوا الْمَلَائِكَةَ الَّذِينَ هُم عِندَ الرَّحْمَٰنِ إِنَاثًا

﴿*They claim that angels,* ***who are with the All-Merciful One****, are females.*﴾

The first reading refutes the notion that the angels are God's daughters and establishes that they are his servants and slaves instead. The second reading supports the notion of Allah's Highness. The angels are described as being so high that they are in the heavens with their Lord, which supports that Allah is in the heavens.[95] Another support for this notion is the description of Paradise, which is in the heavens, as being close to the Lord:

رَبِّ ابنِ لِي عِندَكَ بَيتًا فِي الجَنَّةِ

﴿*[The wife of Pharoah said:] 'My Lord, build for me a house with You in Paradise.'*﴾ (66:11)

---

[94] *Al-Ittiḥāf,* pg 385; *al-Nashr,* vol 2, pg 368.
[95] *Ma'ārij al-qubūl,* vol 1, pg 159.

Describing the Throne of Allah

From the attributes of Allah is that He is 'the owner of a Throne' (40:15), and that He has ascended His Throne. The Throne itself has attributes which point to His Greatness. These attributes appear in the Qur'ān and Sunnah. One of them is that the Throne is mighty:

وَهُوَ رَبُّ العَرشِ **العَظِيمِ**

﴿*And He is the Lord of the **Mighty Throne**.*﴾ (9:129)

قُل مَن رَّبُّ السَّمَاوَاتِ السَّبعِ وَرَبُّ العَرشِ **العَظِيمِ**

﴿*Say: Who is the Lord of the seven heavens, and the Lord of the **Mighty Throne**?*﴾ (23:86)

اللَّهُ لَا إِلَٰهَ إِلَّا هُوَ رَبُّ العَرشِ **العَظِيمِ**

﴿*Allah: none is worthy of worship save He. He is the Lord of the **Mighty Throne**.*﴾ (27:26)

Ibn Muḥayṣin read the word 'Mighty' in the nominative case **[al-ʿaẓīmu]** as a description of Allah ('Mighty Lord of the Throne'), whereas the rest read it in the genitive case as a description of the Throne **[al-ʿaẓīmi]**.[96] In the majority reading, however, the word can also be considered grammatically to be a description of the Lord. In that case, the would be considered to be in the nominative case with an implied ḍammah ending. The reason it carries the kasrah ending is due to its proximity (mujāwarah) to the word *throne* (in Arabic, it is allowed for smoother flow to approximate endings of adjacent words though that would not be their original vowels).

However, its usage as a description of the Throne is more likely since Allah describes in another verse the worldly throne of the Queen Bilqīs in the same way: ﴿*And she has a mighty throne*﴾ (27:23). Therefore, the mightiness of Allah's throne, which is associated with His Independence and Power, is far greater than the throne of a human, which is associated with weakness and incapacity.

Another description of the Throne is its nobility:

لَا إِلَٰهَ إِلَّا هُوَ رَبُّ العَرشِ **الكَرِيمِ**

[96] *al-Ittiḥāf,* pg 246; *al-Qirāʿāt al-shādhdhah,* pg 52.

﴾*There is no true God save Him, the* ***Lord of the Noble Throne.***﴿
(23:116)

Ibn Muḥayṣin read the word 'Noble in the nominative case **[al-karīmu]** as a description of Allah ('Noble Lord of the Throne'), whereas the rest read it in the genitive case as a description of the Throne **[al-karīmi]** (which could also be considered a description of Allah as per the previous discussion):[97]

لَا إِلَٰهَ إِلَّا هُوَ رَبُّ العَرشِ الكَرِيمُ

There is no true God save Him, the ***Noble Lord of the Throne.***

A further description of the Throne is its glory:

ذُو العَرشِ المَجِيدُ

﴾*The* ***Glorious Owner of the Throne.***﴿ (85:15)

Here, the dominant reading is of the adjective in the nominative case **[al-majīdu]** as a description of Allah, whereas Ḥamzah, Kisā'ī, Khalaf, Ḥasan al-Baṣrī and A'mash read it in the genitive case as a description of the Throne **[al-majīdi]** (which could also be considered a description of Allah as per the previous discussion):[98]

ذُو العَرشِ المَجِيدِ

﴾*The* ***Owner of the Glorious Throne.***﴿

---

[97] *al-Ittiḥāf,* pg 246; *al-Qirā'āt al-shādhdhah,* pg 52.
[98] *al-Ittiḥāf,* pg 436; *al-Kashf,* vol 2, pg 369; *Ḥujjat al-Qirā'āt,* pg 757.

Attributes of Negation

There are many attributes that Allah denies for Himself, and the variant readings also add layers of meanings here. For instance, the following verse has variant readings:

لَّا يَضِلُّ رَبِّي وَلَا يَنسَى

﴿*My Lord **does not err**, nor does He forget.*﴾ (20:52)

The dominant reading uses a form of the verb **[yaḍillu]** that would mean to falter or err in His knowledge. Ḥasan al-Baṣrī and Ibn Muḥayṣin read the verb in a derived form **[yuḍillu]**, which would mean to waste, cause to perish, or squander:

لَّا يُضِلُّ رَبِّي وَلَا يَنسَى

﴿*My Lord **does not cause to perish** [His record], nor does He forget.*﴾ [99]

[99] *al-Ittiḥāf,* pg 303; *al-Qirā'āt al-shādhdhah,* pg 67.

Understanding Tawḥīd through Variant Readings

Ulūhiyyah as Worship

The oneness of Godship means the oneness of His exclusive right to be singled out for worship. From the perspective of Allah, it is termed *tawḥīd al-ulūhiyyah* ('Oneness of Godship'), and from the perspective of His servants, it is sometimes termed *tawḥīd al-'ibādah* ('Oneness of worship').[100] It is one of the three types of tawḥīd alluded to in sūrah al-Nās, the final chapter of the Qur'ān:

قُلْ أَعُوذُ بِرَبِّ النَّاسِ

﴾*Say: I seek refuge in the Lord of mankind.*﴿
Tawḥīd al-Rubūbiyyah (Oneness in Lordship)

مَلِكِ النَّاسِ

﴾*The King of mankind.*﴿
Tawḥīd al-Asmā' wa al-Ṣifāt (Oneness in Names and Attributes)

إِلَٰهِ النَّاسِ

﴾*The God of mankind.*﴿
Tawḥīd al-Ulūhiyyah (Oneness in Godship)

The distinction between Lordship and Godship is made in numerous Qur'ānic verses, for instance, where Allah affirms that the idolaters believed that God was 'the Lord of the seven heavens and the Lord of the Mighty Throne' (23:86). At the same time, they rejected that He had the exclusive right to be worshipped.[101]

There is nothing problematic in using new terminologies and classifications such as the three types of tawḥīd for concepts and meanings that are already present in the Qur'ān and Sunnah. This applies to all disciplines. Furthermore, this classification finds support in the words of Ṭabarī, Ibn Baṭṭah al-'Ukburī (d. 387/997)[102] and others, well before Ibn Taymiyyah, who was falsely accused by his detractors of inventing it. Even if we accepted that he originated this classification, it would not be a problem as the concepts are sound and fully in concordance with the Qur'ān and Sunnah. Some of these detractors came up with alternate divisions of Tawḥīd, for instance,

---

[100] *Al-Qawl al-mufīd*, pg 16.
[101] *Fatḥ al-majīd*, vol 1, pg 80-4.
[102] 'Abdullah b. Muḥammad al-'Ukburī was great Ḥanbalī jurist from Baghdad known for his worship and courage.

into: Tawḥīd al-Dhāt (Oneness of Essence), Tawḥīd al-Ṣifāt (Oneness of Attributes), and Tawḥīd al-Af'āl (Oneness of Actions). Ibn Taymiyyah states:

> The tawḥīd that the messengers called to comprised of affirming God's exclusive right to be worshiped. This is by testifying that there is no god but He, that none is worthy of worship except He, that one not place their trust in other than He, that one not associate or disavow others except for His sake, and that one does things only for His sake. This includes all that He affirmed for Himself from Names and Attributes.
>
> Tawḥīd is not simply affirming God's Lordship alone, which is the belief that God alone is the creator of the world. This is the view of certain theologians and people of taṣawwuf, who believed that affirmation of this (that God is the Creator) represented complete tawḥīd.[103]

The word *ilāh,* or 'God,' means object of worship while *ulūhiyyah/ilāhiyyah/ilāhah* refers to worship. From the names of Allah is *al-Ilāh*, as we discussed in the reading of Ḥasan al-Baṣrī of verses (12:31, 12:51). Ibn Taymiyyah comments:

> *Ilāh* refers to the one who is worshipped and deserves to be worshipped. Its meaning is not the one who has power over creation. If it is understood that *ilāh* refers to the one with the power to originate new things, that this is the most specific meaning of god, and that this is the end-result of tawḥīd—as advocated by certain theologians including those who followed Abū al-Ḥasan al-Ash'arī—then the reality of tawḥīd with which Allah sent the Prophet ﷺ will never be known. The idolaters among the Arabs used to affirm that Allah is the creator of everything, but despite that, remained idolaters: ﴾*And most of them do not believe without associating others with Him.*﴿ (12:106). Many of the predecessors affirmed that if you were to ask them who created the heavens and the earth, they would respond: *Allah*. And yet they still worshipped others.[104]

This shows the falsity of the position of some latter-day theologians who made tawḥīd the belief in the oneness of Allah in His Essence, i.e. that His Essence is not composed of parts, that it does not resemble others, and that it is one with His Attributes. In other words, He does not possess more than one attribute in each type, such as having two types of power or multiple types of knowledge. None of His Attributes resemble others. Also, they affirmed that He is one in His Actions. All of

---

[103] *Majmū',* vol 3, pg 97.
[104] *Majmū',* vol 3, pg 97.

creation is created through His power, with no partners in that. As such, His is the only one who acts, with no one else possessing actions.[105] This is obviously incorrect as it does not incorporate the vital notion of worship in their notion of tawḥīd.

As for variant readings that add layers of meaning on this, refer to the following verse:

وَقَالَ الْمَلَأُ مِن قَوْمِ فِرْعَوْنَ أَتَذَرُ مُوسَىٰ وَقَوْمَهُ لِيُفْسِدُوا فِي الْأَرْضِ وَيَذَرَكَ
وَآلِهَتَكَ ۚ قَالَ سَنُقَتِّلُ أَبْنَاءَهُمْ وَنَسْتَحْيِي نِسَاءَهُمْ وَإِنَّا فَوْقَهُمْ قَاهِرُونَ

﴾*The elders of Pharaoh's people said: Will you leave alone Moses and his people to spread mischief in the land, and forsake you and **your gods**? Pharaoh replied: We will kill their male children and spare their female ones. For indeed we hold irresistible sway over them.*﴿ (7:127)

All reciters read the word as plural **[wa ālihatak]** except for Ḥasan al-Baṣrī and Ibn Muḥayṣin, who read the word as a singular verbal noun **[wa ilāhatak]:**

وَقَالَ الْمَلَأُ مِن قَوْمِ فِرْعَوْنَ أَتَذَرُ مُوسَىٰ وَقَوْمَهُ لِيُفْسِدُوا فِي الْأَرْضِ وَيَذَرَكَ
وَإِلَاهَتَكَ ۚ قَالَ سَنُقَتِّلُ أَبْنَاءَهُمْ وَنَسْتَحْيِي نِسَاءَهُمْ وَإِنَّا فَوْقَهُمْ قَاهِرُونَ

*The elders of Pharaoh's people said: Will you leave alone Moses and his people to spread mischief in the land, and forsake you and **your worship**? Pharaoh replied: We will kill their male children and spare their female ones. For indeed we hold irresistible sway over them.* (7:127)

As for the majority reading, one interpretation of that verse is that Fir'awn designated idols for his people to worship in order to gain proximity to God. As such, he proclaimed: ﴾*I am your high lord*﴿ (79:24), meaning I am your lord and the lord of these idols. Another interpretation is that Fir'awn had some gods for himself which he secretly worshiped.

As for the variant reading of Ḥasan, one interpretation is that 'people would leave you and stop worshipping you' since Fir'awn was an object of worship. The second interpretation is that the god being referred to is the sun, for it is reported that he used to worship that as well.

This shādh reading supports the fact that *ilāhah* means worship and this is why one of God's names is *al-ilāh.* Even His proper name *Allah* is derived from this same meaning and root word. They mean the same thing: the one who deserves to be

[105] See, for instance, Ḥusayn Makkī *Sharḥ al-Kharīdah,* vol 1, pg 20.

worshipped in truth. Both Ṭabarī and the author of Fatḥ al-Majīd use this variant reading to support this notion.[106]

[106] *Jāmi' al-bayān,* vol 1, pg 125; *Fatḥ al-majīd,* vol 1, pg 72-3.

Notion of Ikhlāṣ

If tawḥīd of ulūhiyyah is to single out Allah in worship, then the best worship is the purity of intentions towards Allah (ikhlāṣ). Linguistically, *ikhlāṣ* is to purify, preserve, be sincere towards, or choose something. Technically, it refers to the purification of all actions from any tinge of association with God (shirk). The passive participle of the word (*mukhlaṣīn*) appears in the Qur'ān in many verses including the following:

﴿لَقَدْ هَمَّتْ بِهِ وَهَمَّ بِهَا لَوْلَا أَنْ رَأَىٰ بُرْهَانَ رَبِّهِ ۚ كَذَٰلِكَ لِنَصْرِفَ عَنْهُ السُّوءَ وَالْفَحْشَاءَ ۚ إِنَّهُ مِنْ عِبَادِنَا الْمُخْلَصِينَ﴾

﴿And she advanced towards him, and had Yūsuf not perceived a sign from his Lord, he too would have advanced towards her. Thus was Yūsuf shown a sign from his Lord that We might avert from him all evil and indecency, for indeed he was one of Our **chosen servants**.﴾ (12:24)

﴿قَالَ رَبِّ بِمَا أَغْوَيْتَنِي لَأُزَيِّنَنَّ لَهُمْ فِي الْأَرْضِ وَلَأُغْوِيَنَّهُمْ أَجْمَعِينَ ﴿٣٩﴾ إِلَّا عِبَادَكَ مِنْهُمُ الْمُخْلَصِينَ ﴿٤٠﴾﴾

﴿Iblīs said: My Lord! In the manner You led me to error, I will make things on earth seem attractive to them and lead all of them to error, except those of Your servants **whom You have singled out for Yourself**.﴾ (15:39-40)

The singular form (*mukhlaṣ*) appears in one verse:

﴿وَاذْكُرْ فِي الْكِتَابِ مُوسَىٰ ۚ إِنَّهُ كَانَ مُخْلَصًا وَكَانَ رَسُولًا نَبِيًّا﴾

﴿And recite in the Book the account of Mūsā. He was a **chosen one**, a Messenger, a Prophet.﴾ (19:51)

There are variant readings of these words. 'Āṣim, Ḥamzah, Kisā'ī, Khalaf and A'mash read the singular form (*mukhlaṣ*) in their passive participle form [mukhlaṣ], while the rest of the ten along with Ibn Muḥayṣin, Yazīdī and Ḥasan al-Baṣrī read them as active participles [mukhliṣ]:

﴿إِنَّهُ مِنْ عِبَادِنَا الْمُخْلِصِينَ﴾

﴿...he was one of Our **sincere servants**.﴾ (12:24)

As for the plural word, Ibn Kathīr, Abū ʿAmr, Ibn ʿĀmir, Yaʿqūb, Yazīdī, Ḥasan al-Baṣrī, and Ibn Muḥayṣin read all occurrences in the Qur'ān as active participles **[mukhliṣīn]**, whereas Abū Jaʿfar, Nāfiʿ, ʿĀṣim, Ḥamzah, Kisāʾī, Khalaf and Aʿmash read them as passive participles **[mukhlaṣīn]**.[107]

Thaʿlab (d. 291/904)[108] stated: 'The active participle means the one who purifies all worship for Allah, while the passive participle means the one whom Allah purified, i.e. chose them and purified them from sins.'[109] The proofs for the obligation of ikhlāṣ in the Qur'ān and Sunnah are too numerous to list. The variant readings add more evidence, such as the following verse:

وَالْبُدْنَ جَعَلْنَاهَا لَكُم مِّن شَعَائِرِ اللَّهِ لَكُمْ فِيهَا خَيْرٌ ۖ فَاذْكُرُوا اسْمَ اللَّهِ عَلَيْهَا **صَوَافَّ** ۖ فَإِذَا وَجَبَتْ جُنُوبُهَا فَكُلُوا مِنْهَا وَأَطْعِمُوا الْقَانِعَ وَالْمُعْتَرَّ ۚ كَذَٰلِكَ سَخَّرْنَاهَا لَكُمْ لَعَلَّكُمْ تَشْكُرُونَ

*﴾We have appointed sacrificial camels among the symbols of (devotion to) Allah. There is much good in them for you. So pronounce the name of Allah over them **when lined up**, and when they fall down on their sides (after they are slaughtered), eat and also feed them who do not ask and those who ask. Thus, have We subjected these animals that you may give thanks.﴿* (22:36)

The dominant reading **[ṣawāff]** refers to sacrificial animals being arranged in lines or stood up (as camels are slaughtered standing). However, Ḥasan al-Baṣrī read the word **[ṣawāffiya]** which means to be purified for Allah,[110] i.e. do not mention anyone alongside Allah's name:[111]

فَاذْكُرُوا اسْمَ اللَّهِ عَلَيْهَا **صَوَافِيَ**

*So pronounce the name of Allah over them **exclusively**.*

---

[107] *al-Ittiḥāf,* pg 246.
[108] Abū al-ʿAbbās Aḥmad b. Yaḥyā, better known as Thaʿlab, was an early man of literature and Arabic language from Baghdad who was an early proponent of the Kūfan school of grammar.
[109] *Lisān al-ʿArab,* vol 7, pg 26.
[110] *al-Qirāʾāt al-shādhdhah,* pg 72.
[111] *Al-Baḥr al-muḥīṭ,* vol 6, pg 369.

Divine Right of Legislation

To delegate the right of legislation and judgement to Allah is an obligation which no Muslim would dispute. Without doubt, the elimination of divine legislation in favor of man-made laws is one of the most dangerous manifestations of deviation from guidance. Innumerable scholars from the past to present have ruled that replacing divine with manmade legislation is major disbelief (kufr) of the kind that expels one from the religion of Islam, even if the person does not deem it permissible. This is because those actions that are clear disbelief makes its practitioners disbelievers even if they did not intend so, such as prostrating to an idol or cursing Allah. As for sins that do not fall under disbelief, its practitioners do not automatically become disbelievers unless they deem them lawful.

Allah has named those who judge by other than Allah's laws as *ṭāghūt*:

لَمْ تَرَ إِلَى الَّذِينَ يَزْعُمُونَ أَنَّهُمْ آمَنُوا بِمَا أُنزِلَ إِلَيْكَ وَمَا أُنزِلَ مِن قَبْلِكَ يُرِيدُونَ أَن يَتَحَاكَمُوا إِلَى الطَّاغُوتِ وَقَدْ أُمِرُوا أَن يَكْفُرُوا بِهِ وَيُرِيدُ الشَّيْطَانُ أَن يُضِلَّهُمْ ضَلَالًا بَعِيدًا

❴*(O Messenger!) Have you not seen those who claim to believe in the Book which has been revealed to you and in the Books revealed before you, and yet desire to submit their disputes to the judgement of ṭāghūt (false authorities who decide independently of the Law of Allah), whereas they had been asked to reject it. And Satan seeks to make them drift far away from the right way.*❵ (4:60)

The proofs for the impermissibility of judging or ruling by other than Allah's legislation are too numerous to list, and the variant readings establish further evidences, including in the following verse:

وَلَا يُشْرِكُ فِي حُكْمِهِ أَحَدًا

❴*He allows none to share His authority.*❵ (18:26)

The dominant reading of the word is in the third-person present tense as a simple denial **[yushriku]**. Ibn 'Āmir, Ḥasan al-Baṣrī and Muṭawi'ī read the word in the second person as a command **[tushrik]**, i.e. commanding us to not associate anyone with Allah in His rule and authority:[112]

---

[112] *al-Ittiḥāf*, pg. 289.

وَلَا **تُشرِك** فِي حُكمِهِ أَحَدًا

﴿***Do not associate anyone** in His authority.*﴾

This shirk in ḥākimiyyah is not an independent category of shirk but falls within the scope of shirk in rubūbiyyah (Lordship), since one is affirming another legislator other than Allah. It also falls under shirk of Allah's Names and Attributes since one is sharing the divine name al-Ḥakam and the divine attribute al-Ḥukm. It also falls under shirk of ulūhiyyah since one is deflecting to another entity the aspect of worship which represents obedience and delegating authority to Allah's laws.

Another verse with variant readings on the topic is the following:

أَفَحُكمَ الجَاهِلِيَّةِ يَبغُونَ ۚ وَمَن أَحسَنُ مِنَ اللَّهِ حُكمًا لِّقَومٍ يُوقِنُونَ

﴿*(If they turn away from the Law of Allah) do they desire judgement according to the **Law** of Ignorance? But for those who have certainty of belief whose judgement can be better than Allah's?*﴾ (5:50)

The majority read the highlighted word as a verbal noun **[ḥukm]**, whereas Muṭawi'ī reports from A'mash its reading as a different verbal noun **[ḥakam]**:[113]

أَفَحَكَمَ الجَاهِلِيَّةِ يَبغُونَ

*Do they seek the **rulers** of Ignorance?*

Abū Ḥayyān of Andalus stated: Qatādah and A'mash read this verse with **[ḥakam]**, literally meaning 'ruler' but referring to the entire category, as if it was saying 'rulers of Ignorance.' This is referring to the soothsayers and fortune-tellers who used to accept bribes such as sweets and judge between people. The people out of their stupidity wanted the Last Prophet to be a judge very much like those individuals.[114]

Another verse with a variant reading is the following:

وَقَفَّينَا عَلَىٰ آثَارِهِم بِعِيسَى ابنِ مَريَمَ مُصَدِّقًا لِّمَا بَينَ يَدَيهِ مِنَ التَّورَاةِ ۖ وَآتَينَاهُ الإِنجِيلَ فِيهِ هُدًى وَنُورٌ وَمُصَدِّقًا لِّمَا بَينَ يَدَيهِ مِنَ التَّورَاةِ وَهُدًى وَمَوعِظَةً لِّلمُتَّقِينَ ﴿٤٦﴾ **وَلِيَحكُم** أَهلُ الإِنجِيلِ بِمَا أَنزَلَ اللَّهُ فِيهِ ۚ وَمَن لَّم يَحكُم بِمَا أَنزَلَ اللَّهُ فَأُولَٰئِكَ هُمُ الفَاسِقُونَ ﴿٤٧﴾

[113] *al-Ittiḥāf*, pg 200; *al-Qirā'āt al-shādhdhah*, pg 43.
[114] *Al-Baḥr al-Muḥīṭ*, vol 3, pg 505.

﴾*And We sent Jesus, the son of Mary, after those Prophets, confirming the truth of whatever there still remained of the Torah. And We gave him the Gospel, wherein is guidance and light, and which confirms the truth of whatever there still remained of the Torah, and a guidance and admonition for the God-fearing.* ***Let*** *the followers of the Gospel* ***judge*** *by what Allah has revealed therein, and those who do not judge by what Allah has revealed are transgressors.*﴿ (5:46-7)

The majority read the verb as a command **[wal yaḥkum]**, whereas Ḥamzah and Aʿmash read **[waliyaḥkuma]**, which has the following meaning:[115]

وَلِيَحكُم أَهلُ الإِنجِيلِ بِمَا أَنزَلَ اللَّهُ فِيهِ ۚ وَمَن لَّم يَحكُم بِمَا أَنزَلَ اللَّهُ
فَأُولَئِكَ هُمُ الفَاسِقُونَ

﴾***So that*** *the followers of the Gospel* ***may judge*** *by what Allah has revealed therein, and those who do not judge by what Allah has revealed are the transgressors.*﴿

The majority read the verb as a command **[wal yaḥkum]**, meaning that Allah orders the followers of the Gospel to judge according to what was revealed therein just as He commanded the Prophet ﷺ to judge by what Allah revealed to him. The reading of Ḥamzah and Aʿmash **[waliyaḥkuma]** is not a command but for delineating reason or rationale, meaning: We have revealed the Gospel for its followers to judge by.[116]

---

[115] *al-Ittiḥāf,* pg 200.
[116] *Al-Kashf, vol 1,* pg 411.

CHAPTER 4

Heeding the Ties of Kinship/Pleading in their Name

There is a variant reading in the following verse:

يَا أَيُّهَا النَّاسُ اتَّقُوا رَبَّكُمُ الَّذِي خَلَقَكُم مِّن نَّفْسٍ وَاحِدَةٍ وَخَلَقَ مِنْهَا زَوْجَهَا وَبَثَّ مِنْهُمَا رِجَالًا كَثِيرًا وَنِسَاءً ۚ وَاتَّقُوا اللَّهَ الَّذِي تَسَاءَلُونَ بِهِ وَالْأَرْحَامَ ۚ إِنَّ اللَّهَ كَانَ عَلَيْكُمْ رَقِيبًا

﴾*O men! Fear your Lord Who created you from a single being and out of it created its mate; and out of the two spread many men and women. Fear Allah in Whose name you plead for rights and* ***heed the ties of kinship****. Surely, Allah is Ever Watchful over you.*﴿ (4:1)

All of the readings consider the word in the accusative case **[wal-arḥāma]** except for Ḥamzah and A'mash through Muṭawi'ī, who read the word in the genitive case **[wal-arḥāmi]** which produces the following meaning:

وَاتَّقُوا اللَّهَ الَّذِي تَسَاءَلُونَ بِهِ وَالْأَرْحَامِ ۚ إِنَّ اللَّهَ كَانَ عَلَيْكُمْ رَقِيبًا

﴾*Fear Allah, in Whose name* ***and in the name of the ties of kinship****, you plead for rights. Surely, Allah is ever watchful over you.*﴿

This latter reading is supported by the common expression, *I ask you by God and by the familial ties!* This is also the interpretation of Ḥasan al-Baṣrī, 'Aṭā', Ibrāhīm and Mujāhid.[117]

Some grammarians did object to Ḥamzah's reading, but they are excused as this usage was not widespread or established in their eyes. For instance, Zajjāj objected: 'The reading of *al-arḥām* in the genitive case is a grammatical mistake as well as a major mistake in religious matters for the Prophet ﷺ said: *Do not swear oaths by your forefathers*; so how can one plead in the name of ties of kinship?'[118]

Rāzī responded to this objection by saying: 'It could be that the verse is speaking of a pre-Islamic custom (and not necessarily endorsing it) as the pagans used to say, *I ask you by God and by familial ties!* The pre-Islamic custom was not denied, while

[117] *Zād al-Muyassar,* vol 2, pg 3; *al-Durr al-Manthūr,* vol 2, pg 424.
[118] *Ma'ānī al-Qur'ān,* vol 2, pg 6.

the prohibition was intended for future practice.'[119] The Qur'ānic commentator Ibn Kathīr (d. 774)[120] also gave the same response as Rāzī.[121]

Moreover, these objections were brought to the attention of both A'mash and Ḥamzah, and they both responded that this was what they learned from their teachers with continuous chains of transmission back to the Prophet ﷺ and ultimately to Allah.[122]

The majority reading means to fear Allah and heed the familial ties by joining them and not severing them. This is the view of Ibn 'Abbās, Mujāhid, 'Ikrimah, Suddī, and Ibn Zayd.[123]

Grammarians who objected to Ḥamzah's reading were those who followed the Baṣran school and did so on grounds that their principles did not allow the joining of a full noun with a pronoun that is an object of a preposition without repeating the preposition (the reading should have been: *wa bil-arḥāmi*). This was because they did not find precedence for such linguistic usage.

The rebuttal to them is that precedence for such had reached other grammarians and precedence/confirmation is stronger in weight than denial. Such linguistic usage of joining a noun with a pronoun as an object of a preposition is actually found in the Qur'ān in the following verse:

وَجَعَلْنَا لَكُمْ فِيهَا مَعَايِشَ وَمَن لَّسْتُمْ لَهُ بِرَازِقِينَ

﴿*And We have provided sustenance* ***for you*** *on it and also* ***for those*** *of whom you are not the providers.*﴾ (15:20)

Here the noun *man* ('those') is in the genitive case joining the pronoun that is that object of the preposition *lakum* ('for you'), meaning 'for you and for those. . .' The preposition *la* is not repeated for the noun.

Additionally, there is evidence that many early Muslims, including Ja'far al-Ṣādiq, prior to the crystallization of grammar principles read this word in the same way. Ibn Mālik the grammarian alluded to this in his famous 1000-line poem.[124]

---

[119] *Miftāḥ al-Ghayb,* vol 9, pg 164.
[120] Abū al-Fidā' Ismā'īl b. 'Umar b. Kathīr was a great historian, ḥadīth expert, Shāfi'ī jurist, and Qur'ānic commentator from Damascus, who was a student of Ibn Taymiyyah and lived from 701/1300—774/1372.
[121] *Zād al-Muyassar,* vol 2, pg 3; *Tafsīr Ibn Kathīr,* vol 2, pg 179.
[122] Al-Hudhalī, *Al-Kāmil,* manuscript.
[123] 'Abd al-Raḥmān b. Zayd b. Aslam was the son of the Follower Zayd b. Aslam. He died in 82 AH.
[124] *Sharḥ Ibn 'Uqayl,* vol 3, pg 239.

CHAPTER 4

Swearing Oaths

The act of swearing is a noble act of worship which is not allowed to be diverted to anyone other than Allah, as the Prophet ﷺ instructed: *Whoever swears an oath by other than Allah has committed shirk.*[125] This is referring a minor form of shirk which does not expel a person from Islam.

Ḥalf means to swear or take an oath and is done with four letters (bā, wāw, tā and lām) which act as prepositions making their objects take the genitive case. Examples would be: *wallāhi! tallāhi! billāhi!* It carries a sense of amazement and awe of the object of the oath. Sometimes an oath is taken without these letters, in which case the object would simply take the accusative case, as in: *Allāha!* Oaths in the Qur'ān come with the letter wāw in numerous places, and in some places with tā:

وَتَاللَّهِ لَأَكِيدَنَّ أَصْنَامَكُم بَعْدَ أَن تُوَلُّوا مُدْبِرِينَ

❁*By Allah, I shall certainly carry out my plan against your gods after you are gone.*❁ (21:57)

قَالُوا تَاللَّهِ تَفْتَأُ تَذْكُرُ يُوسُفَ حَتَّىٰ تَكُونَ حَرَضًا أَوْ تَكُونَ مِنَ الْهَالِكِينَ

❁*The sons said:* **By Allah!** *You will continue to remember Joseph until you will either consume yourself with grief, or will die.*❁ (12:85)

Ibn Muḥayṣin read every Qur'ānic oath beginning with tā with a bā:[126]

وَبِاللَّهِ لَأَكِيدَنَّ أَصْنَامَكُم بَعْدَ أَن تُوَلُّوا مُدْبِرِينَ

By Allah, I shall certainly carry out my plan against your gods after you are gone.

قَالُوا بِاللَّهِ تَفْتَأُ تَذْكُرُ يُوسُفَ حَتَّىٰ تَكُونَ حَرَضًا أَوْ تَكُونَ مِنَ الْهَالِكِينَ

The sons said: **By Allah!** *You will continue to remember Joseph until you will either consume yourself with grief, or will die.*

In fact, if not for the reading of Ibn Muḥayṣin there would not have been a single Qur'ānic oath with bā except in one case of a non-standard way of stopping in the middle of the following verse:

---

[125] Related by Abū Dāwūd, Tirmidhī, and authenticated by Ḥākim and Dhahabī.
[126] *al-Ittiḥāf*, pg 266.

وَإِذ قَالَ لُقمَانُ لِابنِهِ وَهُوَ يَعِظُهُ
يَا بُنَيَّ لَا تُشرِك بِاللَّهِ إِنَّ الشِّركَ لَظُلمٌ عَظِيمٌ

﴾*And call to mind when Luqmān said to his son while exhorting him: My son, do not associate others with Allah in His Divinity. Surely, associating others with Allah in His Divinity is a mighty wrong.*﴿ (31:13)

By stopping after *lā tushrik*, you can begin *billāhi* as a new sentence which could be understood as an oath with bā:

يَا بُنَيَّ لَا تُشرِك / **بِاللَّهِ** إِنَّ الشِّركَ لَظُلمٌ عَظِيمٌ

My son, do not associate others. By Allah, surely, associating others with Allah in His Divinity is a mighty wrong.

This type of stop is not considered correct, however, for the expression *billāhi* is connected with the command *lā tushrik.*[127] In conclusion, in the reading of Ibn Muḥayṣin there is no Qur'ānic oath with tā, only with wāw and bā. There is no Qur'ānic oath with the letter lām in any reading.

---

[127] *Manār al-hudā fī al-waqf wa al-ibtidā'*, pg 219; Tafsīr Ibn Kathīr, vol 3, pg 587.

Seeking Assistance

There are variant readings of the following verse:

فَاستَغَاثَهُ الَّذِي مِن شِيعَتِهِ عَلَى الَّذِي مِن عَدُوِّهِ فَوَكَزَهُ مُوسَىٰ فَقَضَىٰ عَلَيهِ

﴿*Now the man belonging to Moses' own people* ***cried out to him for help*** *against the man from the foes, and Moses struck him with his fist and finished him.*﴾ (28:15)

All readings utilize the word istighātha **[fastaghāthahu]** whereas Ḥasan al-Baṣrī read read the word in an entirely different form **[fastaʿānahu]**:[128]

فَاستَعَانَهُ الَّذِي مِن شِيعَتِهِ عَلَى الَّذِي مِن عَدُوِّهِ فَوَكَزَهُ مُوسَىٰ فَقَضَىٰ عَلَيهِ

Now the man belonging to Moses' own ***people sought assistance*** *against the man from the foes, and Moses struck him with his fist and finished him.*

Seeking assistance (*istighāthah/istiʿānah*) is normally sought only from Allah but these variant readings prove that they can be directed towards human beings if that assistance is within their capacity.

Excessive Veneration of the Pious

Excessive regard for pious or presumably pious individuals is one of the greatest avenues leading to shirk. The first instance of shirk that occurred in the human race resulted from this among the people the Prophet Nūḥ. The Prophet ﷺ stated: *'Do not exaggerate in praising me as the Christians praised the son of Mary, for I am only a slave. Rather, call me the slave of Allah and His Apostle.'*[129] There are a number of variant readings that add evidence for this:

أَفَرَأَيتُمُ اللَّاتَ وَالعُزَّىٰ

﴿*Have you ever thought about* ***al-Lāt*** *and al-ʿUzzā?*﴾ (53:19)

---

[128] *al-Ittiḥāf*, pg 435.

[129] Ṣaḥīḥ Bukhārī: Kitāb Aḥādīth al-Anbiyā'—Bāb Qawl Allāh: Wadhkur fī al-Kitāb.

Ruways on the authority of Ya'qūb read the word Lāt with a long madd and doubled tā **[al-Lātta]**. This is also related from Ibn 'Abbās, Mujāhid and others:

أَفَرَأَيْتُمُ اللَّاتَّ وَالْعُزَّىٰ

﴿*Have you ever thought about* ***al-Lāt*** *and al-'Uzzā?*﴾ (53:19)

Ibn 'Abbās stated: 'A man was known to knead barley-meal for the pilgrims, and when he died, they began to frequent his grave.' In another report, it is said that he sold barley and butter at a certain rock, over which he would serve it, and when he died, the clan of Thaqīf began to worship the rock out of veneration and esteem for him.[130] In this particular reading, the word *Lātt* would be an active participle of the verb 'to knead.'

The rest of the readers recite it as a proper noun or name **[al-Lāta]**, in which case it is a heretical corruption of God's name *Allah* or *al-Ilāh*, which they derived for their idol. This idol was a large white stone upon which was engraved an image of a house in Ṭā'if which had walls, gates and a courtyard, and which was held in high esteem among the people of Ṭā'if (primarily the Thaqīf clan). The Prophet ﷺ sent Mughīrah b. Shu'bah to destroy it and burn it.[131] In this reading, Kisā'ī stops on the word with hā (*al-Lāh)* and the rest with tā (*al-Lāt*).[132] 'Abd al-Raḥmān b. Ḥasan Āl al-Shaykh[133] stated: There is no contradiction between these two views, for they worshipped the stone and the grave out of esteem and veneration.[134]

---

[130] Ṭabarī, vol 27, pg 35; *al-Durr al-Manthūr*, vol 7, pg 652.
[131] Sīrah Ibn Hishām, vol 4, pg 138.
[132] *al-Ittiḥāf,* pg 402.
[133] He was the grandson of Muḥammad b. 'Abd al-Wahhāb who, after learning from his grandfather, traveled to Egypt to continue his studies at the bequest of Muḥammad Pasha and become the leader of the Ḥanbalī jurists. He died in 1282/1869.
[134] *Fatḥ al-Majīd,* vol 1, pg 255.

Part 2: The Fourteen Readings and Belief in Angels and Scripture

On this topic, I have not found any major influence of variant readings apart from the exact delineation of certain names of angels or books. The angels that are mentioned by name in the Qur'ān are Jibrīl, Mīkāl, Hārūt, Mārūt and Mālik. In addition, the angel of death is mentioned with his title and not by a name. There is also a non-dominant opinion that Sijill is the name of an angel but the truth is that it is a book or register.

Jibrīl

Jibrīl is mentioned by name in the Qur'ān in a number of verses (2:97, 2:98, 66:4) and by various titles in other places, such as *al-Rūḥ* ('Spirit'), *al-Rūḥ al-Amīn* ('Trustworthy Spirit'), and *Rūḥ al-Qudus* ('Holy Spirit'). There are variant readings of the name Jibrīl. Nāfi', Abū 'Amr, Ibn 'Āmir, Ḥafṣ, Abū Ja'far, Ya'qūb and Yazīdī read the word as **[Jibrīl]** and this was the reading of Arabia. Ibn Kathīr and Ibn Muḥayṣin (in one transmission) read it as **[Jabrīl]**. Ḥamzah, Kisā'ī, Khalaf, Shu'bah (in one transmission), and A'mash read it as **[Jabra'īl]**. Shu'bah in another transmission read it as **[Jabra'il]**. Ḥasan al-Baṣrī read it as **[Jabrā'il]**. Shu'bah in one transmission, and Ibn Muḥayṣin in one transmission read it as **[Jabra'ill]**. The basic reason for these differences was the fact that this is a word of non-Arabic origin. Kisā'ī stated: These were foreign words unfamiliar to the Arabs, so they Arabized them in various ways. Aṣma'ī said: 'When the Arabs articulated these foreign names, they played with them in various ways. Some of them applied the words to Arabic meters and scales, while others allowed them to non-conform with standard Arabic measures in order to make their foreign origin clear.'[135]

Mīkāl

This name appears in the following verse:

مَن كَانَ عَدُوًّا لِّلَّهِ وَمَلَائِكَتِهِ وَرُسُلِهِ وَجِبْرِيلَ **وَمِيكَالَ** فَإِنَّ اللَّهَ عَدُوٌّ لِّلْكَافِرِينَ

﴿*Whoever is an enemy of God and His angels and His message-bearers, including Jibrīl and* ***Mīkāl****, [should know that,] verily, God is the enemy of all who deny the truth*﴾ (2:98)

[135] *Kashf,* vol 1, pg 255; *Ḥujjat al-Qirā'āt,* pg 109; *al-Qirā'āt al-Shādhdhah,* pg 32.

Nāfi', Qunbul in one transmission, Abū Ja'far, and Ibn Muḥayṣin in one transmission read the word as **[Mīkā'il]**. Ibn Muḥayṣin in another transmission read it as **[Mīkā'ill]**. Bazzī, Qunbul in another transmission, Ibn 'Āmir, Shu'bah, Ḥamzah, Kisā'ī, Khalaf and A'mash read it as **[Mīkā'īl]**. The remainder read it as **[Mīkāl]**.[136]

Sijill

There is a variant reading as well as variant interpretation of the following verse:

يَومَ نَطوِي السَّمَاءَ كَطَيِّ السِّجِلِّ لِلكُتُبِ

﴿*On that Day We shall roll up the skies as **written scrolls** are rolled up.*﴾ (21:104)

The majority hold the word *sijill* to be a simple noun that refers to a written document or scroll. Some commentators, however, were of the view that Sijill is a proper noun that represents the name of a noble angel. This is the chosen view in *Tafsīr al-Jalālayn.*[137] It is reported from Ibn 'Abbās, Ibn 'Umar, and Suddī that it is the angel assigned to the scriptures.[138] The meaning of this verse according to this interpretation would be that Allah rolls up the skies like the rolling up of the register of human deeds by the angel Sijill. It was also said that Sijill was a Companion who used to write for the Prophet ﷺ but this view is based upon a fabricated report.[139] Ḥasan al-Baṣrī read the word as **[Sijl]** while the rest read **[Sijill]**.[140]

---

[136] *al-Ittiḥāf,* pg 144.
[137] *Tafsīr al-Jalālayn,* pg 431.
[138] Tafsīr Ibn Kathīr, vol 3, pg 100; Tafsīr Qurṭubī, vol 11, pg 302.
[139] Tafsīr Ibn Kathīr, vol 3, pg 100.
[140] *al-Ittiḥāf,* pg 312; *al-Qirā'āt al-shādhdhah,* pg 69.

Other Names

As for the other angels referenced in the Qur'ān (Hārūt, Mārūt, and Mālik), there is no reported difference in their names among the fourteen readings, except for a transmission from Kisā'ī that read the word **[Mālik]** with an imālah vowel: **[Maylik]**.

There is some dispute concerning the terms *raqīb 'atīd* in the following verse:

مَّا يَلْفِظُ مِن قَوْلٍ إِلَّا لَدَيْهِ رَقِيبٌ عَتِيدٌ

﴿*Not even a word can he utter but there is* ***a watcher with him, ever-present.***﴾ (50:18)

The correct view is that these are two attributes of the two recording angels assigned to each human being and not proper names. In any case, there is no variant reading involved in these words.

The Divine Scriptures

The heavenly books mentioned in the Qur'ān are the Qur'ān revealed to Muḥammad ﷺ, the Torah revealed to Mūsā, the Zabūr (Psalms) revealed to Dāwūd, the Injīl (Gospel) revealed to 'Īsā and the *ṣuḥuf* (Pages) of Ibrāhīm which consisted of ten pages, and the *ṣuḥuf* of Mūsā which were also ten pages revealed prior to the Torah.[141] There are some variant readings in these names.

Ibn Kathīr read the word *Qur'ān* with a long-voweled rā and no hamzah and Ḥamzah read it such when stopping on the word **[Qurān]**, while the rest read it in the dominant way with an unvowelled rā followed by a vowelled hamzah **[Qur'ān]**.[142] Ibn Kathīr relied on his reading by considering the word to be a proper noun like *Tawrāh* and not a verbal noun derived from the word *qara'a*. Ḥamzah did consider it to be a verbal noun of *qara'a* but drops the hamzah in stopping as a linguistic convention.[143]

Warsh in one transmission, Abū 'Amr, Ibn Dhakwān, and Ḥamzah in one of his two options all read it with imālah **[Tawrayh]**. Qālūn and Ḥamzah in one of their two options, Warsh in one transmission, and the rest read it without imālah **[Tawrāh]**.[144] Imālah was a known linguistic device of Arabia and was written with yā in the Qur'ānic copies. The absence of imālah was a feature of the region of Najd in central Arabia.

---

141 This appears in a ḥadīth from Abū Dharr related by Ibn Ḥibbān.
142 *Al-Ittiḥāf*, pg 154.
143 *Ḥujjat al-Qirā'āt*, pg 125-6.
144 *Al-Ittiḥāf*, pg. 170.

The word *Injīl* was read by Ḥasan al-Baṣrī with fatḥah **[Anjīl]** and by the rest with kasrah **[Injīl]**.[145] Zamakhsharī asserted that this was proof of the foreign origin of this word since there is no pattern of Arabic that fits with a fatḥah reading.

As for the Zabūr, Ḥamzah, Khalaf, and Aʿmash read it with a ḍammah **[Zubūr]** as a plural of *zubur,* like the word *fulus,* plural *fulūs.* The rest read it with fatḥah **[Zabūr]** on the pattern of *faʿūl*. In the first reading, the word can be considered a plural of the word *zubur*, meaning pages. This would mean that Allah revealed pages to Dāwūd. The dominant reading supports the word as a proper noun for the scripture given to Dāwūd.[146]

---

[145] *Al-Ittiḥāf,* pg. 170.

[146] *Al-Ittiḥāf,* pg. 196; *al-Kashf,* vol 1, pg 403; *Zād al-Muyassar,* vol 2, pg 255.

Part 3: The Fourteen Readings and Belief in Prophethood

Belief in the prophets and messengers sent by God is an essential tenet of belief without which faith can never be complete. Allah says:

آمَنَ الرَّسُولُ بِمَا أُنزِلَ إِلَيْهِ مِن رَّبِّهِ وَالْمُؤْمِنُونَ ۚ كُلٌّ آمَنَ بِاللَّهِ وَمَلَائِكَتِهِ وَكُتُبِهِ وَرُسُلِهِ لَا نُفَرِّقُ بَيْنَ أَحَدٍ مِّن رُّسُلِهِ

﴿*The Messenger has believed in the Guidance which has been sent down to him from his Lord, and those who believe in the Messenger have also sincerely accepted the same. They all believe in Allah, His Angels, His Books and Messengers. And they say, "We do not discriminate against any of His Messengers.*﴾ (2:285)

In addition, the famous ḥadīth of Jibrīl established that when Jibrīl asked about īmān, the Prophet ﷺ replied: '*That you believe in Allah, His angels, His books, His messengers, the Day of Judgement, and in predestination, good and bad.*'[147] There are a number of variant readings that affect some matters pertaining to prophethood.

The Meaning of Prophethood and Messengership

The word *nabīyy* ('Prophet') is linguistically derived either from *anba'a* ('to inform') or from *nabā* ('to raise').

Ibn Zanjalah (d. ~403/1012)[148] said: Nāfiʿ recited the plural with hamzah **[nabī'īn]** as a derivative of *anba'a,* which means that prophets inform people about God, as the verse says: ﴿*Who informed you?*﴾ (66:3) The other readers use a derivative of *nabā* in the pattern of *fa'īl* **[nabiyyīn]**, which means that prophets are elevated and raised people.[149] However, the dominant reading can also be considered to be derived from the word *anba'a*. Makkī b. Abī Ṭālib said: Those who recite it without hamzah do so due to the frequent occurrence of the word and the

---

[147] Ṣaḥīḥ Bukhārī: Kitāb al-Īmān—Bāb su'āl Jibrīl al-nabīyy ʿan al-īmān wa al-islām; Kitāb tafsīr al-Qur'ān: Sūrah Luqmān—Bāb qawl Allah inna Allah ʿindahu ʿilm al-sāʿah; Ṣaḥīḥ Muslim: Kitāb al-Īmān—Bāb bayān al-īmān wal-islām wal-iḥsān (this is the first ḥadīth of Ṣaḥīḥ Muslim); Kitāb al-Īmān—Bāb al-īmān mā huwa wa bayān khiṣāluhu.

[148] Abū Zurʿah ʿAbd al-Raḥmān b. Zanjalah was a great Qur'ānic scholar about whom not much is known, apart from the books he authored. He authored *Ḥujjat al-qirā'āt* on the meanings of the variant readings some time before the year 403 AH.

[149] *Ḥujjat al-qirā'āt,* pg 99.

difficulty of the letter hamzah. The hamzah is simply converted to the letter preceding it, in this case yā.[150]

It should be noted that there is a weak ḥadīth where the Prophet ﷺ reportedly forbade a person from referring to him as the '*nabī'* of Allah' (using the word with a hamzah ending).[151] In addition, Sībawayh stated: It has reached us that some experts of Arabia have deemed *nabī'* with hamzah to be correct, as well as the word *barī'ah* in place of *bariyyah,* but that is not proper.[152] Sībawayh is excused for this lapse as he was likely unaware of the sound transmission of this reading, for had he been aware of it, he would certainly not have rejected it.

Nāfi' recited the word in all its forms in the Qur'ān with hamzah **[nabī'/nabī'īn/nabī'ūn/nubū'ah/anbi'ā']** except for two places in Sūrah al-Aḥzāb where Qālūn from Nāfi' recited without hamzah.[153]

The term *rasūl* comes from the root word r-s-l meaning to follow, and there is no major variant reading of this term, except for the fact that Abū 'Amr, Ḥasan al-Baṣrī, and Yazīdī read it with an unvowelled sīn **[ruslunā/ruslukum/rusluhunm]** while the rest read it with ḍammah on the sīn. The unvowelled sīn reading reflects the dialect of Tamīm, Asad and Qays. It is said that the unvowelled form is the norm while the ḍammah follows it, and vice versa.[154] It is also said that the meanings of *rasūl* and *nabīyy* are synonymous and one term can be substituted for the other.[155] There is at least one verse that has a variant reading affecting this topic:

لَّا تَجْعَلُوا دُعَاءَ الرَّسُولِ بَيْنَكُمْ كَدُعَاءِ بَعْضِكُم بَعْضًا

﴿*O Believers, do not consider the summoning by the* ***Messenger among yourselves*** *like the summoning among you by one another.*﴾ (24:63)

Ḥasan al-Baṣrī read the the expression *al-rasūli baynakum* ('the Messenger among yourselves') as **[al-rasūli nabiyyikum]** ('the Messenger, your Prophet'),[156] which supports the notion that the two terms have the same meaning:

لَّا تَجْعَلُوا دُعَاءَ الرَّسُولِ نَبِيِّكُم كَدُعَاءِ بَعْضِكُم بَعْضًا

O Believers, do not consider the summoning by ***the Messenger, your Prophet****, like the summoning among you by one another.*

---

[150] *Kashf,* vol 1, pg 244.
[151] Al-'Uqaylī reported it in *al-Ḍu'afā'* and Ibn 'Adī in *al-Kāmil.*
[152] *Al-Kitāb,* vol 3, pg 555.
[153] *Al-Ittiḥāf,* pg 138.
[154] *Al-Ittiḥāf,* pg 142-3.
[155] *Tadrīb al-Rāwī,* vol 2, pg 122.
[156] *Ittiḥāf Fuḍalā' al-Bashr,* pg 414.

CHAPTER 4

Some scholars held the view that 'prophet' (nabī) and 'messenger' (rasūl) referred to the same thing. However, the distinction between them is supported by the ḥadīth of Abū Dharr who asked the Prophet how many prophets there were, to which the Prophet responded: '124,000.' When he asked how many of them were messengers, he responded: '313.'[157]

As for the difference between the terms, there are four major views. It is said that the prophet is one who has no revealed scripture while a messenger does. It is also said that the Prophet is not commanded to convey the message whereas a messenger is. It is also said that a prophet does not come with any new divine laws whereas a messenger does bring new divine legislation that abrogates previous ones. This was the view of Ṭaḥāwī. It is also said that the prophet is primarily one who is sent to believers in order to remind them whereas the prophet-messenger is one who is sent to all people, including those who opposed Divine commands. This last view is that of Ibn Taymiyyah. In all of these views, the messenger is more specific than a prophet, for every messenger is also a prophet but not every prophet is a messenger.

---

[157] Related by Ibn Ḥibbān. Ibn Taymiyyah utilized this ḥadīth for evidence in his *Majmū' al-Fatāwā,* vol 16, pg 198.

The Names of Prophets

There are variant readings of a number of prophets mentioned in the Qur'ān. Warsh, for instance, reads the name *Adam* with prolonged madd badal (medium or long) in the beginning as a valid option **[Āādam/Āāādam]**, which the rest read it with a short madd **[Ādam]**.[158]

Ibn 'Āmir, with some differences, reads the name Ibrāhīm with a hā vowelled with fatḥah **[Ibrāhām]** in 33 places in the Qur'ān, all of which are written in the 'Uthmānic codex without the letter yā.[159] Other than these specific positions, all readers read the word in the dominant manner **[Ibrāhīm]**, and the word is written with the letter yā.

There is an interesting historical anecdote concerning this. It was said to Imām Malik that the people of Damascus recited the word as *Ibrāhām*, to which he replied, 'Damascenes have more expertise in eating watermelon than in the recitation of the Qur'ān.' When someone insisted that this was in the 'Uthmānic muṣḥaf, he had the Qur'ān brought out and found that this was indeed the case.[160]

Abū Ja'far and Muṭawi'ī (in one option) read the name *Isrā'īl* with a softened hamzah (tas-hīl) **[Israīl]**. Warsh in one of his options reads with prolonged vowel of the ending madd **[Isrā'īīl/Isrā'īīīl]**. Ḥamzah reads the word when stopping on it, with various ways of softening the hamzah **[Israyīl/Israīl]**. Ḥasan read the word with omission of alif and yā **[Isra'il]**.[161]

Ibn 'Āmir with some differences, Ḥasan al-Baṣrī and Ibn Muḥayṣin in one of his options, read the name *Ilyās*[162] with a definite article **[al-Yās]**, while the rest read it in the dominant way **[Ilyās]**.[163] A related word has a variant reading in the following verse:

سَلَامٌ عَلَىٰ إِلْ يَاسِينَ

﴿*Peace be upon* ***Ilyās.***﴾ (37:130)

Nāfi', Ibn 'Āmir, and Ya'qūb read the word as **[Āli Yāsīn]**, meaning 'family of Yāsīn,' which refers to the children and followers of the prophet Yāsīn:

سَلَامٌ عَلَىٰ آلِ يَاسِينَ

---

[158] *al-Budūr,* pg 28.
[159] *Al-Ittiḥāf,* pg 147.
[160] *Siyar,* vol 8, pg 98.
[161] *al-Ittiḥāf,* pg 135; *al-Qirā'āt al-shādhdhah,* pg 28.
[162] Qur'ān 6:85, 37:123.
[163] *Al-Ittiḥāf,* pg 370.

﴾*Peace be upon the* ***family of Yāsīn.***﴿

The rest of the readers recite the word referring to either a proper name for a prophet **[Ilyāsīn]** or the plural of *Ilyās,* i.e. family and followers of Ilyās.[164]

In the end, there are five variants of the name of this noble prophet, which is a non-Arabic Syriac-origin word that was rendered into Arabic in various ways: Yās, Alyās, Yāsīn, Ilyās, and Ilyāsīn.

The name *Zakariyyā* is read by Ḥafṣ, Ḥamzah, Kisā'ī, Ḥasan al-Baṣrī and A'mash without a hamzah ending **[Zakariyyā]** and by the rest with hamzah **[Zakariyyā']**.[165]

The Prophethood of 'Uzayr is disputed. 'Āṣim, Kisā'ī, Ya'qūb, Ḥasan al-Baṣrī and Yazīdī read the word with tanwīn **['Uzayrun]** and the rest without it **['Uzayr]**. It is also disputed whether the word is of Arabic origin from the root *'azzara*, or a non-Arabic word.[166]

Ḥamzah, Kisā'ī, Khalaf and A'mash read the name *al-Yasa'a*[167] with doubled lām and unvowelled yā **[al-Laysa'a]** as a proper name like *Ḍaygham* to which the definite article is added. The rest read it as **[al-Yasa'a]**.[168]

---

[164] *Al-Ittiḥāf,* pg 371.
[165] *Al-Ittiḥāf,* pg 173.
[166] *Al-Ittiḥāf,* pg 241.
[167] Qur'ān 6:86, 38:48.
[168] *Al-Ittiḥāf,* pg 212.

The Selection of the Prophet

Our Prophet ﷺ is the master of the progeny of Adam. Allah chose him and honored him above the rest of His creation. This is proven by evidence too numerous to list and the variant readings add further clarity to this issue. This includes the following verse:

لَقَدْ جَاءَكُمْ رَسُولٌ مِّنْ أَنفُسِكُمْ

﴿*There has come to you a Messenger* ***from among yourselves.***﴾
(9:128)

Ibn Muḥayṣin in a transmission read the word with fā vowelled with fatḥah **[anfasikum]**, from the root word *nafāsah* ('purity'):

لَقَدْ جَاءَكُمْ رَسُولٌ مِّنْ أَنفَسِكُمْ

There has come to you a Messenger, ***the purest of you****.*

As per the majority reading, the meaning is that the Messenger is from yourselves, i.e. the Arabs as opposed to other groups; or according to some, the progeny of Adam, as opposed to the angels or the jinn.[169]

The Infallibility of Prophets

The infallibility of God's prophets is a Sunnī doctrine concerning which there are two opposing positions: one believing that prophets are protected from every sin, minor and major, as well as forgetfulness and mistakes; while the other denying any absolute protection for the prophets from any sin, forgetfulness or mistake. The middle path is the Sunnī doctrine that they are protected from major sins and not minor ones and that they are not protected from forgetfulness or mistakes. However, since they are under the care of God, they do not persist in their minor sins or mistakes as Divine revelation corrects them. Ibn Taymiyyah defends this position by affirming that it is the view of the vast majority of the scholars of Islam and Muslim groups and that this is the only view soundly transmitted from the Companions and those that followed them.[170]

There are a number of variant readings that support this view. The first is the variant reading of the following verse:

---

[169] *Al-Ittiḥāf,* pg 236.
[170] *Majmū',* vol 4, pg 319.

وَمَا كَانَ لِنَبِيٍّ أَن يَغُلَّ ۚ وَمَن يَغْلُلْ يَأْتِ بِمَا غَلَّ يَوْمَ الْقِيَامَةِ ۚ ثُمَّ تُوَفَّىٰ كُلُّ نَفْسٍ مَّا كَسَبَتْ وَهُمْ لَا يُظْلَمُونَ

﴿*It is not for a Prophet to* ***defraud****; and whoever defrauds shall bring with him the fruits of his fraud on the Day of Resurrection, when every human being shall be paid in full what he has earned, and shall not be wronged.*﴾ (3:161)

Ibn Kathīr, Abū ʿAmr, ʿĀṣim, Ibn Muḥayṣin and Yazīdī read the word in the active tense with fatḥah on the yā **[yaghull]** while the rest read it in the passive tense with ḍammah **[yughall]**:[171]

وَمَا كَانَ لِنَبِيٍّ أَن يُغَلَّ

﴿*It is not for a Prophet* ***to be defrauded.***﴾

In the first reading, the meaning is that the Prophet is protected from a major sin such as defrauding and that it is not possible for a prophet to fall into such a sin. It is not allowed to conceive of such a thing to emanate from a prophet, i.e. to attribute such a thing to a prophet.[172]

The second reading means that a prophet cannot be a victim of such a thing from someone else, i.e. that no one can or should deceive a prophet. This is a statement of fact that is meant as a prohibition ('Do not deceive a prophet.').

Another meaning of this reading could be that fraud cannot be attributed to a prophet, i.e. 'And it is not attributable to a prophet that he would act unfaithfully.' The meaning could also be that a prophet could never be found to act unfaithfully.

Allah is denying the accusation of acting unfaithfully on the part of the prophet and also forbidding us to act unfaithfully, particularly with the Prophet ﷺ. He is also forbidding us from attributing such a thing to the Prophet. With these two variants of one verse, we have an informative statement as well as two prohibitions.

In effect, one verse through simple variant readings of a single word become like three separate verses in a miraculously brief and unique way. Glorified is Allah, whose speech this is![173]

Rāzī lists the wisdom of prohibiting us from defrauding the Prophet ﷺ, though we know that we are prohibited from acting in such a way towards anyone. First of all, the more honorable the object of your treachery, the more monstrous the crime, and the Prophet ﷺ being the best of creation makes this sin even more magnified. Second, since revelation was continuously coming down upon the Prophet ﷺ, acting

---

[171] *Al-Ittiḥāf,* pg 181.
[172] *Al-Kashf,* vol 1, pg 363.
[173] *Al-Qirā'āt wa athruhā,* vol 2, pg 506; *al-Kashf,* vol 1, pg 363.

unfaithfully towards him would carry the grave risk of being mentioned by revelation, thus destroying one's next life along with being disgraced in this one. Lastly, Muslims were extremely indigent and oppressed at the time of this revelation, making this crime even more grave.[174]

Qurṭubī stated: 'The Prophet was specified here because treachery with him is of the utmost seriousness and gravity since sins are magnified in his presence due to his esteemed status, and the rulers who follow the position of the Prophet also have a share in that venerated status.'[175]

Ibn ʿAbbās objected to the passive reading of the verse as unlikely: 'How can that be denied when the prophets were even the subject of murder in the Qur'ān—﴿*And they kill the prophets.*﴾ (3:112)?' The meaning of the verse is that when the hypocrites accused the Prophet ﷺ of something, Allah revealed that the Prophet ﷺ would never defraud others, i.e. defraud his nation in the spoils of war.[176]

What Ibn ʿAbbās denied was the specific meaning of the verse as a statement of fact which denied that the Prophet ﷺ could be the subject of deception or fraud. Since this historically did occur, this is not the meaning of the verse. This misunderstanding could be removed by the previously mentioned interpretation of experts that the reading of the verse as a statement of fact was meant in the sense of a prohibition (i.e. do not do that). This passive-tense reading is soundly established through mass-transmission.

Another variant reading lies in the following verse:

حَتَّىٰٓ إِذَا اسْتَيْأَسَ الرُّسُلُ وَظَنُّوٓا أَنَّهُمْ قَدْ **كُذِبُوا** جَاءَهُمْ نَصْرُنَا فَنُجِّيَ مَن
نَّشَاءُۖ وَلَا يُرَدُّ بَأْسُنَا عَنِ الْقَوْمِ الْمُجْرِمِينَ

﴿*Until the Messengers despaired of their people, and the people also thought that* ***they had been told lies*** *(by the Messengers), then suddenly Our help came to the Messengers. And when such an occasion comes We rescue whom We will; as for the guilty, Our chastisement cannot be averted from them.*﴾ (12:110)

ʿĀṣim, Ḥamzah, Kisāʾī, Abū Jaʿfar, Khalaf and Aʿmash read the verb in the simple passive tense **[kudhibū]**, meaning that the people to whom the messengers were sent believed the messengers were lied to by God with His promises of victory. It could also mean that the people themselves believed that they were lied to by the prophets.

---

174 *Tafsīr al-Rāzī,* vol 9, pg 72.
175 *Tafsīr al-Qurṭubī,* vol 4, pg 256.
176 *Al-Kashf,* vol 1, pg 363.

It is reported from ʿĀ'ishah that she rejected this particular reading since it wasn't soundly established in her eyes, for she presumed the subject of the verb *dhannū* ('they believed') to be the prophets. Since she believed in the infallibility of the prophets, she believed they were protected from having bad thoughts about Allah. It is also alternately reported from ʿĀ'ishah that she read with this variant, perhaps after she had learned of its soundness.[177]

The other readers read this word in its derived form **[kudhdhibū]**, and in this reading the subject are the messengers, who knew with certainty that they had been deemed liars:[178]

حَتَّىٰٓ إِذَا اسْتَيْأَسَ الرُّسُلُ وَظَنُّوٓا أَنَّهُمْ قَدْ كُذِّبُوا

﴾*Until the Messengers despaired of their people and* ***knew that they had been deemed liars*** *. . .*﴿

Another variant lies in the following:

وَمَا كُنتُ مُتَّخِذَ الْمُضِلِّينَ عَضُدًا

﴾***And I*** *do not seek the aid of those who lead people astray.*﴿ (18:51)

Abū Jaʿfar and Ḥasan al-Baṣrī read the pronoun in the second person **[wa mā kunta]** addressed to the Prophet:

وَمَا كُنتَ مُتَّخِذَ الْمُضِلِّينَ عَضُدًا

﴾***And you*** *do not seek the aid of those who lead people astray.*﴿

The intention of this verse was to inform the Muslims that the Prophet was protected from the beginning from seeking the aid of the misguided ones or inclining towards them. More details on this are forthcoming in a subsequent section.

The other readers recite the word in the first person **[wa mā kuntu]** as a statement of fact with Allah informing people that He is free of need and independent from anyone.[179]

A final variant lies in the following verses:

---

177 *Al-Ittiḥāf,* pg 268; *al-Kashf,* vol 2, pg 15.
178 Ibid.
179 *Al-Ittiḥāf,* pg 291.

وَمَا صَاحِبُكُم بِمَجنُونٍ ﴿٢٢﴾ وَلَقَد رَآهُ بِالأُفُقِ المبِينِ ﴿٢٣﴾ وَمَا هُوَ
عَلَى الغَيبِ بِضَنِينٍ ﴿٢٤﴾ وَمَا هُوَ بِقَولِ شَيطَانٍ رَّجِيمٍ ﴿٢٥﴾ فَأَينَ
تَذهَبُونَ ﴿٢٦﴾

﴾*(O people of Makkah), your companion is not mad; he indeed saw the message-bearer on the clear horizon; nor* ***does he withhold*** *(conveying this knowledge about) the Unseen; nor is it a word of an accursed Satan. Where to are you then heading?*﴿ (81:22-6)

The majority reading is with the letter ḍād **[biḍanīn]** from the root *ḍanah* for stinginess. The meaning is that the Prophet ﷺ was never frugal or miserly with conveying the revelation to people but fulfilled his duty by conveying all of revelation to his people.

This proves the infallibility of the Prophet ﷺ in the sense that he was protected from withholding knowledge or information from Allah and not conveying it to others.

Ibn Kathīr, Abū ʿAmr, Kisāʾī, Yaʿqūb through Ruways, Ibn Muḥayṣin and Yazīdī read the word with the letter ẓā **[biẓanīn]**, which has the meaning of being accused:[180]

وَمَا هُوَ عَلَى الغَيبِ بِظَنِينٍ

﴾*Nor is he* ***accused of withholding*** *(conveying this knowledge about) the Unseen.*﴿

[180] *Al-Nashr,* vol 2, pg 398-9; *Al-Ittiḥāf,* pg 434.

CHAPTER 4

The Finality of Prophethood

There is a variant reading on this topic in the following verse:

مَّا كَانَ مُحَمَّدٌ أَبَا أَحَدٍ مِّن رِّجَالِكُمْ وَلَٰكِن رَّسُولَ اللَّهِ وَخَاتَمَ النَّبِيِّينَ ۗ وَكَانَ اللَّهُ بِكُلِّ شَيْءٍ عَلِيمًا

﴿*Muhammad is not the father of any of your men, but he is the Messenger of Allah and the **seal/last** of the Prophets. Allah has full knowledge of everything.*﴾ (33:40)

'Āṣim and Ḥasan al-Baṣrī read the word with fatḥah **[khātam]** as an instrument while the rest read it with kasrah as an active participle **[khātim]**:[181]

مَّا كَانَ مُحَمَّدٌ أَبَا أَحَدٍ مِّن رِّجَالِكُمْ وَلَٰكِن رَّسُولَ اللَّهِ وَخَاتِمَ النَّبِيِّينَ ۗ وَكَانَ اللَّهُ بِكُلِّ شَيْءٍ عَلِيمًا

﴿*Muhammad is not the father of any of your men, but he is the Messenger of Allah and the **seal/last** of the Prophets. Allah has full knowledge of everything.*﴾

Ibn Manẓūr said: '*Khātam* with fatḥah refers to a stamp, ring or seal whereas both *khātam* and *khātim* with kasrah can refer to the last of people. The Prophet Muḥammad ﷺ is both the seal and the last of the prophets.'[182] In the end, both readings support one another to establish the notion that there is no prophet after the Prophet Muḥammad ﷺ.

Ibn Kathīr said: 'This verse is proof that there is no prophet after Muḥammad ﷺ. Since there is no prophet, it is even more established that there is no messenger after him, since messengership is more specific than prophethood.'[183]

Despite that, however, there were many liars and impostors that claimed to be prophets after our Prophet ﷺ by relying on their assertion that the verse refers only to a ring or seal and teaches us that the Prophet Muḥammad ﷺ was the adornment or embellishment of all prophets.

However, there is consensus of Muslim scholars from past to present that the verse establishes the finality of prophethood for Muḥammad ﷺ. Also, it was not customary linguistic usage to utilize the term *khātam* to praise a person in the sense of adornment. Finally, there are numerous proofs from the Sunnah that clarify the

---

[181] *Al-Itti ḥāf,* pg 355.
[182] *Lisān al-'Arab,* vol 12, pg 163-4.
[183] *Tafsīr Ibn Kathīr,* vol 3, pg 474; *Qurṭubī,* vol 14, pg 196.

meaning of the Qur'ān and establish that there would be no more prophets after him, peace be upon him:

وَسَيَخْرُجُ فِي أُمَّتِي كَذَّابُونَ ثَلَاثُونَ كُلُّهُمْ يَزْعُمُ أَنَّهُ نَبِيٌّ، وَأَنَا خَاتَمُ الْأَنْبِيَاءِ، لَا نَبِيَّ بَعْدِي

And indeed there shall be thirty imposters in my nation, each of them claiming that he is a Prophet. And I am the last of the Prophets, there is no Prophet after me.[184]

وَإِنَّهُ لَا نَبِيَّ بَعْدِي

Surely there is no prophet after me.[185]

جِئْتُ فَخَتَمْتُ الْأَنْبِيَاءَ

I have come to finalize the chain of the prophets.[186]

Makkī b. Abī Ṭālib said: "Āṣim read *khātam* with fatḥah meaning that he served as the final prophet, with no more after him, with no action on his part. He is simply the last of all prophets. The rest read *khātim* with kasrah which is an active participle indicating that the Prophet completed the line of prophets, with no more to come after him.'[187]

This proves that restricting the fatḥah reading of ʿĀṣim to mean the 'seal' as an instrument is not correct, but those who interpreted the meaning as an instrumental seal meant it in the sense that a seal formally ends and finalizes a written work.

Qāḍī ʿIyāḍ stated: 'Those who claimed the prophethood of anyone other than Muḥammad ﷺ during his lifetime or after, such as the ʿĪsāwiyyah among the Jews, the Khurramites who believed in continuous messengers, many Rāfiḍī Shīʿah who believed in ʿAlī's share in prophethood, those who claimed prophethood for themselves, or believed it could be attained by purifying one's heart, or even those who claimed to received revelation though they may not claim prophethood, all of these are disbelievers in the Prophet Muḥammad ﷺ who clearly stated that he is the last of the prophets with none to come after him. He also informed us from Allah that He referred to him as the Seal of Prophets and that he was sent to all mankind. The Muslim ummah unanimously held the position that these statements are to be

[184] Tirmidhī: Abwāb al-fitan—Bāb mā jā'a lā taqūm al-sāʿah; Abū Dāwūd : Kitāb al-fitan—Bāb dhikr al-fitan wa dalā'iluhā; Munad Aḥmad; Tirmidhī deemed it ṣaḥīḥ.
[185] Ṣaḥīḥ Bukhārī: Kitāb aḥādīth al-anbiyā'—Bāb mā dhukira ʿan banī Isrāʾīl; Ṣaḥīḥ Muslim: Kitāb al-imārah—Bāb al-amr bi al-wafā' bibaiʿat al-khulafā' al-awwal fal-awwal.
[186] Ṣaḥīḥ Bukhārī: Kitāb al-manāqib—Bāb khātam al-nabiyyīn; Ṣaḥīḥ Muslim: Kitāb al-faḍā'il—Bāb dhikru kawnihī khātam al-nabiyyīn.
[187] *Al-Kashf*, vol 2, pg 199.

taken literally in their overt meanings, without interpreting them away from their apparent meanings and without specifying them.'[188]

[188] *Al-Shifā,* vol 2, pg 1070.

The Father of Ibrāhīm

There is a variant reading in the name of the father of Ibrāhīm:

وَإِذْ قَالَ إِبْرَاهِيمُ لِأَبِيهِ آزَرَ أَتَتَّخِذُ أَصْنَامًا آلِهَةً إِنِّي أَرَاكَ وَقَوْمَكَ فِي ضَلَالٍ مُبِينٍ

﴾*And recall when Abraham said to his father, **Āzar**: 'Do you take idols for gods? I see you and your people in obvious error.*﴿ (6:74)

Ya'qūb and Ḥasan al-Baṣrī read the word with a ḍammah on the rā **[Āzaru]** while the rest read it with fatḥah as a representation of the genitive case since it is indeclinable due to being a non-Arabic origin proper name **[Āzara]**. The ḍammah reading is as an invocation ('O Āzar!'), which is supported by the muṣḥaf of Ubayy b. Ka'b which had the words *Yā Āzaru.*

It is said that Tārakh was his name and Āzar was his title. Some say Āzar was his description, meaning crooked, or old man. There is also an interpretation in tafsīr that Āzar was the name of an idol, but this is refuted by the reading of Ya'qūb and Ḥasan al-Baṣrī.[189]

It was also claimed that Āzar was the name of Ibrāhīm's uncle. Proponents of this view supported this by the fact that Ibrāhīm was forbidden to pray for the idolaters, and it is established that he made the following supplication: ﴾*Our Lord! Forgive me and my parents and the believers on the Day when the reckoning will take place.*﴿ (14:41) Also, the reference to uncles as fathers is established in the Qur'ān as Ismā'īl referred to his fathers: ﴾*And the God of your fathers Ibrāhīm, Ismā'īl and Isḥāq.*﴿ (2:133).

In response, the reference to an uncle as father does not take place categorically but only when the uncle is included among other relatives like fathers and grandfathers, in which case the term *father* would be inclusive of all the relations. In all instances of the Qur'ān, the idolater is referred to as *father* and never as *uncle*. The supplication of Ibrāhīm for his parent's forgiveness occurred before the prohibition. Regarding his mother, some believe she became a believer while others believed she remained an idolater. It is also possible that the reference to parents in the supplication is intended to apply to Adam and Nuh and others prior to Ibrāhīm. There is even a shādh reading variant of the supplication: *Forgive me and my children (wa li waladī) and the believers . . .*[190]

---

[189] *Al-Ittiḥāf,* pg 211; Tafsīr al-Jalālayn, pg 176.
[190] Tafsīr Ibn Kathīr, vol 2, pg 574; Tafsīr al-Jalālayn, pg 336.

CHAPTER 4

The Unity of the Prophetic Messages

There is a variant reading of the following verse:

اللَّهُ أَعْلَمُ حَيْثُ يَجْعَلُ رِسَالَتَهُ

❮*Allah knows best where to place His **message**.*❯ (6:124)

Ibn Kathīr, Ḥafṣ, and Ibn Muḥayṣin read the word in the singular [risālatahu] while the rest read it as plural [risālātihī].[191]

اللَّهُ أَعْلَمُ حَيْثُ يَجْعَلُ رِسَالَاتِهِ

❮*Allah knows best where to place His **messages**.*❯ (6:124)

Also, there is a similar variant in the following:

يَا أَيُّهَا الرَّسُولُ بَلِّغْ مَا أُنزِلَ إِلَيْكَ مِن رَّبِّكَ ۖ وَإِن لَّمْ تَفْعَلْ فَمَا بَلَّغْتَ رِسَالَتَهُ ۚ وَاللَّهُ يَعْصِمُكَ مِنَ النَّاسِ ۗ إِنَّ اللَّهَ لَا يَهْدِي الْقَوْمَ الْكَافِرِينَ

❮*O Messenger! Deliver what has been revealed to you from your Lord, for if you fail to do that, you have not fulfilled the task of His **messengership**. Allah will certainly protect you from the evil of men. Surely Allah will not guide the unbelievers (to succeed against you).*❯ (5:67)

Nāfi', Ibn 'Āmir, Shu'bah from 'Āṣim, Abū Ja'far, Ya'qūb and Ḥasan al-Baṣrī read the word as plural [risālātihī] while the rest read it in the singular [risālatahu].[192] The plural reading here, which refers to the Prophet ﷺ, is an allusion to the fact that His message and mission represented that of all previous prophets. The singular reading reinforces the fact that the message of all prophets was one and the same. The Prophet ﷺ stated: '*I am the closest of people to 'Īsā b. Maryam in this world and the next, for the prophets are paternal brothers with different mothers but the same religion.*'[193]

Dr. Bāzmūl states: The religion of the prophets was the same not only in the doctrine of Tawḥīd, but also in aspects of faith, ethics, fundamentals of worship such as prayer, charity and fasting; and in basic transactions such as trade, marriage,

---

[191] *Al-Ittiḥāf*, pg 216.
[192] *Al-Ittiḥāf*, pg 202.
[193] Ṣaḥīḥ Bukhārī: Kitāb aḥādīth al-anbiyā'—Bāb qawl Allāh wadhkur fī al-kitābi Maryam; Ṣaḥīḥ Muslim: Kitāb al-faḍā'il—Bāb faḍā'il 'Īsā.

slaughter, inheritance, penal law, etc. The difference is only in form and not substance.[194]

[194] *Al-Qirā'āt wa athrihā,* vol 2, pg 538-9.

CHAPTER 4

Part 4: The Fourteen Readings and Belief in the Last Day

Belief in the Hereafter is an essential tenet of Islamic belief and means to affirm with conviction that it will occur and to act accordingly. This includes belief in the signs of the Day of Judgement, death and what lies beyond, the trials, punishments and blessings of the grave, the blowing of the Trumpet, resurrection of bodies from earth, the details of the Gathering, the Register of Deeds, the weighing of deeds, the Bridge, the Fount, Intercession, Paradise and Hellfire. The variant readings add to our understanding of some of these details.

Descent of ʿĪsā

The descent of ʿĪsā towards the end of days is soundly established by the Qur'ān, Sunnah and consensus. Allah says: ﴾*There are none among the People of the Book but will believe in him before his death, and he will be a witness against them on the Day of Resurrection.*﴿ (4:159). The Prophet ﷺ stated: '*By Allah, ʿĪsā b. Maryam shall surely descend to judge with justice.*'[195] The Prophet ﷺ also informed us that ʿĪsā will remain for forty years after killing Dajjāl and die a natural death, with a normal funeral prayer conducted over him by Muslims.[196] A report from Ṣaḥīḥ Muslim establishes that ʿĪsā will descend on a white minaret in eastern Damascus[197] and will perform pilgrimage in Makkah.[198] The reports about the descent of ʿĪsā are mass-transmitted from more twenty five Companions.[199]

There is a variant reading on this issue in the following verse:

وَإِنَّهُۥ لَعِلْمٌ لِّلسَّاعَةِ

﴾*Verily he represents* ***knowledge*** *of the Hour.*﴿ (43:61)

The majority read the word as 'knowledge' **[la ʿilmun]** while Aʿmash read it in the meaning of 'condition' or 'sign' **[la ʿalamun]**:[200]

---

[195] Ṣaḥīḥ Bukhārī: Kitāb al-Buyūʿ—Bāb qatl al-khinzīr; Kitāb al-maẓālim—Bāb kasr al-ṣalīb wa qatl al-khinzīr; Kitāb aḥādīth al-anbiyā'—Bāb nuzūl ʿĪsā; Ṣaḥīḥ Muslim" Kitāb al-īmān—Bāb nuzūl ʿĪsā b. Maryam ḥākiman bi sharīʿat nabiyyinā Muḥammad.

[196] Sunan Abī Dāwūd: Kitāb al-malāḥim—Bāb khurūj al-Dajjāl; Musnad Aḥmad: musnad Abī Hurayrah. This ḥadīth was authenticated by Aḥmad Shākir.

[197] Ṣaḥīḥ Muslim: Kitāb al-fitan wa ashrāṭ al-sāʿah—Bāb dhikr al-Dajjāl wa ṣifatuhū wa man maʿahu.

[198] Ṣaḥīḥ Muslim: Kitāb al-Ḥajj—Bāb ihlāl al-nabī wa hadyihī.

[199] *Ashrāṭ al-sāʿah*, pg 350-1.

[200] *Al-Ittiḥāf*, pg 368; *al-Qirāʿāt al-shādhdhah*, pg 80.

وَإِنَّهُ لَعِلْمٌ لِّلسَّاعَةِ

❧*Verily he represents a **sign** of the Hour.*❧

In the majority reading, the coming of 'Īsā represents the knowledge that the Day of Judgement is close. In the reading of A'mash, his coming is a sign or indication that the Day of Judgment is close. Both readings support the notion that the descent of 'Īsā is a great sign of the Hour, while the reading of A'mash is more explicit.

Emergence of the Beast

The emergence of the beast is another sign of the Hour established by Qur'ān, Sunnah and consensus. In the ḥadīth related through Hudhayfah b. Usayd, the Prophet ﷺ referenced ten major signs, one of them being the beast.[201] There is a relevant variant reading in the following verse:

وَإِذَا وَقَعَ الْقَوْلُ عَلَيْهِمْ أَخْرَجْنَا لَهُم دَابَّةً مِّنَ الْأَرْضِ تُكَلِّمُهُمْ أَنَّ النَّاسَ كَانُوا بِآيَاتِنَا لَا يُوقِنُونَ

❧*And when the time for the fulfilment of Our Word against them will come, We shall bring forth for them a beast from the earth **who will speak to them**, telling them that the people did not believe in Our Signs.*❧ (27:82)

All readers read the variant word as a simple verb 'to speak' **[tukallimuhum]** except for Ḥasan al-Baṣrī who read it as **[tasimuhum]** from the root word *simah*, meaning 'mark' or 'sign':[202]

أَخْرَجْنَا لَهُم دَابَّةً مِّنَ الْأَرْضِ تَسِمُهُمْ أَنَّ النَّاسَ كَانُوا بِآيَاتِنَا لَا يُوقِنُونَ

❧*We shall bring forth for them a beast from the earth **who will serve as a sign** because people did not believe in Our Signs.*❧

The reading of Ibn 'Abbās was very close to this in meaning, for he read the word as **[taklimuhum]** from the root *kalm* meaning to 'wound':[203]

أَخْرَجْنَا لَهُم دَابَّةً مِّنَ الْأَرْضِ تَكْلِمُهُمْ أَنَّ النَّاسَ كَانُوا بِآيَاتِنَا لَا يُوقِنُونَ

---

[201] Ṣaḥīḥ Muslim: Kitāb al-fitan wa ashrāṭ al-sāʿah—Bāb fī al-āyāt allatī takūnu qabla al-sāʿah.
[202] *Al-Ittiḥāf*, pg 339.
[203] *Tafsīr al-Qurṭubī*, vol 13, pg 238.

﴿*We shall bring forth for them a beast from the earth* ***who will wound/mark the people*** *because people did not believe in Our Signs.*﴾

There is even another variant in this verse in the particle *anna*:

وَإِذَا وَقَعَ الْقَوْلُ عَلَيهِم أَخرَجنَا لَهُم دَابَّةً مِّنَ الأَرضِ تُكَلِّمُهُم أَنَّ النَّاسَ كَانُوا بِآيَاتِنَا لَا يُوقِنُونَ

﴿*And when the time for the fulfilment of Our Word against them will come, We shall bring forth for them a beast from the earth who will speak to them,* ***telling them that*** *people did not believe in Our Signs.*﴾

ʿĀṣim, Ḥamzah, Kisāʾī, Yaʿqūb, Khalaf, Aʿmash and Ḥasan read the word with an initial fatḥah **[anna]**, which serves to specify the speech that the beast would utter. The rest of the readers read the word with an initial kasrah **[inna]**:

وَإِذَا وَقَعَ الْقَوْلُ عَلَيهِم أَخرَجنَا لَهُم دَابَّةً مِّنَ الأَرضِ تُكَلِّمُهُم إِنَّ النَّاسَ كَانُوا بِآيَاتِنَا لَا يُوقِنُونَ

﴿*And when the time for the fulfilment of Our Word against them will come, We shall bring forth for them a beast from the earth who will speak to them.* ***Surely,*** *the people did not believe in Our Signs.*﴾

This grammatically creates an independent sentence after the particle which serves as an objection or criticism from Allah to what comes before it.[204]

---

[204] *Al-Ittiḥāf*, pg 339; *Ḥujjat al-Qirāʾāt*, pg 538.

Blowing of the Trumpet

The trumpet (*ṣūr*) is a massive horn that the angel Isrāfīl has placed upon his lips awaiting Allah's command to blow on it. It has been named in the Qur'ān as *Nāqūr*: ﴾*And when the Trumpet (nāqūr) shall be sounded*﴿ (74:8). There are two blowings: the blowing that will signal terror and death (*nafkhat al-faza' wa al-ṣa'iq*) and the blowing that will cause resurrection (*nafkhat al-ba'th*). Between the two is a period of forty days, one month, or one year.

It is also said that Trumpet signaling terror (*faza'*) is separate from the one that signals death (*ṣa'iq*), which would make three soundings of the trumpet in all.[205] However, this opposes the apparent meaning of the verse. In the end, these blowings of the trumpet are established in the Qur'ān, Sunnah and consensus. Its verses include the following:

وَنُفِخَ فِي الصُّورِ فَصَعِقَ مَن فِي السَّمَاوَاتِ وَمَن فِي الْأَرْضِ إِلَّا مَن شَاءَ اللَّهُ ۖ ثُمَّ نُفِخَ فِيهِ أُخْرَىٰ فَإِذَا هُم قِيَامٌ يَنظُرُونَ

﴾*And the **Trumpet** shall be blown and all who are in the heavens and the earth shall fall down dead save those whom Allah wills. Then the Trumpet shall be blown again, and lo! all of them will be standing and looking on.*﴿ (39:68)

وَيَوْمَ يُنفَخُ فِي الصُّورِ فَفَزِعَ مَن فِي السَّمَاوَاتِ وَمَن فِي الْأَرْضِ إِلَّا مَن شَاءَ اللَّهُ ۚ وَكُلٌّ أَتَوْهُ دَاخِرِينَ

﴾*The Day when the **Trumpet** will be blown all those who are in the heavens and on the earth shall be terror-stricken, except those whom Allah wills - and everyone shall come to Him utterly abject.*﴿ (27:87)

وَنُفِخَ فِي الصُّورِ فَإِذَا هُم مِّنَ الْأَجْدَاثِ إِلَىٰ رَبِّهِمْ يَنسِلُونَ

﴾*Then the **Trumpet** shall be blown and lo! they will come out of their graves and be on the move towards their Lord.*﴿ (36:51)

---

[205] The great scholar Abū al-A'lā Mawdūdī, for instance, held the view that there were three signals of the trumpet in all, based upon a reading of all the verses in combination with ḥadīth reports. He considered Qur'ān 27:87 to represent a separate signaling. *The Meaning of the Qur'ān,* vol 4, pg 414. Ibn Kathīr also held this view (*Tafsīr al-Qur'ān al-'Aẓīm*,pg. 1628-9) as did Shaykh Wahbah al-Zuḥaylī in *al-Tafsīr al-Wasīṭ*, vol 3, pg 2253.

وَيَوْمَ يَقُولُ كُن فَيَكُونُ ۚ قَوْلُهُ الْحَقُّ ۚ وَلَهُ الْمُلْكُ يَوْمَ يُنفَخُ فِي الصُّورِ

﴾*And the very day He will say: Be! And there will be. His word is the Truth and His will be the dominion on the day when the **Trumpet** is blown.*﴿ (6:73)

In all these verses, Ḥasan al-Baṣrī read the word in the plural form **[al-ṣuwari]** which would be the plural of the word *ṣūrah* meaning 'images' or 'forms.'[206] For instance:

وَنُفِخَ فِي الصُّوَرِ فَإِذَا هُم مِّنَ الْأَجْدَاثِ إِلَىٰ رَبِّهِمْ يَنسِلُونَ

﴾*Then [the souls] shall be blown into the **forms** (bodies) and lo! they will come out of their graves and be on the move towards their Lord.*﴿

This reading would be referring to the blowing of the souls into bodies. Rāzī comments that the word *ṣūr* refers to a horn and that it is also reported by some that the Qur'ānic word is the plural *ṣuwar* which would be referring to the souls being blown into bodies, as read by Ḥasan al-Baṣrī.[207] Ibn al-Athīr references both views and considers the first (*ṣūr* is a trumpet) to be correct since it is supported by sound ḥadīth reports.[208]

There are two major problems with Ḥasan's reading. First, what is the chronology of the blowing into the bodies in relation to the other known blowings of the Trumpet? Secondly, how does this explanation fit with verse 39:68, where two blowings are mentioned with the second using the masculine pronoun (*thumma nufikha fīhi ukhrā*) whereas *ṣuwar* is a feminine word. Obviously, the blowing of souls into bodies is a one-time event. I have not come across a decisive answer to these two objections in my humble study of tafsīr and Qur'ān literature, so I have endeavored to give my own response.

As to the first, the answer is found in the following ḥadīth: *All human beings will be consumed by the earth except for their tailbones, from which they will sprout [again]. Allah will send life-water which will make them grow out like green vegetation. When the bodies come out, Allah will send the souls, each of which will hasten to its body and will be blown into their forms, while they are standing watching.*[209] This report shows that the blowing of souls takes place between the two blowings.

---

[206] *Al-Ittiḥāf,* pg 340, 377.

[207] *Mukhtār al-ṣiḥāḥ,* pg 373.

[208] *Al-Nihāyah,* vol 3, pg 60.

[209] This ḥadīth is related by Ibn Abī 'Āṣim in *al-Sunnah* with an isnād which al-Albānī deemed good. The basis of this ḥadīth is found in Ṣaḥīḥ Bukhārī: Kitāb al-ādhan—Bāb faḍl al-sujūd; Kitāb al-riqāq—Bāb al-ṣirāṭ jisru jahnnam; Kitāb al-tawḥīd—Bāb qawl Allah wujūh yawma'idhin nāḍirah; and Ṣaḥīḥ Muslim: Kitāb al-īmān—Bāb ma'rifat ṭarīq al-ru'yah.

As for the second objection, the pronoun apparently goes back to the trumpet or to Isrāfīl, even though their names may not immediately appear in the verse. They are understood by the context of blowing into forms, and this is perfectly valid linguistically: a pronoun can refer to something that is understood by the context. An example is the verse: ﴾*Why, then, when it (i.e. the soul) leaps up to the throat?*﴿ (56:83). The subject of the verb *leaps* is not mentioned previously but is understood by the context to be the soul.

Part 5: The Fourteen Readings and Belief in Predestination

Belief in predestination of all events, good and bad, is a basic tenet of faith. The way of the predecessors in this issue was that faith is not complete without affirming predestination at four levels: knowledge, writing, will and creation.

We believe that Allah knows all that was and all that will be, and all that was not and could have been, and exactly how it could have been. We believe that He wrote the decrees of everything in the Preserved Tablets fifty thousand years before the creation of the heavens and earth. We believe that Allah sends an angel to each human being while in the womb and orders it to write the life-span, deeds, sustenance and end-result of every person. We believe that what Allah wills comes to pass and what He does not will never does. We also believe that Allah created human beings as well as their deeds, good and bad: ﴾*And Allah created you and what you do.*﴿ (37:96). The variant readings add to our understanding of this issue. At the same time, deviant groups have clung to their views based upon some of these variants. However, taken together, these variants explain one another and rebut their false notions.

Creation Perform Their Actions in Reality

The Jabarīyyah (determinists)[210] claimed that people do not act in reality and that the ascription of actions to them is only metaphorical. The position of the early Muslims, however, was that human beings are perpetrators of their own actions, good and bad. Had that not been the case, it would not have been correct to describe them through their actions. The actions of one who is compelled is not normally ascribed to the person, nor is he described with those actions, and neither would he be liable for them in terms of reward or punishment.

The Qur'ān is filled with examples of Allah creating means that accomplish certain effects: ﴾*And He revived the earth through it (rain).*﴿ (2:164); and ﴾*Through it (Qur'ān), He guides.*﴿ (5:16).

The variant readings ascribe actions to people at times and to Allah at other times. When ascribing actions to people, it is because they are the ones performing them. When ascribing actions to Allah, then it is because He is the one who created people as well as their actions. There is the following verse, for instance:

[210] The Jabarīyyah (whom Dr Jackson terms 'crass determinists') was an early philosophical school that humans are controlled by God's decree with no choice or free will of their own.

وَعَلَّمنَاهُ صَنعَةَ لَبُوسٍ لَّكُم **لِتُحصِنَكُم** مِّن بَأسِكُم

﴿*It was We Who taught him the art of making armor* ***so that it may protect you*** *from each other's violence.*﴾ (21:80)

In this verse, Ibn ʿĀmir, Ḥafṣ and Ḥasan al-Baṣrī read the word as above **[lituḥṣinakum]**, meaning 'the art of making coats of mail will protect you.' Here the subject could either be the making of armor, the wearing of armor or the armor itself. Shuʿbah and Ruways read the verb in the first-person plural **[linuḥṣinakum]**, meaning 'Allah will protect you:

وَعَلَّمنَاهُ صَنعَةَ لَبُوسٍ لَّكُم **لِنُحصِنَكُم** مِّن بَأسِكُم

﴿*It was We Who taught him the art of making armor* ***so that We may protect you*** *from each other's violence.*﴾

The rest read the verb in the third person **[liyuḥṣinakum]**, whose subject can either be Allah or Dāwūd:[211]

وَعَلَّمنَاهُ صَنعَةَ لَبُوسٍ لَّكُم **لِيُحصِنَكُم** مِّن بَأسِكُم

﴿*It was We Who taught him the art of making armor* ***so that He/he may protect you*** *from each other's violence.*﴾

There is another variant in the following verse:

قَالَ إِنَّمَا أَنَا رَسُولُ رَبِّكِ **لِأَهَبَ** لَكِ غُلَامًا زَكِيًّا

﴿*He said: I am only a messenger of your Lord* ***to grant*** *you a pure boy.*﴾ (19:19)

In this verse, the majority read the word in the first person **[liahaba]** with the subject being the angel, whereas Qālūn with some differences from Nāfiʿ, Abū ʿAmr, Yaʿqūb, Ḥasan al-Baṣrī and Yazīdī read it in the third person **[liyahaba]** with the subject going back to Allah:

قَالَ إِنَّمَا أَنَا رَسُولُ رَبِّكِ **لِيَهَبَ** لَكِ غُلَامًا زَكِيًّا

﴿*He said: I am only a messenger of your Lord so that* ***He may grant*** *you a pure boy.*﴾

[211] *Al-Ittiḥāf,* pg 311.

There is also a variant in the following verse:

يَومَ **يُنفَخُ** فِي الصُّورِ

﴿*On the day the Trumpet **is blown.***﴾ (6:73)

In this verse, the majority read the word in the passive tense **[yunfakhu]** while Abū ʿAmr read it in the active tense first person plural **[nanfukhu]** with the subject being the one who was commanded to blow, i.e. Isrāfīl:[212]

يَومَ **نَنفَخُ** فِي الصُّورِ

﴿*On the day when **We blow into** the Trumpet.*﴾

There is a variant in the following verse:

وَإِنَّ لَكُم فِي الأَنعَامِ لَعِبرَةً **نُّسقِيكُم** مِّمَّا فِي بُطُونِهِ مِن بَينِ فَرثٍ وَدَمٍ لَّبَنًا خَالِصًا سَائِغًا لِّلشَّارِبِينَ

وَإِنَّ لَكُم فِي الأَنعَامِ لَعِبرَةً **نَّسقِيكُم** مِّمَّا فِي بُطُونِهَا وَلَكُم فِيهَا مَنَافِعُ كَثِيرَةٌ وَمِنهَا تَأكُلُونَ

﴿*And indeed there is also a lesson for you in cattle. **We provide you with drink** out of what they have in their bellies; and you have many other benefits in them: you eat of them.*﴾ (23:21)

In this verse, the majority read the word in the first person plural **[nusqīkum or nasqīkum]** while Abū Jaʿfar read it in the third person **[tasqīkum]** with the subject going back to the cattle:[213]

وَإِنَّ لَكُم فِي الأَنعَامِ لَعِبرَةً **تَسقِيكُم** مِّمَّا فِي

﴿*Surely there is a lesson for you in the cattle: **it provides you to drink** out of that which is in their bellies . . .*﴾

---

[212] *Al-Ittiḥāf*, pg 307.
[213] *Al-Ittiḥāf*, pg 279.

Allah is the Creator of the Actions of Creation

There is a variant reading of the following verse:

قَالَ عَذَابِي أُصِيبُ بِهِ مَنْ أَشَاءُ ۖ وَرَحْمَتِي وَسِعَتْ كُلَّ شَيْءٍ ۚ فَسَأَكْتُبُهَا لِلَّذِينَ يَتَّقُونَ وَيُؤْتُونَ الزَّكَاةَ وَالَّذِينَ هُم بِآيَاتِنَا يُؤْمِنُونَ

﴿*He replied: I afflict whomsoever **I will** with My chastisement. As for My mercy, it encompasses everything. I will show mercy to those who abstain from evil, pay Zakat and have faith in Our signs.*﴾ (7:156)

In this verse, the majority read the word in the meaning of Allah's will **[ashāʾu]** while Ḥasan al-Baṣrī read the word with the letter sīn **[asāʾu]** with a different meaning:[214]

قَالَ عَذَابِي أُصِيبُ بِهِ مَنْ أَسَاءَ

﴿*He replied: I afflict whomsoever **does evil** with My chastisement.*﴾

There is some dispute about the authenticity of this reading to Ḥasan al-Baṣrī, with al-Dānī considering it unsound and others accepting it. The dominant reading carries the potential confusion as to whether Allah's punishment will be inflicted only on evildoers, and this reading removes that confusion to establish that Allah inflicts His punishment upon whomever He wills, from those who do evil.[215]

Al-Dānī stated: 'This reading with the letter sīn is not soundly established from Ḥasan, Ṭāwūs, or ʿAmr b. Fā'id, and ʿAmr was an evil man. Sufyān b. ʿUyaynah used to consider this reading sound until ʿAbd al-Raḥmān the Qur'ān expert corrected him. Sufyān then said, 'I was not aware of what the people of innovation used to say.''[216]

Abū Ḥayyān states: 'The Muʿtazilah[217] had an interest in this verse from the perspective of establishing the doctrine of the 'Divine Promise and Threat,'[218] and their belief that humans created their own evil actions with no input from God.'[219]

---

[214] *Al-Ittiḥāf,* pg 231.

[215] *Al-Baḥr al-muḥīṭ,* vol 4, pg 402; *al-Qirāʿāt wa athrihā,* vol 2, pg 667.

[216] *Al-Baḥr al-muḥīṭ,* vol 4, pg 402.

[217] The Muʿtazilah (Rationalists) were a theological school founded by Wāṣil b. ʿAṭā' that believed in, among other things, that the Qur'ān is created, that evil-doers will necessarily be punished with the Fire and doers of good rewarded with Paradise, that God's attributes are metaphorical, and that God cannot be seen in the Afterlife.

[218] This was their belief that God, on the basis of His Justice (ʿadl) which is the master principle in creation, promised reward for good and punishment for evil which He must necessarily carry out, without the unqualified right to do as He pleased.

[219] *Al-Baḥr al-muḥīṭ,* vol 4, pg 400.

It is also mentioned that Shāfiʿī reportedly chose this reading. If this is correct, it still does not support the Muʿtazilī doctrine because all the texts concerning promise and threat must be interpreted in unison and inevitably lead to the following conclusion: All sins lesser than the greatest shirk are under Allah's Will to do as He pleases, to punish or forgive. If He chooses to punish them, it would not be for eternity, but they will be taken out after some time, as ḥadīth reports concerning Intercession prove.

Furthermore, the attribution of evil to human beings does not necessarily prove that humans *created* those actions as the Muʿtazilah supposed, but it proves that they *carried out* those evil actions, whereas the creator is Allah alone.

Part 6: The Fourteen Readings and Other Beliefs

Faith Being Statement and Action

The way of the predecessors is to affirm that īmān (faith) includes both statement and action: statements of heart and tongue, actions of heart and tongue, and actions of the body. This is established by ample evidence from the Qur'ān, Sunnah (including reports in Bukhārī and Muslim) and scholarly consensus.

The Murji'ah school,[220] on the other hand, believed that actions of the heart, tongue or body are not included in the essence of īmān but represent their fruit instead. Some of them believed that īmān was the awareness of God in the heart while others held īmān to be only affirmation alone, and others held that īmān was affirmation by the heart and confirmation by the tongue.

A reading of the following verse proves that while Pharaoh knew that Allah was the one who sent the signs to Mūsā, that knowledge did not benefit him and he remained not only a disbeliever, but a leader of disbelief:

قَالَ لَقَدْ عَلِمْتَ مَا أَنزَلَ هَٰؤُلَاءِ إِلَّا رَبُّ السَّمَاوَاتِ وَالْأَرْضِ بَصَائِرَ وَإِنِّي لَأَظُنُّكَ يَا فِرْعَوْنُ مَثْبُورًا

❴Mūsā replied: **You know well** that no one but the Lord of the heavens and the earth has sent these as eye-opening proofs. I truly think, O Pharaoh, that you are indeed doomed.❵ (17:102)

The majority read the word in the second person **[laqad 'alimta]** whereas Kisā'ī and A'mash read it in the first person **[laqad 'alimtu]**:

قَالَ لَقَدْ عَلِمْتُ مَا أَنزَلَ هَٰؤُلَاءِ إِلَّا رَبُّ السَّمَاوَاتِ وَالْأَرْضِ بَصَائِرَ

❴Mūsā replied: **I know well** that no one but the Lord of the heavens and the earth has sent these as eye-opening proofs.❵

The dominant reading has Mūsā speaking to Pharaoh and reminding him that he knew fully that Allah was the source of these signs.[221] This meaning is supported by the verse: ❴They denied those Signs out of iniquity and arrogance although their

---

[220] They were a now extinct theological school, termed 'Partisans of hope' by Dr. Yaḥyā Michot, which delinked actions from faith to deem the faith of all believers to be the same (sinners, saints and Prophets were identical in faith), and advocated deferring judgement of other people's beliefs (only God had the authority to judge).

[221] Ḥujjat al-qirā'āt, pg 411; Tafsīr al-Qurṭubī, vol 10, pg 337.

hearts were convinced of their truth﴿ (27:14). Ibn Ḥazm commented: 'Both readings are the truth coming from Allah and are not allowed to be rejected, for, yes, both Mūsā and Pharaoh knew that well.'[222] The second-person reading proves that knowledge, awareness and affirmation of the heart is not sufficient to establish real faith that benefits one in this life and the next.[223]

Obligation of Entering Islam and Accepting All of the Sharīʿah

Allah says:

يَا أَيُّهَا الَّذِينَ آمَنُوا ادخُلُوا فِي السِّلْمِ كَافَّةً

﴾*O Believers, enter completely into* ***Islam.***﴿ (2:208)

The majority read the word with kasrah of the sīn **[al-silm]** whereas Nāfiʿ, Ibn Kathīr, Kisāʾī, Abū Jaʿfar and Ibn Muḥayṣin read it with fathah **[al-salm]**:[224]

يَا أَيُّهَا الَّذِينَ آمَنُوا ادخُلُوا فِي السَّلْمِ كَافَّةً

﴾*O Believers, enter completely into* ***peace/Islam.***﴿

It is said that *silm* refers to Islam whereas *salm* refers to peace and reconciliation. It is also said they are synonyms for the same meanings, which could be either Islam or peace.[225] A similar difference has arisen in 8:61 and 47:35. Qurṭubī stated:

> The meaning of the word in this verse is Islam and not reconciliation, for the believers have never been commanded to enter a state of reconciliation in an absolute way. Rather, they were ordered to incline to reconciliation if the enemy does so and not to initiate it.
>
> It is also said that the meaning here is for the believers to enter Islam with their hearts after they had entered with their tongues (i.e. their professions of belief). Ṭāwūs and Mujāhid said it means to enter into the affair of religion. Sufyān al-Thawrī said it means to enter into all types of good.[226]

---

[222] *Al-Faṣl fī al-milal wa al-ahwāʾ wa al-naḥl,* vol 3, pg 203.
[223] *Al-Ittiḥāf,* pg 156.
[224] *Al-Qirāʿāt wa athruhā,* vol 2, pg 595-6.
[225] *Ḥujjat al-qirāʿāt,* pg 130; *Al-Kashf,* vol 1, pg 287.
[226] *Al-Jāmiʿ li aḥkām al-Qurʾān,* vol 3, pg 23.

Ibn Kathīr stated:

> Allah is commanding the believers, who have believed in Him and accepted His Messenger, to accept all the ties of faith and all the laws of Islam, to practice all the commandments and leave all the prohibitions to the best of their ability. Ibn ʿAbbās (as reported by al-ʿAwfā), Mujāhid, Ṭāwūs, Ḍaḥḥāk, ʿIkrimah, Qatādah, Suddī and Ibn Zayd all said that *silm* refers to Islam. Also, Ibn ʿAbbās (in another report through Ḍaḥḥāk), Abū al-ʿĀliyah, and Rabīʿ b. Anas all reported that it means obedience. Qatādah also reported that it meant gentleness.
>
> As to the word *kāfatan,* Ibn ʿAbbās, Mujāhid, Abū al-ʿĀliyah, ʿIkrimah, Rabīʿ b. Anas, Suddī, Muqātil b. Ḥayyān, Qatādah and Ḍaḥḥāk reported that it means, 'all of it' (i.e. enter into the entirety of Islam). Mujāhid reported that the verse meant: *practice all the aspects of good works.*
>
> On the other hand, there were commentators who considered the meaning of the term to refer to the state of the believers, i.e. enter *all of you* into Islam.
>
> The correct view is the former, for all believers were commanded to believe in and to practice all the branches of īmān and laws of the Sharīʿah, which are numerous indeed, to the best of their abilities. Ibn Abī Ḥātim reports through his isnād from ʿIkrimah from Ibn ʿAbbās that he read the word *salm* with fatḥah. In other words, the verse was addressing the believers who were formerly from the People of the Book who still believed in parts of the Torah and previous laws. They were commanded to enter all the laws of the religion of Muḥammad ﷺ, without leaving any of them. And they were reminded that their belief in the [original revealed] Torah was sufficient [and that they no longer had to follow its laws which were abrogated and replaced by the Sharīʿah of Muḥammad ﷺ].[227]

[227] *Tafsīr Ibn Kathīr,* vol 1, pg 335.

CHAPTER 4

Prior Good Deeds of Disbelievers

When a disbeliever embraces Islam with a history of doing good prior to that, then Allah recognizes those deeds and does not let them go to waste. The variant readings support this notion in the following verse:

وَمَا يَفعَلُوا مِن خَيرٍ فَلَن يُكفَرُوهُ

﴿*Whatever good* ***they do*** *shall not go unappreciated, and Allah fully knows those who are pious.*﴾ (3:115)

Ḥafṣ, Ḥamzah. Kisā'ī, Khalaf, Dūrī from Abū 'Amr in one narration, and A'mash read the word in the third person **[yaf'alū]** with the subject being the People of the Book, whereas the rest read it in the second person **[taf'alū]** which refers to Muslims:[228]

وَمَا تَفعَلُوا مِن خَيرٍ فَلَن يُكفَرُوهُ

﴿*Whatever good* ***you do*** *shall not go unappreciated, and Allah fully knows those who are pious.*﴾

The Prophet ﷺ stated: *There is no slave who accepts Islam in a good way except that Allah records for him all the good deeds he performed and wipes out all the evil deeds he committed.*[229] He ﷺ also said to Ḥakīm b. Ḥazim: *You have embraced Islam with all the good that you previously did.*[230] Ibn Ḥajar stated:

> Al-Māzirī states that piety is not accepted from a disbeliever nor are his good deeds rewarded while he is in a state of shirk, because one of the conditions of nearness to Allah is to know who you are becoming close to, which is not the case with a disbeliever. Qāḍī 'Iyāḍ agreed with him on that, while Nawawī disagreed and stated:
>
> > The truth according to experts, with some even reporting consensus on this, is that the disbeliever who embraces Islam and dies upon that is rewarded for all his prior good deeds like charity and familial ties. As for the claim that this is contrary to established principles since the person was

---

[228] *Al-Ittiḥāf,* pg 178.

[229] Related by Dāruquṭnī from Ṭalḥah b. Yaḥyā from Malik. The basis of this ḥadīth appears in Ṣaḥīḥ Bukhārī: Kitāb al-īmān—Bāb ḥusn al-islām al-mar'.

[230] Ṣaḥīḥ Bukhārī: Kitāb al-zakāh—Bāb man taṣaddaqa fī al-shirk thumma aslama; Kitāb al-buyū'—Bāb shurrā' al-mamlūk min al-ḥarbī; Kitāb al-'itq—Bāb 'itq al-mushrik; Kitāb al-adab—Bāb man waṣala raḥimahu thumma aslama; Ṣaḥīḥ Muslim: Kitāb al-īmān—Bāb bayān ḥukm 'amal al-kāfir idhā aslama ba'dahu.

> not a Muslim, then that does not hold since certain compensations and expiations by previous non-Muslims are counted when they embrace Islam and do not need to be repeated.

The truth is that the recording of reward for a Muslim even for his prior good deeds, as a grace from Allah, does not have to be because those prior good deeds were acceptable. The ḥadīth report establishes the recording of reward alone. It is possible that the acceptance of those prior deeds is linked to the submission of that person, i.e. that they are accepted and rewarded only because the person accepted Islam. This is a strong position that was held by—in addition to Nawawī—Ibrāhīm al-Ḥarbī (d. 285 AH),[231] Ibn Baṭṭāl (d. 449 AH),[232] Qurṭubī and Ibn al-Munayyar (d. 683 AH).[233] Ibn al-Munayyar stated:

> What would be contrary to principles would the case that a person be rewarded for their deeds while being a disbeliever. As for Allah increasing the rewards for good deeds for believers, even those they previously did and considered good, there is no problem with that. This is similar to the case of someone who had no prior good deeds and began anew, or the case of those who continue to be rewarded for previous good deeds that they are now incapable of performing. If reward for deeds that have not been performed is acceptable, then the reward for deeds that were performed without their full conditions would also be acceptable.[234]

---

[231] Ibrāhīm b. Isḥāq al-Ḥarbī was a prolific scholar in all Islamic sciences from Baghdad.
[232] Abū al-Ḥasan ʿAlī b. Khalaf b. Baṭṭāl, a great jurist, ḥadīth expert and scholar of Cordoba who wrote a commentary on Ṣaḥīḥ Bukhārī.
[233] Al-Shihāb Aḥmad b. Muḥammad b. al-Munayyar, a great Mālikī jurist and ḥadīth scholar of Alexandria.
[234] *Fatḥ,* vol 1, pg 133-4.

CHAPTER 4

How a Disbeliever is Deemed Muslim

There is a variant reading in three locations of the following verse:

يَا أَيُّهَا الَّذِينَ آمَنُوا إِذَا ضَرَبْتُمْ فِي سَبِيلِ اللَّهِ **فَتَبَيَّنُوا** وَلَا تَقُولُوا
لِمَنْ أَلْقَىٰ إِلَيْكُمُ **السَّلَامَ** لَسْتَ **مُؤْمِنًا** تَبْتَغُونَ عَرَضَ الْحَيَاةِ الدُّنْيَا
فَعِنْدَ اللَّهِ مَغَانِمُ كَثِيرَةٌ

﴾*Believers! When you go forth in the way of Allah,* ***discern*** *(between friend and foe), and do not say to him who offers you the* ***greeting of peace****: 'You are not a* ***believer****.' If you seek the good of this worldly life, there lies with Allah abundant gain.*﴿ (4:94)

Most read the word as **[fatabayyanū]** from the root *tabayyana,* whereas Ḥamzah. Kisā'ī, Khalaf, A'mash and Ḥasan al-Baṣrī read the word as **[fatathabbatū]** from the root *tathabata*:

يَا أَيُّهَا الَّذِينَ آمَنُوا إِذَا ضَرَبْتُمْ فِي سَبِيلِ اللَّهِ **فَتَثَبَّتُوا**

﴾*Believers! When you go forth in the way of Allah,* ***verify*** *(between friend and foe . . .*﴿

In addition, all readers read the second word as **[al-salāma]** except for Nāfi', Ibn 'Āmir, Ḥamzah and Khalaf, who read it as **[al-salama]**:

وَلَا تَقُولُوا لِمَنْ أَلْقَىٰ إِلَيْكُمُ **السَّلَمَ** لَسْتَ مُؤْمِنًا

﴾*. . . And do not say to him who offers you* ***surrender****: 'You are not a believer.'*﴿

Finally, most readers the third word as 'believers' **[lasta mu'minan]**, whereas Abū Ja'far, with some differences, read the word **[lasta mu'manan]** as a passive participle of the root word *security*:[235]

وَلَا تَقُولُوا لِمَنْ أَلْقَىٰ إِلَيْكُمُ السَّلَمَ لَسْتَ **مُؤْمَنًا**

﴾*. . . And do not say to him who offers you surrender: 'You are* ***not granted security****.'*﴿

---

[235] *Al-Ittiḥāf,* pg 193.

The variant readings serve to clarify the ruling of the disbelieving enemy when he accepts Islam or surrenders in front of Muslims.

Makkī b. Abī Ṭālib stated: 'The meaning of the reading with *salam* is that one should not say to the enemy who has surrendered to you that you have not surrendered and thereby kill them. The reading with *salām,* which is the greeting of Muslims, is that one should not reject those who greet you as Muslims or doubt their faith and thereby kill them for their possessions. Another meaning could be to not reject those who withhold from fighting you.'[236]

Based on this, it is agreed upon without dispute that the disbeliever who pronounces the testimony of faith must be considered a believer. However, what about the one who alludes to Islam through other words, or through Islamic practices such as prayer? Qurṭubī answers that in his commentary of this verse:

> This verse was revealed after a group of traveling Muslims came across an individual possessing a camel and other spoils who uttered the testimony of faith but was still killed. When this was brought to the Prophet's attention, it vexed him greatly, and then this verse was revealed. Bukhārī relates from 'Aṭā' from Ibn 'Abbās that he confirmed this. And Ibn 'Abbās used to read the verse with the word *salām.* In ḥadīth reports from other books, the Prophet paid the blood-money to the family and returned the person's possessions.
>
> This verse contains six issues. First, the word *salam, silm* and *salām* are the same, and each one was read. Abū 'Ubayd al-Qāsim b. Sallām read *salām,* and some scholars opposed him considered *salam* to be more correct, as it is in the meaning of surrender and submission, like the verse: *they will proffer their submission saying: 'We were engaged in no evil'* (16:28). In other words, the meaning is that if one comes to you with his hands extended, surrendering, and professing your faith, do not reject his faith.
>
> It is also said that *salām* refers to the Muslim greeting *al-salāmu 'alaikum.* This goes back to the previous meaning because his use of the Muslim greeting indicates his obedience and submission. It is also possible that this indicates his retreat. Al-Akhfash said that *salām* refers to a person who is alone and does not mix with anyone while *silm* refers to reconciliation.
>
> Secondly, Abū Ja'far read the word *mu'min* as *mu'man* as one who was granted protection.

[236] *Al-Kashf,* vol 1, pg 395; *Hujjat al-qirā'āt,* pg 209.

> . . . Fifthly, as for the one who prays or does an overt Muslim act, our scholars disagreed on that. Ibn al-ʿArabī[237] said: We see that these overt actions do not make them believers. They should be tested as to why they are performing these acts and if they express allegiance to Islam, they would be asked to profess the testimony. If they do so, they are considered truthful; and if they refuse, they were toying with their actions.[238]

These Qur'ānic and ḥadīth texts prove that we consider as believers all those who verbally profess, in any way, the testimony of faith or perform overtly Muslim actions if it is clear that they intended through them to be within the faith.[239] Ibrāhīm Ḍūyān al-Ḥanbalī said:

> The statement that 'I am a Muslim' is considered repentance because it includes the testimony of faith. Miqdād asked the Prophet ﷺ about the case of a disbeliever who, in the course of his fighting with the believer, utters the testimony. The Prophet ﷺ replied: 'Don't kill him, for if you kill him, he would surely be in a position where you had been before killing him, and verily you would be in a position where he had been before uttering it.'[240]
>
> ʿImrān b. Ḥuṣayn reports that the Companions of Allah's Messenger ﷺ took one person from the clan of ʿUqayl as prisoner and brought him to the Prophet ﷺ. The man said, 'O Muḥammad, I am Muslim!' The Prophet ﷺ replied to him: 'Had you said this when you had been the master of yourself, you would have gained every success.'[241]
>
> The author of al-Mughnī said: It could be that this text is speaking about the real disbeliever or the one who rejects the oneness of God. As for the one who rejects a prophet, Book, or commandment, he does not become a Muslim by that because he might already think that he is Muslim like all the deviant groups who believe they are believers when some of them are not.
>
> The disbeliever who writes out the testimony of faith becomes a believer because writing is like verbalizing. If he says, 'I have embraced Islam,' or 'I am Muslim,' or 'I am a believer,' then he also

---

[237] Muḥammad b ʿAbdullah Abū Bakr b. al-ʿArabī was a Mālikī jurist and judge of Andalus who died in Fez in 543 AH.

[238] *Al-Jāmiʿ li aḥkām al-Qur'ān,* vol 5, pg 339.

[239] *Nayl al-Awṭār,* vol 7, pg 198.

[240] Ṣaḥīḥ Bukhārī: Kitāb al-maghāzī—Bāb ḥaddathanī khalīfah; Kitāb al-diyāt—Bāb qawl Allah wa man yaqtul mu'minan; Ṣaḥīḥ Muslim: Kitāb al-īmān—Bāb taḥrīm qatl al-kāfir baʿda an qāla lā ilāha illa Allah.

[241] Ṣaḥīḥ Muslim: Kitāb al-nadhr—Bāb lā wafā' li nadhrin fī maʿṣiyat Allah.

becomes a Muslim through those expressions even if he does not verbalize the testimony.[242]

The Faith of Minors

The child of Muslim parents is also considered Muslim since that child is born on the innate nature of Islam and continues that faith upon transitioning to adulthood. As for the child of non-Muslim parents in the case that the child, or one of the parents, embraced Islam, then there is a variant reading of the following verse that instructs us on the matter:

وَالَّذِينَ آمَنُوا وَاتَّبَعَتهُم ذُرِّيَّتُهُم بِإِيمَانٍ أَلحَقنَا بِهِم ذُرِّيَّتَهُم

﴿*And as for those who have attained to faith and* ***whose offspring will have followed them in faith****, We shall unite them with their* ***offspring.***﴾ (52:21)

All readers recite the word as **[wattabaʿathum dhuriyyathuhum]** while Abū Amr and Yazīdī read **[wa atbaʿnāhum dhurriyyātihim]**:

وَالَّذِينَ آمَنُوا وَأَتبَعنَاهُم ذُرِّيَّاتِهِم بِإِيمَانٍ أَلحَقنَا بِهِم ذُرِّيَّاتِهِم

﴿*And as for those who have attained to faith and* ***whom We followed (with) their offspring in faith****, We shall unite them with their* ***offsprings.***﴾

Ibn al-Jawzī references three interpretations of this verse. The first is that it refers to children who will join in Paradise their parents who were believers, even if the children themselves did not reach the level of their parents in deeds. This represents an honoring of the believing parents by Allah. Saʿīd b. Jubayr related this view from Ibn ʿAbbās.

The second interpretation is that the believing parents' minor children who have not believed will join them in Paradise. This is reported from al-ʿAwfī from Ibn ʿAbbās and Ḍaḥḥāk. This means that while elder children who were believers are known to join their believing parents in Paradise, all minor children who have not formally believed will also join them since the judgment of their faith will follow that of their parents.

The third interpretation, also reported from Ibn ʿAbbās, is that the children will join their parents based upon the faith of their parents.[243]

---

[242] *Manār al-sabīl fī sharḥ al-dalīl*, vol 2, pg 285-91.
[243] *Zād al-muyassar,* vol 8, pg 50.

It should be noted that the term *children* in the verse cannot apply to all of the progeny of human beings until the Day of Judgement, for this would necessitate that every single human being join their father Adam in Paradise and that all human beings be of the same level. The texts, on the other hand, establish that Paradise is composed of many levels. The verse is speaking about children that lived with their parents in the same home. In other words, the believing homes of parents and children will be reconstructed in Paradise just as they lived in this world in order to recreate and complete their family unit. This point was affirmed by Shaykh al-ʿUthaymīn and others.

The Arabic term *dhurriyah* can mean various things based upon context, and in Qurʾānic verses it has been used for fathers, mothers, grandmothers, grandfathers, children, and grandchildren. Shaykh al-ʿUthaymīn states:

> The term *dhurriyyah* is taken from the root *dhara'a* meaning 'create' or 'multiply,' as Allah used in the verse: ﴾*Thus does He multiply you (yadhra'akum fīh)*﴿ (42:11). It is also said that it comes from the root *wadhara* meaning 'to leave.' In the first meaning, the term could include ancestors and descendants, while in the latter meaning, it would refer to descendants only.
>
> The proof that Allah used the term in the sense of ancestors lies in the verse: ﴾*Another Sign for them is that We carried all their offspring ('dhurriyyatahum') in the laden vessel.*﴿ (36:41). The verse is addressed to human beings and refers to the carrying of their *dhurriyyah* in the ship, i.e. at the time of Nuh, which refers to ancestors.[244]

Here, he responded to the confusion of many Qurʾānic commentators, including that of his own teacher al-Saʿdī who once confessed, 'This verse was one of the most difficult for me to comprehend.'

As for the scope of the term *dhurriyah* in verse 52:21, it can be said that Allah through His Grace will join parents and grandchildren with their righteous children and grandchildren with whom they lived in the same house. Conversely, Allah will join children and grandchildren with their righteous parents and grandparents with who they used to live. Ibn al-ʿArabī stated:

> The readings support two meanings. In the first reading, the verb goes to the children, who must have independently attained faith in order to meet their parents. In the other reading, the verb goes back to Allah, who through His mercy will join the minor children of believing parents to their parents. As for the single parent-believer, there is no

[244] *Majallah al-bayān,* No. 160, pg 48.

dispute that minor children will join their believing fathers, but regarding the believing mothers, it is disputed, and two conflicting views are attributed to Imām Malik.

The truth is that the minor children will join any of their believing parents, based upon the ḥadīth of Ibn 'Abbās who admits that he and his mother were both oppressed believers at one point, as his father 'Abbās had not yet embraced Islam. He had followed his mother in Islam and was considered Muslim.

As for the case of the minor of two disbelieving parents who embraces Islam as a minor, there are great differences among scholars. The dominant view [of the Mālikī school] is that they are considered Muslim. The issue is a complex one, which centers on this verse (52:21). Since the verb is ascribed to the children in one reading, this indicates that Allah accepted their faith and ruled them as believers. Also, many scholars pointed to the Islam of 'Alī b. Abī Ṭālib as a child whose both parents were disbelievers.[245]

[245] *Al-Aḥkām al-Qur'ān,* vol 4, pg 1732.

CHAPTER 4

Magic

Magic is defined as a transaction based upon writing something, uttering some expressions, or performing certain actions, to influence another person in his body, heart or mind.[246]

There are two types of magic: that which has a real influence and effect on another person, such as causing disunion between spouses, and that which is essentially an illusion that foils the sights but does not alter reality. Allah refers to the first type in this verse: ﴾*Those people used to learn from the angels the art which caused division between husband and wife*﴿ (2:102); and the second type in this: ﴾*So when they threw [their rods], they enchanted the eyes of the people, and struck them with awe, and produced a mighty sorcery.*﴿ (7:116).

Magic is explicitly forbidden by the Qur'ān, Sunnah and consensus. It is deemed one of the seven deadly sins in a Prophetic ḥadīth report. Magic itself only harms by the permission of Allah: ﴾*It was obvious that they could not do any harm to anyone by means of this magic without Allah's permission.*﴿ (2:102).

The Mu'tazilah sect rejected the possibility of magic, and perhaps even considered those who affirmed it to be disbelievers. Others rejected the notion that magic could have any effect at all and considered it to be only illusory in nature. Many of them were driven by the idea that affirming any effect for magic would muddle the notion of Prophetic miracles.

The truth as established by the Qur'ān and Sunnah is that magic does indeed have a reality and effect, through the permission and decree of Allah. We have been commanded to seek refuge in Allah from the evil of magic and those who practice it, in a verse with some variant reading:

قُل أَعُوذُ بِرَبِّ الفَلَقِ ﴿١﴾ مِن شَرِّ مَا خَلَقَ ﴿٢﴾ وَمِن شَرِّ
غَاسِقٍ إِذَا وَقَبَ ﴿٣﴾ وَمِن شَرِّ النَّفَّاثَاتِ فِي العُقَدِ ﴿٤﴾ وَمِن
شَرِّ حَاسِدٍ إِذَا حَسَدَ ﴿٥﴾

> ﴾*Say: I seek refuge in the Lord of daybreak (1) From the evil of that which He created (2) And from the evil of darkness when it settles (3) And from the evil of the blowers in knots (4) And from the evil of an envier when he envies.*﴿ (113:1-5)

The relevant word has four variant readings. The first was read by Ruways in some of his transmissions as **[al-nāfithāt]**, as a plural of *nāfithah,* which would simply refer

---

[246] *Al-Mughnī,* vol 8, pg 150.

to magicians. Rawḥ in some of his transmissions read **[al-nufāthāt]**, plural of *nufāthah,* which refers to exhaled breath. Ḥasan al-Baṣrī read it as **[al-nuffāthāt]** on the pattern of *tuffāḥah/tuffāḥāt* ('apple/apples'). The fourth and final one is the dominant reading of **[al-naffāthāt].** The last two readings are derived from the intensive derived form *naffāth* and refer to magicians who pursue their craft extensively.[247]

These readings teach us that the art of magic is real and has a real effect by God's decree, for He ordered us to seek refuge from its evil. Moreover, the last two sūrahs (al-Falaq and al-Nās, also known as *al-muʿawwadhatān*, 'the two sought refuge with') were revealed when the Prophet ﷺ was affected by magic by the Jewish Labīd b. al-Aʿṣam and his daughters, who had tied a cord with eleven knots. When the Prophet would recite each verse of these sūrahs, one knot would get untied with each verse until each one was untied,[248] and then the Prophet got up as if he had been released from a bond.[249]

Taqiyyah

Taqiyyah comes from the root t-q-y which means to take precautions. Allah uses the word in the following verse:

لَّا يَتَّخِذِ الْمُؤْمِنُونَ الْكَافِرِينَ أَوْلِيَاءَ مِن دُونِ الْمُؤْمِنِينَ ۖ وَمَن يَفْعَلْ
ذَٰلِكَ فَلَيْسَ مِنَ اللَّهِ فِي شَيْءٍ إِلَّا أَن تَتَّقُوا مِنْهُمْ **تُقَاةً**

﴾*The believers may not take the unbelievers for their allies in preference to those who believe. Whoever does this has nothing to do with Allah unless he does so in order to* ***protect himself*** *from their wrong-doing.*﴿ (3:28)

The majority read the the word as **[tuqāh]** while Yaʿqūb and Ḥasan al-Baṣrī read **[taqiyyah]**, both of them from the same root *ittaqā*:[250]

وَمَن يَفْعَلْ ذَٰلِكَ فَلَيْسَ مِنَ اللَّهِ فِي شَيْءٍ إِلَّا أَن تَتَّقُوا مِنْهُمْ **تَقِيَّةً**

﴾*Whoever does this has nothing to do with Allah unless he does so in order to* ***protect himself*** *from their wrong-doing.*﴿

[247] *Al-Ittiḥāf,* pg 335; *al-Qirāʾāt al-shādhdhah,* pg 94.
[248] These two sūrahs have 11 verses in total.
[249] *Tafsīr Ibn Kathīr,* vol 1, pg 476.
[250] *Al-Ittiḥāf,* pg 172.

Ibn Kathīr clarified that the meaning of the verse is that those who fear the evil of disbelievers in some lands or times may protect themselves by concealing their external actions while maintaining inward belief and purity of intentions. Bukhārī relates that Abū al-Dardā' said: 'We used to smile at certain people while cursing them inside.'[251]

Ibn ʿAbbās said: '*Taqiyyah* is not with actions but with the tongue alone.' This was reinforced by Abū al-ʿĀliyah, Abū al-Shaʿthā', Ḍaḥḥāk, and Rabīʿ b. Anas. It is also supported by the following verse: ﴿*Except for those who were forced to engage in infidelity to Allah after believing the while their hearts remained firmly convinced of their belief.*﴾ (16:106) Bukhārī reports from Ḥasan al-Baṣrī that he said: '*Taqiyyah* is valid until the Day of Judgment.'[252] This is the limited scope and extent of *taqiyyah* for Sunnī Muslims—simply a concession allowed in extreme duress—which is unlike its more elaborate and central treatment in other Muslim denominations.

There is a variant reading of the verse:

ثُمَّ إِنَّ رَبَّكَ لِلَّذِينَ هَاجَرُوا مِن بَعدِ مَا **فُتِنُوا** ثُمَّ جَاهَدُوا وَصَبَرُوا إِنَّ
رَبَّكَ مِن بَعدِهَا لَغَفُورٌ رَّحِيمٌ

> ﴿*And surely your Lord will be Most Forgiving and Most Merciful towards those who left their homes after they* ***were wronged/tried/tested****, and who thereafter struggled hard and remained constant.*﴾ (16:110)

The majority read the word in passive tense **[futinū]** while Ibn ʿĀmir read it in active tense **[fatanū]**:[253]

ثُمَّ إِنَّ رَبَّكَ لِلَّذِينَ هَاجَرُوا مِن بَعدِ مَا **فَتَنُوا** ثُمَّ جَاهَدُوا وَصَبَرُوا
إِنَّ رَبَّكَ مِن بَعدِهَا لَغَفُورٌ رَّحِيمٌ

> ﴿*And surely your Lord will be Most Forgiving and Most Merciful towards those who left their homes after they* ***wronged [others]/ wronged [themselves]/put [themselves] through trials****, and who thereafter struggled hard and remained constant.*﴾

---

[251] This is a suspended, isnād-less (muʿallaq) report related by Bukhārī in his chapter heading in Ṣaḥīḥ Bukhārī: Kitāb al-adab—Bāb al-mudārāt ma'a al-nās. These are not considered part of the primary corpus of the work and are meant as supporting and explanatory reports.

[252] Another muʿallaq report from Ṣaḥīḥ Bukhārī: Kitāb al-ikrāh.

[253] *Al-Ittiḥāf,* pg 280-1; *Al-nashr,* vol 2, pg 305.

The active-tense reading refers to those idolaters who persecuted and wronged believers but later embraced Islam themselves like ʿIkrimah and Suhayl b. ʿAmr. It could also refer to those persecuted believers who uttered expressions of disbelief to protect themselves out of taqiyyah, and that by these false utterances they were overtly wronging themselves prior to the revelation allowing taqiyyah. It could also mean that the believers were testing and purifying themselves through the extreme hardships they were experiencing, just as gold and precious metals emerges from extreme heat.

The passive-tense reading supports the meaning that the believers were persecuted by idolaters and forced to utter expressions of disbelief while their hearts were content with faith. It could also mean that the believers were tried and tested by Allah.[254]

Companions

A major Sunnī belief is loyalty and love for the Companions of the Prophet ﷺ, mentioning them with good, being merciful towards them, praying for their forgiveness, deceasing from abusing them or mentioning their internal struggles, and believing in their virtue and preeminence. Allah said: ﴿*Those who came after them, and pray: Lord, forgive us and our brethren who have preceded us in faith, and do not put in our hearts any rancor towards those who believe. Lord, You are the Most Tender, Most Compassionate.*﴾ (59:10). He also said: ﴿*Muḥammad is Allah's Messenger, and those who are with him are firm with the unbelievers but compassionate with one another.*﴾ (48:29).

Ibn Taymiyyah said: 'A central principle for Sunnīs is to have sound hearts and tongues for the Prophet's Companions, in compliance with the wishes of the Prophet ﷺ: *'Do not revile my Companions, for I swear by the One in Whose grasp is my soul, were one of you to spend the amount of Mount Uḥud in charity, you would not reach their status.'*[255] They accept all that has come in the Qur'ān, Sunnah and consensus regarding their virtues and merits.'[256]

There is a relevant variant reading here:

وَمَا كُنتُ مُتَّخِذَ المُضِلِّينَ عَضُدًا

﴿***And never was I*** *to take the misguiding people for assistants.*﴾ (18:51)

[254] *Al-Kashf,* vol 2, pg 41; *Hujjat al-qirāʿāt,* pg 395.
[255] Ṣaḥīḥ Bukhārī; Kitāb ; ṢaḥīḥMuslim
[256] *Sharḥ al-Fawzān,* pg 184.

The majority read the word in the first-person **[kuntu]** while Abū Ja'far and Ḥasan al-Baṣrī read it in the second-person **[kunta]**:

وَمَا كُنتَ مُتَّخِذَ الْمُضِلِّينَ عَضُدًا

﴾***And never were you*** *to take the misguiding people for assistants.*﴿

The second-person reading is addressed to the Prophet ﷺ, i.e. that he is protected from following those who would deviate him.[257] This runs counter to the allegations of some members of the Shī'ah denomination that Abū Bakr, 'Umar and others from the closest Companions of the Prophet ﷺ were individuals who could lead him astray, or to even hide or distort the truth. Ibn Taymiyyah said:

> It is known through mass-transmission that Abū Bakr, 'Umar and 'Uthmān had exclusive, special and esteemed rank with the Prophet ﷺ. They were the dearest and closest of people to him. He was related to each one of them by marriage. He was never known to have blamed or rebuked them. On the contrary, he loved them and praised them.
>
> They must have been rightly-guided and sincere in his lifetime and afterwards. Had they been misguided, either in his lifetime or afterwards, then either the Prophet was unaware of that or was insincere towards them. Both of these possibilities are an incredible affront to the personality of the Prophet ﷺ as the poet said: *If you were not aware, then that would be a great calamity, but if you were, then the calamity is far greater!*
>
> If they became misguided after his passing, then that would be a failure on the part of Allah regarding his closest and most senior Companions. Who would have greater knowledge of what they would do afterwards than Allah? Where would be Allah's care for the ummah that misguided people were able take over so soon after the Prophet? Who promised to make the religion manifest other than Allah? How could that be if the most senior followers were misguided?[258]

Some people objected to this variant reading by pointing to the protection of Abū Ṭālib, the idolater, for the Prophet ﷺ and, after his death, that of Muṭ'im b. 'Adīyy. The response is that the Prophet ﷺ, though he entered into their protection, did not make them his primary support, his intimate or close associates, or the recipients of his close love or good pleasure. To the contrary,

---

[257] *Al-Ittiḥāf,* pg 291.
[258] *Minhāj al-sunnah al-nabwiyyah,* vol 7, pg 365.

he always fled idolatry and freed himself from all of its aspects, as his migration proved.

Chapter 5: The Influence of Variant Qur'ānic Readings on Jurisprudence

المصحف العثماني وعلاقته بالقراءات

The Meaning of Fiqh

Before discussing the impact of the variant readings on specific issues of jurisprudence, we must first start with definitions.

Linguistically, *fiqh* refers to comprehending or knowing a matter. Examples of such usage in the Qur'ān includes the following verses:

قَالُوا يَا شُعَيْبُ مَا نَفْقَهُ كَثِيرًا مِّمَّا تَقُولُ

They said: O Shu'ayb! We do not ***understand*** *much of what you say.* (11:91)

يَفْقَهُوا قَوْلِي

so that they may ***understand*** *my speech.* (20:28)

The verb *faqiha* means to understand something, while the verb form *faquha* is used for deeper comprehension of something, especially knowledge of the Sharī'ah. The one who possesses such knowledge of Sharī'ah is termed *faqīh*. The derived form *faqqaha* means to grant understanding and is used for Allah granting someone deep knowledge.[1] *Tafaqqaha* is used for the process of attaining knowledge[2] and *fāqaha* for the process of inquiry and investigation.

In the early period, fiqh was used for deep insight in religion and knowledge of Qur'ān and Sunnah. It was not confined to a specific discipline.[3] Later scholars settled on particularizing it to a specific branch of knowledge. They gave it the following definition: *knowledge of the practical rulings of Sharī'ah that are acquired from its detailed evidence.*[4] This definition was constructed in order to distinguish it from other Islamic sciences.

---

[1] This usage is found in a Prophetic ḥadīth: 'Whomever Allah desires good for, he makes them learned in religion (*yufaqqih-hu fī al-dīn*).' Ṣaḥīḥ Bukhārī: Kitāb al-'ilm—Bāb man yuridillāhu bihī khayran; Kitāb al-I'tiṣām bi al-kitāb wa al-sunnah—Bāb qawl al-nabī lā tazālu ṭā'ifah; Ṣaḥīḥ Muslim: Kitāb al-zakāh—Bāb al-nahy 'an al-mas'alah.

[2] See Qur'ān 9:122—*that they may grow in religious understanding (li yatafaqqahū fī al-dīn).*

[3] See *Tārīkh al-fiqh al-islāmī,* pg 11-20.

[4] Al-Āmidī, *Al-Iḥkām,* vol 1, pg 5; *Sharḥ al-kawkab al-munīr,* vol 1, pg 41; *al-Ta'rīfāt,* pg 14.

CHAPTER 5

The Relationship Between the Readings and the Rulings of Fiqh

Each Qur'ānic reading in relation to the others are like individual verses in relation to the other verses. One reading can explain something more ambiguous in another, restrict something unrestricted, specify something general, or even abrogate something in another. For that reason, the Qur'ānic readings have a great impact on deriving jurisprudential rulings. As the early Muslim jurists differed over reconciling various verses, so too did they differ over reconciling the readings with one another, as the subsequent discussions in this chapter will reveal.

From another angle, the relationship between the Qur'ānic readings and fiqh is similar to the relationship between Qur'ānic experts and jurists. The particular readings that were chosen by each of the Imāms of fiqh had an inevitable effect on their jurisprudential understandings.

Abū Ḥanīfah, for instance, read the Qur'ān to A'mash and 'Āṣim. He also used to admit to Ḥamzah: 'There are two things you have overpowered us in: Qur'ān and knowledge of rulings of inheritance (farā'iḍ).'[5]

Because he read the Qur'ān to A'mash, whose reading is considered among the shādh ones, the Ḥanafī jurists accepted such readings for evidentiary purposes. Also, because of his interaction with Ḥamzah, the Ḥanafī school does not have the dislike for reciting the reading of Ḥamzah in prayer as other schools did.

As for Imām Mālik, he recited to Nāfi' of Madīnah and referred to his reading as 'the Sunnah.' Because of that, the Nāfi' reading has a prominent position in the Mālikī school. When Mālik was asked about reciting basmalah aloud, he replied, 'Ask Nāfi', for each answer is sought from the people of that discipline.'[6] Mālik said about Imām Abū Ja'far, 'He was a pious man that taught Qur'ān in Madīnah.'[7]

Because Imām Shāfi'ī read by the reading of Ibn Kathīr of Makkah,[8] he preferred to recite basmalah aloud in prayer and preferred articulating takbir in the ending sūrahs of the Qur'ān. This was simply following the practice of the reading of Ibn Kathīr.

Imām Aḥmad would prefer the Readings of Abū 'Amr, 'Āṣim and the Imāms of Madīnah because these were the readings he recited by.[9] He disliked the readings of Ḥamzah and Kisā'ī because they weren't mass transmitted in his eyes,[10] although

---

[5] *Siyar,* vol 7, pg 9.
[6] *Laṭā'if al-ishārāt,* vol 1, pg 94; *al-Rawḍ al-naḍīr,* pg 9.
[7] *Ghāyat al-nihāyah,* vol 2, pg 382.
[8] *Al-Nashr,* vol 2, pg 310.
[9] *Ghāyat al-nihāyah,* vol 1, pg 112.
[10] *Al-Mughnī,* vol 2, pg 165.

other Imāms like Abū Ḥanīfah and Sufyān al-Thawrī accepted them. Sufyān even said: 'Ḥamzah never read any single letter without precedence.'[11]

[11] *Al-Nashr,* vol 1, pg 133.

CHAPTER 5

Relying on Shādh Readings[12]

Scholars differed over the evidentiary-value of the shādh (anomalous) readings. The anomalous readings are those that were transmitted through solitary rather than mutawātir chains or differed from the ʿUthmānic orthography. From a practical standpoint, they represented all those readings which were outside of the ten mutawātir ones. These anomalous readings include some that have strong chains and others with weaker ones. The point of contention revolves around those of them that have sound chains. There are two scholarly opinions as to their usage.

The first view is that these readings are fully acceptable for evidence purposes, and this represented the view of Ḥanafī and Ḥanbalī jurists. The Mālikī scholar Ibn ʿAbd al-Barr even reported consensus on this, as reported by Shāfiʿī.[13]

For them, just as a sound chain is sufficient for a ḥadīth, so too is a sound chain sufficient for a reading. Those anomalous readings that are affirmed as Qur'ān through sound chains represent two scenarios: either they represent the Qur'ān or an explanation of the Qur'ān by the Prophet which was mistakenly considered by a Companion as the Qur'ān. In either case, they can be used as evidence.[14]

The second view is that the shādh readings cannot be used as evidence. This was the view of most Shāfiʿī jurists and attributed to Shāfiʿī by assumption based upon the fact that he had not utilized these readings in some of his rulings. However, it was explicitly reported from him that he had accepted their evidentiary status. It is more likely the case that his abstaining from their use in some matters was simply due to that particular reading not being established in his eyes or due to some stronger evidence on that particular issue.

This view of not accepting shādh readings was also reported from Imām Aḥmad, though what is more known from him was to accept them.[15] Other scholars who did not accept these readings for evidence included al-Āmidī (d. 631/1233),[16] Ibn al-Ḥājib, Juwaynī (d. 478/1085),[17] and Nawawī.

These latter scholars do not consider these anomalous readings to represent the Qur'ān because the Qur'ān for them is only established through tawātur and consensus. They also do not consider them to be ḥadīth since they were not

---

[12] See chapter one for the initial discussion on shādh readings.

[13] See *Mukhtaṣar al-Buyūṭī*; *Rawḍat al-nāẓir,* vol 1, pg 34.

[14] *Al-Mughnī,* vol 7, pg 752.

[15] *Al-Iḥkām,* vol 1, pg 83.

[16] Sayf al-Dīn ʿAlī b. Muḥammad b. Sālim al-Thaʿlabī al-Āmidī was the leading theologian of his time and great scholar of Baghdad who started out as Ḥanbalī and converted to the Shāfiʿī school. He died in 631.

[17] Ḍiyā' al-Dīn Abū al-Maʿālī ʿAbdullah b. Malik b. Yūsuf was a great scholar and head of the Shāfiʿī jurists of Naysābūr known as 'Imām al-Ḥaramayn' who lived from 410 to 478.

transmitted as such. They consider them to possibly represent abrogated portions of the Qur'ān or exegetical explanations of the Qur'ān by Companions.[18]

The stronger view, and Allah knows best, is the first one because the basic principle is to accept from trustworthy and reliable transmitters. So long as reliable reporters transmit a report as the Qur'ān, we cannot assume that it is a ḥadīth report or a statement of a Companion. Such a practice would also open the door to considering any sound ḥadīth to be a statement of a Companion instead of the Prophet that was mistakenly added.

As for not relying on shādh readings due to them not being mutawātir, then this was previously addressed in chapter 1. As for rejecting them due to the lack of consensus, then it must be pointed out that those who rejected them did so only because these readings were not established in their eyes as opposed to others who considered them established. And on this, the principle is that affirmation takes precedence over rejection.

[18] Nawawī's commentary of Ṣaḥīḥ Muslim, vol 3, pg 502.

CHAPTER 5

Part 1: Issues of Purification

Sexual Relations and the Cessation of Menses

Jurists have differed over the permissibility of sexual relations with a wife who has ended her menses but has not yet performed the ritual bath (ghusl). The variant readings concerning the following verse have an influence on the understanding of this issue:

وَيَسأَلُونَكَ عَنِ المَحِيضِ ۖ قُل هُوَ أَذًى فَاعتَزِلُوا النِّسَاءَ فِي المَحِيضِ ۖ وَلَا
تَقرَبُوهُنَّ حَتَّىٰ **يَطهُرنَ** ۖ فَإِذَا تَطَهَّرنَ فَأتُوهُنَّ مِن حَيثُ أَمَرَكُمُ اللَّهُ ۚ إِنَّ
اللَّهَ يُحِبُّ التَّوَّابِينَ وَيُحِبُّ المُتَطَهِّرِينَ

﴿*They ask about the monthly course. Say, 'It is a state of impurity; so keep apart from women during their monthly course and do not go near them* ***until they are clean****. When they have cleansed themselves, then you may go to them in the manner Allah has enjoined you." Most surely Allah loves those people who refrain from evil and keep themselves pure and clean.*﴾ (2:222)

The word **[yaṭhurna]** is the reading of Ibn Kathīr, Nāfiʿ, Abū ʿAmr, Ibn ʿĀmir, Ḥafṣ from ʿĀṣim, Yaʿqūb, Abū Jaʿfar, Ḥasan and Yazīdī, while **[yaṭṭahharna]** is the reading of Abū Bakr from ʿĀṣim, Ḥamzah, Kisāʾī, Khalaf, Ibn Muḥayṣin, and Aʿmash:[19]

وَلَا تَقرَبُوهُنَّ حَتَّىٰ **يَطَّهَّرنَ** ۖ فَإِذَا تَطَهَّرنَ فَأتُوهُنَّ مِن حَيثُ أَمَرَكُمُ اللَّهُ ۚ
إِنَّ اللَّهَ يُحِبُّ التَّوَّابِينَ وَيُحِبُّ المُتَطَهِّرِينَ

﴿*So keep apart from women during their monthly course and do not go near them* ***until they have cleansed themselves****. When they have cleansed themselves, then you may go to them in the manner Allah has enjoined you." Most surely Allah loves those people who refrain from evil and keep themselves pure and clean.*﴾
[20]

---

[19] *Al-Ittiḥāf,* pg 157.

[20] The first variant carries a simple meaning: 'until they are clean,' while the second has a more active sense: 'until they have cleansed themselves.'

The view of most jurists, including Mālik, Awzā'ī, Shāfi'ī, Sufyān al-Thawrī, Aḥmad, is that the wife is not lawful for the husband until she has used water upon cessation of her monthly course.

The more widespread view of Abū Ḥanīfah is that if her menses stops before ten days, then she carries the ruling of the menstruating woman until she has performed the ritual bath—so long as she can find water or the time of the obligatory prayer has not passed. With either of these scenarios (she performs the bath, or the time of the obligatory prayer has passed), she exits from the state of menses and is now lawful for the husband. If her menses is for the full duration of the ten days or more, then the ruling of menses is lifted by the passing of the ten days. In that state, sexual relations are permissible for her as she is simply in the state of ritual impurity (janābah) and not menses. The reason for the limitation of ten days is because this is considered to be the maximal duration of menses by Ḥanafī jurists.[21]

Ṭabarī states: 'Scholars have differed over the cleansing mentioned by Allah in this verse which makes sexual relations lawful. Some consider it to refer to the full ritual bath—and that relations are not permitted until she has cleaned her entire body with water—while others held that it refers to simple ablution (wuḍū') for prayer, and others that it refers simply to washing of the private parts, after which sexual relations would become lawful.'[22]

This third view that cleansing refers to washing the private parts is the view of 'Aṭā' and Qatādah. Ibn Ḥazm held that all three are valid ways of cleansing: 'All of this is considered in the Sharī'ah as the Arabic language to represent cleaning. So the adoption of any of these means would suffice for cleaning. God says, '*In it are people who love to purify themselves, and Allah loves those that purify themselves.*'[23] The texts as well as consensus prove that this refers to cleaning the private parts with water.'[24]

Al-Albānī states: 'In sum, there is no proof to restrict the meaning of 'cleansing' in this verse to the ritual bath alone, but rather, it encompasses all three meanings, all of which are valid to allow sexual relations upon termination of menses. I am not aware of any evidence from the sunnah to prove or deny this, except for the Prophetic ḥadīth related from Ibn 'Abbās, which happens to be weak: 'If one of you has relations with his wife during menses, he must give one dīnār in charity; and if he does so after the bleeding has stopped but she has not yet taken the bath, then half a dīnār.''[25][26]

---

[21] Al-Jaṣṣāṣ, *Aḥkām al-Qur'ān*, vol 1, pg 348; Mohammad Akram Nadwi. *Al-Fiqh al-Islami,* vol 1, pg 69.
[22] Tafsīr Ṭabarī, vol 2, pg 385.
[23] Qur'ān 9:108.
[24] *Al-Muḥallā*, vol 10, pg 82..
[25] Abū Dāwūd —Kitāb al-nikāḥ—Bāb fī kaffārat man atā ḥāi'iḍan.
[26] Al-Albānī, *Ādāb al-zifāf,* pg 198.

CHAPTER 5

Washing the Two Feet in Ablution

There exists consensus among Sunnī scholars that the feet are to be washed in wuḍūʾ, whereas those of the Shīʿah school permit wiping of the bare feet, basing their erroneous view on an established reading of the following verse:

﴿يَا أَيُّهَا الَّذِينَ آمَنُوا إِذَا قُمْتُمْ إِلَى الصَّلَاةِ فَاغْسِلُوا وُجُوهَكُمْ وَأَيْدِيَكُمْ إِلَى الْمَرَافِقِ وَامْسَحُوا بِرُءُوسِكُمْ وَأَرْجُلَكُمْ إِلَى الْكَعْبَيْ﴾

❦Believers! When you stand up for Prayer, wash your faces and your hands up to the elbows, and wipe your heads, and **[wash] your feet** up to the ankles.❧ (Qurʾān 5:6)

A review of the readings supports the Sunnī position, as another variant opposes this view. There are three ways of reading the lām on the above word. The above variant is that of Nāfiʿ, Ibn ʿĀmir, Ḥafṣ from ʿĀṣim, Kisāʾī, and Yaʿqūb, who read the word in the accusative case **[wa arjulakum]**. Abū Jaʿfar, Abū ʿAmr, Ibn Kathīr, Shuʿbah from ʿĀṣim, Ḥamzah, Khalaf, Ibn Muḥayṣin, Aʿmash and Yazīdī read the word in the genitive case **[wa arjulikum]**:

﴿يَا أَيُّهَا الَّذِينَ آمَنُوا إِذَا قُمْتُمْ إِلَى الصَّلَاةِ فَاغْسِلُوا وُجُوهَكُمْ وَأَيْدِيَكُمْ إِلَى الْمَرَافِقِ وَامْسَحُوا بِرُءُوسِكُمْ وَأَرْجُلِكُمْ إِلَى الْكَعْبَيْ﴾

❦Believers! When you stand up for Prayer, wash your faces and your hands up to the elbows, and **wipe your heads and your feet** up to the ankles.❧

Ḥasan al-Baṣrī read the word in the nominative case **[wa arjulukum]**:[27]

﴿يَا أَيُّهَا الَّذِينَ آمَنُوا إِذَا قُمْتُمْ إِلَى الصَّلَاةِ فَاغْسِلُوا وُجُوهَكُمْ وَأَيْدِيَكُمْ إِلَى الْمَرَافِقِ وَامْسَحُوا بِرُءُوسِكُمْ وَأَرْجُلُكُمْ إِلَى الْكَعْبَيْ﴾

❦Believers! When you stand up for Prayer wash your faces and your hands up to the elbows, and wipe your heads, **and as for your feet, [wash them]** up to the ankles.❧

Reading the word in the accusative form (*arjulakum*) makes the word the object of the command 'wash' and supports the obligation of washing the feet up to the ankles

---

[27] Al-Ittiḥāf, pg 198.

in wuḍū'. This position is further supported by the mention of 'ankles' since wiping cannot encompass the ankles and by sound ḥadīth reports, including what was related by Bukhārī and Muslim that the Prophet saw people performing wuḍū' without washing their feet fully and said, 'Save your heels from the Hellfire!'[28] This ḥadīth proves that washing the entire feet is obligatory. Finally, this position enjoys the consensus of Muslims scholars. Ibn Ḥajar states:

> This ḥadīth clarifies Allah's command in the Qur'ān. There is also a lengthy ḥadīth of 'Amr b. 'Abasah as reported by Ibn Khuzaymah and others that *'the Prophet then washed his feet as Allah had commanded.'* No Companion is established to have differed on this practice save for 'Alī, Ibn 'Abbās and Anas, and it is established that they recanted from their positions.
>
> 'Abd al-Raḥmān b. Abī Laylā said: The Companions unanimously held that the feet are to be washed, as reported by Sa'īd b. Manṣūr.[29]

Ibn Rushd said the following:

> The scholars agree that the feet are subject to washing in wuḍū', though they differed in the details of their washing. The majority held that this means complete washing, while others held that it meants wiping, and yet others that either option is equally valid.
>
> These differences go back to the readings. Reading the word in the accusative case (arjulakum) apparently goes back to washing, while the genitive case (arjulikum) goes back to wiping.
>
> Those who held either position relied on their respective explicit reading of the verse, while interpreting the alternate reading in a manner to support their preferred view. Those who held the apparent meaning of both readings to be equally valid interpreted it as a type of obligation in which one has the choice of either options. Ṭabarī and Dāwūd al-Ẓāhirī held this latter view.[30]

However, this is not Ṭabarī's position at all, for he held the position of washing along with rubbing the hands (in Arabic, *dalk*) over the feet, relying on both readings. He said the following: 'Washing is the pouring of water over the feet while wiping is the rubbing of the hands (or their equivalent) over them, and whoever does that is fulfilling both washing and wiping.'[31]

---

[28] Ṣaḥīḥ Bukhārī: Kitāb al-wuḍū'—Bāb ghusl al-a'qāb; Kitāb al-wuḍū'—Bāb ghusl al-rijlayn wa lā yamsaḥ 'alā al-qadamayn.
[29] *Fatḥ al-bārī*, vol 1, pg 353.
[30] *Bidāyat al-mujtahid*, vol 1, pg 283.
[31] Tafsīr Ṭabarī, vol 6, pg 130.

Ibn Ḥajar points out that the position attributed to Ṭabarī is actually that of another individual named Muḥammad b. Jarīr b. Rustum al-Ṭabarī, who was a Shīʿī scholar and contemporary of the similarly named Sunnī commentator Muḥammad b. Jarīr b. Zayd al-Ṭabarī. Their similar names caused them to be confused for one another.[32]

The third reading of the word in the nominative case (*arjulukum*) creates a sentence with an implied predicate that is not explicitly mentioned: 'As for your feet up to the ankles . . .', which could refer to both washing and wiping. Perhaps this is the reason for the position of choosing either option. However, other evidence, including historical precedence from the Prophet and Companions, as well as scholarly consensus decisively establish that washing, and not wiping, the feet is the correct position and the correct implicit predicate of this variant: *'and as for your feet, [wash them] up to the ankles'*.

Scholars have accepted the validity of the second reading in the genitive case while still maintaining the obligation of washing with the following arguments.

First, Sībawayh, Akhfash and others point out that in Arabic language construction, an object or conjunction can be physically removed from its antecedent while still referring to it, as is the case in this verse. The word 'feet' appears immediately after 'and wipe your heads' and can thus be read with the same case-ending (*ruʾūsikum/arjulikum*) to maintain flow. However, it can still be considered to be in the accusative case as the object of the earlier removed command 'and wash.' There are many similar examples in the Qurʾān as well as Arabic poetry. In this case, while read in the genitive case to maintain flow with its neighbor, it is actually in the accusative case with the meaning being to wash the feet.

Secondly, Abū ʿAlī al-Fārisī points out that 'feet' can grammatically be a conjunction to 'heads' and understood to be the object of 'wipe' (in which case it would mean: 'and wipe the heads and feet'), while the understood meaning could still be to 'wash the feet' since Arabs considered wiping (masḥ) to be a lesser form of washing. They would often refer to a concept by using a word for a lesser form, as in 'I wiped myself for prayer,' which means 'I washed myself for prayer.'[33]

It is also possible that 'wiping' is used here rather than 'washing' to imply frugality of water during washing since wastage and extravagance of water is common when it comes to the feet. Also, the preposition *bi* ('with') with the feet is implicitly understood here ('*with* your heads and *with* your feet') to indicate actual touching and not pouring excess water, further supporting the notion of frugality. This portion of the verse delineates the full extent of the feet ('to the ankles') to

---

[32] *Lisān al-mīzān,* vol 5, pg 103.

[33] An English equivalent would be a complement, popular in my own college days—'Nice threads!' referring to a person's clothes.

make clear that washing is the intent, since wiping does not encompass every portion of the feet.

Thirdly, it is possible to assume that the reading supporting wiping the feet is referring to a specific case, such as when one is wearing khuffayn (a type of foot covering).[34] In this case, the verse would allow wiping the feet when wearing leather socks only.

Finally, those who considered it difficult to reconcile these readings simply dismissed the reading supporting wiping as being abrogated by the notion of washing, which was the persistent practice of the Prophet. This was the view of Ṭaḥāwī and Ibn Ḥazm. However, the sound position is that the readings can be easily reconciled as the above indicates and there is no need for resorting to abrogation.[35]

Does Touching a Female Nullify Ablution?

There exists a long history of difference on this issue, from past to present, between those who believe that touching a female unconditionally nullified one's ablution those that believe it never does so in any case, and those who qualify it depending upon conditions. These differences are influenced upon varying readings of the following verse:

وَإِن كُنتُم مَّرْضَىٰ أَوْ عَلَىٰ سَفَرٍ أَوْ جَاءَ أَحَدٌ مِّنكُم مِّنَ الْغَائِطِ أَوْ لَامَسْتُمُ النِّسَاءَ فَلَمْ تَجِدُوا مَاءً فَتَيَمَّمُوا صَعِيدًا طَيِّبًا

❧*If you are either ill or travelling or have satisfied a want of nature or* **have had contact with women** *and can find no water, then betake yourselves to pure earth, passing with it lightly over your face and your hands.*❧ (4:43, 5:6)

There are two ways of reading the highlighted word: All readers recite the read it with alif as above **[lāmastum]**, apart from Ḥamzah, Kisā'ī, Khalaf and A'mash read it without alif **[lamastum]**:

وَإِن كُنتُم مَّرْضَىٰ أَوْ عَلَىٰ سَفَرٍ أَوْ جَاءَ أَحَدٌ مِّنكُم مِّنَ الْغَائِطِ أَوْ لَمَسْتُمُ النِّسَاءَ فَلَمْ تَجِدُوا مَاءً فَتَيَمَّمُوا صَعِيدًا طَيِّبًا

---

[34] The khuff was a type of shoe that covered the entire foot that early Arabs wore in order to walk on the ground, as opposed to the na'l (sandal), which was also a type of shoe that did not cover the entire feet. Dr. Mohammad Akram Nadwi points out that it is a mistake to translate the khuff as leather socks because they were really a type of shoe meant to walk in.
[35] *Fatḥ al-bārī*, vol 1, pg 353.

> ﴿*If you are either ill or travelling or have satisfied a want of nature or* ***have had contact with women*** *and can find no water, then betake yourselves to pure earth, passing with it lightly over your face and your hands.*﴾ (4:43, 5:6)

Many scholars believed that both readings carry the same meaning, which refers to either skin-to-skin contact between a man and woman, or to sexual relations. Others made a distinction between the readings, where **[lamastum]** refers to sexual relations while **[lāmastum]** to physical contact.

Bayḍāwī[36] (d. 685/1286) states, 'The word *lamastum* is used as an allusion to sexual relations.'[37] Makkī b. Abī Ṭālib said: 'The reading of Ḥamzah and Kisā'ī (*lamastum*) uses a single-doer verb that is addressed to men only and means rubbing a portion of the body over another, which can occur without sexual relations. The reading of the others (*lāmastum*) uses a reflexive verb that involves two parties and means sexual relations, which is an act necessarily involving two parties. However, both can convey the same meanings also, in which case the readings converge.' Ibn Zanjalah also affirmed the view that *lamastum* is touching while *lāmastum* is sexual relations. Ibn Rushd stated:

> Scholars differed over the obligation of performing ablution for the one who has touched a woman with his hand or any other body part. Some held the view that a man who touches a woman with his open hand without any barrier must perform ablution. They also said that a kiss would necessitate the same, since it is a type of touching. This is the case whether it is accompanied by desire or not. This was the view of Shāfi'ī and his companions, although he did distinguish in one report between the one who touched (who must perform ablution) and the recipient (her ablution is not nullified). In another report, he considered the two individuals to be alike (in their requiring ablution). In one report, he also distinguished between one's spouse (in which case ablution is necessary) and other female relatives (in which case it is not), and in another report, he considered the two cases to be similar.
>
> Other scholars considered physical contact to nullify ablution only if accompanied by desire or intended desire, in which case it would not matter if there were a barrier during the contact, or which body part was involved (other than kissing). In the case of kissing, they

---

[36] Abū Sa'īd Nāṣir al-Dīn 'Abdullah b. 'Umar al-Bayḍāwī was a Shāfi'ī jurist and Qur'ānic commentator who died in Tabriz in 685/1286.

[37] Tafsīr al-Bayḍāwī, vol 2, pg 76.

did not stipulate desire to be a condition for ablution to be nullified. This is the view of Imām Mālik and most of his followers.

Imām Abū Ḥanīfah denied that physical contact nullified ablution at all.

All three views have precedence from the Companions, except for the stipulation of desire, for I do not know of any single Companion that was known to have considered that a condition.

The reason for these differences is the usage of the word *'lamasa'* in Arabic. Sometimes it is used for touching with the hand, and sometimes it is used as an allusion to refer to sexual intercourse. Hence, there are two ways of interpreting the use of that term in this verse. Additionally, some considered this to be a general verse whose meaning is subject to specification, and hence stipulated desire as condition for physical contact to nullify ablution. Others considered the verse to remain general and hence considered all physical contact, irrespective of desire, to nullify ablution. Those who stipulated desire as a condition pointed to the contradiction between this unrestricted understanding of the verse with the practice of the Prophet who used to touch his wife ʿĀ'ishah—and she may have touched him as well—during his prostration in prayer. Ḥadīth scholars relate the report of Ḥabīb b. Abī Thābit from ʿUrwah from ʿĀ'ishah that the Prophet would kiss some of his wives and then leave for prayer (immediately). ʿUrwah stated, 'Who could that be but you?' upon which she smiled.[38] Abū ʿUmar b. ʿAbd al-Barr states that this ḥadīth was deemed acceptable by the people of Kūfah and rejected by the people of Makkah and Madīnah, and that he was inclined to accept it. He also states that this ḥadīth was related additionally through Maʿbad b. Nabātah.

Shāfiʿī said: If the ḥadīth of Maʿbad concerning kissing is sound, then I would not view kissing or touching to require ablution.' Those who stipulated ablution relied on the fact that the word 'lamasa' is used literally for touching with the hand and metaphorically for sexual relations. In the case that a meaning vacillated between literal and metaphorical meanings, the literal meaning is preferred unless there is evidence to indicate otherwise. If the metaphorical meaning, for instance, becomes more widespread, then that could be preferred, as in the case of the term in this same verse: 'satisfied a want of nature.' Here, the Qur'ānic term 'ghā'iṭ' literally refers to the hollow region

[38] Tirmidhī: Kitāb al-ṭahārah—Bāb tark al-wuḍū' min al-qublah; Nasā'ī (Sunan al-Kubrā): Kitāb al-ṭahārah—Bāb tark al-wuḍū' min al-qublah; Abū Dāwūd: Kitāb al-ṭahārah—Bāb al-wuḍū' min al-qublah; Ibn Mājah: Kitāb al-ṭahārah wa sunanihā— Bāb al-wuḍū' min al-qublah.

> within the ground where one relieves themselves but is used more commonly for the metaphorical sense for 'excrement,' which is deposited into that.[39]

In summary, there are three views on this issue: the Shāfiʿī school considers physical touching to nullify ablution in all cases, the Ḥanafī school does not consider it to do so in any circumstance, and the Mālikī school considers touching to nullify ablution only if accompanied by desire. The Ḥanbalī school has all three positions reported from Imām Aḥmad.

[39] *Bidāyat al-mujtahid,* pg 41-2..

Part 2: Matters Related to Prayer

The Obligation of Isti'ādhah in Ṣalāh

There are a number of jurisprudential issues which are related to the views of the Qur'ānic Imāms concerning isti'ādhah, which is based upon the following verse:

فَإِذَا قَرَأْتَ الْقُرْآنَ فَاسْتَعِذْ بِاللَّهِ مِنَ الشَّيْطَانِ الرَّجِيمِ

﴿*Whenever you read the Qur'ān, seek refuge with God from Satan, the accursed.*﴾ (16:98)

The first issue concerns the exact ruling of isti'ādhah. Almost all Imāms advocate it at the beginning of each recitation. There is a report from Isḥāq al-Musayyabī (d. 206),[40] that Nāfi' did not practice isti'ādhah or the recitation of basmalah aloud. Makkī b. Abī Ṭālib responds that he may have left them out on occasion only in order to make it clear that they are not part of the Qur'ān, because his widespread practice was to recite them like every other Imām.[41]

As for the jurists, some have deemed it obligatory to recite isti'ādhah at every recitation, including in prayer, while others considered it obligatory only in prayer. The majority considered it sunnah (preferred) at every recitation, whether within or without the prayer. The Mālikīs advocate not reciting it within prayer. The Ḥanafī scholar Sarakhsī (d. 483/1090)[42] said: 'Based upon the apparent meaning of the verse, 'Aṭā' considered isti'ādhah obligatory at the beginning of every recitation, including in prayer. This opposed the consensus of early Muslims that it is sunnah.'[43] The Mālikī jurist Ibn 'Abd al-Barr said: 'Some of our companions relied on Mālik's answer to the question of how he began his prayers: 'I recite al-Fātiḥah,' as an evidence of not reciting isti'ādhah at the beginning of the sūrah.'[44] The Shāfi'ī scholar al-Shāshī (d. 365/976)[45] said: 'Isti'ādhah is recited at the beginning of recitation,

---

[40] Abū Muḥammad Isḥāq b. Muḥammad b. 'Abd al-Raḥmān al-Musayyabī al-Makhzūmī of Madīnah was among the best students of Imām Nāfi'.

[41] *Al-Nashr,* vol 1, pg 146, 251; *al-Kashf*, vol 1, pg 12.

[42] Shams al-a'immah Muḥammad b. Aḥmad b. Abī Sahl was a prolific writer who authored the 15-volume al-Mabsūṭ in Ḥanafī jurisprudence, which he dictated from memory while imprisoned.

[43] *Al-Mabsūṭ*, vol 1, pg 13.

[44] *Al-Tamhīd*, vol 2, pg 220.

[45] Abū Bakr Muḥammad b. 'Alī b. Ismā'īl al-Qaffāl al-Ka'bīr al-Shāshī of the ancient city of Chach (later Persianized to Chachkand, 'city of Chach,' and later Russianized to Tashkent) was a major Shāfi'ī scholar whose teachers included Ṭabarī, Baghawī, and Ibn Khuzaymah. He is credited with spreading the Shāfi'ī school in Transoxania. He lived from 291/904—365/976.

though Mālik said it is not uttered in obligatory prayers but only in the recitation of the Ramadan night prayers.'[46] The Ḥanbalī Ibn Qudāmah (d. 620/1223)[47] said:

> Isti'ādhah is sunnah before recitation in prayer, and that is also the position of Ḥasan al-Baṣrī, Ibn Sīrīn, 'Aṭā', Sufyān al-Thawrī, Awzā'ī, Shāfi'ī, Isḥāq, and the school of opinions (Kūfah).' Mālik, however, held the view that It is not recited due to the ḥadīth of Anas.[48] But our position follows the Qur'ānic verse 16:98.
>
> There is also the ḥadīth of Abū Sa'īd al-Khudrī that when the Prophet stood for prayer, he began with the following supplication:
>
> أَعُوذُ بِاللهِ السَّمِيعِ العَلِيمِ مِنَ الشَّيطَانِ الرَّجِيمِ مِن هَمزِهِ وَنَفخِهِ وَنَفثِهِ
>
> *I seek refuge in God, All-Hearing and All-Knowing, from the accursed devil, from his evil whispers, inhaling and exhaling.*[49] [50]

Ibn Ḥazm said: 'For us, there is no doubt about the obligation of isti'ādhah in prayer, for many Companions did so before their recitations, as was soundly narrated to us with no report to the contrary from any of them.'[51]

These are the various positions of jurists along with their evidence concerning isti'ādhah with the majority deeming it either obligatory or recommended, and so, caution would warrant its practice.

---

[46] *Ḥilyat al-'ulamā',* vol 2, pg 83.

[47] Muwaaq al-Dīn Abū Muḥammad 'Abdullah b. Aḥmad b. Qudāmah al-Maqdisī (541/1147—620/1223) was a prolific Ḥanbalī scholar from Palestine who produced a large body of works and a warrior who participated in the expeditions of Ṣalāḥ al-Dīn. Among his teachers was 'Abd al-Qādir Jīlānī of Baghdad.

[48] Anas reported: I prayed behind the Prophet, Abū Bakr and 'Umar, and they began their recitations (in prayer) with al-Fatihah. They did not recite basmalah either before or after the recitation. Related by Ṣaḥīḥ Muslim: Kitāb al-ṣalāh—Bāb ḥujjah man qāla lā yajhar bi al-basmalah. Also related by Ṣaḥīḥ Bukhārī: Kitāb al-adhān—Bāb mā yaqūlu ba'da al-takbīr, without the second sentence.

[49] Abū Dāwūd: Kitāb al-ṣalāh—Bāb man ra'ā al-istiftāḥ bi subḥānakallāhumma wa bi ḥamdik; Also see Tirmidhī, Ibn Mājah and Aḥmad. This report was authenticated by Albānī in *al-Irwā' al-ghalīl*.

[50] *Al-Mughnī,* vol 1, pg 283.

[51] *Al-Iḥkām,* vol 2, pg 196.

The Wording of Isti'ādhah

The Imāms of the Readings had varying practices in the wording of isti'ādhah. Most of them followed the basic Qur'ānic expression:

أَعُوذُ بِاللهِ مِنَ الشَّيطَانِ الرَّجِيمِ

I seek refuge with God from Satan, the accursed.

Ḥasan al-Baṣrī used to use the following expression:

أَعُوذُ بِاللهِ السَّمِيعِ العَلِيمِ مِنَ الشَّيطَانِ الرَّجِيمِ، إِنَّ اللهَ هُوَ السَّمِيعُ العَلِيمُ

I seek refuge with God, All-Hearing, All-Knowing, from Satan, the accursed. Surely God is All-Seeing, All-Knowing.

Nāfi', Ibn 'Āmir, Kisā'ī, and A'mash used the following expression:

أَعُوذُ بِاللهِ مِنَ الشَّيطَانِ الرَّجِيمِ، إِنَّ اللهَ هُوَ السَّمِيعُ العَلِيمُ

I seek refuge with God from Satan, the accursed. Surely God is All-Seeing, All-Knowing.

Ḥamzah, as reported by Sahl al-Sijistānī, and Ibn Sīrīn used to use the following expression:

أَستَعِيذُ بِاللهِ مِنَ الشَّيطَانِ الرَّجِيمِ

I seek refuge with God from Satan, the accursed.

Ḥamzah is also reported to have used the following expression:

أَستَعِينُ بِاللهِ مِنَ الشَّيطَانِ الرَّجِيمِ

I seek assistance with God from Satan, the accursed.

Ḥafṣ through the transmission of Hubayrah adds the following:

أَعُوذُ بِاللهِ العَظِيمِ السَّمِيعِ العَلِيمِ مِنَ الشَّيطَانِ الرَّجِيمِ

I seek refuge with God, Majestic One, All-Hearing, All-Knowing, from Satan, the accursed.

Jurists considered this a flexible issue and relied on the Prophet ﷺ as well as the Imāms of the readings for its exact form. Sarakhsī, after relating the various expressions in use by these Qur'ānic Imāms, comments, 'All of these differences have reports establishing them.'[52] Sufyān al-al-Thawrī used to recommend the expression

[52] *Al-Mabsūṭ*, vol 1, pg 13.

used by Nāfi' above. Ḥasan b. Ṣāliḥ b. Ḥayy (d. 167)[53] recommended using the following form:

أَعُوذُ بِاللهِ السَّمِيعِ العَلِيمِ مِنَ الشَّيطَانِ الرَّجِيمِ

I seek refuge with God, All-Hearing, All-Knowing, from Satan, the accursed.

Imām Aḥmad recommended the expression of Ḥasan al-Baṣrī. Nawawī, after recommending the most basic form in the beginning of prayer and admitting that other scholars have other forms, comments: 'The purpose of isti'ādhah is fulfilled by anything that contains the notion of seeking refuge in God from the devil.'[54]

Ibn Qudāmah states that the basic expression fulfills the Qur'ānic command and that this was the view of Abū Ḥanīfah and Shāfi'ī, based on the verse. Aḥmad preferred the additions of Ḥasan al-Baṣrī due to the report of Abū Sa'īd al-Khudrī. Ibn Qudāmah then concludes that the matter is flexible, and that all such forms were good.[55]

In the end, it would be preferable to confine oneself to one of the forms that have been established as coming from the Prophet ﷺ, which are the following:

أَعُوذُ بِاللهِ السَّمِيعِ العَلِيمِ مِنَ الشَّيطَانِ الرَّجِيمِ مِن هَمزِهِ وَنَفخِهِ وَنَفثِهِ

I seek refuge in God, All-Hearing and All-Knowing, from the accursed devil, from his evil whispers, inhaling and exhaling.[56]

اللَّهُمَّ أَعُوذُ بِكَ مِنَ الشَّيطَانِ الرَّجِيمِ مِن هَمزِهِ وَنَفخِهِ وَنَفثِهِ

Oh God, I seek refuge in you from the accursed devil, from his evil whispers, inhaling and exhaling.[57]

Both of these expressions were uttered by the Prophet ﷺ in prayer as established by ḥadīth reports. Albānī comments that he does not know of any ḥadīth report from the Prophet ﷺ containing the basic form of isti'ādhah without the above additions.[58]

However, the widespread transmission of these other forms from the Qur'ānic Imāms, all of whom read them upon their own teachers from the Companions and Followers, makes their usage acceptable. And Allah knows best.

---

[53] He was a great jurist and worshipper of Kūfah who lived from 100—167. Abū Nu'aym commented that he had met 800 ḥadīth scholars but found no one better than him.
[54] *Rawḍah al-ṭālibīn*, vol 1, pg 240.
[55] *Al-Mughnī*, vol 1, pg 283.
[56] See footnote 49.
[57] Ḥadīth of Jubayr b. Muṭ'im in Abū Dāwūd: Kitāb al-ṣalāh—Bāb ma ustaftaḥu bihi al-ṣalāh min al-du'ā', Musnad Aḥmad; Ibn Mājah: Kitāb iqāmat al-ṣalāh wa al-sunnah fīhā—Bāb al-isti'ādah fī al-ṣalāh. It was authenticated by Albānī in *al-Irwā' al-ghalīl*.
[58] *Al-Irwā' al-ghalīl*, vol 2, pg 53.

Verbalizing Isti'ādhah Aloud

The practice of most Qur'ānic Imāms is to utter isti'ādhah silently in prayer in all cases, and outside of prayer to match the recitation: if reciting aloud, isti'ādhah is uttered aloud, and vice versa. However, it is reported from Nāfi' and Ḥamzah that they advocated uttering isti'ādhah silently even with loud recitation. It is also reported from Ḥamzah, through one report, that he articulated isti'ādhah silently in sūrah al-Fātiḥah but aloud with the other sūrahs.[59]

Sarakhsī says: 'The one who is praying, whether he is following or leading, utters isti'ādhah to himself because uttering isti'ādhah aloud is not transmitted from Allah's Messenger ﷺ. The practice of loud isti'ādhah which was transmitted from 'Umar represented his own personal application, which was either incidental and without intent, or for the purpose of teaching those who were around him. In this same manner, it is related from him that he also recited the opening prayer of ṣalāh aloud. Muḥammad al-Shaybānī held the view that the followers in prayer do not utter isti'ādhah whereas for Abū Yūsuf, they are to do so.'[60]

Qaffāl states: 'There are two views on this issue.'[61] Nawawī states: 'The predominant view is that isti'ādhah is not uttered aloud in any prayer, whether the prayer itself is silent or loud. A second view is that it is uttered aloud in the same manner as basmalah and āmīn. The third view is that both are equally valid options. It is also said that silent isti'ādhah is always preferable.'[62] Ibn Qudāmah said: 'Isti'ādhah is always uttered silently, and I do not know of any difference on this.'[63] Here, he means the case of isti'ādhah in prayer, for outside of prayer there are well-known differences, as previously mentioned.

Isti'ādhah for Each Rak'ah

As for the issue of whether isti'ādhah is for the beginning of prayer in the first rak'ah or for every rak'ah, there are various juristic views. Sarakshī states: 'It is preferred to utter isti'ādhah for every rak'ah, and this is the view of Abū Ḥanīfah. In the first rak'ah, it is more certain. And there are other scholars in our school who say that for the other rak'ahs apart from the first, there are two practices.'[64] Ibn Ḥajar said: 'The generality of the verse commanding isti'ādhah supports uttering it in every single rak'ah, and this was the view of Ḥasan al-Baṣrī, 'Aṭā' and Ibrāhīm.'[65] Nawawī said: 'The school's position is that isti'ādhah is preferred in every rak'ah, though the first

[59] *Al-Ittiḥāf,* pg 20; *al-Kashf,* vol 1, pg 11.

[60] *Al-Mabsūṭ,* vol, pg 14.

[61] *Ḥilyat al-'ulamā',* vol 2, pg 83.

[62] *Rawḍat al-ṭālibīn,* vol 1, pg 241.

[63] *Al-Mughnī,* vol 1, pg 283.

[64] *Al-Mabsūṭ,* vol 1, pg 14.

[65] *Talkhīṣ al-ḥabīr,* vol 1, pg 230.

one is certain. This is reported from Shāfiʿī, and was adopted by Qāḍī Abū al-Ṭayyib, Juwaynī, Rūyānī and others. Another view in the school is that it is only for the first rakʿah and if it is left out in the first, forgetfully or intentionally, then it is uttered in the subsequent rakʿah.'[66] Ibn Mufliḥ (d. 769/1367)[67] said: 'Istiʿādhah after the first rakʿah has two views.'[68] Al-Buhūtī (d. 1051/1641)[69] said: 'If istiʿādhah is left out in the first rakʿah, intentionally or forgetfully, it is done in the second.'[70]

The Place of Istiʿādhah

The practice of nearly all Qur'ānic scholars is to utter istiʿādhah before recitation and not at its end, and this is the correct view based upon the practice of the Prophet ﷺ as found in the ḥadīth reports from Abū Saʿīd al-Khudrī and Jubayr b. Muṭʿim.

Here, the Prophetic practice, or sunnah, clarifies the intent of the verse commanding istiʿādhah. When God says, ﴿*And when you recite the Qur'ān, seek refuge in God*﴾, He means that when you intend to recite, utter the istiʿādhah first. This is similar to the command: ﴿*And when you stand for prayer, wash your faces . . .* ﴾, which obligates ablution before prayer.

However, it is narrated from some early Muslims that istiʿādhah is uttered after the completion of recitation, but this is a weak view. Qaffāl states that it is reported from Ibrāhīm al-Nakhaʿī and Ibn Sīrīn that they would both utter istiʿādhah after recitation.[71] Sarakhsī states:

> The adherents of the Ẓāhirī school take the overt meaning of the verse and stipulate istiʿādhah after recitation because they consider the verse to list the sequence through the conjunction *fā*: ﴿*Whenever you read the Qur'ān, then seek refuge with Allah from Satan, the accursed.*﴾
>
> But this is not correct, for the conjunction here in our view is for stipulating a state, as in the statement: 'When you come into the company of a king, *then* be on your guard.' This means that when you are about to enter upon royal company, be on your guard, i.e. before you enter, not afterwards. Thus, the real meaning of the verse is that

---

[66] *Rawḍat al-ṭālibīn,* vol 1, pg 241.
[67] Shams al-Dīn Abū ʿAbdullah Muḥammad b. Mufliḥ al-Maqdisī was a great Ḥanbalī scholar from Damascus about whom Ibn al-Qayyim remarked: 'There is none under the skies more knowledgeable about the Ḥanbalī school than him.' He lived from 700/1300—769/1367.
[68] *Al-mubdiʿ,* vol 1, pg 241.
[69] Manṣūr b. Yūnus b. Ṣalāḥ al-Buhūtī was leader of the Ḥanbalī scholars of Egypt who lived from 1000/1592—1051/1641.
[70] *Kashshāf al-qināʿ,* vol 1, pg 356.
[71] *Ḥilyat al-ʿulamāʾ,* vol 2, pg 83.

when you intend to recite the Qur'ān, then first seek refuge in God. This is explained in the ḥadīth report about the incident of the slander of ʿĀ'ishah when the Prophet lifted the cloak from his face, he uttered the istiʿādhah and recited verse 11 of sūrah al-Nūr: ﴾*Those who have invented the slander, are some of your own people . . .*﴿ (24:11)[72] [73]

Qur᾽ānity of Basmalah

All scholars agree that the basmalah is a portion of a verse in sūrah al-Naml: ﴾*[The letter] is from Sulaymān, and it says: 'In the name of Allah, the Most Merciful, the Most Compassionate.'*﴿ (27:30) and that it is not a verse in the beginning of sūrah al-Tawbah. Beyond, that, they differ over whether it is the first verse of al-Fātiḥah or any other sūrah.

Mālik did not consider it to be a verse of any sūrah.[74] Shāfiʿī and Aḥmad considered it to be a verse that is a part of every single sūrah except Barā'ah.[75] Abū Ḥanīfah considered it to be an independently revealed verse which serves to separate the sūrahs (apart from al-Anfāl and al-Tawbah), but that it is not the first verse of any sūrah.[76]

As for the Imāms of the Qur'ānic readings, the Makkan and Kūfan readers considered it to be the first verse of al-Fātiḥah. They did not consider the portion [*anʿamta ʿalayhim*] to be the end of a verse.[77] In contrast, the other Imāms (the readers of Madīnah, Baṣrah, and Syria) hold the opposite position and consider [*anʿamta ʿalayhim*] to be serve as the verse.

All of them agree that al-Fātiḥah is composed of seven verses, since it has been referred to as the 'seven oft-repeated verses' in the Qur'ān 15:87 as well as by the Prophet. The position of basmalah being the first verse of al-Fātiḥah is supported by the ḥadīth of Abū Hurayrah that the Prophet ﷺ said: '*When you recite al-Fātiḥah, recite basmalah, for this sūrah represents the foundation of the Qur'ān, the*

---

[72] *Al-Mabsūṭ*, vol 1, pg 13.

[73] Abū Dāwūd: Kitāb al-ṣalāh—Bāb man lam yara al-jahr bi bismillāh al-Raḥmān al-Raḥīm. Abū Dāwūd relates this alone among the Sunan, and deems the ḥadīth munkar.

[74] Ibn al-ʿArabī, *Aḥkām al-Qur'ān*, vol 1, pg 20.

[75] *Al-Muhadhdhab,* vol, pg 71; *Al-Mughnī,* vol 1, pg 476.

[76] Al-Jaṣṣāṣ, *Aḥkām al-Qur'ān*, vol 1, pg 11.

[77] Because sūrah al-Fātiḥah has been referred to in the Qur'ān as the 'seven oft-repeated verses' in 15:87, all scholars agree on the number of verses in the sūrah. Those who consider the basmalah to be the first verse of the sūrah designate the final verse to begin with *ṣirāṭ alladhīna* . . .in order to maintain seven total verses.

foundation of the Book, the 'seven-oft repeated verses,' and the basmalah is one of its verses.'[78]

Beyond al-Fātiḥah, all transmitters agree that basmalah does not represent the first verse of the other sūrahs.

Reciting Basmalah in the Beginning of Each Sūrah

All fourteen Qur'ān transmitters apart from Ḥasan al-Baṣrī consider reciting basmalah in the beginning of each sūrah apart from al-Tawbah to be legislated. Ḥasan advocated reciting basmalah in the beginning of al-Fātiḥah only and not in the other sūrahs for fear that it would be considered a verse of the other sūrahs, for he did not consider it to be so except in al-Fātiḥah.[79]

The schools of jurisprudence have four basic positions on the matter. Shāfi'ī and Aḥmad (through one narration) held that it is obligatory in the beginning of al-Fātiḥah and recommended before the other sūrahs apart from al-Tawbah. The Ḥanafī school considered it recommended in the beginning of al-Fātiḥah alone. The more popular opinion of Aḥmad was that it is recommended at the beginning of each sūrah including al-Fātiḥah. In the Mālikī school it is disliked to be recited at the beginning of any sūrah during the obligatory prayers, and either permitted or recommended in the supererogatory prayers.[80]

Reciting Basmalah Between Two Sūrahs

The differences among Qur'ānic experts on the issue of reciting basmalah when joining between two sūrahs in recitation are detailed in works on the Qur'ānic readings. These differences can be summarized into three basic positions. Qālūn, Ibn Kathīr, 'Āṣim, Kisā'ī and Abū Ja'far advocated reciting basmalah between surahs. Ḥamzah and Khalaf joined sūrahs without basmalah. Warsh, Abū 'Amr, Ibn 'Āmir and Ya'qūb allowed the recitation of basmalah as well as its omission, and the joining of the sūrahs with or without a brief pause (sakt).

There were some scholars who made an exception for two sūrahs that begin with the negative particle *lā* (al-Qiyāmah[81] and al-Balad[82]) and two sūrahs that begin

---

[78] Related by Dāruquṭnī: Kitāb al-ṣalāh—Bāb fī al-jahr bi bismillāh al-Raḥmān al-Raḥīm; Bayhaqī (Sunan al-Kubrā): Kitāb al-ṣalāh—Bāb al-dalīl 'alā anna bismillāh al-Raḥmān al-Raḥīm āyah tāmah min al-Fātiḥah; Ṭabarānī (Mu'jam al-Awsaṭ): Bāb man ismuhū Muḥammad. It was deemed authentic by Albānī in *Ṣaḥīḥ al-Jāmi'*.

[79] *Al-Budūr al-zāhirah,* pg 13; *al-Qirā'āt al-shādhdhah,* pg 24.

[80] Ibn al-'Arabī, *Aḥkām al-Qur'ān,* vol 1, pg 20; *Nayl al-Awṭār,* vol 3, pg 50; Jaṣṣāṣ, *Aḥkām al-Qur'ān,* vol, pg 11; *Al-Mughnī,* vol 1, pg 476.

[81] Sūrah 75.

[82] Sūrah 90.

with the particle *wayl* (al-Muṭaffifīn[83] and al-Humazah[84]): these sūrahs are joined with their preceding sūrahs with basmalah for those who are joining other surahs with a pause; and with a pause for those joining the other surahs without any pause or stop. However, those who have researched this issue do not accept these distinctions and consider the case of these sūrahs to be the same as the rest.

These rules apply to adjacent surahs in the muṣḥaf sequence (like joining sūrah 2 with 3, or 77 with 78) as well as those that are not adjacent but follow one another in the muṣḥaf sequence (like joining sūrah 2 with 4). However, when joining sūrahs in a non-mushaf sequence, like the end of sūrah 2 with the beginning of sūrah 1, all Qur'ān transmitters advocate basmalah as a separation and disallow joining with a pause or continuously. In addition, when a single sūrah is repeated more than once, then the basmalah is recited at each beginning of the sūrah.[85]

Reciting from within a Sūrah

The Qur'ān transmitters allow the option of starting from within a sūrah—even if it is one word after the beginning—with and without basmalah. Imām Shāṭibī alludes to this in his poem:

ولاَ بُدَّ مِنها فِي ابتِدائِكَ سُورَةً / سِواهاَ وفِي الأجزاءِ خَيَّرَ مَن تَلا

[Basmalah] is mandatory when you begin a sūrah,
Apart from [al-Tawbah], but starting from within, it is optional.[86]

The author of *al-Ittiḥāf* states: The basmalah is optional in starting the recitation of a sūrah from anywhere after its beginning, even if by a word, as indicated by Shāṭibī and al-Dānī in al-Taysīr. Most reciters of Iraq adopted the basmalah in these cases, while most reciters from the west omitted it. There were also some scholars (like Ibn Kathīr) that stipulated basmalah for those who considered it to separate sūrahs and omitted it for those who did not consider it a separation (for instance, Ḥamzah).[87]

Basmalah with Sūrah al-Tawbah

The Qur'ānic experts as well as jurists are agreed that basmalah is not recited in the beginning of sūrah al-Tawbah[88] even when it is joined with the previous sūrah because it simply was not revealed as such through Jibrīl by God's command. The

[83] Sūrah 83.
[84] Sūrah 104.
[85] *Al-Ittiḥāf,* pg 121; *Al-Budūr al-zāhirah,* pg 14.
[86] Al-Shāṭibīyyah line 106.
[87] *Al-Ittiḥāf,* pg 121.
[88] This sūrah is also known as Barā'ah.

basmalah represents God's safety, while al-Tawbah was revealed 'with the sword.' Shāṭibī alludes to this in line 105 of his poem:

ومَهما تَصِلها أو بَدَأت بَراءَةً / لِتَنزيلِها بالسَّيفِ لَستَ مُبَسمِلا

However you recite Barā'ah, from its beginning or through joining
Because of its being revealed with the sword, do not recite basmalah.

As for the exact ruling on doing so (beginning sūrah al-Tawbah with basmalah), jurists consider it either forbidden or disliked. As for beginning the recitation from within the sūrah, they considered it either sunnah like the case of the other sūrahs or disliked. The author of Itḥāf states:

> The correct view is what appears in al-Nashr (of Ibn al-Jazarī): that whoever adopts the practice of leaving the basmalah when reciting from within sūrahs, also does so in this sūrah without any problem. For those who consider the basmalah to separate sūrahs, then the basmalah in the middle of the sūrah follows the beginning of it, and hence, there is no basmalah in al-Tawbah even when reading from its middle.
>
> As for those who adopt basmalah when beginning from within every sūrah, then the case of al-Tawbah goes back to their view on its exclusion in the beginning. If they believe that the reason for its exclusion is the theme of the sword in the sūrah and that this reason applies to the entire sūrah, as Shāṭibī does, then they would drop it within the sūrah as well. If they don't consider this to be the reason for the omission of basmalah at all, or if they believe this reason does not apply to the entire sūrah, then they would begin with basmalah within the sūrah with no problem. And Allah knows best.[89]

Audible Basmalah in Prayer

A group of early Muslims held that it was preferred to recite basmalah aloud in the loud prayers before al-Fātiḥah and other sūrahs. This was reported from 'Umar, 'Alī, Ibn 'Umar, Ibn 'Abbās, Ibn al-Zubayr, 'Ammār b. Yāsir and a large group of the Followers. This is the dominant opinion among the jurists and Qur'ānic scholars of Makkah, including Imām Shāfi'ī and his followers.

On the other hand, the majority of scholars did not consider audible basmalah to be sunnah. Among these, some considered it sunnah to recite it silently while others advocated not reciting it all, as per the previous discussion.

---

[89] *Al-Nashr,* vol 1, pg 259; *Al-Ittiḥāf,* pg 121; *Al-Budūr al-zāhirah,* pg 13.

What is worthy of mention here is that Abū al-Qāsim al-Hadhalī, the author of al-Kāmil, narrates that Mālik asked Nāfiʿ about this issue, and he replied, 'It is sunnah to recite it aloud.' Mālik accepted this fully and said, 'In every field, we ask its experts.'[90]

Ibn Taymiyyah discussed this issue at length in a treatise that is part of his *Majmūʿ al-Fatāwā,* where he states that ḥadīth reports supporting audible basmalah are either reported by jurists who weren't experts in ḥadīth narration or by ḥadīth transmitters who did not stipulate authenticity in their reporting. Hence these reports could vacillate between strong or weak:

> More astonishing than that is the fact that some esteemed jurists who never reference any ḥadīth from Bukhārī in their works quote one ḥadīth reportedly from Bukhārī on the basmalah which was not related by him at all. If this is the extent of their ḥadīth expertise, then what would be the state of their understanding on the rest of the matter? Such reports were related by those who attempted to compile everything on this topic, such as Dāruquṭnī and Khaṭīb, who were known to collect everything that is reported [without verification]. When asked about the soundness of these reports, they could only answer based on the extent of their knowledge. When Dāruquṭnī came to Egypt, for instance, he was asked to narrate all ḥadīth on reciting basmalah aloud and did so. He was then asked, 'Are these reports sound?' He replied, 'From the Prophet ﷺ they are not, but from the Companions, some of them are sound and some are weak.'
>
> Khaṭīb was asked the same and related two ḥadīth reports concerning an incident involving Muʿāwiyah leading prayers in Madīnah. Shāfiʿī reported with his isnād that Anas b. Mālik said: Muʿāwiyah led us in prayer in Madīnah and recited basmalah aloud prior to al-Fātiḥah. In the next sūrah, he did not, and when going down, he did not utter takbīr. After he finished the prayer, many of the Muhājirīn that were present asked, 'O Muʿāwiyah, did you steal from the prayer, or did you forget?' He repeated the prayer, this time reciting basmalah before the second sūrah and uttering takbīr when going down to prostration. Shāfiʿī also related his isnād through ʿUbayd b. Rifāʿah that Muʿāwiyah came to Madīnah and led the prayer . . .[91]

---

[90] *Al-Rawḍ al-naḍīr,* pg 9.

[91] Related by Bayhaqī (Sunan al-Kubrā): Kitāb al-ṣalāh—Bāb iftitāḥ al-qirāʿah fī al-ṣalāh; Dāruquṭnī: Kitāb al-ṣalāh—Bāb fī al-jahr bi bismillāh al-Raḥmān al-Raḥīm; Muṣannaf ʿAbd al-Razzāq: Kitāb al-ṣalāh—Bāb qirāʿah bi bismillāh al-Raḥmān al-Raḥīm; Mustadrak Ḥākim: Kitāb

Khaṭīb commented that this report is the strongest evidence on the issue, but that is not the case at all.

Since ḥadīth experts agree that there is no sound or explicit ḥadīth on the issue of reciting basmalah aloud, not to mention widespread or mutawātir reports, it is unlikely that the Prophet ﷺ would recite the basmalah aloud, just as it is not possible that he would utter the other opening supplications of prayer aloud and that they simply were not transmitted. . . .

With all of this, we are forced to admit that the Prophet ﷺ did not verbalize basmalah aloud as he did al-Fātiḥah. It is possible that he did it early on and abandoned it later, as Abū Dāwūd relates in his Marāsīl from Sa'īd b. Jubayr and Ṭabarānī in his Mu'jam from Ibn 'Abbās that the Prophet ﷺ would recite it aloud in Makkah, until the mushrikīn began to curse al-Raḥmān after hearing it, after which he stopped saying it aloud until he died.

As for incidentally uttering things aloud, there are many such reports in the Ṣaḥīḥ. He ﷺ would sometimes recite verses aloud (in Ẓuhr and 'Aṣr prayers). On some occasions, certain Companions behind him uttered some supplications aloud, such: *Rabbanā laka al-ḥamdu ḥamdan kathīran ṭayyiban mubārakan fīh* ('Our Lord, praise belongs to You, praise that is frequent, pure and blessed.'[92]. . . Sometimes Ibn 'Umar and Abū Hurayrah recited isti'ādhah aloud. Once, Ibn 'Abbās even recited the funeral prayer aloud to show that it is sunnah. It can be said that in all these cases, the Companions uttered these things aloud only to teach and demonstrate that they were sunnah, not that the recitation aloud itself is sunnah.

Whoever reflects over the entirety of established narrations on this topic would know that basmalah is a verse of God's Book and that those who recited it aloud intended only to demonstrate this and not to show that it was a part of al-Fātiḥah. Reciting it aloud is only sunnah in the line of what Ibn Wahb mentioned in his Jāmi': A number of teachers have related to me from Ibn 'Abbās, Abū Hurayrah, Zayd b. Aslam, and Zuhrī a similar report, other than that of Ibn 'Umar: that he would begin his recitation with basmalah. Zuhrī points out: He wanted to show through this that this was a verse of the Qur'ān and that God had revealed it. And the jurists began to practice this as well as time passed on.

---

al-imāmah wa ṣalāh al-jamā'ah—ḥadīth al-jahr bi bismillāh al-Raḥmān al-Raḥīm. Ḥākim deemed it ṣaḥīḥ on Bukhārī and Muslim's conditions, and Dhahabī agreed with him.

[92] Ṣaḥīḥ Bukhārī: Kitāb al-adhān—Bāb ḥaddathanā Mu'ādh b. Faḍālah.

The ḥadīth of Ibn 'Umar is known through the report of Ḥammād b. Zayd from Ayyūb from Nāfi' from Ibn 'Umar that when he prayed, he recited basmalah aloud, and when he reached the end of al-Fātiḥah, he again recited basmalah aloud. This was mentioned by Zuhrī, who was the most knowledgeable one of his time in the sunnah, in order to elucidate the reality of the matter.

So the issue rests upon the reports of Ibn 'Abbās, Abū Hurayrah and Ibn 'Umar; and the reality of the practice of Abū Hurayrah and others is well known, may God be pleased with them all.

The weakness of the ḥadīth of Mu'āwiyah is clear, based upon various pieces of evidence. First, more sound, explicit and widespread reports are transmitted from Anas to the contrary of this. Second, the ḥadīth rests upon 'Abdullah b. 'Uthmān b. Khaytham who was a weak reporter. Third, it does not possess a sound, connected chain free of weak and contradictory elements. Fourth, Anas resided in Baṣrah, and there is no one as far we know that confirmed his presence with Mu'āwiyah when he came to Madīnah. Fifth, such an incident should have been widely transmitted, but no Madīnans transmitted nor did any of the reliable students of Anas. What was transmitted from the Madīnans and from Anas was the opposite of this. Finally, if indeed Mu'āwiyah's practice was to have reverted to uttering basmalah aloud, it would have been widely known among his students and companions in Syria. But in fact, the unanimous practice in Syria was to not recite the basmalah aloud. Awzā'ī's school in Syria, for instance, was the same as the Mālikī school in Madīnah: to not recite basmalah.

Reflecting over these points makes any scholar realize decisively that the ḥadīth of Mu'āwiyah was either entirely false without any basis at all or an incident that was altered in its reporting. In the end, this report, were its transmission to be sound, would be considered shādh (anamalous) as it contradicts what the reliable experts related from Anas, from the Madīnans, and from the Syrians.[93]

[93] *Majmū' al-Fatāwā* (Dār al-Kutub al-'Ilmiyah), vol 22, pg 205-12.

CHAPTER 5

Takbīr in the Final Sūrahs

The practice of takbīr in the final sūrahs refers to reciting either of the following formulas at the beginning or end of each sūrah from al-Ḍuḥā to the end of the Qur'ān:[94]

الله أكبَر

Allāhu akbar

لَا إِلهَ إِلّا الله وَالله أكبَر

Lā ilāha illallāh wallāhu akbar

لَا إِلهَ إِلّا الله وَالله أكبَرُ وَلِلَّهِ الحَمد

Lā ilāha illallāh wallāhu akbar wa lillāh al-ḥamd

This practice has also been transmitted as a valid practice by Ibn al-Jazarī in his book al-Nashr through his isnāds to the ten readings, with the first wording ('*Allāhu akbar*') in the beginning of all sūrahs of the Qur'ān except for al-Tawbah.

This is a practice established from the Prophet ﷺ who used to practice it on occasion, as reported by Ḥākim in his Mustadrak:

> Abū Yaḥyā Muḥammad b. ʿAbdullah b. Muḥammad b. ʿAbdullah b. Yazīd the Qur'ānic expert and Imām of the Grand Masjid of Makkah reported to us: Abū ʿAbdullah Muḥammad b. ʿAlī b. Zayd b. al-Ṣā'igh reported to us: Aḥmad b. Muḥammad b. al-Qāsim b. Abī Bazzah (the Qur'ānic expert al-Bazzī) reported to us: I read upon ʿIkrimah b. Sulaymān and he related to me: I read upon Ismāʿīl b. ʿAbdullah b. Qusṭanṭīn and Shibl b. ʿAbbād, and when I reached sūrah al-Ḍuḥā, both of them said: 'Recite takbīr until the end of the Qur'ān, after you complete each sūrah, for we read so upon Ibn Kathīr and he ordered us to do so. He informed us that he read upon Mujāhid who ordered him to do the same. Mujāhid informed him that he read upon Ibn ʿAbbās who ordered him to do the same. Ibn ʿAbbās informed him that he read upon Ubayy b. Kaʿb who ordered him to do the same. And Ubayy informed him that he read upon the Prophet ﷺ who ordered him to do the same.[95]

---

[94] Last 22 sūrahs of the Qur'ān.

[95] Related by Ḥākim in al-Mustadrak: Kitāb maʿrifat al-ṣaḥābah—Bāb dhikr manāqib Ubayy b. Kaʿb. Ḥākim deemed it ṣaḥīḥ on the conditions of Bukhārī and Muslim but Dhahabī disagreed and pointed to the criticism about al-Bazzī.

This practice is also traced to Ibn ʿAbbās, as reported by Abū ʿAmr al-Dānī, Abū al-ʿUlā al-Hamadānī and Ibn Mujāhid, all of them from Abū Bakr al-Ḥumaydī who said: Ibrāhīm b. Abī Ḥayyah al-Tamīmī reported to me: Ḥumayd al-Aʿraj reported to me: from Mujāhid, who said: I completed the Qur'ān nineteen times with Ibn ʿAbbās, and each single time he ordered me to utter the takbīr with each sūrah starting with al-Sharḥ.[96]

This practice is also traced to several Successors, including Mujāhid, Aʿraj, Ibn Muḥayṣin and Ibn Kathīr.[97]

At the same time, the practice has not been adopted by many scholars due to the fact that it is only reported through al-Bazzī, who was deemed a weak narrator of ḥadīth. Ibn Kathīr said: 'This practice is related in a solitary fashion from al-Bazzī, who was an expert in Qur'ānic reading. As for his status in ḥadīth, Abū Ḥātim al-Rāzī considered him weak and did not narrate from him.' Abū Jaʿfar al-ʿUqaylī considered him to report munkar ḥadīth.[98]

However, Shihāb al-Dīn Abū Shāmah in his commentary on al-Shāṭibīyah relates that when Imām Shāfiʿī saw someone adopting this practice in prayer, he said to him, 'You have done well and adopted the Prophetic sunnah.' This indicates his acceptance of this ḥadīth.[99] This statement of Shāfiʿī is also related by Abū ʿAmr al-Dānī with his isnād to al-Bazzī, who said, 'If you had left this practice of takbīr, you would have abandoned a sunnah of your Prophet.'[100]

Those who adopted the practice of takbīr responded with a number of arguments to their opponents who either did not consider it sunnah or went further to deem it an innovation. First, scholars are unanimous in accepting al-Bazzī as an authority in transmitting the Qur'ānic readings, and since the practice of takbīr belongs to the domain of the readings, his practice is accepted even if he is alone in narrating it. Second, some ḥadīth experts pointed out that al-Bazzī was not really alone in narrating this report but was joined by Shāfiʿī, for Shams al-Dīn Sakhāwī (d. 907/1497)[101] relates in his musalsal narrations with an isnād to Imām Shāfiʿī who said: 'I read the Qur'ān to Ismāʿīl b. ʿAbdullah b. Qusṭanṭīn, who said: I read upon Ibn Kathīr,' and he mentioned the ḥadīth on the practice of takbīr.[102] However, Ḥākim also related in his Mustadrak a report with an isnād to Imām Shāfiʿī that he read upon Ismāʿīl who read upon Ibn Kathīr who read upon Mujāhid who read upon Ibn ʿAbbās who read upon Ubayy b. Kaʿb who read upon the Prophet ﷺ, and they did not

---

[96] *Al-Nashr,* vol 2, pg 310.
[97] *Al-Nashr,* vol 2, pg 311.
[98] *Al-Ḍuʿafāʾ,* vol 1, pg 127.
[99] Tafsīr Ibn Kathīr, vol 4, pg 522; Abū Shāmah, *Sharḥ Shāṭibīyyah,* pg 735.
[100] *Al-Nashr,* vol 2, pg 310.
[101] Muḥammad b. ʿAbd al-Raḥmān al-Sakhāwī was a prolific Shāfiʿī scholar, historian, ḥadīth expert and Qur'ānic scholar who was born in Cairo in 831/1428 and died in Madīnah in 902/1497.
[102] *Al-Manāhil al-silsilah,* pg 252.

mention the takbīr.[103] Finally, they point out that even if the practice does not have precedence to the Prophet ﷺ, it does have precedence in the practice of Ibn ʿAbbās. And since this is a matter not based on reasoning or opinion in any way, a Companion's practice would be considered to have originated from the Prophet.

Ibn al-Jazarī states: 'Know that takbīr is established as a practice of the scholars, reciters, and experts of Makkah, and those that narrate from them are so numerous that they reach the level of mass-transmission (tawātur).'[104]

Ibn Qudāmah states in al-Mughnī: 'Abū Bakr (d. 363/974)[105] adopted the takbīr in the ending sūrahs from al-Ḍuḥa to al-Nās because this was narrated from Ubayy b. Kaʿb that he recited upon the Prophet, who ordered him to do the same. Al-Qāḍī reports this with a connected chain in al-Jāmiʿ.[106]

The takbīr is universally practiced in the reading of Ibn Kathīr of Makkah, and in some narrations of the readings of Abū ʿAmr and Abū Jaʿfar. In addition, many Qur'ānic scholar adopted the practice in all the Qur'ānic readings based upon the notion that takbīr is a form of remembering God (dhikr) and not part of the Qur'ān in any way, and so, it need not be confined to strict narrated practice.[107]

The takbīr was reported in multiple forms by specific Qur'ānic transmitters, and specific details are found in books of the readings.

Reciting Certain Readings in Prayer

Scholars are unanimous on the soundness of reciting any of the seven readings in prayer or outside of it.[108] This consensus is not violated by the fact that some early scholars disliked reciting by the reading of Ḥamzah in prayer or outside of it, including Aḥmad b. Ḥanbal, ʿAbd al-Raḥmān b. Mahdī, and Yazīd b. Harun.[109] Ḥammād b. Zayd even went to extent of stating, 'If someone led the prayer in the Reading of Ḥamzah, I would repeat the prayer.'[110]

Despite that, Imām Aḥmad was asked about the soundness of prayer behind someone who recited by the Reading of Ḥamzah and replied, 'That does not reach the entire matter (the prayer).' Ibn Qudāmah and Abū ʿAmr explained that Aḥmad disliked certain elements in the Ḥamzah Reading such as the imālah vowel, frequent assimilated letters, prolonged madd vowels and the alteration of the hamzah letters.

---

[103] Related by Ḥākim in al-Mustadrak: Kitāb al-tafsīr—Bāb min kitāb qirāʿāt al-nabī, as ṣaḥīḥ on the conditions of Bukhārī and Muslim.

[104] *Al-Nashr,* vol 2, pg 310.

[105] Abū Bakr ʿAbd al-ʿAzīz b. Jaʿfar b. Aḥmad b. Yazdād, better known as Ghulām al-Khallāl after his teacher al-Khallāl (d. 311/923), was a great Ḥanbalī scholar.

[106] *Al-Mughnī,* vol 1, pg 458.

[107] *Al-Nashr,* vol 2, pg 306.

[108] *Majmūʿ al-fatāwā,* vol 13, pg 397; *Al-Nashr,* vol 1, pg 15.

[109] See section on the biography of Imām Ḥamzah in chapter two.

[110] *Mīzān al-I'tidāl,* vol 1, pg 605; *Al-Tahdhīb,* vol 2, pg 28.

Since these were also part of the Reading of Kisā'ī, Imām Aḥmad also disliked that Reading.

However, the fact is that each of these 'disliked' elements are also present in other readings and that these two Imāms (Ḥamzah and Kisā'ī) were not alone in reciting by them. Also, they were reading these elements with sound, connected chains going back to the Prophet. They explicitly pointed out that they did not come up with these elements based on their own reasoning but were reciting them in the manner in which they were taught by their teachers. To this, Sufyān al-Thawrī said, 'Ḥamzah never recited a single thing without having precedence.'

These two readings contain all the essential ingredients which qualify a sound Qur'ānic reading. These readings correspond to the 'Uthmānic orthography, have sound chains, and correspond to proper Arabic grammar. Each of their word linguistic variants have been traced by scholars of Arabic to early Arab tribes (for precedence).

Those who objected to these readings did so simply because they were not established in their eyes in the same vein that some Companions had objected to certain readings, as in the case of 'Umar rejecting the reading of Hishām b. Ḥakīm. However, the affirmation of a reading based upon knowledge takes precedence over its denial based upon an absence of it.

In addition, certain transmitters of these two readings were not accurate and made some mistakes in transmission, which caused scholars to reject these readings entirely whereas the mistakes had originated from these transmitters and not the Imāms themselves.

Finally, there is consensus on accepting these readings and not validating the view of those who rejected them.[111]

As for the other three readings that complete the ten canonical readings, most scholars do not consider them to be any different from the seven. These three are also mass-transmitted like the seven. In fact, one of the three—Khalaf—does not contain any unique elements and only contains features which were already part of the seven. So how could it not be on the same level of transmission?

Some jurists objected to these three readings based upon their incomplete study on the issue and mistakenly considered these three readings to be anomalous, whereas, in fact, they are not so at all. Baghawī reports that there is consensus on the validity of reading by the readings of Ya'qūb and Abū Ja'far along with the seven.[112]

Ibn Taymiyyah states: "Scholars of Iraq, for whom the ten or eleven readings were as established as the seven that were collected in these books, recited by them

[111] *Mīzān al-I'tidāl,* vol 1, pg 605; *Siyar,* vol 7, pg 91.

[112] *Ma'ālim al-tanzīl,* vol 1, pg 30.

in prayer and outside of prayer, and this was agreed upon by these scholars with no dissenting opinions.'[113]

Ibn al-Jazarī had a dialogue with Taj al-Dīn al-Subkī (d. 771/1370),[114] author of *Jamʿ al-jawāmiʿ fī al-uṣūl*, on this issue, which he referenced in his own al-Nashr:

> The erudite scholar and judge Abū Naṣr ʿAbd al-Wahhab asl-Subki was asked why he referenced in his book the seven mass-transmitted readings rather than ten?
>
> He replied, 'First, our reason for not mentioning the ten, despite our claim that they are mutawātir, is that these seven are unanimously considered to be so, and we were mentioning the points of agreement followed by disputed points. Despite the dispute, the claim that the other three are not mutawātir is one that falls short and is not valid from anyone whose opinions are valuable in religion. These additional three readings (Yaʿqūb, Khalaf, Abū Jaʿfar) do not contradict the ʿUthmānic orthography.'
>
> A long debate ensued between us, in which I insisted that he should have made reference to the ten mutawātir readings. He replied, 'I only wanted to point out the difference.' I responded, 'What difference? Who claims that the readings of Abū Jaʿfar, Yaʿqūb and Khalaf are not mutawātir?' He replied: 'It is understood from the words of Ibn al-Ḥājib, 'the seven mutawātir readings.''
>
> I replied, 'Which seven then? If we suppose they refer to these seven—and his statement does not necessarily indicate that—then the reading of Khalaf does not depart from these seven, nor even from the Kūfan readings, in the least. So how can anyone deny that Khalaf's reading is mutawātir while claiming that the seven are? Also, if we suppose he meant these seven, then which of their narrations, chains or books did he consider? The specifics were not indicated by him, and had they been, it would not be accepted from him. In the end, his statement remains general and includes everything that comes from the seven, and the reading of Yaʿqūb comes from ʿĀṣim and Abū ʿAmr, and Abū Jaʿfar was the teacher of Nāfiʿ and does not depart from the seven through their other chains.'
>
> He replied, 'Because of this, I have said that the truth is that what is beyond the ten is considered anomalous (shādh) and what opposes the sound is false.'

[113] *Majmūʿ al-fatāwā,* vol 13, pg 397.
[114] Tāj al-Dīn ʿAbd al-Wahhāb b. ʿAlī was a prolific Mamluk-era Shāfiʿī scholar, jurist and judge who was born in Cairo in 727 and died in Damascus in 771.

After that, I wrote to him formally requesting this in writing, and he wrote the following:

> Praise belongs to God. The seven readings chosen by Shāṭibī along with the three readings of Abū Ja'far, Ya'qūb and Khalaf, are all mutawātir and known from the religion by necessity. They were revealed upon Allah's Messenger ﷺ, and no one disputes that except the ignorant one. Their tawātur is not confined to those who recite them with chains of transmission but it extends to every Muslim that affirms the faith of Islām, even those who are ignorant and have not memorized a single letter of the Qur'ān. A prolonged discussion or lengthy proofs are not allowed by these limited pages. It is the right and duty of each Muslim to adopt Allah's religion and affirm what we mentioned as mutawātir and well-known, without any shred of suspicion or doubt.[115]

The consensus that was reported by these scholars allows the recitation of any of the ten readings, whether they are famous in a region or not. However, some scholars considered it disliked to recite by a reading which was not known in a region, under the principle, *'Speak to people in a manner they can comprehend, for would you like for people to reject God and His Messenger?'*[116] This was so that those who were unaware would not reject these verses and fall into something prohibited.

Dhahabī, who was both a scholar of fiqh and Qur'ān, disliked reciting in front of people with unfamiliar readings: 'There are some who, when reciting in gatherings or in the miḥrāb, bring out all the strange and exotic ways of reading, including pauses, alterations of hamzah, and highlighting all types of differences, effectively announcing to people that they are *Abū Fulān* ('so and so'), that everyone should know them because they know the seven readings.[117]

However, what Dhahabī apparently meant to rebuke those who seek to show off by these practices. Those who do so sincerely for God's sake and for the purposes of teaching and reviving Prophetic practices, then there is no compelling reason to prohibit this. If leaders were to avoid all Prophetic practices which are considered strange by people, then many of these sunnah practices would die out.

---

[115] *Al-Nashr,* vol 1, pg 41-2.

[116] Statement of 'Alī quoted by Bukhārī in his mu'allaqāt narrations of the Ṣaḥīḥ (supporting, secondary reports).

[117] *Bayān zaghal al-'ilm wa al-ṭalab,* pg 4-5; *Bida' al-qurrā',* pg 25.

Reciting Anomalous Readings in Prayer

What are known as the shādh (anomalous) readings[118] today were the readings of many Companions and Followers, who considered them fully sound and established, and recited by them in their prayers and outside of it. Because of this, many jurists from each of the four schools allowed reading by them in prayer and outside of it, if two conditions were fulfilled: they had sound and connected chains and they did not contradict the ʿUthmānic codex.

This is one of the two views on the issue reported in each of the four schools, but the majority of scholars disallowed reciting by them in prayer in all circumstances. Majd al-Dīn b. Taymiyyah (d. 652/1255)[119] disallowed reciting sūrah al-Fātiḥah by them but allowed the other surahs.[120]

Based upon this, scholars rejected Muḥammad b. Aḥmad Shannabūdh's (d. 328/939)[121] practice of reciting anomalous readings in prayer which he considered sound, because that reading opposed the ʿUthmānic codex. Dhahabī stated:

> The dispute over its permissibility is well known among past and present scholars. This man was trustworthy, pious, religious and an expert of this field. However, he was brought to trial by the minister Ibn Muqlah, where he affirmed his alternate readings of various verses:
>
> فَامضُوا إِلَىٰ ذِكرِ اللَّهِ
>
> *And **proceed** to the remembrance of Allah.*
>
> in place of:
>
> فَاسْعَوا إِلَىٰ ذِكرِ اللَّهِ
>
> ﴾*And **hasten** to the remembrance of Allah.*﴿ (62:9)
>
> وَتَجْعَلُونَ شُكرَكُمْ أَنَّكُمْ تُكَذِّبُونَ
>
> *And you make it your **form of gratitude** to call the truth a lie?*
>
> in place of:
>
> وَتَجْعَلُونَ رِزْقَكُمْ أَنَّكُمْ تُكَذِّبُونَ

---

[118] Refer to section on shādh readings in chapter 1 for more details, along with scattered discussions on the issue in other relevant chapters.

[119] The grandfather of the more well-known Ibn Taymiyyah, Abū al-Barakāt Majd al-Dīn ʿAbd al-Salām b. Taymiyyah was a great Ḥanbalī scholar who lived from 590/1194—652/1255.

[120] *Al-Nashr,* vol 1, pg 15; *Majmūʿ al-fatāwā*, vol 13, pg 398; Tafsīr al-Qurṭubī, vol 1, pg 47.

[121] Also known as Ibn Shannabūdh, and alternately read as Ibn Shanbūdh. See footnote number 28 on page 127.

﴾*And you make it **your daily bread** to call the truth a lie?*﴿ (56:82)

وَكَانَ وَرَاءَهُم مَّلِكٌ يَأْخُذُ كُلَّ سَفِينَةٍ صَالِحَةٍ غَصْبًا

*Behind them was a king who is wont to seize **every sound boat** by brute force.*

in place of:

وَكَانَ وَرَاءَهُم مَّلِكٌ يَأْخُذُ كُلَّ سَفِينَةٍ غَصْبًا

﴾*Behind them was a king who is wont to seize **every boat** by brute force.*﴿ (18:79)

وَتَكُونُ الْجِبَالُ كَالصُّوفِ الْمَنفُوشِ

*And the mountains will be like carded **wool**.*

in place of:

وَتَكُونُ الْجِبَالُ كَالْعِهْنِ الْمَنفُوشِ

﴾*And the mountains will be like carded **wool**.*﴿ (101:5)

> He was ruled to receive a physical punishment of seven lashes. It was there that he prayed against the minister and asked God to cut his hands and frustrate his plans. His prayer was answered, for the minister's hand was ultimately cut and his home destroyed. He was thus humiliated and lived out the rest of his days confined in the worst state.[122]

The correct view is that it is not allowed to read by such readings, as were read by Ibn Shannabūdh, even if they had sound chains because they have been abrogated by the Last Rehearsal and by the consensus of Companions on the ʿUthmānic codex. Ibn al-Jazarī quotes Ibn Taymiyyah:

> There is absolutely no dispute among reputable scholars over the belief that the Qur'ān's revelation in seven modes as referred to by the Prophet ﷺ is *not* the same as the seven popular readings. Rather, the first one to list these seven readings was Ibn Mujāhid who did so simply to match the number of modes, not to consider them synonymous or to confine valid readings to these seven alone. Because of that, scholars have criticized Ibn Mujāhid by saying, for example: 'If Ibn Mujāhid had not preceded me in including Ḥamzah

[122] *Ghāyat al-nihāyah,* vol 2, pg 54-5.

> [among the seven], I would have substituted his name with Ya'qūb, the Imām of the Grand Mosque of Baṣrah and leader of Baṣran reciters in the beginning of the 200s.'
>
> Because of this, the reputable scholars of Islām from the past did not dispute the belief that Ibn Mujāhid was not recommending that these seven readings be exclusively read in all Muslim lands. Rather, for whomsoever the reading of A'mash (the teacher of Ḥamzah) or the reading of Ya'qūb was as established in their eyes as the readings of Ḥamzah and Kisā'ī, then they could recite them without any scholarly dispute. Many scholars who had personally witnessed the reading of Ḥamzah—like Sufyān b. 'Uyaynah, Aḥmad b. Ḥanbal, and Bishr b. al-Ḥārith—still preferred the Madīnan readings of Abū Ja'far and Shaybah b. Naṣṣāḥ and the Baṣran readings of the teachers of Ya'qūb over the readings of Ḥamzah and Kisā'ī. There is well-known scholarly debate on this. Because of this, scholars of Iraq, for whom the ten or eleven readings were as established as the seven which are gathered in those books, recited by these readings in prayer and outside of prayer. This was agreed upon by scholars with no dispute.[123]

Ibn Taymiyyah's view may be summarized as follows:

1. It is allowed, based on scholarly consensus, to recite the ten readings, in prayer and outside of it, including the readings of Abū Ja'far and Ya'qūb.
2. It is allowed, without scholarly dispute, to recite by the reading of A'mash for those who consider it soundly established in the same manner as the seven readings.
3. It is even allowed, according to many scholars, to recite anything beyond the fourteen readings, such as the reading of Shaybah b. Naṣṣāḥ, if it happened to be soundly established in the eyes of the individual.

[123] *Majmū' al-fatāwā,* vol 13, pg 390-3; *al-Nashr,* vol 1, pg 15.

Combining Multiple Readings in Recitation

In prayer, the summary of the position of jurists is that if a portion of the Qur'ān is connected to the next then it must continue in one consistent reading. However, if the portion ends in a complete manner with no strong connection to the next then it is allowed to switch to another reading for the new passage, though it is still recommended to maintain one consistent reading for a prayer or a single session of reading.[124]

Ibn Taymiyyah was asked about this issue and answered: 'It is allowed to recite a portion of the Qur'ān in the reading of Abū 'Amr, for instance, and another in the reading of Nāfi'. This is allowed whether it is within one or across multiple rak'ahs, or within prayer or outside of it.'[125] Ibn al-Jazarī provided an excellent clarification here:

> The correct view in our eyes requires elaboration and balance. It would not be allowed—in the sense of being forbidden—to mix readings of portions that are superimposed on one another. For instance, if a verse allows two divergent and different readings of the same sentence, it would not be allowed to mix them up by taking features from each to construct a new reading that could violate the norms of Arabic and language. For instance, examples of corruption of language would be the verse, *'Adam received the words from His Lord'* (2:37), where the verse structure includes *Adam* as the subject and *words* as the object. Here, it can be reversed (*Adam* as the object and *words* as the subject) but both words cannot be read as subjects nor as objects.
>
> In other cases, we differentiate between reciting by transmission (riwāyah), where it would not be allowed to mix readings since that would be equivalent to dishonesty about the transmission, and general recitation, where there is no impediment to such mixing. When we criticize experts of readings for doing so, we are not doing this due to the fact that it is forbidden but due to their standing as scholars and experts in contrast to laymen.
>
> In the end, all of these variations come from God, revealed by Jibrīl upon the heart of the Prophet ﷺ in order to facilitate matters for this nation. If we obligated each person to restrict themselves to an individual, specific transmission with all its limits, it would be difficult

[124] *Majmū' al-fatāwā,* vol 22, pg 445; Nawawī, *Al-Tibyān,* pg 136.
[125] *Majmū' al-fatāwā,* vol 22, pg 445; *Al-Fatāwā al-kubrā,* vol 1, pg 220.

> and tantamount to reversing the aim of facilitation that these readings sought to realize.[126]

For purposes of teaching, there is no problem with combining multiple readings as done by professional teachers for instruction and practice, all done for the purposes of efficiency.[127]

We may conclude in the following manner. For a single session of recitation or rakʿah of prayer, it is always preferred to recite in a single reading. However, if portions of the Qur'ān are not inter-connected, then one may switch to different readings in the same session. This was the view of Ibn Taymiyyah, Ibn al-Jazarī, and Nawawī.

As for reciting a single word in multiple ways in a single session, like reciting *'māliki maliki yawm al-dīn'* and its likes, this requires further elaboration. If this is for the purpose of instruction, such as a student learning multiple readings from a professional teacher, then it is allowed. This has been the continuing practice of Qur'ānic scholars, who taught multiple readings in a single completion of the Qur'ān in various specific ways. Also, the Prophet ﷺ would recite the entire Qur'ān to Jibrīl once in the month of Ramadan, and this single reading encompassed all the ways the Qur'ān was revealed. Ibn Ḥajar inclined to the view that this reading encompassed all that is contained in the various readings.

If this is for another purpose, such as the public recitation sessions in various occasions or on broadcast media, many scholars considered that an innovation and forbade it. This amounts to combining multiple things which are really meant as substitutes for one another, which is not a normative practice. The norm is to select one of multiple options, not all of them at one time. This practice amounts to an innovation and has the potential to corrupt verses in the ears of listeners. It should be noted, however, that Dr. ʿAbd al-ʿAzīz allowed it in his book *Sunan al-qurrā' wa manāhij al-mujawwadīn,* as well as ʿAbd al-Fattāḥ al-Hunaydī in his treatise entitled *al-Adillah al-ʿaqliyah ʿalā jawāz jamʿ al-qirā'āt al-naqliyah.*

---

[126] *Al-Nashr,* vol 1, pg 19.

[127] For more details, see ʿAbd al-Fattāḥ al-Hunaydī's work entitled *al-Adillah al-ʿaqliyyah ʿalā jawāz jamʿ al-qirā'āt al-naqliyyah; Bidaʿ al-qirā'āt,* pg 18; *Sunan al-qurrā' wa manāhij al-mujawwadīn.*

Reading Mistakes

The Arabic word *laḥn* linguistically refers to mistakes in language and is used specifically by Qur'ānic scholars to refer to two types of mistakes: major (jalīyy) and minor (khafīyy). Major mistakes are those that are recognizable by experts as well as others, such as alteration of vowels or letters, which potentially lead to changes in meaning. Minor mistakes are generally recognized only by experts and include things such as not assimilating a letter (idghām), articulating heavy letters as light, or shortening prolonged vowels (madd).

Generally, Qur'ānic scholars considered major mistakes forbidden if done deliberately. Minor mistakes, on the other hand, take away from the beauty of language but were not necessarily forbidden, which would lead to great hardship upon believers. This was the view of Mullā 'Alī Qārī (d. 1014).[128] Other scholars, however, including Ibn al-Jazarī and Nāṣir al-Dīn Ṭablāwī (d. 966 AH),[129] considered minor mistakes forbidden since the ummah was ordered to transmit the words of the Qur'ān in the same manner they had received them from the Companions, from the Prophet ﷺ, from Jibrīl, from the Lord.

As for the jurists, they discussed this issue at length in their discourse on the leadership of prayer. Apart from Ḥanafī jurists, those of the other three schools stipulated the reading of sūrah al-Fātiḥah without mistakes for the validity of the imām in prayer for others. If he read with mistakes, he could only lead prayers for those who make similar, or worse, mistakes. This is built upon their view that this sūrah is a pillar of prayer, based upon the ḥadīth of Bukhārī and Muslim who related that the Prophet said, *There is no prayer for the one who does not recite al-Fātiḥah*. Because of this, jurists of the three schools apart from the Ḥanafī school were quite strict in this regard. Al-Dassūqī (d. 1230/1815)[130] said:

> Is it obligatory to recite al-Fātiḥah, even for the one who makes mistakes in its reading? If we believe that mistakes do not nullify prayer even if they change meanings, as is the relied upon position, then it would be obligatory to recite al-Fātiḥah for everyone, since the person making mistakes would have the same status as the one who does not make mistakes.
>
> If we believe that mistakes do nullify prayer, then the person should not recite al-Fātiḥah. If the mistakes are in some portions of the sūrah to the exclusion of others, then he recites the portions that are sound and leaves the ones that are not. Our teacher said, 'The

---

[128] Mullā 'Alī b. Sulṭān al-Harawī was a great Ḥanafī scholar and Qur'ānic expert who was born in Iraq and died in Makkah.

[129] Nāṣir al-Dīn Muḥammad b. Sālim al-Ṭablāwī was a great Egyptian Shāfi'ī scholar who studied under Zakariyyā al-Anṣārī.

[130] Muḥammad 'Arafah al-Dassūqī was the senior Mālikī scholar of Egypt in his time.

> view that it is obligatory to recite even a mistaken articulation of al-Fātiḥah, built upon the view that mistakes do not nullify prayer, is far-fetched since recitation with mistakes is not allowed. In fact, this is not considered recitation, and such a person is in the position of the one who has inability.'[131]

Imām Shāfi'ī said:

> If a non-Arab or one who makes mistakes leads the prayer, then if he recites al-Fātiḥah correctly or makes mistakes which do not change meanings, the prayer is valid for him and the followers. If he makes mistakes which change meanings, then his prayer is not valid for the followers, but is valid for himself so long as there is no one who can recite better than him, just as it is valid for him to pray without reciting if he is not able to recite correctly.[132]

Al-Shirbīnī (d. 977/1570)[133] writes:

> If the mistake is in other than al-Fātiḥah, like changing the ending vowel of the word *rasūl,* for instance, then his prayer is valid as well as his leadership of prayer, so long as he is unable to learn, unaware of its prohibition, or forgetful. As for the one who is able to recite correctly, knows better, and does so deliberately, then his prayer is not sound nor is his leadership for the one who knows his state.[134]

Ibn Qudāmah wrote: 'There are three types of people whose leadership of prayer is only sound for those who are of their level and not for others. . . The second type is the unlettered one, who is not able to recite al-Fātiḥah correctly and winds up corrupting the order of its verses, or letters, or changing them entirely.'[135] Al-Mardāwī stated:

> It is forbidden for one to deliberately recite al-Fātiḥah in a way that alters its meaning while possessing the ability to correct it, but the one who is unable to correct it should recite only what is obligatory and not more than that. The prayer of the one who recites incorrectly is voided if done deliberately and is tantamount to disbelief if one

---

[131] *Ḥāshiyah al-Dasūqī,* vol 1, pg 373.
[132] *Al-Umm,* vol 1, pg 166.
[133] Muḥammad b. Aḥmad al-Shirbīnī was a Shāfi'ī jurists, theologian and grammarian from Egypt.
[134] *Al-Iqnā',* vol 1, pg 167.
[135] Ibn Qudāmah, *al-Kāfī,* vol 1, pg 183.

> believes that it is correct. But if done out of ignorance or forgetfulness, the prayer is not voided.[136]

All of this shows the importance of the science of Tajweed, which is the way to safeguard oneself from such mistakes.

---

[136] *Al-Inṣāf,* vol 2, pg 279.

CHAPTER 5

Pagans Maintaining the Mosques

Allah says about the polytheists maintaining the mosques:

مَا كَانَ لِلْمُشْرِكِينَ أَن يَعْمُرُوا مَسَاجِدَ اللَّهِ شَاهِدِينَ عَلَىٰ أَنفُسِهِم بِالْكُفْرِ

﴾*It is not for the polytheists to maintain the **mosques** of Allah [while] witnessing against themselves with disbelief.*﴿ (Qur'ān 9:17)

Most read the word 'mosques' in the plural **[masājid]**, whereas Ibn Kathīr, Abū ʿAmr, Yaʿqūb, Ibn Muḥayṣin, and Yazīdī read the word in the singular number **[masjid]**:

مَا كَانَ لِلْمُشْرِكِينَ أَن يَعْمُرُوا مَسجِدَ اللَّهِ شَاهِدِينَ عَلَىٰ أَنفُسِهِم بِالْكُفْرِ

﴾*It is not for the polytheists to maintain the **mosque** of Allah [while] witnessing against themselves with disbelief.*﴿

In the very next verse, Allah continues to say:

إِنَّمَا يَعْمُرُ مَسَاجِدَ اللَّهِ مَنْ آمَنَ بِاللَّهِ وَالْيَوْمِ الْآخِرِ وَأَقَامَ الصَّلَاةَ وَآتَى الزَّكَاةَ وَلَمْ يَخْشَ إِلَّا اللَّهَ

﴾*The **mosques** of Allah are only to be maintained by those who believe in Allah and the Last Day and establish prayer and give zakāh and do not fear except Allah.*﴿ (9:18)

All readers read this in the plural, except for Ibn Muḥayṣin who read it as singular:

إِنَّمَا يَعْمُرُ مَسجِدَ اللَّهِ مَنْ آمَنَ بِاللَّهِ وَالْيَوْمِ الْآخِرِ وَأَقَامَ الصَّلَاةَ وَآتَى الزَّكَاةَ وَلَمْ يَخْشَ إِلَّا اللَّهَ

*The **mosque** of Allah is only to be maintained by those who believe in Allah and the Last Day and establish prayer and give zakah and do not fear except Allah.*

The singular form can imply a reference exclusively to Masjid al-Ḥarām of Makkah. This usage would be supported by the very next verse which references that explicitly (with no variant readings):

أَجَعَلْتُمْ سِقَايَةَ الْحَاجِّ وَعِمَارَةَ الْمَسْجِدِ الْحَرَامِ كَمَنْ آمَنَ بِاللَّهِ وَالْيَوْمِ الْآخِرِ وَجَاهَدَ فِي سَبِيلِ اللَّهِ ۚ لَا يَسْتَوُونَ عِندَ اللَّهِ

> ﴾Have you made the providing of water for the pilgrim and the **maintenance of al-Masjid al-Haram** equal to [the deeds of] one who believes in Allah and the Last Day and strives in the cause of Allah? They are not equal in the sight of Allah.﴿ (9:19)

The singular word can refer to Masjid al-Ḥarām but it can also serve as a reference to all mosques in general, as the singular can be used in Arabic to refer to an entire species. The plural reading supports a reference to all mosques while the singular reading can be general to all mosques or specific to Makkah alone.[137] This led to the development of many differences among jurists on the issue of polytheists tending to mosques. Jaṣṣāṣ said:

> The notion of maintaining (ʿimārah) mosques can have two meanings: first, visiting or spending time therein; and second, building or renovating them. When one simply visits a mosque, the Arabic word *iʿtamara* is often used, and the religious journey to Makkah is called *ʿumrah* from the same root. One who spends frequent time in mosques becomes known as *ʿummār*. So the verse necessitates the forbidding of polytheists from entering mosques, building them, or being responsible for their restoration or maintenance in any way. This is because the word encompasses all of these meanings.[138]

Qurtubi says:

> The word 'mosques' is read in the singular by Ibn ʿAbbās, Saʿīd b. Jubayr, ʿAṭāʾ, Mujāhid, Ibn Kathīr, Abū ʿAmr, Ibn Muḥayṣin and Yaʿqūb. The rest read it in the plural implying a general meaning. This is the preference of Abū ʿUbayd. This can have a general meaning which would also include specific mosques such as the one in Makkah. It is also possible that the plural is used while the reference is for the specific mosque in Makkah, which is also grammatically valid. One can use a general word when intending something more specific, as in saying 'He rode an animal,' when that person is riding a horse.[139]

---

[137] *Al-Qirāʾāt al-shādhdhah*, pg 50; *al-Kashf*, vol 1, pg 500.
[138] *Aḥkām al-Qurʾān*, vol 2, pg 87.
[139] *Tafsīr Qurṭubī*, bol 8, pg 89.

These views can be summarized in the following way. Maintenance (ʿimārah) can be used physically for construction and renovation, or in an implied sense meaning prayer, worship and remembering God therein. All jurists agree that the latter is not valid for disbelievers. Both readings ('mosque of God' and 'mosques of God') can be used for the generality of all mosques or specifically for the Sacred Mosque of Makkah. Moreover, Masjid al-Ḥarām can refer to the Sacred Mosque (Kaʿbah) alone or to all mosques in the sanctuary precincts of Makkah. As for actual maintenance of mosques like construction, laying foundations and building, the majority of jurists allow the service of polytheists for that so long as they are not given leadership roles or independent management of its affairs.

Ḥanafī jurists restrict polytheists from entering the precincts of Makkah during the Ḥajj season but allow them to enter in other seasons, including into the Sacred Mosque itself. Mālikī jurists disallow polytheists from entering any mosque in the world on any occasion. Shāfiʿīs disallow polytheists from entering the Sacred Mosque at any time but allow them to enter any other mosque or site in Makkah or elsewhere. Ḥanbalīs disallow polytheists from entering the precincts of Makkah, including its mosques but allow them to enter all other mosques. Shāfiʿīs and Ḥanbalīs rely on the verse:

يَا أَيُّهَا الَّذِينَ آمَنُوا إِنَّمَا المشرِكُونَ نَجَسٌ فَلَا يَقرَبُوا المسجِدَ الحَرَامَ بَعدَ عَامِهِم هَٰذَا

﴿*O you who have believed, indeed the polytheists are unclean, so let them not approach al-Masjid al-Haram after this, their [final] year.*﴾ (9:28)

They allow the entry into other mosques based upon the practice of the Prophet ﷺ who accepted the entry of delegations of polytheists into his mosque in Madīnah when they were holding prisoners of war.[140]

[140] See Tafsīr Ibn Kathīr, vol 2, pg 340; *Zād al-muyassar*, vol 3, pg 417; al-Baḥr al-muḥīṭ, vol 5, pg 28; Jaṣṣāṣ, *Aḥkām al-Qur'ān*, vol 2, pg 87; *Rawāʾiʿ al-bayān,* vol 1, pg 538; *Rūḥ al-maʿānī,* vol 10, pg 65-77; Tafsīr al-Nasafī, vol 2, pg 119.

Part 3: Issues Related to Fasting

The Obligation of Fasting

The obligation of fasting in Ramadan and the fact that it is a pillar of Islam is established by the Qur'ān, Sunnah and scholarly consensus. It is also supported by Ḥasan al-Baṣrī's reading of the following verse:

شَهرُ رَمَضَانَ الَّذِي أُنزِلَ فِيهِ القُرآنُ

﴿*The month of Ramadan is that in which the Qur'ān was sent down.*﴾ (2:185)

While everyone else read the word month in the nominative case **[shahru]**, Ḥasan reads the first word in the accusative case **[shahra]**, which makes it the object of an implied command 'fast,' making the meaning of the verse as follows:

شَهرَ رَمَضَانَ الَّذِي أُنزِلَ فِيهِ القُرآنُ

﴿***[And fast]*** *the month of Ramadan in which the Qur'an was sent down.*﴾

Iʿtikāf in other than the Three Mosques

Allah says:

وَلَا تُبَاشِرُوهُنَّ وَأَنتُم عَاكِفُونَ فِي المَسَاجِدِ

﴿*But you should not have relations with your wives while you confine yourselves to **mosques** (for iʿtikāf).*﴾ (2:187)

The word 'mosques' is read in the plural **[al-masājid]** by everyone except for Aʿmash, who read it in the singular **[al-masjid]**:

وَلَا تُبَاشِرُوهُنَّ وَأَنتُم عَاكِفُونَ فِي المَسجِدِ

*But you should not have relations with your wives while you confine yourselves to **the mosque**.*

The plural reading obviously refers to all mosques while the singular usage can refer to a specific one or still support the majority reading referring to all mosques, since the singular form is often used in Arabic to refer to the entire species. The Qur'ān, Sunnah and consensus establish that the practice of iʿtikāf is a sunnah in all mosques. Scholarly consensus also establishes that it is not valid in places other than mosques, like homes or marketplaces, except for an aberrant opinion of the Mālikī scholar of Spain Muḥammad b. ʿUmar b. Lubābah (d. 314 AH)[141] who allowed it in any place.[142]

However, jurists differ over which are the types of mosques in which the practice of iʿtikāf is permissible, and their views can be summarized into six positions, in order of leniency.

The most lenient view is that it is allowed in any mosque, even if prayers are not conducted within them, including Jumuʿah. This is the view of Imām Mālik, Shāfiʿī, and Dāwūd al-Ẓāhirī.[143]

Next is the view that it is permissible in any large mosque in which Jumuʿah is conducted, even if other prayers are not. This is the view of Zuhrī, al-Ḥakam, Ḥammād, one of the statements of ʿAṭā'[144] and one of the reported views of Mālik.

Abū Ḥanīfah, Aḥmad and others hold the view that it is allowed in any mosque holding congregational prayers.[145] The reason for this stipulation is so that the congregational prayers are not abandoned due to the performance of iʿtikāf, or that one would not have to leave their site of iʿtikāf to perform congregational prayers elsewhere, all of which would detract from iʿtikāf. This is the correct view, God-willing.

Hudhayfah b. al-Yamān viewed that iʿtikāf is only allowed in the three mosques: Masjid al-Ḥarām of Makkah, the Prophet's Mosque in Madīnah and al-Aqṣā Mosque. This is apparent from his discussion with ʿAbdullah b. Masʿūd in which he related that the Prophet said, *'There is no iʿtikāf save in the three mosques.'* Shaykh Albānī held this view from contemporary scholars. The full report is as follows:

Hudhayfah said to ʿAbdullah b. Masʿūd: 'Do you think that iʿtikāf between your house and the house of Abū Mūsā al-Ashʿarī is sound? You know that the Allah's Messenger ﷺ said: *'There is no iʿtikāf except in the three mosques.''* ʿAbdullah replied to him, 'Perhaps you forgot while the rest have preserved the matter correctly, or you might have been mistaken while the rest are correct.''[146]

قَالَ حُذَيْفَةُ لِعَبْدِ اللهِ يَعْنِي ابْنَ مَسْعُودٍ رَضِيَ اللهُ عَنْهُ: عُكُوفًا بَيْنَ دَارِكَ وَدَارِ أَبِي مُوسَى وَقَدْ عَلِمْتَ أَنَّ رَسُولَ اللهِ صَلَّى اللهُ عَلَيْهِ وَسَلَّمَ قَالَ: لَا اعْتِكَافَ إِلَّا فِي الْمَسْجِدِ الْحَرَامِ، أَوْ قَالَ: إِلَّا فِي الْمَسَاجِدِ الثَّلَاثَةِ؟ فَقَالَ عَبْدُ اللهِ: لَعَلَّكَ نَسِيتَ وَحَفِظُوا، أَوْ أَخْطَأْتَ وَأَصَابُوا.

[141] Muḥammad b. ʿUmar b. Lubābah was a Mālikī jurist of Andalus who was a student of the renowned ḥadīth expert of Spain and student of Aḥmad Baqīyy b. Makhlad.

[142] It should also be noted that some Ḥanafī jurists, including Shaykh Muḥammad Yūsuf Iṣlāḥī allowed iʿtikāf in the homes for women.

[143] *Fatḥ al-bārī*, vol 4, pg 272; *al-Mughnī*, vol 3, pg 183.

[144] See Muṣannaf ʿAbd al-Razzāq, vol 4, pg 364.

[145] *Al-Mughnī*, vol 3, pg 189; *Badāʾiʿ al-ṣanāʾiʿ*, vol 2, pg 114.

[146] Related by Bayhaqī, Ṭabarānī (Muʿjam al-kabīr), Muṣannaf ʿAbd al-Razzāq, and Muṣannaf Ibn Abī Shaybah. Al-Albānī authenticated it in *Qiyām Ramaḍān*, pg 36.

However, there is significant scholarly dispute over this particular ḥadīth report. First, the ḥadīth has been reported by three ḥadīth experts from Sufyān b. ʿUyaynah as a statement of Ḥudhayfah and not the Prophet. Second, the same ḥadīth documents Ibn Masʿūd's disagreement and disavowal of this position ('Perhaps you forgot while the rest have preserved the matter correctly, or you might have been mistaken while the rest are correct.'). In addition, there are variant narrations of the ḥadīth report that mention the other mosques. Saʿīd b. Manṣūr's version states that the Prophet either stated, *'There is no iʿtikāf except in the three mosques,'* or *'in the congregational mosques.'* Ṭabarānī' version only mentions *'except in the congregational mosques.'* All of this weakens the strength of the argument that restricts iʿtikāf to the three mosques and strengthens the position of Abū Ḥanīfah and Aḥmad.

Abū Jaʿfar al-Ṭaḥāwī held the view that the restriction of iʿtikāf to the three mosques was abrogated:

> We have contemplated the ḥadīth and found that Ḥudhayfah informed Ibn Masʿūd that he already knew about the Prophet's statement. Ibn Masʿūd did not deny that. His response indicates that it was likely abrogated: *'Perhaps you forgot (that it was abrogated) while the rest have preserved the matter correctly (by allowing it all the mosques).'* This unrestricted view of iʿtikāf is supported by the apparent meaning of the Qur'ānic verse ﴿*And do not approach your wives while you are in iʿtikāf in mosques*﴾ which does not specify the three mosques and the practice of Muslims in every region who have been performing iʿtikāf in their own mosques.[147]

Al-Kāsānī (d. 587/1191)[148] states that the ḥadīth report, if authentic, can support the view that it is preferred to perform iʿtikāf in the three mosques. He concludes: 'The best iʿtikāf is that which is performed in Masjid al-Ḥarām, then in the Prophet's Mosque, then in al-Aqṣā Mosque, and then in the large mosques elsewhere.'[149]

Another view is attributed to ʿAṭā'—and this is the last view reported from him—that iʿtikāf is only valid in the two Mosques of Makkah and Madīnah.

It is also reported from Saʿīd b. al-Musayyab that it is only allowed in the Prophet's Mosque, as he said, 'There is no iʿtikāf except in the mosque of the Prophet

---

[147] *Mushkil al-āthār,* vol 4, pg 20.

[148] Abū Bakr ʿAlā' al-Dīn b. Masʿūd b. Aḥmad al-Kāsānī was a great Ḥanafī scholar from the ancient city of Kāsān (Kosonsoy/Kasansay) in present-day Uzbekistan. He worked in the Seljul court in Konya and served as an ambassador to Nūr al-Dīn Zengī in Aleppo. He married the daughter of his teacher ʿAlā' al-Dīn Samarqandī, and the dowry was his authorship of a comentary on his teachers fiqh work *Tuḥfat al-fuqahā'*. The final result was *Badā'iʿ al-ṣanā'iʿ*, a celebrated work in Ḥanafī jurisprudence.

[149] *Badā'iʿ al-ṣanā'iʿ*, vol 2, pg 113.

ﷺ.'[150] However, there is a version of this report which states: 'There is no iʿtikāf except in the mosque of a prophet,'[151] which may be liberally interpreted to include all three mosques.

---

[150] Muṣannaf ʿAbd al-Razzāq, vol 4, pg 346; *Majmūʿ*, vol 6, pg 483; *al-Muḥallā,* vol 5, pg 194.
[151] Muṣannaf Ibn Abī Shaybah, vol 3, pg 91; *Fatḥ,* vol 4, pg 272; *al-Muḥallā,* vol 5, pg 195.

Part 4: Matters Pertaining to Ḥajj

Argument during Ḥajj

Allah states concerning the Ḥajj pilgrimage:

الْحَجُّ أَشْهُرٌ مَّعْلُومَاتٌ ۚ فَمَن فَرَضَ فِيهِنَّ الْحَجَّ فَلَا رَفَثَ وَلَا فُسُوقَ وَلَا جِدَالَ فِي الْحَجِّ

﴿*Hajj is [during] well-known months, so whoever has committed to performing Ḥajj,* ***there should never be intimate relations, foul language, or arguments*** *during the pilgrimage.*﴾ (2:197)

This is the reading of the majority is of the three nouns in the accusative case without tanwīn **[fa lā rafatha wa lā fusūqa wa lā jidāla]**, while Abū Ja'far and Ḥasan al-Baṣrī read all three nouns in the nominative case with tanwīn **[fa lā rafathun wa lā fusūqun wa lā jidālun]**:

الْحَجُّ أَشْهُرٌ مَّعْلُومَاتٌ ۚ فَمَن فَرَضَ فِيهِنَّ الْحَجَّ فَلَا رَفَثٌ وَلَا فُسُوقٌ وَلَا جِدَالٌ فِي الْحَجِّ

﴿*Hajj is [during] well-known months, so whoever has committed to performing Ḥajj,* ***there should be no intimate relations, foul language, or arguments*** *during the pilgrimage.*﴾

Ibn Kathīr, Abū ʿAmr and Yaʿqūb read the first two nouns in the nominative case ending with tanwīn and the third in the accusative case without tanwīn **[fa lā rafathun wa lā fusūqun wa lā jidāla]**:[152]

الْحَجُّ أَشْهُرٌ مَّعْلُومَاتٌ ۚ فَمَن فَرَضَ فِيهِنَّ الْحَجَّ فَلَا رَفَثٌ وَلَا فُسُوقٌ وَلَا جِدَالَ فِي الْحَجِّ

﴿*Hajj is [during] well-known months, so whoever has committed to performing Ḥajj,* ***there should be no intimate relations or foul***

[152] *Al-Ittiḥāf,* pg 155.

> ***language, and there is absolutely no dispute concerning*** *the pilgrimage.*﴾ [153]

The meaning of reading the three nouns in one consistent case is that sexual relations, foul language[154] and arguments are all prohibited during Ḥajj.[155]

The reading of distinguishing the case endings of the first two nouns from the third implies that sexual relations and foul language are forbidden during Ḥajj, while *jidāl* ('dispute') is a separate statement belonging to the remainder of the verse: *'There is no dispute about Ḥajj,'* i.e. *'There is no dispute about the fact that Ḥajj is in the month of Dhū al-Ḥijjah.'* The prohibition of disputing over worldly matters or argumentation leading to fighting among pilgrims during Ḥajj is not supported by this reading, but only supported by the reading of the three nouns in one consistent grammatical case. Ibn Zanjalah said:

> Abū Ubayd said: Some readings distinguished the first two nouns implying prohibition of sexual relations and foul language, from the third, which would mean that there is no doubt about Ḥajj and no dispute about its month. The rest read the three nouns as one case, implying the prohibition of all three things. They are supported by the statement of Ibn ʿAbbās (in the tafsīr of this verse): 'Do not argue with your companion to the point of angering him.' Ibn ʿAbbās did not have the prior view but considered disputing to be prohibited like the first two.[156]

In the end, all the various readings support alternate meanings, all of which are correct.

---

[153] Translation of the three variants adapted from the Bridges translation of the Qur'ān.

[154] *Fusūq* in the verse has been interpreted to refer to either foul language or all forms of disobedience.

[155] The difference between negation with the nominative versus accusative cases is that the accusative case negation is simply more emphatic ('there should *never* be intimate relations, foul language, or arguments').

[156] *Ḥujjat al-qirā'āt,* pg 128-9.

Two Rak'ahs after Ṭawāf

Allah states the following:

وَإِذْ جَعَلْنَا الْبَيْتَ مَثَابَةً لِّلنَّاسِ وَأَمْنًا وَاتَّخِذُوا مِن مَّقَامِ إِبْرَاهِيمَ مُصَلًّى

﴿Remember when We made the House a sanctuary for people and place of security. ***And take from*** *the standing place of Ibrāhīm a place of prayer.﴾* (2:125)

Most readers recited the variant word in command form **[wattakhidhū]** referring to a divine command, while Nāfi', Ibn 'Āmir and Ḥasan al-Baṣrī read the verse in the past tense **[wattakhadhū]** meaning that the progeny of Ibrāhīm 'took from the standing place of Ibrāhīm a place of prayer':[157]

وَإِذْ جَعَلْنَا الْبَيْتَ مَثَابَةً لِّلنَّاسِ وَأَمْنًا وَاتَّخَذُوا مِن مَّقَامِ إِبْرَاهِيمَ مُصَلًّى

﴿Remember when We made the House a sanctuary for people and place of security. ***And they took from*** *the standing place of Ibrāhīm a place of prayer.﴾*

The majority of scholars including Mālik, Aḥmad, and Shāfi'ī through one of his reported positions, considered praying behind the station of Ibrāhīm a recommended sunnah practice based upon the second reading in the past tense. They also based their position on an incident involving a bedouin who asked the Prophet ﷺ if he needed to pray anything beyond the obligatory prayers. The Prophet ﷺ replied, 'No, unless you wish to offer voluntary prayers.'[158] Finally, because there is no congregation stipulated for this prayer, it shows that it is not obligatory like the rest of the supererogatory prayers.[159]

Those who read the verse in the command form consider the prayer obligatory since commands generally imply obligations. This was the view of Abū Ḥanīfah and Shāfi'ī through his other reported position.[160]

---

[157] *Al-Ittiḥāf,* pg 147; *Ḥujjat al-qirā'āt,* pg 113; Tafsīr Qurṭubī, vol 2, pg 111; *al-Baḥr al-muḥīṭ,* vol 1, pg 380.

[158] Ṣaḥīḥ Bukhārī: Kitāb al-shahādāt—Bāb kayfa yustakhlaf; Muslim: Kitāb al-īmān—Bāb bayān al-ṣalawāt allatī hiya aḥad arkān al-islām.

[159] *Al-Mughnī,* vol 3, pg 384.

[160] *Sharḥ fatḥ al-qadīr,* vol 2, pg 456; *al-Muhadhdhab,* vol 1, pg 223.

The Mālikī scholar al-Abharī (d. 375/996)[161] held the view that this prayer is obligatory after any obligatory ṭawāf and recommended after any recommended ṭawāf.[162]

The ʿUmrah

Allah states concerning ʿUmrah:

وَأَتِمُّوا الحَجَّ وَالعُمرَةَ لِلَّهِ

﴿*And complete the Ḥajj* ***and ʿUmrah*** *for God.*﴾ (2:196)

All readers recited the word *ʿUmrah* in the accusative case **[wa al-ʿumrata]**, making it the object of the command, except for Ḥasan al-Baṣrī who read the word in the nominative case **[wa al-ʿumratu]**, which makes it the subject of a separate sentence whose object is 'for God.':[163]

وَأَتِمُّوا الحَجَّ وَالعُمرَةُ لِلَّهِ

﴿*And complete the Ḥajj,* ***while ʿUmrah*** *is for God.*﴾

The meaning of the command *'and complete'* has been deliberated by scholars. ʿUmar, Ḥasan al-Baṣrī and ʿAṭā' considered it to mean separation of Ḥajj from ʿUmrah, i.e. perform Ḥajj in its month, and ʿUmrah in the other months. ʿAlī, Ṭāwūs and Ibn Jubayr considered it to mean that one refrain from relations with one's spouse during Ḥajj and ʿUmrah. Ibn ʿAbbās viewed it to mean that once a person starts either Ḥajj or ʿUmrah, he must complete it. Mujāhid believed it meant that one is to follow Allah's commands within Ḥajj and ʿUmrah.[164]

The legal ruling on ʿUmrah is a matter of difference among scholars, with the manner of reading the verse exerting an influence over that. Many scholars considered ʿUmrah obligatory, relying on the default reading above which makes both the objects of the command. These include Shāfiʿī, Aḥmad, Dāwūd al-Ẓāhirī from the jurists. Early Muslims who held this view included ʿAlī, Ibn ʿUmar, Ibn ʿAbbās, Ḥasan al-Baṣrī, and Ibn Sīrīn.

Those who differ point out that the command is to 'complete' the pilgrimage which does not necessarily obligate the beginning of a deed. These scholars also rely on the ḥadīth of ʿĀ'ishah that the Prophet said, 'Women are enjoined a jihād that

---

[161] Abū Bakr Muḥammad b. ʿAbdullah b. Muḥammad b. Ṣāliḥ al-Tamīmī al-Abharī was a Persian-origin Mālikī scholar who became the leader of the Mālikīs in Baghdad and lived from 289—375.

[162] *Sharḥ al-Zarqānī,* vol 2, pg 274.

[163] *Al-Ittiḥāf,* pg 155; *al-Qirā'āt al-shādhdhah,* pg 35.

[164] *Zād al-muyassar,* vol 1, pg 369-73.

doesn't involve fighting: Ḥajj and 'Umrah.'[165] They also rely on the ḥadīth of a man who came to 'Umar after embracing Islam and said that when he found that Ḥajj and 'Umrah were due from him, he made the intention for both. 'Umar said to him, 'You have been guided to the sunnah of your Prophet ﷺ.'[166]

Abū Ḥanīfah and Mālik, on the other hand, view 'Umrah as a voluntary practice, and this is supported by the reading of Ḥasan al-Baṣrī which implies the obligation of Ḥajj alone while pointing to the need for sincerity in 'Umrah.[167]

---

165 Related by Aḥmad and Ibn Mājah: Kitāb al-manāsik. It was authenticated by al-Albānī in al-Irwā'.

166 Related by Abū Dāwūd: Kitāb al-manāsik—Bāb fī al-iqrān, and authenticated by al-Albānī in al-Irwā' under number 981.

167 *Badā'i' al-ṣanā'i',* vol 2, pg 226; Tafsīr al-Qurṭubī, vol 2, pg 368; *al-Majmū',* vol 7, pg3; *al-Mughnī,* vol 3, pg 223.

Part 5: Matters Pertaining to Sales

The Scribe and Witness to the Debt Contract

Allah says in the verse on loans:

وَأَشْهِدُوا إِذَا تَبَايَعْتُمْ ۚ وَلَا يُضَارَّ كَاتِبٌ وَلَا شَهِيدٌ

﴿*And have witnesses whenever you trade with one another, but neither scribe nor witness* ***must harm their clients.***﴾ (2:282)

The majority read the verb ending in doubled rā and fatḥah **[*yuḍārra*]**, while Abū Ja'far in one of his transmissions reads the word ending in a single unvowelled rā **[*yuḍār*]**:

وَأَشْهِدُوا إِذَا تَبَايَعْتُمْ ۚ وَلَا يُضَارْ كَاتِبٌ وَلَا شَهِيدٌ

﴿*And have witnesses whenever you trade with one another, but neither scribe nor witness* ***must suffer harm.***﴾

Ibn Muḥayṣin reads the ending with a doubled rā vowelled with ḍamma **[*yuḍārru*]**:

وَأَشْهِدُوا إِذَا تَبَايَعْتُمْ ۚ وَلَا يُضَارٌّ كَاتِبٌ وَلَا شَهِيدٌ

﴿*And have witnesses whenever you trade with one another, but neither scribe nor witness* ***are to be harmed.***﴾

The single versus undoubled rā reflects a different root verb form. All three forms could be understood as prohibitions. Alternatively, the *lā* could be one of simple negation for the nominative case (ḍamma ending), or one of prohibition for the accusative case (fatḥa ending).

The reading of the majority in the accusative case (fatḥa ending) supports the meaning that it is prohibited for the writer or witness to harm their client (the contractor of the debt or transaction), either by their refusal to serve or by their negligence during service.

The reading in the nominative case could mean that 'the one who contracts the debt will not harm or burden the scribe or witness by inviting them to the task if they are already preoccupied and worthy of being excused.[168] In any event, harming and reciprocating harm are generally prohibited.

[168] Ibn al-'Arabī, *Aḥkām al-Qur'ān,* vol 1, pg 259; Jaṣṣāṣ, *Aḥkām al-Qur'ān,* vol 1, pg 522.

Part 6: A Case of Inheritance Law

Allah states concerning inheritance:

فَإِن لَّمْ يَكُن لَّهُ وَلَدٌ وَوَرِثَهُ أَبَوَاهُ فَلِأُمِّهِ الثُّلُثُ ۚ فَإِن كَانَ لَهُ إِخْوَةٌ فَلِأُمِّهِ السُّدُسُ

﴿*but if he has left no child and his parents are his [only] heirs, then his mother shall have one-third; and if he has* ***siblings****, then his mother shall have one-sixth . . .*﴾ (4:11)

This verse establishes that if an heir has a number of siblings then the mother's share is reduced from one-third to one-sixth. There exists consensus on this. However, there is a difference over what constitutes a plurality of siblings— a minimum of two to three?

The four Imāms and the majority of early scholars considered a minimum of two to qualify as plural. There is a report in Lisān al-ʿArab that two siblings means three or more, but this was considered weak by Ibn Kathīr and al-Albānī.[169] Zayd b. Thābit said: 'The term siblings (*ikhwah*) according to Arabs means two or more siblings.'[170]

Proof for a minimum of two constituting plural comes from a variant reading of the following verse:

رَبَّنَا وَاجْعَلْنَا مُسْلِمَيْنِ لَكَ وَمِن ذُرِّيَّتِنَا أُمَّةً مُّسْلِمَةً لَّكَ

﴿*Our Lord,* ***make us both Muslims*** *[in submission] to You and from our descendants a Muslim nation [in submission] to You.*﴾ (2:128)

The supplicant in the verse-context are two individuals: Ibrāhīm and Ismāʿīl, and hence the dual form in the majority reading **[muslimayn]**. Ḥasan al-Baṣrī, however, read the word in the simple plural **[muslimīn]**:[171]

رَبَّنَا وَاجْعَلْنَا مُسْلِمِينَ لَكَ وَمِن ذُرِّيَّتِنَا أُمَّةً مُّسْلِمَةً لَّكَ

---

[169] Tafsīr Ibn Kathīr, vol 1, pg 610; *Irwā' al-ghalīl,* vol 6, pg 122.
[170] Related by Ḥākim and authenticated by Dhahabī and al-Albānī in *al-Irwā'*, vol 6, pg 123.
[171] *Al-Ittiḥāf,* pg 148; *al-Qirā'āt al-shādhdhah,* pg 33.

﴾*Our Lord,* ***make us all Muslims*** *[in submission] to You and from our descendants a Muslim nation [in submission] to You.*﴿

Ḥasan al-Baṣrī use of the plural for two individuals proves that two is also considered plural.

Part 5: Matters Pertaining to Marriage and Divorce

Consent in the Marriage Contract

Allah states:

يَا أَيُّهَا الَّذِينَ آمَنُوا لَا يَحِلُّ لَكُمْ أَن تَرِثُوا النِّسَاءَ كَرْهًا

﴿*Believers! It is not lawful for you to inherit women* ***against their will.***﴾ (4:19)

The majority read the variant word as **[karhā]**, while Ḥamzah, Kisā'ī, Khalaf, Ḥasan al-Baṣrī and A'mash read it as **[kurhā]**. A group of scholars of language held the opinion that *kurh* refers to doing something one would abhor while *karh* refers to doing something out of coercion. Other believed the meanings of the two forms are different words for the same meaning.[172]

There are a number of jurisprudential differences that stem from these variant readings. For those who take the meaning of abhorring or loathing, the ruling that would result from that is that it would not be allowed for a husband to restrict the affairs of his wife or harm her in interactions such as forcing her to ransom herself from him through separation (khula'). For the meaning of coercion, it would mean that a man may not force a woman to marry someone of his relatives, for instance, as there was a pagan practice that after the death of a husband, his wives were treated like property that belonged to the husband's relatives to dispense as they wished. The relatives of the deceased husband would marry those women against their will, and Allah forbade that.[173] This is supported by the following ḥadīth: *A previously married woman should not be given in marriage except after consulting her, and a virgin should not be given in marriage except after her permission*.[174] In another case, Khidhām al-Anṣārī married off his daughter Khansā', who happened to be previously married, against her wishes, and the Prophet ﷺ rejected that marriage.[175]

[172] *Al-Ittiḥāf,* pg 188.
[173] Jaṣṣāṣ, *Aḥkām al-Qur'ān,* vol 2, pg 109; *al-Mughnī,* vol 7, pg 56.
[174] Ṣaḥīḥ Bukhārī: Kitāb al-nikāḥ—Bāb lā yunkiḥ al-abb wa ghayruhu al-bikr wa al-thayyib illā bi riḍāhā; Ṣaḥīḥ Muslim: Kitāb al-nikāḥ—Bāb isti'dhān al-thayyib fī al-nikāḥ bi al-nuṭq wa al-bikr bi al-sukūt.
[175] Jaṣṣāṣ, *Aḥkām al-Qur'ān,* vol 2, pg 109; *al-Mughnī,* vol 7, pg 56.
[175] Ṣaḥīḥ Bukhārī: Kitāb al-nikāḥ—Bāb idhā zawwaja ibnatahu wa hiya kārihah fa nikāḥuhā mardūd; Kitāb al-ikrāh—Bāb lā yajūz nikāḥ al-mukrah; Kitāb al-ḥiyal—Bāb fī al-nikāḥ.

CHAPTER 5

The Need for a Judge or the Condition of Fear in Khulʿ Divorce

Allah states concerning divorce:

الطَّلَاقُ مَرَّتَانِ ۖ فَإِمْسَاكٌ بِمَعْرُوفٍ أَوْ تَسْرِيحٌ بِإِحْسَانٍ ۗ وَلَا يَحِلُّ لَكُمْ أَن
تَأْخُذُوا مِمَّا آتَيْتُمُوهُنَّ شَيْئًا إِلَّا أَن يَخَافَا أَلَّا يُقِيمَا حُدُودَ اللَّهِ ۖ فَإِنْ خِفْتُمْ
أَلَّا يُقِيمَا حُدُودَ اللَّهِ فَلَا جُنَاحَ عَلَيْهِمَا فِيمَا افْتَدَتْ بِهِ ۗ تِلْكَ حُدُودُ اللَّهِ
فَلَا تَعْتَدُوهَا ۚ وَمَن يَتَعَدَّ حُدُودَ اللَّهِ فَأُولَٰئِكَ هُمُ الظَّالِمُونَ

﴿*Divorce may be pronounced twice, then either the wife is kept honorably or parted with gracefully. And it is not lawful for you to take back anything you have given them, **unless they both fear** that they may not maintain Allah's limits. So if you fear that they may not maintain Allah's limits, then there is no harm if both agree mutually that the wife should obtain divorce by giving something as compensation to the husband. These are the bounds set by Allah, so do not violate them, for those who violate the bounds of Allah are the unjust.*﴾ (2:229)

All Imāms recite the word in the active form with fatḥah **[yakhāfā]** except for Abū Jaʿfar, Ḥamzah, Yaʿqūb, and Aʿmash, who read it in the passive form with ḍammah **[yukhāfā]**:[176]

وَلَا يَحِلُّ لَكُمْ أَن تَأْخُذُوا مِمَّا آتَيْتُمُوهُنَّ شَيْئًا إِلَّا أَن يُخَافَا أَلَّا يُقِيمَا حُدُودَ
اللَّهِ

﴿ *And it is not lawful for you to take back anything you have given them, **unless it is feared** that they may not maintain Allah's limits.*﴾

The active form refers to the fear of both spouses that they may not be able to establish Allah's laws while the passive form does not specify the subject ('unless it is feared such . . .'), which could be the leader, judge, or mediator between the couple.[177]

There are two separate issues that stem from these variant readings concerning khulʿ (wife-initiated divorce).

---

[176] *Al-Nashr,* vol 2, pg 227; *al-Ittiḥāf,* pg 158.
[177] Tafsīr Qurṭubī, vol 3, pg 138; *Fatḥ al-bārī*, vol 9, pg 394.

The first is whether the consent of both spouses is sufficient to carry out such a separation without resort to a judge.

Abū 'Ubayd stated, relying on the ḍammah (passive tense) reading: 'This is evidence for the position that khul' is the right of the authorities, which is the view Ḥasan al-Baṣrī, Ibn Jubayr, and Ibn Sīrīn.'[178]

It is also soundly reported from 'Umar, 'Uthmān, and Ibn 'Umar that they viewed the validity of khul' without resort to the authorities in the same way marriage and divorce was valid without the authorities. This is the position of the majority of scholars, that khul' can be effected by the consent of both spouses, or their representatives, without recourse to a judge. However, in case the consent of both parties does not exist, then it must be taken to a judge.[179]

The second issue is whether the fear of not being able to maintain Allah's limits is necessary for khul'. The majority of scholars did not stipulate that such fear, whether on the part of the spouses or from others, be necessary for the validity of khul'. Ibn Ḥazm, Ibn Taymiyyah, and Shawkānī, however, maintained that such fear was necessary, either from both of them, based upon the active reading of the verse (*'unless they both fear . . .'*), or from others, based upon the passive reading of the verse (*'unless it is feared . . .'*). Fakhr al-Dīn Rāzī stated the following:

> The majority of jurists held the view that khul' is valid with and without this fear. The proof for this position is the verse: ﴿*And give the women [upon marriage] their [bridal] gifts graciously. But if they give up willingly to you anything of it, then take it in satisfaction and ease.*﴾ (4:4) If it fully allowed for her to freely gift back her dowry from her husband without keeping anything for herself, then that is even more applicable in khul', through which she demonstrates control of her own affairs.[180]

Ibn Taymiyyah stated:

> Khul' as it appears in the Qur'ān and Sunnah is that a woman who despises her husband and desires separation returns back her dowry, or a portion of it, as if to free herself.[181]

Shawkānī stated:

> Allah restricted the permissibility of khul' due to differences to the fear of not maintaining Allah's limits. The overt meaning of the verse

---

[178] *Al-Muḥallā,* vol 10,. 237; *al-Mughnī,* vol 7, pg 51.

[179] Tafsīr Qurṭubī, vol 3, pg 138; *Fatḥ al-bārī,* vol 9, pg 394; *Al-Mugni,* vol 7, pg 55; *al-Qirā'āt wa athrihā,* vol 1, pg 489.

[180] Tafsīr al-Rāzī, vol 6, pg 100.

[181] *Majmū',* vol 32, pg 282.

> indicates that such khulʿ is not allowed except when this fear exists on behalf of both of them: that the husband fears not being able to keep her in kindness, and that the wife fears not being able to obey him as is her duty. However, since the ḥadīth of Ibn ʿAbbās related by Bukhārī that the wife of Thābit b. Qays came to the Prophet ﷺ and complained: 'Allah's Messenger, I do not blame Thābit b. Qays for his character or religion, but I fear being guilty of ingratitude.' He asked her if she would give him back his garden. When she replied that she would, the Prophet ﷺ asked the husband to accept the garden and divorce her once.[182]
>
> This proves that the fear of not maintaining Allah's limits from her is sufficient for khulʿ.[183]

The views of Ibn Ḥazm, Ibn Taymiyyah, and Shawkānī conform with the obvious meanings of the verse, and Allah knows best.

[182] Ṣaḥīḥ Bukhārī: Kitāb ṭalāq—Bāb al-khulʿ wa kayfa al-ṭalāq fīh.
[183] *Al-Sayl al-Jarār,* vol 2, pg 364; *al-Muḥallā,* vol 10, pg 235-243.

Part 6: Matters Pertaining to Vows

Oaths Requiring Expiation

Allah states concerning vows:

لَا يُؤَاخِذُكُمُ اللَّهُ بِاللَّغْوِ فِي أَيْمَانِكُمْ وَلَٰكِن يُؤَاخِذُكُم بِمَا عَقَّدتُّمُ الْأَيْمَانَ ۖ فَكَفَّارَتُهُ إِطْعَامُ عَشَرَةِ مَسَاكِينَ مِنْ أَوْسَطِ مَا تُطْعِمُونَ أَهْلِيكُمْ أَوْ كِسْوَتُهُمْ أَوْ تَحْرِيرُ رَقَبَةٍ ۖ فَمَن لَّمْ يَجِدْ فَصِيَامُ ثَلَاثَةِ أَيَّامٍ ۚ ذَٰلِكَ كَفَّارَةُ أَيْمَانِكُمْ إِذَا حَلَفْتُمْ ۚ وَاحْفَظُوا أَيْمَانَكُمْ ۚ كَذَٰلِكَ يُبَيِّنُ اللَّهُ لَكُمْ آيَاتِهِ لَعَلَّكُمْ تَشْكُرُونَ

﴿*Allah does not take you to task for the oaths you utter vainly, but He will certainly take you to task* ***for the oaths you have sworn in earnest****. The expiation (for breaking such oaths) is either to feed ten needy persons with more or less the same food as you are wont to give to your families, or to clothe them, or to set free from bondage the neck of one man; and he who does not find the means shall fast for three days. This shall be the expiation for your oaths whenever you have sworn (and broken them.) But do keep your oaths. Thus does Allah make clear to you His commandments; maybe you will be grateful.*﴾ (5:89)

The majority read the word with a shaddah **['aqqadtum]**, whereas Shu'bah, Ḥamzah, Kisā'ī, and Khalaf read it with a single qāf **['aqadtum]**:

لَا يُؤَاخِذُكُمُ اللَّهُ بِاللَّغْوِ فِي أَيْمَانِكُمْ وَلَٰكِن يُؤَاخِذُكُم بِمَا عَقَدتُّمُ الْأَيْمَانَ

﴿*Allah does not take you to task for the oaths you utter vainly, but He will certainly take you to task* ***for the oaths you have sworn****.*﴾

Ibn Dhakwān alone read it with an extra alif **['āqadtum]**:[184]

لَا يُؤَاخِذُكُمُ اللَّهُ بِاللَّغْوِ فِي أَيْمَانِكُمْ وَلَٰكِن يُؤَاخِذُكُم بِمَا عَاقَدتُّمُ الْأَيْمَانَ

[184] *Al-Nashr*, vol 2, pg 255; *al-Ittiḥāf*, pg 202.

﴾*Allah does not take you to task for the oaths you utter vainly, but He will certainly take you to task* ***for the oaths you have sworn between yourselves.***﴿

The dominant reading with shaddah indicates that the oath requiring expiation is one that is willfully intended by a person and not out of heedlessness or jest. It also indicates frequency, meaning that if one swears an oath to something repeatedly, there is expiation for that and that a single expiation would suffice.

The reading with a single qāf indicates that a single oath that is broken requires expiation, even if it is not repeated.

The reading with alif has a reflexive meaning and indicates that oaths requiring expiation are those that involve two parties (i.e. the one who swears does so because of an argument with another person).[185]

Agreements of Disbelievers

Allah states concerning vows:

وَإِن نَّكَثُوا أَيْمَانَهُم مِّن بَعْدِ عَهْدِهِمْ وَطَعَنُوا فِي دِينِكُمْ فَقَاتِلُوا أَئِمَّةَ الْكُفْرِ ۙ
إِنَّهُمْ لَا أَيْمَانَ لَهُمْ لَعَلَّهُمْ يَنتَهُونَ

﴾*But if they break their pledges after making them and attack your faith, make war on the leaders of unbelief that they may desist, for* ***they have no regard for their pledges.***﴿ (9:12)

All readers recite the word as above **[aymān]** except for Ibn ʿĀmir and Ḥasan al-Baṣrī in one report, who read it with kasrah **[īmān]**:[186]

وَإِن نَّكَثُوا أَيْمَانَهُم مِّن بَعْدِ عَهْدِهِمْ وَطَعَنُوا فِي دِينِكُمْ فَقَاتِلُوا أَئِمَّةَ الْكُفْرِ ۙ
إِنَّهُمْ لَا إِيمَانَ لَهُمْ لَعَلَّهُمْ يَنتَهُونَ

﴾*But if they break their pledges after making them and attack your faith, make war on the leaders of unbelief that they may desist, for* ***they have no faith/can give no assurance of safety.***﴿

The latter reading of *īmān* goes back to the root *āmana* meaning to believe, or according to some, to *amina* meaning to be secure or safe. This would mean that

---

185 *Ḥujjat al-qirā'āt,* pg 234; Ibn al-ʿArabī, *Aḥkām al-Qur'ān,* vol 2, pg 644; Tafsir Ṭabarī, vol 7, pg 13; Tafsīr Qurṭubī, vol 6, pg266.

186 *Al-Ittiḥāf,* pg 240.

they have no faith or religion, or that they never feel secure, or that they cannot assure anyone else's safety. Makkī b. Abī Ṭālib said:

> It is far-fetched that meaning of *īmān* here would be faith for their previous description is that of disbelief (kufr). In this context, īmān must have a different meaning to provide any meaningful sense to the word right after the description of kufr. This indicates that meaning must be security or safety (amān), as supported by the verse: ﴿*They neither have any respect for kinship nor for agreement in respect of the believers. Such are indeed transgressors.*﴾ (9:10) In other words, they do not fulfill their agreements with others nor do they guarantee anyone's safety.[187]

Abū Ḥanīfah relying on the reading with fatḥah held the view that the vow of a disbeliever has no legal effect. Hence, if a such a person were to swear an oath, then accept Islam and later break the oath, there is no expiation.

The majority of jurists, however, held that the oaths and agreements of disbelievers are binding, for the beginning of the verse says: ﴿*if they break their pledges after making them.*﴾ The meaning of ﴿*They have no regard for their pledges*﴾ is that the habit of such people is not to fulfill their promises and pledges. Were these people to pledge to something and break it after embracing Islam, there would be expiation.[188]

[187] *Al-Kashf,* vol 1, pg 500.

[188] *Al-Baḥr al-muḥīṭ,* vol 5, pg 15; *Rūḥ al-ma'ānī,* vol 10, pg 59; *Badā'i' al-ṣanā'i',* vol 3, pg 10; *al-Mughnī,* vol 8, pg691.

Conclusions

الخاتمة

Conclusions

For this meager effort of mine, I pray that I have succeeded in elucidating the impact of the fourteen Qur'ānic readings on various issues affecting understandings of creed and jurisprudence. The most important conclusions of this study may be divided into three: the broad and general ones, those than deal with creedal studies, and those that deal with matters of jurisprudence. I have summarized those conclusions here.

Broad Conclusions

The discipline of the Qur'ānic readings is an esteemed one which includes many different facets: articulating the words of the Qur'ān, writing them in script, identified those passages that enjoyed the agreement of the Qur'ān's transmitters and those that were subject to differences, meticulous referencing of each word and variant to its transmitter, and distinguishing sound (whether mass-transmitted or otherwise) from unsound transmissions of the Qur'ān. For this reason, Allah utilized the experts of the Qur'ānic readings to preserve the Qur'ān, in the same way that he used the masters of ḥadīth and reports to preserve the sunnah. Both the Qur'ān and Sunnah comprise the 'Admonition' (*dhikr*) that Allah promised to safeguard: ﴾*As for the Admonition, indeed it is We Who have revealed it and it is indeed We Who are its guardians.*﴿ (15:9)

The established sound variants among Qur'ānic readings represent complementary, not contradictory, differences. This multiplicity of readings contains great benefits such as increasing the eloquence of language, adding to the uniqueness and inimitability of the Qur'ān, facilitating the process of memorization and transmission, and magnification of spiritual rewards. Each reading explains and elaborates the others, bringing new layers of meaning and insight so that, in their entirety, they serve to increase the overall clarity of the message to the highest degree. These readings compared to one another are like Qur'ānic verses compared to each other.

These seven, ten, and fourteen readings represent portions of the seven modes with which the Qur'ān was originally revealed. The reason for the large number of these readings is due to the personal choices of the individuals to whom each reading was attributed. These individuals chose from the range of sound revealed modes of the Qur'ān they had learned. If a verse were to contain three words, each of which was revealed in three ways, that would represent 27 possible variations of the verse. Each scholar chose a particular way of reciting, and this way came to be attributed to him. The attribution of a reading to an individual represents transmission and personal practice, not a new invention or creation. There exists scholarly consensus over the belief that it is not allowed for a person to recite the

Qur'ān without having sound precedent from the Prophet ﷺ, through Jibrīl, to God Himself. Reciting in a way that conforms to language alone without a chain of transmission is not sufficient, for although each reading has a linguistic basis, not every linguistic possibility is found in these readings.

The Qur'ānic readings continue to be transmitted in our times through sound chains throughout the world, connected through the process of reciting and hearing, and composed of trustworthy individuals. As ʿUmar and Zayd b. Thābit affirmed, recitation is a followed practice taken from those before us.

The ʿUthmānic codices compiled by the Companions utilized a skeletal script without vowels or markings which could accommodate multiple readings established from the Prophet ﷺ. In the event that a reading could not be accommodated by a single script, they compiled multiple copies, each designed to accommodate a different reading. There is no basis for the claim of some Orientalists that it was these codices themselves that led to the rise of the multiple readings.

The Islamic sciences complement and explain one another and it is important for a student, even if he intends to specialize in one discipline, to be familiar with the others and to begin with the foundations of each. This study was intended to highlight the manner in which knowledge of the discipline of the Qur'ānic readings has a strong bearing on our understanding of theology and jurisprudence. These readings are like a precious treasure-chest containing concealed pearls which require extraction by qualified individuals.

Conclusions in Theology

The creed of the pious predecessors was one and the same, and there is nothing in any of the established readings that detracts from these beliefs in any way. In fact, the multiplicity of readings only serves to affirm their theology and increases its evidence.

Conclusions in Jurisprudence

The Qur'ānic readings can potentially aid in preferring some juristic views over others in matters of dispute in many subsidiary matters. Since the established readings are like the multiple verses of the Qur'ān, we must believe in all of them without rejecting any. The jurist must strive to reconcile them in the same manner that they reconcile all Qur'ānic verses, so that their juristic conclusions do not oppose any of them.

Proposals for Research

Before I put down my pen, I would like to put forward some proposals for fellow researchers.

It became apparent to me in the course of my personal experience and correspondence with specialists from various lands that no one after Ibn al-Jazarī (d. 833/1429) endeavored to compile an exhaustive history of Qur'ānic experts, especially those who comprise the Qur'ānic isnāds that transmitted the Qur'ān to the Islamic lands, and especially in light of the frequent mistakes and errors that appear in contemporary ijāzahs. Despite that, there still exist many sound and connected isnāds today and many worthy biographies of these figures scattered throughout books of history, biography and other fields. I must acknowledge that since the publication of the Arabic edition of this book, I have come across of a work of Shaykh Ilyās Burmāwī published by Dār al-Nadwah in 1421 entitled *Imtāʿ al-fuḍalāʾ bi tarājim al-qurāʾ*. It is an excellent work though it still misses out on biographies of latter-day scholars.

It is hoped that there be some individuals who take up the task of exhaustively compiling the biographies of these experts of Qur'ānic readings, including interviewing those that are still alive to learn about their teachers from the recent past and collating these scattered biographies together. This work should serve as an addendum to the ṭabaqāt works of the past with the additional aim of preserving the Qur'ānic isnāds to the multiple readings. It should also strive to preserve the various Qur'ānic ijāzahs, published and unpublished, and to correlate them critically with biographical works in order to uncover mistakes and errors.

Another worthy project would be to lend clarity to the connection and impact of Arabic on various Islamic sciences, the impact of Qur'ānic readings upon each of these fields, and the inter-connection of all Islamic disciplines. This a field entirely open to study, with much work yet to be done.

There also remain many reading variants beyond the fourteen which are soundly transmitted in books of ḥadīth and tafsīr, which are waiting to be uncovered in order to study their impact on theology and jurisprudence.

Index

ʿ

ʿAbd al-ʿAzīz al-Zayyāt, 93
ʿAbd al-Fattāḥ al-Qāḍī, 8
ʿAbd al-Raḥmān b. Ḥasan Āl al-Shaykh, 185
ʿAbd al-Raḥmān b. Muḥammad b. Qāsim al-ʿĀṣimī of Najd, 127
ʿAbd al-Razzāq al-ʿAfīfī, 131
ʿAbdullah b. ʿAbbās, 65
ʿAbdullah b. al-Mubārak, 45
ʿAbdullah b. al-Sā'ib, 65
ʿAbdullah b. ʿAyyāsh, 66
ʿAbdullah b. Masʿūd, 62
ʿAbdullah b. Wahb, 18

A

Abrogation in the Qur'ān, 112–15
Abū ʿAbd al-Raḥmān al-Sulamī, 66
Abū al-ʿĀliyah al-Riyāḥī, 66
Abū al-Aswad al-Du'alī, 66
Abū al-Dardā', 62
Abū ʿAmr al-Dānī, 25, 45
Abū ʿAmr of Baṣrah, 78–79
Abū Ḥātim of Sijistān, 18
Abū Ḥayyān of Andalus, 8
Abū Hurayrah, 64
Abū Isḥāq al-Shāṭibī, 142
Abū Jaʿfar al-Ṭaḥāwī, 18
Abū Jaʿfar of Madīnah, 86
Abū Mūsā al-Ashʿarī, 63
Abū Rajā' al-ʿUṭāridī, 66
Abū Shāmah, 17
Abū ʿUbayd al-Qāsim b. al-Sallām, 18
Aḥmad al-Marzūqī, 92
Aḥmad b. Ḥanbal, 46
Aḥmad Salāmūnah, 93
al-Abharī, 286
Al-Aswad b. Yazīd, 65
Al-Buhūtī, 254
Al-Dassūqī, 273
al-Hamadhānī, 46
al-Ḥulwānī, 92
al-Ḥulwānī al-Kabīr, 92

ʿ

ʿAlī al-Rumaylī, 92
ʿAlī b. Abī Ṭālib, 60
ʿAlī b. Ghānim al-Maqdisī, 92

A

Al-Kāsānī, 281
al-Mādhirī, 54
Al-Mughīrah b. Abī Shihāb, 65
al-Qabāqibī, 94

ʿ

ʿAlqamah b. Qays, 66

A

al-Samanūdī al-Munayyar, 92
al-Samīn al-Ḥalabī, 134
Al-Shirbīnī, 274
al-Ṭarābīshī, 47
Aʿmash, 91
Āmidī, 238

ʿ

ʿĀṣim of Kūfah, 80–81

A

Aṣmaʿī, 77

ʿ

ʿAṭā b. Abī Rabāḥ, 65

A

Āzar, 203

B

Badr al-Dīn Zarkashī, 8
Baghawī, 143
Bāqillānī, 123
Battle of Yamāmah, 56
Bayḍāwī, 246
Bayhaqī, 130
Buzzī, 77

D

Dhahabī, 46
Dūrī, 78

F

Final Rehearsal, 23

G

Ghulām al-Khallāl, 264

Ḥ

Ḥafṣ, 81
Ḥamzah of Kūfah, 82–84
Ḥasan al-Baṣrī, 90–91
Ḥasan b. Ṣāliḥ b. Ḥayy, 252

H

Hishām, 80

Ḥ

Ḥiṭṭān b. ʿAbdullah al-Raqqāshī, 65

I

Ibn ʿAbd al-Barr, 60
Ibn Abī al-ʿIzz, 130
Ibn al-ʿArabī, 224
Ibn al-Athīr, 7
Ibn al-Jazarī, 8, 46
Ibn al-Munayyar, 221
Ibn ʿĀmir of Damascus, 79–80
Ibn ʿĀshūr, 98
Ibn Baṭṭah al-ʿUkburī, 171
Ibn Baṭṭāl, 221
Ibn Dhakwān, 80
Ibn Kathīr of Makkah, 77
Ibn Khaldūn, 123
Ibn Mufliḥ, 254
Ibn Mujāhid, 27, 95
Ibn Qudāmah, 250
Ibn Qutaybah, 18
Ibn Ṭāwūs, 96
Ibn Taymiyyah, 24, 310
Ibn Zanjalah, 190
Ibn Zayd, 181
Ibrāhīm al-Ḥarbī, 221
Ibrāhīm al-Nakhaʿī, 74
Ibrāhīm al-ʿUbaydī, 92
Ibrāhīm b. Shaḥātah al-Samanūdī, 94
Idrīs, 88
Īhāb Fikry, 93

ʿ

ʿIkrimah, 78

I

imālah, 11, 14, 31, 37, 41, 83, 97, 118, 129, 162, 188, 264
iqrā', 12

ʿ

ʿĪsā b. Wardān, 86

I

Isḥāq, 88
Isḥāq al-Musayyabī, 249

ʿ

ʿIzz b. ʿAbd al-Salām, 123

J

Jabarīyyah (determinists), 212
Jaṣṣāṣ, 41
Jurjānī, 127
Juwaynī, 238

K

Khalaf, 82
Khalaf of Baghdad, 87–89
Khallād, 82
Khaṭṭābī, 53
Khuzaymah b. Thābit, 103
Kisā'ī of Kūfah, 84–86

M

Majd al-Dīn b. Taymiyyah, 268
Makkī b. Abū Ṭālib, 95
Muḥammad b. Aḥmad al-Mutawallī, 93
Muḥammad b. Aslam, 46
Muḥammad b. Ibrāhīm al-Samadīsī, 92
Muḥammad b. Qāsim al-Baqarī, 92
Muḥammad b. ʿUmar b. Lubābah, 280
Muḥammad Salīm al-Ḥulwānī, 47
Muḥammad ʿUmar Bāzmūl, 3, 9, 10, 204, 309
Mullā ʿAlī Qārī, 273
muqri', 11
Murji'ah, 217
Muʿtazilah, 215, 216, 228
Muṭṭawiʿī, 129

N

Nāfiʿ, 75–76
Nawawī, 74

Q

Qālūn, 75
qāri', 11
Qasṭallānī, 13
Qunbul, 77
Qur'ānic commentator Ibn Kathīr, 181

R

Rawḥ, 87
Ruways, 87

Ṣ

Ṣafāqisī, 70

S

Sa'īd b. al-Musayyab, 63
Sa'īd b. Jubayr, 65
Sakhāwī, 70, 263
Sāmir al-Naṣ, 94
Sarakhsī, 249
Sayyid Aḥmad al-Durrī al-Tihāmī, 93
shādh readings, 23, 39, 40, 64, 238, 239, 268
Shaḥādhah al-Yamanī, 92
Shannabūdh, 268, 269
Shannabūdhī, 132, 151, 162
Shāshī, 249
Shāṭibī, 24
Shāṭibīyyah, 24
Shawkānī, 35
Shu'bah, 81
Suddī, 140
Sufyān al-al-Thawrī, 45
Sufyān b. 'Uyaynah, 18
Sulaymān b. Jammāz, 86
Sūsī, 78

Ṭ

Ṭabarī, 18
Ṭablāwī, 273

T

taḥqīq, 70
Taj al-Dīn al-Subkī, 266

Ṭ

Ṭarābishī, 92

T

tas-hīl, 129, 130, 193
tawātur, 34–36, 35
Tawātur, 9
Tha'lab, 176

U

Ubayy b. Ka'b, 60

'

'Umar b. al-Khaṭṭāb, 59
'Uthmān b. 'Affān, 60

W

Warsh, 75
well of Ma'ūnah, 56, 58

Y

Ya'qūb of Baṣrah, 86–87
Yazīdī of Baṣrah, 89–90
Yūnus Ghalbān, 47

Z

Zajjāj, 143
Zayd b. Thābit, 61
Zayn al-Dīn al-Rāzī, 7

Bibliography

'Abd al-Ra'ūf, Ṣabrī. *Athr al-qirā'āt fī al-fiqh al-islāmī*. Riyad: Dār Aḍwā' al-Salaf. 1997.

Abū Ḥayyān al-Andalūsī, Muḥammad b. Yūsuf. *Al-Baḥr al-muḥīṭ*. Beirut: Dār al-Fikr. 2nd edition. 1403.

Al-Albānī, Muḥammad Nāṣir al-Dīn. *Ādāb al-zifāf*. Amman: Al-Maktabah al-Islāmiyyah. 1409.

—*Irwā' al-ghalīl fī takhrīj aḥādīth Manār al-Sabīl*. Beirut: Al-Maktabah al-Islāmiyyah. 2nd edition. 1405.

Al-Andalusī, Abū Ḥayyān. *Tafsīr al-Baḥr al-Muḥīṭ*. Beirut: Dar al-Kutub al-'Ilmiyyah. 1413/1993.

Al-'Aql, Nāṣir 'Abd al-Karīm. *Mujmal uṣūl ahl al-sunnah wa al-jamā'ah fī al-'aqīdah*. Riyad: Dār al-Waṭan. 1412.

Al-Azmīrī, *Nūr al-i'lām bi infirādāt al-arba'at al-a'lām*, manuscript: Azhar University. Number 302454.

Al-Baghdādī, 'Abd al-Qāhir. *Uṣūl al-dīn*. Beirut: Dār al-Kutub al-'Ilmīyyah. 1st edition. 1346.

Bayḍāwī, Nāṣir al-Dīn. *Anwār al-tanzīl wa asrār al-ta'wīl (Tafsīr Bayḍāwī)*. Beirut: Dār Iḥyā' al-Turāth al-'Arabī. 1418.

Bayhaqī, Aḥmad b. al-Ḥusayn. *Al-I'tiqād*. Beirut: Dār al-Āfāq al-Jadīdah. 1401.

Bāzmūl, Muḥammad 'Umar. *Al-qirā'āt wa athruhā fī al-tafsīr wa al-aḥkām*. Riyad: Dār al-Hijrah. 1417/1996.

Dānī, Sharḥ qaṣīdah Abī Muzāḥim.

Al-Burmāwī, Ilyās Aḥmad Ḥusayn. *Imtā' al-fuḍalā' bi tarājim al-qurrā'*. Madīnah: Dār al-Nadwah al-'Ālamīyyah. 1st edition. 1421.

Al-Dānī, Abū 'Amr 'Uthmān b. Sa'īd. *al-Taḥdīd fī al-itqān wa al-tajwīd*. Baghdad: Dār al-Anbār. 1407/1988.

Al-Dasūqī, Muḥammad 'Arafah. *Ḥāshiyah al-dasūqī 'alā al-sharḥ al-kabīr*. Beirut: Dar al-Fikr. 2017.

Dhahabī, Shams al-Dīn. *Tārīkh al-Islām*. Beirut: Dār al-Gharb al-Islāmī. 2003.

Al-Dimyāṭī, Aḥmad b. 'Abd al-Ghanī. *Ittiḥāf fuḍalā' al-bashar fī al-qirā'āt al-arba'at 'ashar*. Beirut: Dār al-Nadwah al-Jadīdah. 1357.

Al-Dimyāṭī, al-Sayyid al-Bakrī b. Muḥammad. *I'ānah al-ṭālibīn 'alā ḥall alfāẓ Fatḥ al-Mu'īn*. Beirut: Dār al-Fikr.

Mawdūdī, Sayyid Abū al-A'lā. *The Meaning of the Qur'ān*. Lahore: Islamic Publications Ltd. 1999.

Al-Ḥayānī, Dr. Usāmah 'Abd al-Wahhāb Ḥamd. "Al-'Arḍah al-akhīrah lil-Qur'ān al-karīm wa al-aḥādīth wa al-āthār al-wāridah fīhā jam'an wa dirāsatan." Algeria: Emir Abdelkader University Journal. 2016.

Al-Qāḍī, ʿAbd al-Fattāḥ. *Al-budūr al-zāhirah fī al-qirāʿāt al-ʿashr al-mutawātirah min ṭarīqay al-shāṭibīyyah wa al-durrah.* Beirut: Dār al-Kutub al-ʿIlmiyah. 1439/2018.

Al-Qasṭalānī, Shihāb al-Dīn. *Laṭāʾif al-ishārāt li funūn al-qirāʿāt.* Cairo: Lajnah Iḥyāʾ al-Turāth al-Islāmīyy. 1392.

Al-Rāzī, Muḥammad b. Abībakar. *Mukhtār al-Ṣiḥāḥ*. Beirut: Al-Maktabah al-ʿAṣriyyah. 1420/1999.

Ibn ʿAbd al-Barr. *al-Istīʿāb fī maʿrifat al-aṣḥāb*. Beirut: Dār al-Jayl. 1412/1992.

—Cairo: Maṭbaʿah al-Saʿādah. 1st edition. 1328.

Ibn al-ʿArabī, Abū Bakr Muḥammad b. ʿAbdullah. *Aḥkām al-Qurʾān.* Beirut: Dār al-Maʿrifah.

Ibn ʿĀshūr, *Tafsīr al-taḥrīr wa al-tanwīr.* Tunis: al-Dār al-Tūnisīyyah li al-Nashr. 1984.

Ibn al-Athīr. *Al-nihāyah fī gharīb al-ḥadīth wa al-athar.* Beirut: al-Maktabah al-ʿIlmiyyah. 1399/1979.

Ibn Baṭṭāl, *Sharḥ Ṣaḥīḥ al-Bukhārī.* Riyad: Maktabah al-Rushd. 1423/2003.

Ibn Baṭṭah al-ʿUkburī. *Al-Ibānah ʿan sharīʿah al-firqah al-nājiyah.* Riyad: Dār al-Rāyah. 1409.

Ibn Ḥajar al-ʿAsqalānī, Aḥmad b. ʿAlī. *Fatḥ al-bārī.* 2nd edition. Egypt: Dār al-ʿĀlamiyyah. 1436/2015.

—*Fatḥ al-bārī.* 1st edition. Riyad: Maktabat al-Mālik Fahd al-Waṭanīyyah. 1421/2001.

—*Fatḥ al-bārī.* Beirut: Dār al-Maʿrifah. 1379.

—*al-Iṣābah fī tamyīz al-ṣaḥābah.* Cairo: Maṭbaʿah al-Saʿādah. 1st edition. 1412.

Ibn Ḥazm, ʿAlī b. Aḥmad. *Al-Iḥkām fī uṣūl al-aḥkām.* Cairo: Dār al-Ḥadīth. 1404.

Ibn Hunaydī, ʿAbd al-Fattāḥ. *al-Adillah al-ʿaqlīyyah fī ḥukm jamʿ al-qirāʿāt al-naqlīyyah.* Cairo: Maṭbaʿah al-Jundī. 1344.

Ibn Kathīr, Abū al-Fidāʾ Ismāʿīl. *Al-Bāʿith al-ḥathīth sharḥ ikhtiṣār ʿulūm al-ḥadīth.* Damascus: Dār al-Fayḥāʾ. 1994.

—*al-Bidāyah wa al-nihāyah.* Beirut: Maktabah al-Maʿārif. 1st edition. 1966.

—*Tafsīr al-Qurʾān al-ʿAẓīm.* Beirut: Dār Ibn Ḥazm. 1420/2000.

Ibn al-Jazarī. *Al-munjid al-muqriʾīn wa murshid al-ṭālibīn.* Beirut: Dār al-Kutub al-ʿIlmiyah. 1420/1999.

Ibn al-Jazarī. *Al-Nashr fī al-Qirāʾāt al-ʿAshr.* Beirut: Dār al-Kutub al-ʿIlmiyah. 1427/2006.

Ibn Mujāhid, *Kitāb al-sabʿah fī al-qirāʿāt.* Egypt: Dār al-Maʿārif. 1400/1980.

Ibn Rajab al-Ḥanbalī, Zayn al-Dīn ʿAbd al-Raḥmān. *Ikhtiyār al-ūlā fī sharḥ ḥadīth ikhtiṣām al-malaʾ al-aʿlā.*

Ibn Rushd. *Bid āyat al-mujtahid.* Beirut: Dār al-Kutub al-ʿIlmiyah. 1416/1996.

Ibn Sallām, Abū ʿUbayd al-Qāsim. *Faḍāʾil al-Qurʾān.* Damascus: Dār Ibn Kathīr. 1415/1995.

Ibn Taymiyyah. *Majmūʿ al-fatāwā.* Madīnah, Saudi Arabia: Majmaʿ al-Mālik Fahd. 1425/2004.

Jaṣṣāṣ, Abū Bakr Aḥmad. *Aḥkām al-Qur'ān.* Beirut: Dār Iḥyā' al-Turāth al-'Arabī. 1412.

Al-Kāsānī, Alā' al-Dīn. *Badā'i' al-ṣanā'i' fī tartīb al-shar ā'i'. Beirut: Dār al-Kutub al-'Ilmīyyah.* 2nd edition. 1406.

Al-Mardāwī, ali b. Sulaymān. *Al-Inṣāf fī ma'rifah al-rājiḥ min al-khilāf 'alā madhhab al-imām Aḥmad.* Beirut: Dār Iḥyā' al-Turāth al-'Arabī.

Al-Meneese, Waleed Edrees. *Athr Ikhtilāf al-Qirā'āt al-Arba'at 'Ashr fī Mabāḥith al-'Aqīdah wa al-Fiqh*. Cairo: Maktabah Dār al-Ḥijāz. 1436/2014.

Al-Meneese, Waleed Edrees. *Al-Khayr al-kathīr sharḥ al-naẓm al-ḥabīr fī 'ulūm al-Qur'ān wa uṣūl al-tafsīr*. Minnesota, USA: Islamic University of Minnesota. 1438/2016.

Al-Meneese, Waleed Edrees. *Al-Khayr al-kathīr sharḥ al-naẓm al-ḥabīr fī 'ulūm al-Qur'ān wa uṣūl al-tafsīr*. Minnesota, USA: Islamic University of Minnesota. 1438/2016.

Al-Meneese, Waleed Edrees. *Al-Qamar al-munīr fī sharḥ al-zamzamīyah*. Minnesota, USA: Islamic University of Minnesota. 1441/2020.

Mundhirī, Muḥammad b. Ibrāhīm. *Al-Ijmā'.* Alexandria: Dār al-Da'wah. 1402.

Nadwi, Mohammad Akram. *Al-Fiqh al-Islami*. Istanbul: Angelwing Media. 2012.

Al-Qāḍī, 'Abd al-Fattāḥ 'Abd al-Ghanī. *Al-Budūr al-zāhirah fī al-qirā'āt al-'ashar al-mutawātirah.* Beirut: Dār al-Kitāb al-'Arabī. 1st edition. 1401.

Ṣafāqisī, 'Alī al-Nūrī. *Ghayth al-naf' fī al-qirā'āt al-sab'.* Beirut: Dār al-Kutub al-'Ilmiyah. 1425/2004.

Shāfi'ī, Muḥammad b. Idrīs. *Al-Umm.* Beirut: Dār al-Ma'rifah. 2nd edition. 1393.

Shalbī, 'Abd al-Fattāḥ Ismā'īl. *Al-Ikhtiyār fī al-qirā'āt.* Makkah: Umm al-Qurā University. 1417.

Al-Sharbīnī al-Khaṭīb, Muḥammad. *Al-Iqnā' fī ḥall alfāẓ Abī Shujā'.* Beirut: Dār al-Fikr. 1415.

Al-Shawkānī, Muḥammad b. 'Alī. *Al-Badr al-ṭāli' bi maḥāsin man ba'd al-qarn al-sābi'.* Egypt: Maktabah al-Sa'ādah. 1st edition. 1348.

Suyūṭī, Jalāl al-Dīn. *Al-Itqān fī 'ulūm al-Qur'ān.* Beirut: Dār al-Nadwah al-Jadīdah.

Ṭabarī, Abū Ja'far Muḥammad b Jarīr. *Jāmi' al-bayān fī ta'wīl al-Qur'ān.* Edited by Aḥmad Shakir. Beirut: Mu'assasat al-Risālah. 1420/2000.

Ṭabarī, 'Imād al-Dīn. *Aḥkām al-Qur'ān.* Beirut: Dār al-Kutub al-Ḥadīthah.

Al-Wābil, Yūsuf 'Abdullah. *Ashrāṭ al-sā'ah.* Riyad: Dār Ibn al-Jawzī. 2nd edition. 1416.

Al-Zarkalī, Khayr al-Dīn. *Al-A'lām.* Beirut: Dār al-'Ilm. 1984.

Al-Zarkashī, Badr al-Dīn Muḥammad b. Bahādur. *Al-burhān fī 'ulūm al-Qur'ān.* Beirut: Dār al-Kutub al-'Ilmiyah. 1439/2018.

Al-Zarqānī, 'Abd al-'Aẓīm. *Manāhil al-'urfān fī 'ulum al-Qur'ān.* Beirut: Dār al-Kitāb al-'Arabī. 1415/1995.

Al-Zuḥaylī, Wahbah. *Al-Tafsīr al-Wasīṭ.* Damascus: Dār al-Fikr. 1422/2001.

Yasin Dutton. ORALITY, LITERACY AND THE ‘SEVEN AḤRUF’ ḤADĪTH. *Journal of Islamic Studies* 23:1 (2012): pg 1-49.

www.ingramcontent.com/pod-product-compliance
Lightning Source LLC
Chambersburg PA
CBHW070233240426
43673CB00044B/1772
* 9 7 8 1 7 3 3 8 3 7 4 2 2 *